THE HOUSE THAT JILL BUILT:
A LESBIAN NATION IN FORMATION

The decade of the 1970s is commonly remembered for its kitschy contributions to popular culture – bean-bag chairs, platform shoes, bell-bottoms, disaster movies, disco, hot tubs, and hot pants. In *The House That Jill Built*, Becki Ross offers a rare view of this decade – one that shows community-based activism challenging the prevailing tenets of individualism and conspicuous consumerism. Ross explores the dedicated struggle of a largely white, middle-class group of lesbian feminists to subvert the history of lesbian invisibility and persecution by claiming a collective, empowering, public presence in Toronto during the mid- to late 1970s.

Gathering information from archival sources and numerous interviews with lesbians who were active in the feminist, left, and gay-liberation movements in the 1970s, Ross provides a window onto complex developments in community, identity, and visionary politics. She uses the Lesbian Organization of Toronto (LOOT, 1976–80) as a centrepiece, tracing the route that LOOT members took in enacting their desire to politicize the personal, in order to be lesbian in all aspects of their lives. Ross investigates the properties intrinsic to 'lesbian nationalism': fashion, sexuality, relationships, living arrangements, group membership, service provision, cultural production, and political strategy-making.

The House That Jill Built convincingly analyses the significant achievements of lesbian feminism in the 1970s as well as the limitations of identity-based organizing. The book is especially useful for those interested in the fields of women's studies, cultural studies, queer theory, and social movements.

BECKI ROSS is an assistant professor in the Departments of Sociology/ Anthropology and Women's Studies, University of British Columbia.

BECKI L. ROSS

The House
That Jill Built:
A Lesbian Nation
in Formation

UNIVERSITY OF TORONTO PRESS
Toronto Buffalo London

© University of Toronto Press Incorporated 1995
Toronto Buffalo London
Printed in Canada

ISBN 0-8020-0460-1 (cloth)
ISBN 0-8020-7479-0 (paper)

Printed on acid-free paper

Canadian Cataloguing in Publication Data

Ross, Becki, 1959–
    The house that Jill built : a lesbian nation
    in formation

    Includes bibliographical references and index.
    ISBN 0-8020-0460-1 (bound)   ISBN 0-8020-7479-0 (pbk.)

    1. Lesbian Organization of Toronto.   2. Lesbians –
    Ontario – Toronto – Societies, etc.   I. Title.

    HQ75.6.C3R6 1995   306.76′63′060713541   C95-930331-6

University of Toronto Press acknowledges the financial assistance to its
publishing program of the Canada Council and the Ontario Arts Council.

This book has been published with the help of a grant from the Social
Science Federation of Canada, using funds provided by the Social Sciences
and Humanities Research Council of Canada.

Contents

Acknowledgments

This book began as a Ph.D. thesis in the Sociology Department at the Ontario Institute for Studies in Education. The original manuscript is available from libraries at OISE and the University of Toronto. *The House That Jill Built,* in substantially revised form, was conceived in the company of many colleagues and friends at OISE, among them Anne-Louise Brookes, Mary Ann Coffey, Julia Creet, Kari Dehli, Jane Haddad, Susan Heald, Didi Khayatt, Gary Kinsman, Mary Ann MacFarlane, Susan MacEachern, Heather MacDonald, Judy Millen, Rusty Neal, and Anita Sheth. For four years, my sex/history group provided a context to read theory, critique each other's work, and challenge ourselves to construct and deconstruct 'the sexual' in history. I want to thank Mary Louise Adams, Debi Brock, Karen Dubinsky, Julie Guard, Margaret Little, and Carolyn Strange for pushing me to accomplish a more textured and balanced account. Over many years, Dorothy E. Smith's political acumen, her unwavering commitment to struggle, and her passion for rigorous, sociological scholarship have guided me and inspired me in countless ways. Ruth Roach Pierson and Deanne Bogdan have also offered generous encouragement over the years. I want to thank them for their valuable insight. I also want to thank the late Audre Lorde for *Zami: A New Spelling of My Name;* Joan Nestle for *A Restricted Country* and for being an out, proud, and rebellious femme; and Alice Echols for daring to write *Daring to Be Bad: Radical Feminism in America, 1967–1975* – a text that showed me that scholarship on second-wave women's liberation was not only possible, but critically necessary.

Virgil Duff, my editor at the University of Toronto Press, believed in and supported this manuscipt from the moment I deposited it on his desk. Thank you, Virgil. And thank you to Agnes Ambrus at the Press, and to John St James for his expert copy-editing. At various points over the years, I received financial support from the Ontario Arts Council, the Toronto Lesbian and Gay Community Appeal, and the Social Sciences and Humanities Research Council of Canada, from which I greatly benefited. Don McLeod of the Canadian Lesbian and Gay Archives devoted hours to much-appreciated photo research.

In different and immeasurable ways, Mary Millen and Cynthia Wright have sustained me in intimate friendship over the bumps and bruises, around the bends, and through the bogs of writing. Their unswerving companionship has helped to keep me sane and sure of my vision. For three-and-a-half years, Nancy Kelly offered me a Montréal home, her unconditional, loving support at all times, her unflagging sense of humour, her financial generosity, and her belief in me as a writer. Ingrid Stitt, my partner in life, has shared the process of preparing the revisions for this book. I thank her for the everyday/everynight joy she brings me.

Finally, I dedicate *The House That Jill Built* to the women I interviewed. Those who appear in this account, and whose actual names (except for two) have been used with their consent, welcomed me graciously into their lives and their memories. I am enormously grateful for their willingness to participate in the research. This book is indebted to and built on their courage to live as sexual and political outlaws. Their stories have taught me the power and the glory of lesbian history.

The notorious Brunswick Four in 1974, following their group rendition of 'I Enjoy Being a Dyke' at the downtown Toronto tavern The Brunswick House. *Left to right*: Adrienne Potts, Pat Murphy, Susan Wells, and Heather (Beyer) Elizabeth.

Jane Rule, British Columbia–based lesbian writer and outspoken defender of *The Body Politic*, 1974.

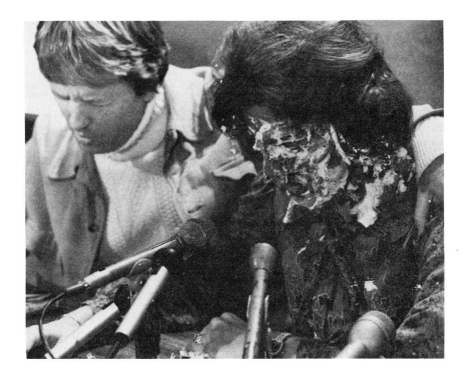

At a press conference in Des Moines, Iowa, on 14 October 1977, former Miss America Anita Bryant had a banana cream pie thrown in her face by a gay man, Tom Higgins. In January 1978, Bryant travelled to Toronto to spread her antigay and antilesbian gospel.

Mama Quilla II, a Toronto-based lesbian rock 'n' roll band in performance, 1980.

Take Back the Night demonstration, Toronto, May 1980.

Members of Women Against Violence Against Women (WAVAW) protest
Anita Bryant's 'Save Our Children' crusade in Toronto, 1978.

Chris Bearchell (*left*) and Konnie Reich in Toronto, 1976.

Lesbian mothers and kids.

Cover from the English-language lesbian periodical *Long Time Coming,*
published by a collective of lesbians in Montréal.

Becki Ross impersonating Emily Ruth, a fictitious 1970s lesbian feminist in full uniform, at 'Strange Sisters,' a Buddies in Bad Times Theatre event, Toronto, 1988.

LESBIAN DROP-IN
FROM
MAY 3rd

POT LUCK SUPPER
TUESDAYS AT 7pm.
DROP-IN FRIDAYS
Lesbian Organization
of Toronto
342 Jarvis Street
960-3249

WOMEN ONLY

Advertisement for the Lesbian Organization of Toronto, 1977.

ABOVE: Marie Robertson of Gays of Ottawa (GO) addresses a demonstration on Parliament Hill in Ottawa, October 1975.

OPPOSITE: Advertisement for the Fly by Night Lounge, a lesbian-managed bar that opened in Toronto in April 1981, at the back of the Stage 212 tavern of Filmore's Hotel.

a bar catering to women

open noon to 1 a.m.   Monday to Saturday
northeast corner George & Dundas, side door

- pool table   · 3´ x 5´ TV screen
- women's music   · backgammon
          · munchies, and more!

ABOVE: *The Body Politic*, an influential gay-liberation journal published in Toronto, 1971–87.

OPPOSITE: Maureen Fitzgerald, lesbian member of the International Women's Day Committee, preparing a 'Lesbian Rights Are Women's Rights' banner, Toronto, 1979.

A FINE KETTLE OF FISH!

THE LAVENDER HERRING   THE HETERO-MACKEREL

LESBIANS AND FEMINISTS IN THE WOMEN'S MOVEMENT

A workshop to explore our commonalities and our differences

- Is the personal political?
- Politically correct - Politically Incorrect?
- Bi-sexual - Bi-Issual?
- Skit: "Will the <u>real</u> feminist please stand up!"

Saturday 24 March 1979
2:00 - 6:00 P.M.
Niagara Centre   700 Wellington St. W.
(3 Blcks W. of Bathurst 1 s. of King)

Refreshments + Light Supper

Women Only $1.00

Sponsored by: Lesbian Organization of Toronto, Women Against Violence Against Women, International Women's Day Committee.

'A Fine Kettle of Fish' (Toronto, March 1979) was a raucous community-based event intended to heal feminist political splits.

THE HOUSE THAT JILL BUILT

Introduction

Being bold is like life in general. It's like a thistle: if you grab a thistle hard, it caves in; touch it gently and it half kills you, you know. You have to grab life. If you are gay or if you are doing something against the norm, you gotta do it boldly. If you do it boldly, you're less likely to suffer for it.
Lois Stuart[1]

In 1993, *Newsweek* featured two lesbians 'stepping out front and center'; *New York* magazine made a spectacle of 'lesbian chic' and assured all non-queers that it's all white, professional, Armani-draped style and no substance. And the August cover of *Vanity Fair* showed singer/songwriter k.d. lang and supermodel Cindy Crawford playfully acting out lang's lesbian sex fantasy.[2] Sandra Bernhard and Morgan Fairchild appeared as a lesbian couple on the TV sitcom 'Roseanne' and a lesbian articling student appeared on the now-defunct CBC series 'Street Legal.' Hollywood films such as *Three of Hearts* and *Basic Instinct* that sport stereotyped lesbian characters continue to draw huge audiences. The tabloid *National Enquirer* recently stirred up considerable fuss with its report on '10,000 lesbians' living in North Hampton, Massachusetts, and *Glamour* ran a feature story about two teenaged lesbian lovers who attended their high school prom together, in matching tuxedos.[3] North American lesbians, predominantly white and middle-class, seem to have reached a level of public visibility and personal confidence un-imaginable in earlier decades. How is it that the lesbian love that dared not speak its name is now, in the 1990s, refusing to shut up?

In Canada and the United States, lesbian and gay community-based institutions abound in large urban centres. They include books, newsletters, and magazines; presses; lesbian and gay studies courses; sports leagues and outdoors clubs; counselling centres; theatre troupes; 'dyke nites' at straight bars; film/video festivals; Asian, Latina, First Nations, and Black lesbian groups; support groups for lesbian parents, lesbian youth, and older lesbians; 'wild, wet, and well' safe-sex workshops; 'fuckerware' parties; community radio programs; the style wars of lea-thered '90s butches and mini-skirted, lipsticked femmes, sports dykes, punks, and gay-boy clones.[4]

Among those of us privileged enough to be out and to have access to these resources, there is little collective knowledge of how they came to exist, who was responsible for their genesis, and how fragile they continue to be. When I first came out, even the immediate lesbian past seemed remote; I joined a collective state of unknowing that is both personally disabling and politically dangerous. Dismayed, Latina lesbian Cherrie Moraga recently observed: 'Anyone can open up a les-bian/gay rag and it could be ten years ago. There's a new breed of 27-year-olds asking the same questions.'[5] The inference to be drawn is that if they are asking the same questions, they are making some of the same mistakes.

Slowly, I recognized that, as a white, middle-class lesbian of the 1980s, I was defining myself against my own heritage without realizing that greater choice was available because lesbian, straight, and bisexual feminists had fought long and hard for it. Given that present conditions arise from historical precedents, and that the past informs and gives meaning to the present and projects its trajectory into the future, I became aware that we must engage with what we remember, indiv-idually and collectively. *Village Voice* columnist Alisa Solomon reminds us: 'After all, it's not as though we have overcome; we just have a little more room.'[6] In the tough times of the 1990s, we will need to know what worked in the 1970s and 1980s, what didn't, and how to proceed differently. Unquestionably, this knowledge will empower us in the present and affect the possibilities for political change in the future.

Young lesbians and feminists in the 1980s and 1990s have a tendency to generational chauvinism: radical lesbians of the 1970s are carica-tured as shrill and humourless sexual prissies, fanatical about political correctness. Seventies-dykedom is often comically reduced to excessive flannel, vigilantly practised downward mobility, cramped collective liv-ing, ugly second-hand workboots, shared socks and underwear, angry manifestos, strict vegetarianism, and syrupy, sentimentalized fiction. In the 1990s style of young, urban, and sophisticated queer girls, why listen to the simply arranged, overly earnest, unmistakably lesbianized music of Holly Near, Cris Williamson, and Alix Dobkin when there is the gender-neutral raunchiness of rocker Melissa Etheridge, the racy gender and sexual fuck of Madonna, the torch and twang of cowgirl k.d. lang, the haunting, husky croon of African-American Tracy Chapman, and the searing ballads of bald-headed and Doc-Martened Sinead O'Connor?[7] Why endure Katherine Forrest's sexually circumspect *Curious Wine* when Pat Califia's *Macho Sluts* is guaranteed to pass the 'wet test'?[8]

Over the past twenty years, a generation of scholars has emerged to lead the work of uncovering, preserving, and expanding our knowledge of lesbian identities and communities, past and present.[9] Part of a broader field of the social history of sexuality, lesbian and gay socio-historical research has spawned conferences and university/college courses, projects, theses, anthologies, special issues of journals, and caucuses within a range of academic disciplines.[10] Like gay men's history, much 'lesbian' history began outside the university in local communities – oral-history projects and independent archival work – and it continues to depend on this political support.[11] However, as the work is gradually introduced into the academy, it presents a profound challenge to the heterosexist assumptions embedded in the fields of women's social history and the sociology of social movements.

Indebted to grass-roots, community-based lesbian and gay political/cultural activism over the past two decades, the reconstruction of female (and male) homoerotic history demands a reconceptualization of the 'normal' and 'natural' social organization of gender and sexuality. This is an expressly political project devoted to creating a history and a sociology *for* lesbians, gay men, and other oppressed peoples, with the broader purpose of transforming the world we live in.

Researching sexuality in history presupposes that sex is a subject-matter separate and detachable from other aspects of human life. Indeed, as Robert Padgug notes, conceiving of sex as a discrete entity coincided with emerging capitalist divisions into public (political and economic) and private (familial and sexual).[12] And the popularizing of Freud's analysis of sex in the 1920s served to consolidate notions of individual personality and behaviour dominated or even determined by one's sexuality in the twentieth century. Feminist historians Kathy

Peiss and Christina Simmons argue that 'sexuality has increasingly become a core element of modern social identity, constitutive of being,
consciousness and action.'[13]

Since the mid-1970s, the new scholarship has advanced the theory
of sexuality as a historical and social construction, rather than a private
experience, an intrinsically biological phenomenon, or a 'thing in itself.'
Carole Vance, Gayle Rubin, Jeffrey Weeks, Frank Mort, Pratibha Parmar, Isaac Julien, and others convincingly argue that sexual identities,
practices, and meanings are produced and regulated by political, social,
economic, and cultural processes at different times and in different
places.[14] Critical of feminist attempts to subsume sexuality under the
study of gender, Rubin also emphasizes the need to analyse the social
construction of sexuality and gender separately.[15] For example, lesbians
have been and are subjected to gender oppression as women, but also
to sexual oppression as perverts and queers.

Clearly, lesbians have stood and continue to stand in a different social
position with regard to official sexual discourse, legislation, and police
practices than have gay men. As Jeffrey Weeks notes, 'Lesbianism and
male homosexuality have quite different, if inevitably interconnected,
social histories, related to the social evolution of distinct social identities.'[16] More likely to be accused of being witches or anarchists, lesbians have been much less directly managed by the Criminal Code
and police activity through obscenity and gross-indecency statutes.
State-administered legislation is anchored in the institutionalization
of compulsory heterosexuality, for instance, child-custody laws, tax
and probate laws, and laws that govern medical/health insurance, in-
heritance, pensions, and immigration in ways that have negatively affected lesbians.[17]

Lesbian oppression is also organized through hegemonic apparatuses
of the media, the church, the medical profession, social-welfare agen-
cies, and the educational system.[18] In these instances, the sexual and
moral regulation of lesbian existence is accomplished in a more diffuse
manner than the police entrapment and arrest of other 'sex deviants'
like gay men and sex-trade workers, whose bodies have been/are more
overtly criminalized. In effect, the state sanctioning of the male-
dominated, heterosexual nuclear family and of the corresponding forms
of masculinity and femininity figures centrally in the social organization of lesbian lives.

In spite of the very different social and historical bases of the subordination of male and female homosexuality, some theorists have at-

tempted to treat lesbianness and gayness as indistinguishable.[19] Yet the inclusion of lesbians in one seamless, undifferentiated gay/lesbian movement, community, or minority obliterates and distorts the specificity of lesbian lives. Rather than collapse gay and lesbian under the unitary category of homosexual, thereby implying that lesbians are simply female counterparts of homosexual men, sociohistorical analysis must address the particularities of female same-gender experience. Moreover, critical attention to differences among lesbians along lines of class, race/ethnicity, age, region, and ability disrupts singular notions of 'lesbian identity' as universal, transhistorical, and transcultural.

The discovery and analysis of lesbian histories, therefore, works against the legacy of the destruction of records and memorabilia documenting female same-gender desire and the bowdlerization of texts by biographers intent on protecting the reputation of their authors. According to Lillian Faderman, Martha Bianchi Dickinson systematically excised references to the passionate, mutual love between her aunt, poet Emily Dickinson, and Emily's sister-in-law, Sue Gilbert.[20] In the early 1960s, American lesbian poet Judy Grahn burned her own diaries, letters, and journals for fear of being court-martialled and expelled as an 'undesirable' from the U.S. armed forces.[21] African American lesbian academic Gloria Hull stumbled on references to homoerotic love while reading the diary of early-twentieth-century African American writer and suffragist Alice Dunbar-Nelson.[22] Dependence on bricolage – a process of piecing together fragments from disparate and incomplete sources – attests to the difficulty of elaborating a same-gender erotic heritage. And yet recovering largely disregarded histories provides us with resources for reconstituting the present and imagining the future. As lesbian historian Judith Schwarz asserts, 'Uncovering our history is going to take enormous amounts of time, energy, money, dedication, inspiration, imagination and resourcefulness. What we will gain is a cure for our cultural amnesia: a past.'[23]

A primary focus to date is the construction of lesbian identity and the development of lesbian subcultures in the pre-Stonewall period, for instance, same-gender relationships among women in pre-contact First Nations cultures; working-class female cross-dressers in the late-nineteenth and early-twentieth centuries in the United States and Britain; African American lesbian and bisexual networks during the Harlem Renaissance in the 1920s and 1930s; lesbian reformers and artists in pre-Nazi Germany; 'man-royals' and 'sodomites' in Jamaica in the

1950s; and working-class lesbian bar culture of the 1930s to the 1960s.[24] The consolidation of identity and community in the 1970s, in the context of a predominantly white, middle-class lesbian-feminist movement, has yet to figure strongly in the study of contemporary social movements.[25]

Among the books and articles written on the second-wave women's movement, the majority allot only perfunctory treatment to lesbian-feminist organizing.[26] The almost twenty-five-year history of lesbian-feminist theorizing and institution-building, including political and cultural centres, community-based publishing, service provision, and cultural production, has fallen largely outside the feminist scholarly gaze. Sociologist Susan Krieger describes the lesbian community as 'the range of social groups in which the lesbian individual may feel a sense of camaraderie with other lesbians, a sense of support, shared understanding, shared vision, shared sense of self "as a lesbian" vis-à-vis the outside world. Some lesbian communities are geographically specific ... some exist within institutions ... some exist only in spirit; some are ideological ... some, primarily social. All are groups in which an individual may share her distinctively lesbian way of being with other lesbians.'[27] Yet Krieger admits that 'we do not know very much, in the social sciences, about lesbian communities, or about their interconnection with lesbian identity.'[28] Nor, I would add, do we know much about past attempts made by lesbian-feminist activists to build an autonomous political movement. Lillian Faderman devotes sixty pages to lesbian feminism in the 1970s in her survey text *Odd Girls and Twilight Lovers: A History of Lesbian Life in Twentieth Century America* (1991), and Shane Phelan addresses the same decade in her book *Identity Politics: Lesbian Feminism and the Limits of Community* (1989), though her analysis is limited by the absence of interview material. In addition, a number of provocative essays have contributed to my own project.[29] In English Canada, I have discovered only scanty accounts of the history of post-Stonewall lesbian identity and community formation.[30] *The House That Jill Built* intends to redress this gap by offering a full-scale, original case-study of lesbian-feminist nation-building in Toronto during the period between 1976 and 1980. Comparisons with developments in other cities in Canada, the United States, Britain, and western Europe await similar book-length investigations.

I began my study of 1970s lesbian feminism convinced that clues to the strengths and weaknesses of lesbian-feminist organizing in

North America today lie in our collective reclamation and analysis of the past. Unlike gay women in the 1940s and 1950s, I don't expect routine bar raids and police beatings, I don't carry a knife, and I don't fear incarceration in a mental institute. In fact, in the 1990s, I proudly combat antilesbian and antiwoman rhetoric that positions me as pervert, deviant, or sinner. None the less, the safety and security I feel as an out lesbian at times seems contingent and precarious, even temporary. Most lesbians are not out. Approximately nine-tenths of the 'lesbian population' continue to live in fear of disclosure and the attendant loss of family, friends, jobs, and the custody of children.

I contend that there is considerable urgency in excavating the substance of what worked and what didn't in the ongoing fight against forces determined to contain and even obliterate lesbian and gay realities. In my body over the past several years, I have registered the escalating fear of queer-bashing on the streets, on the subway, in movie theatres, at cafés, on the beach. The almost total lack of response to the elimination of the Secretary of State Women's Program funding to lesbian groups in 1988 attested to the fragmented, diffuse state of organized lesbianism in Toronto and across the country.[31] Local school boards continue to obstruct the introduction of lesbian- and gay-positive curriculum, and municipalities continue to block the extension of benefits to the partners of their lesbian and gay employees.

The regulation of sexually explicit materials in Canada has intensified on myriad levels since the mid-1980s. State obscenity legislation – Section 168 of the Criminal Code (popularly known as the Butler decision) – has been deployed successfully in decisions by Judge Hayes (1992) and Judge Paris (1993) in Ontario to censor images made by and for lesbians and gay men. Memorandum D-9-1-1 continues to instruct seizures and confiscation of 'obscene' lesbian/gay/bisexual materials at the Canada/U.S. border. Project P – the joint OPP/Metro Toronto police anti-pornography squad – continues to prowl alternative bookstores in search of 'smut for smut's sake.' In the summer of 1993, Metro Toronto Council voted to withdraw cultural funding from Inside/Out, Toronto's lesbian and gay film/video collective, and the AIDS Committee of Toronto and Buddies in Bad Times theatre troupe have been repreatedly threatened with loss of funds; printers in various locales across Canada and the United States have rejected controversial jobs; film review boards continue to edit out so-called harmful sex; newspapers such as the *Toronto Sun* have publicly vilified lesbians and gays as 'sickos,' 'child molesters,' and 's/m freaks.' Artists themselves have described the impact of the 'obscenity chill' on their imaginations and on their willingness to break rules and court penalties.

Federal conservative politicians are resistant to amending the Charter of Rights and Freedoms to prohibit discrimination on the basis of sexual orientation. And the state's criminal negligence regarding AIDS-related treatments and resources continues to punish not only gay men, IV drug-users, and, increasingly, ethnic and racial communities, but also women – the fastest-growing HIV-positive population in Canada.

Internal to the women's movement, problems concerning lesbianism remain. There was no mention of the word 'lesbian' at the four-hour 'Women Say No to Racism' rally at Toronto's International Women's Day in 1986. At the time, I wondered about lesbian visibility and the extent to which radical sexual politics had been truly integrated into a class-conscious and antiracist feminist agenda. Now I wonder whether such an oversight could happen again. With respect to coalition-building, in the summer of 1990 a demonstration was called by Montréal's newly formed Lesbians and Gays Against Violence for the same afternoon that the Mohawks of Kanasatake had organized a mass protest against the invasion of their territories by police and the Canadian armed forces. Similar inattention to the links between oppressions was beginning to surface among young, politically inexperienced activists drawn to the direct-action mandate of Queer Nation in Toronto (1990–1) and elsewhere. Thus, tentative efforts to articulate alliances have been impeded by the absence of an already established infrastructure of communication and collaboration among progressive constituencies – as much a comment on the history of counter-hegemonic organizing as it is a comment on the present.

In view of the difficulties of devising a politics of lesbian organizing, it is 'small wonder,' Lorna Weir argues, 'that lesbian politics has as a rule taken the form of the festival – an outpouring of spontaneous musical solidarity.'[32] Today, Valentine's Day dances, sex cabarets, and porn goddess Annie Sprinkle's workshops sell out; local bars are jam-packed on weekends; and vanloads travel to the Michigan Womyn's Music extravaganza every August. Looking around me, I can see that the intense collective rage that saturated lesbian-feminist writings in the 1970s has virtually disappeared. In the mid-eighties, critiques of feminist and lesbian organizing made by lesbians and women of colour exposed the limitations of a white lesbian and feminist political praxis. Today, lesbians of all political persuasions, ages, colours, and ethnicities are sharply split on questions of prostitution, butch/femme, gay liberation, S/M, public and intergenerational sex, pornography, censorship, bisexuality, and transsexuality, as well as class, race, and coalitional politics.

Lesbian community, or, more accurately, communities, tend to revolve around small friendship groups, some of which self-identify loosely as anarchist, socialist, gay liberationist, environmentalist, anti-racist, separatist, or radical, while others, such as the bar community, have no overt political affiliation. I have trouble imagining a distinctly lesbian-feminist, anti-heterosexist project that would galvanize members of increasingly diffuse, decentred, and multifaceted lesbian communities. Hence, when I discovered mention of Toronto's first openly lesbian-feminist group, the Lesbian Organization of Toronto (LOOT) – founded in late 1976 and closed in the spring of 1980 – I was intrigued.[33] How did an organization that set out to meet all the social, cultural, recreational, *and* political needs of lesbians in Toronto survive for over three years? What did it accomplish? How did LOOT members feel about their organization at the time, and how do they remember it today?

The House That Jill Built is about the dedicated struggle of a distinct group of largely white, middle-class lesbian feminists to claim a collective, empowering public presence in Toronto during the mid- to late 1970s. The Lesbian Organization of Toronto (LOOT) was founded in late 1976. In February 1977, along with two other feminist groups – *The Other Woman* newspaper and the Three of Cups Coffeehouse – LOOT members rented a spacious, run-down three-storey house in the city's downtown. Under the roof of 342 Jarvis Street, these ventures combined to constitute the first, largest, and best-known lesbian-feminist centre in Canada during the 1970s, with LOOT at its core.

THE 'ME' DECADE?

The decade of the 1970s marked the first ten years of lesbian-feminist social, cultural, and political activism in North America, Britain, and parts of western Europe. It also marked the crystallization of First Nations organizing, environmental/peace activism, antinuclear energy agitation, organizing for Third World liberation, independent left politics, and arts organizing.[34] During this heady period, I was a teenager growing up in the mining town of Sudbury, Ontario, largely unaware of alternative social movements. I was amused to hear that the decade was officially revived in all its chaotic splendour by CBC radio host Peter Gzowski in May 1991.[35] Several weeks later, in his *Globe and Mail* review of Daniel Richler's novel *Kicking Tomorrow*, cultural critic Geoff Pevere synthesized his interpretation of the 1970s: 'The utopian, ill-formulated ideals of the sixties had collapsed, and it was a rainy Monday morning all over again. In retrospect, the politics of collectivism seemed like a scam: a pretext for a decade-long party that had left us, the inheritors, not with a new order, but a pile-driving, soul-splintering hangover. Unwitting counter-revolutionaries, we rejected the future wholesale (and any program for improving it), and we rearranged the political universe so that Me and not We reigned supreme at its centre. We elevated cynicism and narcissism to creed, and we made pleasure a matter of principle. We boogied, we got down and we got off. And, since we didn't give a damn what anyone thought, we dressed very badly.'[36] When I began to delve into the history of social movements of the 1970s, with a central focus on lesbian activism, I discovered that there was much more to the decade than the summaries provided by Pevere and others. In fact, the decade could not be justly captured via an inventory of its popular consumer/cultural trappings: bean-bag chairs, panelled rec-rooms, platform shoes, fishnet stockings, bell bottoms, velour, hot tubs, hot pants, 'Saturday Night Fever,' K.C. and the Sunshine Band, 'The Gong Show,' disaster movies, Annie Hall, and acid trips. Contrary to Pevere's (and Richler's) equation of the seventies with bleakly amoral and thoughtless self-indulgence, I discovered a vibrant community of lesbian feminists who were deeply committed to each other, to the ideology of collectivism, and to their utopian vision for a transformed world.

Inside the Lesbian Organization of Toronto (LOOT), the emergence of a radically innovative, counter-hegemonic lesbian-feminist discourse marked a shift from a negative (that is, pervert) to a positive identity. In the 1950s and 1960s, before modern-day gay liberation and the women's movement, gay women often lived in fear, shame, and self-loathing, with little or no access to lesbian-positive space beyond local bars and weekend house parties. If a gay woman discovered any depiction of homosexuality at all, she likely found patriarchal myths of the Lesbian as a predatorial, sexually insatiable, and hyper-masculine monster. Sexological and psychoanalytic discourse, dating from the late-nineteenth century, depicted female homosexuality as a congenital, 'mannish' abnormality and/or a pathological sickness born of complex neuroses.[37] In 1954, popular American psychoanalyst Frank Caprio described lesbians as unhappy, sexually maladjusted, and prone to extreme jealousy, sexual immaturity, and sadomasochistic tendencies. He concluded that lesbians 'can be restored to normal sex outlook by sympathetic and expert treatment, usually at the hands of a psychiatrist or psychoanalyst who believes in cure.'[38] In 1965, University of Toronto psychiatry professor Daniel Cappon stated in his book *Toward an Understanding of Homosexuality*: 'I have never known a happy homo ... Their aim is ultimately self-destruction to limit the unbearable disorder that makes them hate themselves. They say they become adjusted to it and they believe it, but it's not true.'[39]

In their path-breaking sourcebook, *Lesbian/Woman* (1972), Martin and Lyon list fifty-four causes of lesbianism proposed by medical professionals from 'penis envy,' 'orality and sadism,' and 'castration complex,' to overidentification with the mother coupled with a weak father image.[40] By the 1950s, the medical model became entrenched as the dominant sexual ideology and the received wisdom within the social sciences. Treatments such as electroshock, behaviour modification and aversion 'therapy,' hypnotism, and chemical intervention were developed to 'cure' multiple features of sexual abnormality, including lesbianism, and were routinely performed on imprisoned and institutionalized populations.[41] In the 1960s, lesbians, some of whom were prostitutes, sought out women-only hostels and half-way houses such as Toronto's Street Haven, only to be prohibited entry altogether or to be subtly encouraged to convert to 'proper' feminine heterosexuality.[42]

Throughout the 1950s and early 1960s, motivated by alleged communist and sexual 'threats to the nation,' the RCMP collected the names of thousands of 'suspected homosexuals.' The ruling Pearson government sponsored research into means to detect 'sexual perversion' (such as the 'fruit machine') and hundreds of lesbians and gay men were purged from their jobs in the federal civil service and the military.[43] Through myriad avenues, from the regulation of 'sexual psychopaths' and 'indecent literature' to the sex education of adolescents, heterosexual 'normality' was produced as *the* central organizer of postwar sexual and moral identities.[44]

In the broad context of an ever-expanding commercial (hetero)sex industry, voyeuristic portrayals of lesbianism were popularized in mass-market pornography (*Playboy* was launched in 1952) and lurid pulp fiction. A vast array of dime-store paperback novels were published in the United States and distributed across Canada in the 1950s and 1960s under such titles as *Forbidden Love, Satan Was a Lesbian, Daytime in Suburbia,* and *Black Nylon Lovers.* Written largely by men, the pulps featured gay female characters, all-female settings (such as Greenwich Village bars, sororities, and women's barracks), and themes of 'strange' seduction, violence between women, suicide, alcoholism, and heterosexual conversion. In 1952, an Ottawa judge declared that the lesbian pulp novel *Women's Barracks,* by Tereska Torres, was 'exceedingly frank' and the distributor was convicted under obscenity law.[45]

In *The Joy of Lesbian Sex,* Sisley and Harris describe the dominant theme of fifties and sixties lesbian pulp novels: 'femme meets butch (usually in Greenwich Village); drunkenness, violence and heavy (but very unspecified) sex ensues; femme ponders the problems of being "different" and outcast; the young man in the background quickly replaces the butch in the foreground and we close on a vision of a heterosexual cottage covered with heterosexual ivy. The butch either commits suicide straight off, begins to drink herself to death or finds a new "innocent" to corrupt.'[46] In contrast to the titillation peddled by predominantly male authors, lesbian writers like Paula Christian, Ann Bannon, and Valerie Taylor also wrote strong, rebellious lesbian characters into their 1950s and 1960s paperbacks. They offered readers positive role models as well as information about gay clothing styles, argot, bars, coffee-shops, resorts like Fire Island and Provincetown, and neighbourhoods like San Francisco's Barbery Coast.[47] Similarly, in Montréal and Toronto, the tabloids or the 'yellow press' (*Justice Weekly, Flash, Hush, True News Times, Flirt, Flirt et Potins,* and *Frivolo*) provided lesbian (and gay male) readers with clues to local gay codes and milieux. For years, the Toronto-based *Rocket, TNT,* and *Tab* carried gay gossip columns under the headings, 'Toronto Fairy Go-Round,' 'A Study in Lavender,' and 'Fairy Tales Are Retold,' along with personal ads placed by those seeking same-sex partners. At the same time, they published lewd tales of frustrated lesbian housewives, evil lesbian prostitutes, and vice-squad raids on 'homo' bars and clubs.[48] These sensational tabloids – the precursors to the modern-day *National Enquirer, Globe,* and *Star* – sought to expose the encroachment of the 'cult of homosexuality' or the 'society of sexual inverts' on unsuspecting, 'normal' citizens. As such, they contributed to a growing awareness of, and fascination with, 'unorthodox sex exponents,' while playing on heterosexual fears that male and female 'queers' were busily taking over cities.

In the 1970s, in the wake of New York's Stonewall Inn rebellion – the catalyst of modern-day gay liberation – new constituencies of lesbian feminists, or 'dyke warriors,' sought to rid themselves of negative stereotypes and the compulsion to hide or compromise. They scorned practices of 'passing' in straight society, sustaining closeted lesbian relationships in suburbia, and relying on what they felt was seedy, 'apolitical,' and 'regressive' butch/femme bar life.[49] Unaware of the earlier feats of courage, love, and determination by gay women (and men) whose proto-political, pre-Stonewall struggles prepared the ground for liberation movements, members of the Lesbian Organization of Toronto (LOOT) were devoted to transcending sex and gender norms. It was not good enough to be a proud lesbian feminist. LOOT faithfuls endeavoured to politicize and publicize the personal – clothing, work, relationships, housing arrangements, and sexuality – in ways that enabled them to *be* lesbian in all facets of their lives, just as heterosexual women are presumed to *be* heterosexual in every facet of their lives. Against the dual legacy of invisibility and persecution, self-consciously naming oneself a lesbian feminist enacted a direct blow to the hegemonic discourse of female homosexual deviance and perversion. As film critic Shari Zeck observes, 'The ability to make oneself heard or seen and the ability to alter what others hear and see is necessary to the very survival of lesbians and gay men.'[50]

Defining a lesbian-feminist identity in the context of a re-emerging women's movement and Black Power that recast symbols of black pride and brotherhood became requisite to the process of positive self-definition.[51] The invention of a lesbian feminist praxis, a Lesbian Nation, made possible both the integration of previously dichotomized public and private lives and the articulation of lesbian identity as a basis for political and cultural organizing. Throughout this book, I use the highly politicized term 'nation.' Globally in the 1990s, ethnic, political, and religious nationalisms have deepened, and in some cases have provoked bloody warfare, excessive ideological dogma, and brutal 'ethnic cleansing' within and across state borders. Over twenty years ago, a kind of North American lesbian nationalism inspired by Jill Johnston's book *Lesbian Nation* (1973) embodied much more innocent, even quixotic, notions of non-violent militancy, feminist utopia, and the power of women-only collective agency. Speaking sameness, commonality, and the unity of a lesbian-feminist sisterhood not only promised cohesion, it also offered the possibility of discovering individual and collective empowerment, beauty, and knowledge in public, once-tabooed settings.

In other words, to lesbian activists in the 1970s, whether they identified as separatists or not, 'nation' served as a potent metaphor for the visible maturation of a subculture once consigned to debilitating secrecy. 'Lesbian Nation' signified shared language, ideology, cultural capital (including symbols and aesthetics), and collective identity – the very discursive elements that theorists such as Alberto Melucci, Barbara Epstein, David Plotke, and others associate with the emergence of 'new social movements' in the postwar period.[52] Though neither *Social Movements / Social Change* (1988) nor *Organizing Dissent* (1992) offer critical accounts of lesbian activism, authors in both Canadian collections note that a Marxist analysis devoted solely to political economy is ill equipped to explicate the vitality of the lesbian/gay, feminist, aboriginal, peace/antinuclear, and ecology movements of the 1970s and 1980s.[53] In centring lesbian-feminist discourse and practice, *The House That Jill Built* tests social-movement theory that emphasizes the importance of identity, aesthetics, and culture as terrains of struggle and the construction of community as a basis for changing society. It also puts into play Antonio Gramsci's definition of counter-hegemony as a *dis*organization of consent, a disruption of (sexist and heterosexist) hegemonic discourses and practices.[54] In all, this book aims to contribute new insights to scholarly fields of social-movement research, contemporary intellectual history, cultural theory, and lesbian/gay/queer studies.

METHODOLOGIES

The House That Jill Built draws on the eclectic mix of fiction, poetry, coming-out stories, and non-fiction manifestos published in the 1970s by largely white, middle-class lesbian feminists in the small-scale feminist, lesbian, and gay press. Overwhelmingly American in origin, the materials include the periodicals *off our backs, Sinister Wisdom, The Furies,* and *Lesbian Connection;* books released by the presses of Diana, Inc., Daughters, and Naiad; and albums from Olivia Records. Also useful to this study are personal and organizational files, journals, sound recordings, mimeos and newsletters, posters, buttons, T-shirts, chapbooks, conference programs, graffiti, photographs, and essays, most of which is housed at the Canadian Women's Movement Archives at the University of Ottawa, and the Canadian Lesbian and Gay Archives in Toronto. Mainstream newspapers, mass-circulation women's magazines, television shows, films, and police commissions offer diverse clues to textually mediated lesbian identity formation and community development.

In addition to plumbing archival sources, between the fall of 1988 and the spring of 1991 I conducted taped interviews (average length: two hours) with thirty-one women who were former members of the Lesbian Organization of Toronto. I also interviewed three women (two bisexuals, one heterosexual) who were non-lesbian feminists during LOOT's existence (see appendix). And I draw on interviews I did with sixteen lesbians who did not consider themselves to be full-time members of LOOT. None of these samples is exhaustive as there were many more women whom I did not interview and who were active lesbian feminists at the time. The thirty-one former LOOT members ranged in age from thirty-one to forty-eight, which means that the majority were in their late teens, twenties, and early thirties when LOOT first opened its doors in 1977. Twenty-six women identify as middle-class and five identify as working-class. Twenty-eight women are white; I also interviewed two Native women and one Black woman. Religious beliefs among the women varied: some are Jewish, a number were raised as Catholics. Though several participated in diverse forms of feminist spiritualism and one woman identified as a Buddhist at the time of the interviews, most had not practised any form of organized religion since the 1970s. When interviewed, all of them lived in downtown Toronto and over a third owned their own homes. The others lived in cooperative housing or apartments; about half lived with lovers and two couples were raising A.I. babies.[55]

Influenced by Davis and Kennedy's work on Buffalo lesbian bar culture between 1940 and 1960, I chose oral history, not simply as a way to collect individual life stories, but as a basis to construct the history of a community. The ups and downs of building an 'army of lovers' *and* ex-lovers are far more likely to be communicated via oral histories than they are in print. Furthermore, few groups recorded the internal workings of their collectives, for instance, consensus decision making, the dynamics of 'trashing,' and the problems of leadership and membership. Only through in-depth interviews was I able to tap my subjects' often emotional recollections of a time they equate with unparalleled exuberance and growth, as well as vigorous, sometimes immobilizing, controversy.

Most researchers who have interviewed lesbians have found it necessary to deploy sophisticated mechanisms in order to safeguard the identities of their subjects. For the most part, if a woman is not out, she likely feels compelled to orchestrate a 'double life.' In fact, she may build her emotional, physical, and sexual life with another woman and yet not identify as either lesbian or gay. All but one of the former LOOT members I interviewed wanted their real names to appear in the book. They argued strongly for visibility on strictly political grounds as a way of lesbianly claiming pride in themselves and their community.

It seems to me that we need to map all the peaks and valleys of lesbian-feminist culture in the 1970s before travelling prematurely 'beyond the lesbian nation.'[56] I am not convinced by decontextualized, ahistorical, and dismissive equations of lesbian feminism, 1970s-style, with a prudish, backwards, humour-free, selfish, and ill-conceived separatism. In *Odd Girls and Twilight Lovers: A History of Lesbian Life in Twentieth Century America*, historian Lillian Faderman emphasizes the 'fanaticism' of 'excessively idealistic lesbians' who 'failed' because of 'youthful inexperience and inability to compromise unbridled enthusiasms.'[57] By contrast, *The House That Jill Built* explores the *meanings* that LOOT members themselves attributed to public lesbian culture in the 1970s – what they learned, what they gained, what mistakes they made, and how they now make sense of their successes and shortcomings. The poststructuralist thought of Judith Butler, Diana Fuss, Jackie Goldsby, Pratibha Parmar, and Eve Sedgwick encourages me to abandon notions of a stable, monolithic, and immutable lesbian-feminist identity in the service of an approach supple enough to capture the dominant ideological underpinnings of Lesbian Nation alongside the lived discontinuities, contradictions, and complexities of identity and community formation. As such, my aim is neither to patronize nor to romanticize white, middle-class lesbian feminism, but to illuminate the richness and density of one historic moment of courageous resistance.

In describing and analysing the complex processes of lesbian-feminist identity formation and community development in Toronto during the 1970s, I am deeply aware of the desire among the women I interviewed for a celebratory reclamation of this period. Co-author of *Sappho Was a Right-On Woman* (1972) Sidney Abbott contends that 'a group that is just raising its head after centuries of bowing it under the weight of prejudice, cruelty and exclusion wants to celebrate, not conduct self-criticism.'[58] Lesbian (and gay) grass-roots activists have long relied upon the assertion of a positive 'minority group identity.' Hence, a number of lesbian scholars, myself included, have wondered whether investigating the achievements *and* the limitations of lesbian-feminist organizing will lead to a sense of group frailty instead of robustness.[59] At the Berkshire Women's History Conference at Rutgers University in June 1990, historian Judith Schwarz advised: 'I think we have to construct lesbian identity before we deconstruct it.'

Yet it feels necessary to describe the often-unforeseeable pitfalls that unsettled, contained, and in some instances disorganized efforts to make manifest a downtown Lesbian Nation in the 1970s. At the same time, documenting experiences of alienation, extreme disappointment, and loss of self internal to lesbian-feminist communities may be seen to undermine the ideologically preferred image of these communities as open, stable, and conflict-free. Furthermore, it could be argued that turning our postmodern attention to the strength *and* the fragility of lesbian-feminist identity and community formation is a politically dangerous enterprise given our present climate of moral and economic conservatism. However, it is this very fundamental (and unresolvable?) tension that runs through the story of *The House That Jill Built*.

OUTLINING THE FRAMEWORK

This book is divided into four sections. Part One is devoted to forms of lesbian feminist social and political organization that predate and prefigure the emergence of LOOT. In chapter 1, I explore the ways in which definitions of lesbian feminism were initially articulated in contradistinction to women's liberation, gay liberation, the left, and lesbian 'closetry.' In chapter 2, I examine the small-scale cultural, social, and political ventures launched by and for lesbian feminists in the early-to-mid 1970s as a means to experiment with the notion of an autonomous lesbian movement. Chapter 3 maps the impetus for the foundation of an independent lesbian-feminist centre in Toronto, as well as the vision that those involved brought to the planning meetings.

In Part Two, I examine the processes through which largely white, urban, university-educated, and young LOOT members invented modes of living that integrated all aspects of lesbianism into their everyday/everynight worlds. A key focus of these two chapters is the extent to which LOOT members created a set of 'politically correct' standards of life/style and sexuality that gave shape and definition to their desire for a downtown Lesbian Nation. At the same time, a central contradiction to be problematized concerns the claim made by LOOT members to universality and diversity, and the ways in which inward-looking community norms and attempts to establish ideological conformity undercut and undermined their original pledge to inclusiveness.

Part Three focuses on LOOT's social, cultural, and political accomplishments. Questions of the internal dynamics of LOOT's decision-making processes, leadership, structure, and priorities are explored in chapter 6, as are the successes of LOOT-based initiatives, from music to poetry to the monthly newsletter. In chapters 7 and 8, I reconstruct the participation of LOOT members in four major political debates that placed the sensitive, vexing question of coalition politics on the LOOT agenda. Chapter 7 addresses the varied lesbian-feminist positions that emerged upon confronting two crises that arose in the context of gay-male liberation struggles, that is, the Anita Bryant crusade and 'Men Loving Boys Loving Men.' In chapter 8, I examine the splits between radical and socialist feminist lesbians in and outside of LOOT that deepened in the context of broader ideological struggles within the women's movement, that is, International Women's Day and the 'Fine Kettle of Fish' forum. Both chapters demonstrate how the desire for a coherent lesbian-feminist politic became disrupted by the articulation of competing political positions among Toronto lesbian feminists.

In the final section, Part Four, chapter 9 is devoted to an analysis of LOOT's closure: why it closed when it did, how the women felt about its demise, what they learned, and where they next directed their activist energies. To conclude, chapter 10 points to prospects for the defence, sustenance, and future of lesbian-feminist institutions as well as the prospects for alliance building across lines of sexuality, gender, race, and class in deeply conservative economic, political, and moral times.

PART ONE

1

Shaking the ground: The emergence of lesbian-feminist discourse

Lesbian is the word, the label, the condition that holds women in line. When a woman hears this word tossed her way, she knows she is stepping out of line. She knows that she has crossed the terrible boundary of her sex role. She recoils, she protests, she reshapes her actions to gain approval. Lesbian is a label invented by the man to throw at any woman who dares to be his equal, who dares to challenge his prerogatives (including that of all women as part of the exchange medium among men), who dares to assert the primacy of her own needs.
Radicalesbians, 'Woman Identified Woman' (1970)[1]

The general social and economic destablization that began in the immediate post–Second World War period persisted throughout the 1960s. It involved the continued expansion of capitalist markets, the tremendous growth in university and college enrolments, the increasing numbers of women entering the labour force, the introduction of the birth-control pill, new abortion technology, a declining birth rate, and the increased attention to sex-related issues in the media and advertising. By the late 1960s, a climate of reform prevailed in Canada as liberalism promised a more equitable allocation of material resources. Poverty was 'discovered,' as were 'regional disparities,' and the welfare state expanded, primarily through health, education, and social programs. In this context of economic, social, and gender/sexual *bouleversement*, a heady, intoxicating rush of political protest erupted across Canada, the United States, Britain, and parts of western Europe. Black civil-rights activism (with roots in the 1950s), Native-rights organizing, student-led anti–Vietnam War resistance, the new left, the struggle for Québec's right to self-determination, gay liberation, and the second-wave women's movement emerged as organized, angry challenges to what was perceived as a fundamentally corrupt, unequal, and disempowering social, economic, and political system.[2]

In their book on contemporary Canadian feminism, Adamson, Briskin, and McPhail argue that 'the women's liberation movement emerged as a separate activist movement in Canada in the late 1960s and the early 1970s, as feminists put forward analyses of women's oppression, proposed strategies for change, and formed organizations.'[3] By 1968 in cities like Vancouver, Montréal, and Toronto, mostly white, middle-class feminists (many of whom had experience in the new left), set up consciousness-raising groups, study groups, newsletters/journals, and women-only services, though this happened unevenly and with clear regional specificity. The vast range of topics presented for debate and action in the early years of the second wave included abortion, contraception, child care, support for working and immigrant women, the gendered division of labour, wages for housework, sexism in advertising, and the relationship of feminism to the left. Because no one segment of the grass-roots movement possessed the power to dominate, the issue of lesbianism (and the oppression specific to lesbians) was taken up differently by different segments.

Toronto Women's Liberation Movement (TWLM) – a multi-issue feminist organization with roots in the new left of the 1960s – was formed by a group of white, heterosexual, university-educated women in 1969.[4] With virtually no mention of lesbian issues in the early TWLM's records and newsletters, the relationship of lesbianism to the women's movement, and to a broad socialist vision, sprung to the fore in the fall of 1970. At the Indo-Chinese Conference sponsored by members of TWLM that October, the bitterness and divisions that erupted in response to 'the lesbian question' revealed the lack of clarity, the confusion, and the need for debate within TWLM itself. Angered by the unspoken assumption that it was not possible to be lesbian, feminist, and anti-imperialist, Mary Bolton reported on the conference for the *TWLM Newsletter*: 'The lack of sisterhood was apparent in the paranoia regarding "feminists" and "lesbians," the totally appalling and inexcusably rude treatment given our sisters in the Chicago Women's Liberation Rock Band (who donated their time and energy and then were not allowed to play except a couple of numbers ... because there was no time for them) and the lack of understanding given the lesbian demands (after all it *had* been announced that there *would* be lesbian workshops – which were canceled at the last minute – and many women had come expecting them) ..: Women became categories [at this conference] not people ... and began to polarize.'[5] In the spring of 1971, sparked by critiques posed during and in the wake of the fall conference, a 'lesbian educational' was set up to facilitate discussion within TWLM.[6] Following this forum, a lesbian collective was founded and operated under the umbrella of TWLM. However, confusion about the links between working-class struggle, women's oppression, and sexuality (that is, lesbianism) plagued members until the demise of the TWLM in 1972.

Toronto New Feminists (NF), a radical feminist organization that left TWLM in 1969, also struggled to face the divisive issue of lesbianism. According to Holly Devor, the leadership of the NF warned against the negative influence of lesbians internal to their own (closed) ranks. And as Devor recalls in an interview with me, NF spokeswoman Bonnie Kreps denied the presence of lesbians in the organization to the mainstream press. Even in the feminist press years later, not one of the NF leaders profiled addressed the subject of lesbianism or lesbian oppression.[7] And in their own bimonthly newsletter, *The New Feminist* (1969–72), the invisibility or nonexistence of lesbians prevailed. In 1972, having challenged the 'bourgeois, anti-lesbian attitude' of the New Feminists, Devor reports that she and several other 'shit disturbing' lesbians were eventually instructed by 'the management' to 'get out.'

Toronto Women's Caucus (TWC) was formed by members of the League for Socialist Action who broke from the New Feminists after the Abortion Caravan in the summer of 1970. Committed to establishing a mass women's movement 'without party affiliations and independent of men,' they made access to safe, accessible abortion in free-standing clinics across the country their primary focus. On the subject of lesbianism, in the twelve issues of their newspaper *Velvet Fist* published between 1970 and 1972, there is one editorial mention of 'the double oppression of black and gay women' (1972), two short pieces, 'Growing Up Gay' (1971) and 'Gay Sisters' (1971), and a list of quotes 'on lesbianism' culled from American feminist anthologies.[8] *Bellyfull*, a newspaper published by women with former links to TWLM but intent on producing an 'independent feminist' paper, was published between May and October of 1972 before it amalgamated with *Velvet*

Fist to form *The Other Woman*. In the four issues of *Bellyfull* that were produced, there is only one mention of lesbianism – a short prose poem reprinted from Judy Grahn's *Edward the Dyke* collection.[9]

Without question, the lack of lesbian-related discussion 'on the record' does not accurately reflect the passionate debates and discoveries that rocked virtually all participants in women's liberation during this period. Based on her experience in British Columbia, Dorothy E. Smith notes that straight feminists were very nervous about how an explicit avowal of lesbianism would affect the involvement of women who were not yet members of the women's movement. Debates raged within feminist organizations and concerned questions of whether or not to identify with lesbianism, and at what cost.[10] Smith recalls that straight feminists tended to live a striking disjuncture: they recognized the personal and political significance of lesbianism and yet they denied its significance on the level of public policy and ideology.

In large part, relationships between straight feminists and lesbians who identified as feminists during the late sixties and early seventies in Toronto (and elsewhere) were fraught with tension, suspicion, and confusion. Feminists I interviewed, both straight and lesbian, told me that too much fear and not enough honesty repeatedly clogged communication channels. Lesbians just out of the closet didn't anticipate marginalization or the fear of guilt by association. Nor did they expect the (unspoken) desire of some straight feminists to suppress a visible lesbian-feminist presence. In 1972, Pat Murphy and Linda Jain capsulized their conundrum: 'Even though we are all sisters, many women in Women's Lib reject their own gay contingent ... If our own sisters do not realize our double struggle as gay women, then whom do we get support from?'[11] The same year, in *The Other Woman*, a lesbian summed up her disenchantment this way: 'I resent being put in the position of being a token lesbian, a strange species who must always be defining to other women why I am gay, while no heterosexual women are put in the position of having to define why they are straight ... They say that being gay is just a "personal matter" and of course everyone has worked those [personal matters] out already somewhere else.'[12] Members of women's liberation organizations tended to rely on American print materials or speakers from homophile groups rather than attempt to name and strategize around the particulars of lesbian oppression within their own local constituencies. In fact, what was not clear was the extent to which straight feminists' discomfort with lesbianism was a measure of internalized antilesbian attitudes and/or a sign of political disagreement over the nature of women's oppression and the appropriate strategies to combat it. If, as many feminists with roots in the left argued, class was the primary contradiction, how was one to reconcile the 'men are the enemy' claim made by some self-declared radical feminists and some increasingly vocal lesbians by the early 1970s?

Clearly, the wariness and anger that marked most encounters between straight and lesbian feminists was not restricted to the Canadian scene. Gay/straight splits, or what Alice Echols calls 'the first sex war,' were beginning to heat up and become even more acrimonious in the United States.[13] Purges of lesbians wracked the National Organization of Women (NOW) between 1969 and 1971. Commonly disparaged as the lavender menace, the lavender herring, or the Achilles heel of the women's movement, lesbians encountered humiliation and oppression within women's liberation organizing.[14]

In 1972, Rita Mae Brown called for the establishment of an autonomous lesbian-feminist movement. A charismatic, influential member of New York's Radicalesbians and a founder of the separatist collective The Furies, Brown pondered: if lesbianism was a choice, then those who continued to relate to men could be defined as those who refused to choose.[15] Later, in essays published in *The Furies* newspaper, she elaborated: 'You do not free yourself by polishing your chains, yet that is what heterosexual women do.'[16] 'And,' she continued, 'the terms heterosexual and lesbian mark the difference between reform and revolution. It is the woman who loves women who will make the next revolution. It is the woman who sells out to men who will betray her.'[17]

To many who shared Brown's rage, 'feminism is the theory and lesbianism is the practice' – the dictum attributed to Ti-Grace Atkinson – best encapsulated the claim to the superior praxis of lesbian feminism. Or as American theorist Katie King argues, for many lesbian activists, this discursive 'fact' constituted 'a magical sign through which political identity was constructed.'[18] Importantly, however, not all lesbians agreed with an unambiguously pro-lesbian, separatist strategy.

In 1970, New York's Radicalesbians published their manifesto, 'The Woman-Identified Woman,' which was widely circulated and reprinted in the English Canadian feminist press.[19] In this powerful, clever treatise, the tendency to view lesbianism as a private, personal, and sex-related lifestyle issue is recast as the quintessential act of woman-to-woman solidarity. Lesbianism is not, however, championed as the truest feminist identity and politic. Building on the Radicalesbians' position, in 1971, Anne Koedt warned against 'the false implication that to have no men in your personal life means you are therefore living the life of fighting for radical feminist change ... Sex roles and male supremacy,' she argued, 'will not go away simply by women becoming lesbians.'[20] In other words, there is an implication in both texts that lesbians must struggle as feminists within the broad context of the women's movement.

Yet not always welcomed into the movement in the early-to-mid 1970s, lesbians grappled with the vexing question of political location – from where and with whom to struggle. Indeed, the prickly relationship of lesbianism to feminism is evident in some Canadian writings from this period. In March 1973, Karol's article 'Dyke Power' was published in *The Other Woman*, and it reflects the influence of Rita Mae Brown and The Furies: 'Little has been heard from the radical, man-hating dyke simply because we will not allow ourselves to become Liberalized ... [but] I want to repeat that Dykes are organizing: this being the only group of Females who are threatening to the male structure, and who can create agony within.'[21] Conversely, more hesitant and more ambivalent about the positioning of lesbians in relation to social protest movements, Lorna reported on the 1974 Lesbian Conference in Montréal for *The Other Woman*: 'Should we work with the gay liberation movement or the women's movement? Which comes first, our status as lesbians or our status as women? A group of strong women, lesbian and straight, but all feminist, is needed. Alone we cannot begin to accomplish, politically and socially, what we could do as a group.'[22] In spite of the spotty history of joint lesbian/heterosexual feminist activity, some lesbians not only desired collaboration, but argued for its merits. In the fall of 1973, writing for *The Other Woman*, Adrienne Potts claimed: 'It's time for women to get together to struggle for our lives and our freedom, so that we can feel strong and build a strong community of women that can change and grow with other sisters.'[23] Echoing Potts's words, Pat Leslie stated: 'The true woman-identified woman is out to change the world, to make the world over into an angry but loving woman's image! We can be powerful if only we were Sisters!'[24] Unlike calls for lesbian separatism made by The Furies and other groups in the United States at this time, Canadian lesbian feminists seemed committed to a gay/straight reconciliation. In the summer 1974 issue of Vancouver's *The Pedestal*, Judi Morton stressed the inclusiveness of 'lesbian' as a political category: 'In my opinion, a lesbian is a woman-identified woman ... all women fully committed to the cause of freeing themselves and other women from oppression are "lesbians". Feminism and lesbianism are in no way mutually exclusive terms. A true feminist is by definition a lesbian, in the political sense. Lesbianism is not just another issue of feminism; a lesbian is simply a full-time feminist.'[25] For other lesbian activists, embracing straight feminists on equal terms, both personally and politically, without reservation, was easier said than done. Underneath the ideological weight of an abstract, rhetorical 'sisterhood,' most lesbian feminists carried memories of scorn, purges, and snubs. To Pat Murphy, 'It was like the lesbians were always at the back of the bus.' In the Montréal lesbian periodical *Long Time Coming*, an anonymous contributor recounted stories heard at the Montréal lesbian conference in 1974: 'A lesbian who was helping organize a straight CR group was told that her services were not desired since women coming to terms with their feminism don't need a gay woman around. In another city, lesbians can't touch each other in the front room of the Woman's Centre. In another city, lesbians asked to change the night of their Drop-In and they were told that if they had the Drop-In the same night as a straight activity they would have to have it on the top floor and stay there. After all, what if a lesbian made a pass at a straight woman?'[26] A year following the purge of herself and friends from the Toronto New Feminists in 1972, Holly Devor recalls that she suffered another round of humiliation at A Woman's Place. Advised that she and other lesbians were 'too affectionate' and would 'scare off' straight women, Devor was once again reminded of the hostility and fear vis-à-vis lesbianism that had been simmering inside feminist circles for several years. The drama of the conflict is especially vivid in Pat Leslie's memory: 'There was this huge trauma that went rippling through North America, it was like a plague, and we had this gay/straight split finally, and it nearly destroyed us. [At A Woman's Place] we were literally coming in and going out separate doors.'

Contrarily, between 1974 and 1975, the Lesbian Caucus of the British Columbia Federation of Women (BCFW) forged a position on the desirability and the necessity of personal and political unity among heterosexual and lesbian feminists.[27] Yet this was not accomplished without often agonizing struggle. At first, when some straight feminist members of the BCFW saw the newsletter that included the list of lesbian demands, they recoiled: 'One woman said that she had to hide her copy of the newsletter under her mattress so that nobody would see it. Another woman said that she had to burn hers for fear that the garbage man would see it when he picked up her garbage and would see the word lesbian right there in the paper.'[28]

The BCFW standing committee received a two-page letter from Terrace, a small northern community. It addressed the lesbians as 'green slime who should go back to the bars where you came from.' And, 'left unchecked,' the Terrace feminists warned, 'the lesbians would bring the organization down to their gutter level.'[29] In the face of fear and dissent, Lesbian Caucus members urged reconciliation: 'Laws and attitudes oppressive to lesbians are used to threaten and control all women. Every woman must have the right to choose for herself a lifestyle suitable to her needs as an individual ... Women's fear of themselves and each other clearly divides our strength as a group. Until such fear is no longer used to control and manipulate us, women will not be free to choose alternative lifestyles.'[30] Unlike the BCFW or the National Organization of Women (NOW) in the United States, there was no centralized, broad-based feminist organization in Ontario within which Toronto lesbians might agitate for the inclusion of a lesbian platform (however defined).[31] And without this body, there was no urgent, immediate, and irrefutable need for lesbian and straight feminists to work together in pursuit of conflict resolution.[32] Writing of her experience in Toronto, Amy Gottlieb remembered 'the fearful and often hysterical response to open lesbians in the early 70s.' The issue of lesbian rights, as she recalls, 'was considered or treated by much of the women's movement as a divisive or touchy issue, to be treated (or obliterated) with the utmost tactical agility, thus covering us in a cloud of mystery and uncertainty.'[33]

In the early 1970s, collaboration with gay men appealed to a number of lesbian feminists. To these women, the promise of accepting their own gayness, finding other lesbians (as friends and lovers), and working to contest negative images of homosexuality resided in the project of gay liberation. Indeed, a small number of women discovered meaningful work and friendships in what for them became a collective, gender-mixed venture. For others, as the seventies wore on, the struggle to find their own voice and to be taken seriously as lesbians *and* political actors by 'gay brothers' posed dilemmas no less intense or wrenching than those internal to grass-roots feminism.

By 1970, gay-liberation groups had sprung up like spring tulips across Canada. Organizations like the University of Toronto Homophile Association (1969), le front de libération homosexuelle in Montréal (1970), the Vancouver Gay Liberation Front (1970), the York University Homophile Association (1970), the Community Homophile Association of Toronto (CHAT, 1970), Gays of Ottawa (1971), Gay Alliance for Equality in Halifax (1972), and the Gay Community Centre of Saskatoon (1973) signalled a new, militant generation of (largely white, middle-class) gay activists. On most college and university campuses, gay groups lobbied for access to funds, resources, and office space. Convinced that 'the liberation of homosexuals must be the work of homosexuals themselves,'[34] a small group of young gay male members of Toronto Gay Action (a direct-action faction of CHAT) published the first issue of *The Body Politic* in November 1971. In Vancouver, the *Gay Tide* newspaper was launched shortly thereafter. Numerous newsletters were produced by members of mixed lesbian and gay organizations across Canada and served as cultural/political/social lifelines to people living in small towns.

During these early years, the public announcement of one's homosexual identity with pride, bravado, and considerable nose-thumbing became *the* mobilizing strategy. Borrowing from Black civil-rights and Black Power movements in the sixties, slogans like 'gay is good,' 'gay is beautiful,' and, later, 'gay is just as good as straight' and 'hey, hey what do you say, try it once our way' captured the spirit of defiance and signified the shedding of psychological subordination that gay men and women had internalized. It also marked a sharp dissociation with the assimilationist position of early homophile activists who were concerned to emphasize the similarities between homosexuals and heterosexuals.

Homosexuality, gay liberationists argued, was as natural and normal as heterosexuality (if not more so). Once a private decision was made to accept one's homosexual desires and admit one's sexual identity to other gay men and women, the meaning of coming out in the militant post-Stonewall period was transformed. American historian John D'Emilio argues: 'To come out of the "closet" quintessentially expressed the fusion of the personal and the political that the radicalism of the 1960s exalted.'[35] A continual process through which identity is claimed and embraced, coming out was seen to represent the first step to both personal and collective liberation. Early gay activists declared: 'We must start coming out on television, on the radio, in newspapers, in public – everywhere!'[36] Writing for the *Rat* in 1970, Martha Shelley warned: 'Understand this – that the worst part of being a homosexual is having to keep it secret. Not the occasional murders by police or teenage

queer beaters, not the loss of jobs or explusion from schools or dis-
honorable discharges – but the daily knowledge that what you are is
so awful that it cannot be revealed.'[37]

Varied in scope, mandate, and activities, the foundation of gay
groups made possible both the surge in, and the response to, increasing
numbers of out gay people. Some groups were dedicated to the provision of self-help, support initiatives, and social services. Others concentrated their energies and resources on developing and implementing
educational, cultural, and political programs. In Toronto (and elsewhere), by the early-to-mid 1970s, gay activists had identified civil
rights–related strategies as key to their collective liberation. Building
on networks and projects nurtured by homophile associations, the Gay
Alliance Toward Equality (1973), Gay Youth of Toronto (1972), the
John Damien Defence Committee (1975), and the Coalition for Gay
Rights in Ontario (1975) focused on legal reforms. Among the central
demands were the inclusion of sexual orientation in the Ontario
Human Rights Code and the Canadian Bill of Rights, the elimination
of all references to homosexuality in the Immigration Act, the abolition
of 'age of consent' laws, and the unequivocal decriminalization of homosexuality in the Canadian Criminal Code.

Police raids of baths and bars, the entrapment of gay men in washrooms, the refusal of mainstream newspapers and radio stations to
carry gay-related advertising, the firings in 1975 of John Damien, a
racing steward with the Ontario Racing Commission, and Doug Wilson, a teaching assistant at the University of Saskatchewan, together
with the seizure of *The Body Politic* from newsstands by the Metro Toronto morality squad that same year, brought home the intrusive, coer-
cive force of state and social repression. The National Gay Rights Coalition (NGRC) was formed in Quebec City in 1973 for the purpose
of organizing an annual conference and facilitating the coordination
of movement tactics, techniques, and priorities.[38]

To counter and neutralize the depth and breadth of gay oppression,
as well as encourage the expansion of gay resistance, activists designed
multiple, inventive manoeuvres. At times, they borrowed from the
1960s shock specialties of guerilla demonstrations, street theatre, 'gay-
ins,' and kiss-ins. The more traditionally political procedures of lobbying, picketing, gathering petitions, letter writing, and fund raising
were also employed. At other times, activists pursued education-related
initiatives like television and radio appearances, talks in high schools,
universities, and community centres, and the distribution of leaflets

and handouts, in addition to highly public celebrations like Gay Pride Week in Toronto (first established in 1972).[39]

THE TROUBLE WITH GAY LIBERATION

In 1969, following from then Justice Minister Pierre Trudeau's famous declaration, 'The state has no place in the bedrooms of the nation,' the Canadian criminal code was amended or liberalized to include the partial decriminalization of homosexuality and the partial legalization of abortion.[40] Unhappy with the limitations of the reforms, activist lesbians sought out relationships to gay men, gay-liberation organizations, and the movement more generally. For the most part, from the beginning, they encountered the reality that gay organizations and the gay press were led and controlled by men. The difficulty of attracting and then sustaining an active female membership was acknowledged by women and some men as an almost universal problem. To women, this was not an altogether unfamiliar state of affairs. Before the Canadian criminal code reforms of 1969, a number of homophile organizations were founded, though it was rare that women were centrally involved.[41] The Canadian Council on Religion and the Homosexual (formerly the Social Council on Hygiene) was formed in Ottawa in 1965. In Vancouver in 1964, the Association for Social Knowledge (ASK) was founded as an 'educational society' by a mixed group of homosexual and heterosexual men, though several lesbians joined later and made significant contributions.[42]

Reflecting on their experience of homophile activism in the 1950s and 1960s, Del Martin and Phyllis Lyon – co-founders of the Daughters of Bilitis – commented that 'the movement as a whole ... meant male-dominated, male-oriented, male chauvinistic policies and attitudes.'[43] In the early 1970s, recalls Sue Wells, who would later become a key figure in Toronto lesbian-feminist circles: 'I went to a gay liberation CR group. Gerald Hannon and *The Body Politic* boys were in my group. I was the only woman.' In the March 1971 issue of the *York University Homophile Association Newsletter*, the following unsigned, critical comment echoes several of these concerns: 'An inordinate amount of time is spent at some homophile meetings on rather tedious discussions concerning police activities and sex in public washrooms. Members thus begin to lose their interest and girls especially become alienated and have been known to exclaim exasperatedly, "If you guys would just stay out of the johns, we'd have time to discuss really important things."'[44] In early 1971, conscious of the dearth of gay women at CHAT, the editor of *Backchat* admitted, 'We need the support of women and would like to see more of them at our functions.'[45] By the spring of 1972, the women who were involved with CHAT contested their underrepresentation on the executive board and they succeeded in securing five of the ten seats for women members. Still, they were reluctant to push gay men for more fundamental, far-reaching (and potentially threatening) changes. They were more likely to protest 'the classic male chauvinism' of bar owners who prohibited the entrance of gay women who wore jeans and/or lacked a male escort.[46]

Gay women and lesbians also felt collectively under siege, alongside their gay male friends and co-workers at CHAT, when their centre was bombed by a Molotov cocktail in the spring of 1972, and they coordinated a 'round-the-clock defence plan.' Shortly thereafter, representatives of the right-wing Western Guard – the same ones who threw the bomb – used Protect U gas (a form of mace) and anti-homosexual slogans to disrupt a St Lawrence Town Hall forum on the 'Myths and Realities of Homosexuality.'[47] Moderated by journalist Barbara Frum, the panel included CHAT members Kathleen Brindly and Pat Murphy.

In effect, for a handful of women, their emotional and political investment in the ongoing work and stability of the organization extended far beyond a mere 'support' role. Women like Pat Murphy, Aline Gregory, Stephanie St John, Judy Masters, Linda Jain, and Chris Fox already had spent several years doing joint speaking engagements with gay men, taking calls on the distress line (as many as 200–300 per day), offering peer counselling, appearing at police commissions and city council meetings, organizing the library, and participating in the CHAT television show 'Coming Out' on Metro Cable, among innumerable other tasks. According to Fox, before CHAT was awarded a $14,000 grant from the Local Initiatives Program (LIP) in March 1972, 'women used to come to the meetings and look around and see there were no women there and go away. Since the project, the [women's] membership has increased to 15 to 20 per cent.'[48]

In the spring of 1972, at the first meeting of the CHAT Women's Committee, those in attendance decided to 'integrate with all or most existing committees ... and work with them in the interest of the entire membership and community, not just in the interest of women.'[49] It was not until 1973 that several members of CHAT, naming themselves the CUNTS, stormed out of the organization and left behind a one-page declaration of dissent: 'As lesbians we are oppressed both as cunts and dykes. Until the gays of CHAT see the necessity of struggling against sexism, until the structure of CHAT is revolutionized, then CHAT will reflect the status quo through legalization and acceptance. Our energies will not be wasted on raising the consciousness of the members of CHAT who should be raising their own. An independent lesbian group has been started. It is imperative that CHAT confront its own sexism ... It's up to you.'[50] In this bulletin, the CUNTS not only announced their genuine disillusionment with CHAT men; they also demonstrated their own growing, self-conscious commitment to feminist language and analysis. These women were not interested in the designation of CHAT's 'women's night' every Thursday for dances and discussion groups (which began in the summer of 1973), or in *Backchat* (given its historically negligible lesbian content), or in what they perceived to be the hollow promises of some men to take their criticisms into account. Early treatment of the 'men loving boys loving men' issue in *The Body Politic* began to divide the CHAT membership along gender lines (a division that only sharpened in the late 1970s). To Sue Wells, the difference was more than theoretical or political: 'Most of the gay men at CHAT were typical men – they only wanted to counsel the cute, young guys. So all the real bad cases got dumped on the women – the transsexuals, the transvestites, a Hungarian "princess." It became so blatantly obvious that the men were into the work to have sex. Finally, after we saw that we were dealing with all the frigging men's problems, we split.'

While the CHAT community centre, and Thursday nights in particular, continued to meet the needs of many gay women and lesbians, others, including CUNTS' leaders Pat Murphy, Holly Devor, and Ellen Woodsworth, vented their vexation with the 'impossibly sexist thoughts and practices' of (most) gay men. Their stories picked up steam and momentum as they reverberated across the country and resonated with the anger shared by increasing numbers of gay women and lesbian feminists.

In January 1974, Pat Smith levelled this scathing attack against gay men in *The Pedestal* (reprinted in the April/May issue of *Long Time Coming*): 'Gays are men, and their asses won't be pinched and their breasts won't be grabbed and they won't be verbally assaulted while minding their own business. Homosexual men have a lot more in common with straight men than they do with lesbian women. Even if a gay man doesn't extend his male privilege over a woman in bed, he uses and benefits from that privilege every time he walks down the street, applies for credit, finds a job, takes his shirt off in public.'[51] In one of the most most widely circulated Canadian feminist newspapers, *The Other Woman*, Gillean Chase made crystal clear her political and personal allegiances in the 1974 summer issue: 'I do not identify with the issue of homosexuality, I identify with the issue of gender. I am a woman, and it is with women's condition that I am concerned. And I cannot allow gay males to determine for me what my priorities should be or where my commitment lies ... Gay women know instinctively, even if not yet politically, that they are being oppressed, and that they are oppressed by their so-called homosexual brothers.'[52]

Two year later, following several regional and national lesbian conferences and countless tussles in her own community of Ottawa, Marie Robertson had reached a boiling point. In the pages of *The Body Politic*, her sarcasm-laden indictment targeted gay men's groups who boasted a number of female members in order to shore up their credibility and status, hence qualifying them for the 'Most Together Gay Liberation Group of the Year.'[53] Concerned that lesbians who maintained active connections to gay men would only alienate feminist sisters, and keen to enunciate lesbian and gay differences further, Robertson twisted the knife: 'I'm beginning to perceive a clear conflict of interest. Gay liberation, when we get right down to it, is the struggle for gay men to achieve approval for the only thing that separates them from the "Man" – their sexual preference. The point is, if all you self-proclaimed "male feminists" were not gay, you would be part of the powerful prestigious male ruling class that oppresses women, whether you choose to face that reality or not. Your birth as males defines that; you don't. My female birthright places me on the bottom rung, regardless of my sexual orientation and that is where I must fight from. Thanks for letting me take a step up to your rung on the ladder, but no thanks.'[54] By the mid-1970s, especially in large urban centres like Toronto, many lesbian feminists extended their distaste for gay male political culture and personal politics to what they viewed as signs of a rising gay capitalism.[55] A burgeoning commercial and residential district, complete with established cruising grounds, businesses, a publishing company, local bars, baths and clubs, and a pornography/sex industry, signified the expansion of an openly gay men's market. In short, and in general, an infrastructure of economic, political, social, and cultural institutions was set in place by and for (some) white, privileged gay men – the future members of a 'professional/ managerial élite.'[56] Despite the highly charged contests within gay male communities over the meaning and direction of gay-oriented consumerism, this phenomenon had virtually no lesbian equivalency.

For most lesbians, especially those who were parents, working-class, or of colour, access to fewer material resources meant fewer bars and social spaces to frequent. Lesbian sexuality rarely assumed public expression and was not regulated by police and the courts in the same way, hence the liberation of *sexual practice* was not the locus of political battle for lesbians in ways that it was for gay men. Gay men's 'right to (sexual) privacy' campaigns did not, and could not address the *privatization* of lesbian existence within gay liberation, the women's movement, and the wider society. Nor, lesbian feminists argued, was a civil-rights platform and its 'equality with straights' mandate able to bring into view the full complexity of their oppression as homosexuals *and* as women.

Through the mid-1970s, a number of lesbians continued to work with CGRO, the John Damien Defense Committee, *Esprit!* magazine (launched and folded in 1975), GATE (and its Lesbian Caucus, formed in the summer of 1976), the Metropolitan Community Church, and *The Body Politic*, among other joint political/cultural ventures. However, by 1975, many of the women initially involved in gay-liberationist projects had retreated from the fold, whereupon they began to investigate the meaning of feminist ideas and practices in their own lesbian lives, in earnest.

THE REVOLUTIONARY LEFT: FRIEND OR FOE?

Between 1970 and 1975, upon the demise of the large student-led, antiwar organizations, Toronto's grass-roots left splintered, withered, and then regrouped in the form of small revolutionary sects of Marxist-Leninists, Trotskyists, and Maoists.[57] Debates within these organizations ranged from the character and contradictions of state capitalism to the priority of economic issues and the place of the working class in revolutionary struggle. With the virtual dormancy of earlier Marxist and socialist feminist study/action groups, women on the left were faced with few alternatives to the newly constituted formations of the new left intelligentsia. Yet once inside, many (though not all) of them were routinely angered by the men's sexist posturing, the lack of feminist collective process, the hierarchical nature of sect leadership, the abstractions of obtuse 'male theory,' and their own feelings of disconnection from the struggle.

Raising 'the woman question' or the relationship of women's oppression to capitalism and class oppression often provoked open hostility among male comrades, though many women believed in class struggle as fundamental to the struggle for socialism. Some organizations, like Red Morning, the Spartacus League, and the International Socialists, were known to belittle feminism and the counterrevolutionary, bourgeois women's movement. Again, as Dorothy E. Smith recalls her experience, there is/was a clear socialist position that identified the emancipation of women with the struggle for socialism.[58] However, the position ordinarily postponed emancipation until socialism had been achieved. Meanwhile, the potential divisiveness of feminism (and lesbianism) had to be subordinated to class struggle in the interest of longer-term goals.

In March 1972, nine women (the majority of whom were lesbians) entered the office of *Guerilla*, Toronto's 'most well-known left underground newspaper.'[59] Having articulated their intention to negotiate the publication of a 'women's issue' in recognition of International Women's Day, the women were shocked that the 'Gorilla men' responded by calling the police. Openly humiliated by the Gorillas and then badgered by four policemen, *guns drawn*, Pat Leslie concluded that 'all men are conservative authorities fearing loss of their prerogatives over women. The dominant group will fight to conserve its supremacy with whatever means necessary.'[60]

By the mid-seventies, many feminists, like Leslie, Eve Zaremba, Susan Cole, Darlene Lawson, Phil Masters, and Chris Lawrence, among waves of others across North America and Britain who had earlier experience in (or sympathy with) the left, turned away from what they saw as its 'glaring, intractable limitations.'[61] The few dedicated members of the Toronto chapter of Wages for Housework did attempt to combine a Marxist analysis of production and a radical-feminist analysis of reproduction – the unpaid, exploitative work women do in servicing men and children in the home. Formed after a tour by international leaders Selma St James and Maria Dellacosta in 1973, the Toronto chapter struggled to demand wages from the capitalist state for all women. They articulated links to 'unwaged' peoples of the Third World, immigrant women in Canada, prostitutes, and welfare mothers (or all those 'ignored by the rest of the women's movement').[62] In part, because of the organization's apparent 'women should stay at home' platform and its structure and tactics, few feminists joined forces with Wages for Housework, though some did join the subgroup Wages Due Lesbians (see chapter 2).

A small number of Marxist/socialist feminists continued to wrestle with theorizing the interrelated systems of capitalism and patriarchy. Still, even in light of this bold theorizing, acknowledgment of lesbian (and gay) oppression was not clear – in part, a consequence of the left's historical reluctance to allot energy and resources to issues of sexuality.[63] In an unsigned letter to *The Other Woman* in 1972, a woman offered this biting observation: 'While everyone is always crying out that we must relate to the perenially absent working class women and Third World women, lesbians are the scum of the earth. Many women have too much Marxist analysis to come to an exclusively gay meeting, a gay bar or party.'[64]

In Toronto, the Canadian Women's Educational Press was one of the only self-identified socialist-feminist groups active in the early-to-mid 1970s. A collective of white, university-educated straight women, the Press was seen by many lesbian feminists, including Eve Zaremba, as not only 'too closely allied with the left,' but resistant to 'lesbian input.' (In fact, apart from the short lesbian essay in *Women Unite!* [1972], the first overtly lesbian text they ever published was *Dykeversions*, in 1986.) Indeed, it wasn't until the formation of the gay-liberation caucus (or 'Tendency Z') within the Revolutionary Marxist Group in 1976 that several lesbians and gay men began to formulate (against much opposition) the integration of a sexual-liberation politic with a Marxist and feminist vision for a transformed world.[65]

In all, during this period, lesbians who began to identify themselves as feminists began to experience augmenting levels of exasperation at the heterosexual bias of straight feminists, the sexism of gay and straight men, and the class determinism of the left. Yet the exasperation was not always experienced in the same ways. On the one hand, a small number of lesbians, like Sandy Fox and Cynthia Wright, shared the intense conflict between a commitment to class struggle and a commitment to lesbian feminism. On the other hand, increasingly plagued by feelings of political and cultural 'homelessness,' Toronto lesbians who were more closely aligned with radical-feminist critiques of women's oppression and less concerned with class struggle began to contemplate the practicality and desirability of independent, lesbian-only initiatives. In effect, the wish to explore, name, and flesh out the specificities of their lives as women and as lesbians meant placing this complexly gendered and sexed experience (in all its multiple expressions) *at the centre* rather than on the periphery of discourse and organized action. Once recognized, the need to find venues wherein social, cultural, and political projects by and for lesbian feminists might root and flourish began to take shape.

2

Independent lesbian-feminist organizing

Neither heterosexual nor 'gay' culture has offered lesbians a space in which to discover what it means to be self-defined, self-loving, woman-identified, neither an imitation man nor his objectified opposite.
Adrienne Rich, 1977[1]

In the early 1970s, American groups like the Radicalesbians in New York, the Furies in Washington, DC, and the Gutter Dykes in Ann Arbor, Michigan, announced the birth of autonomous lesbian-feminist cultural and political organizing. Through discussions, printed manifestos, women-only music, and public demonstrations, 'new lesbians' gave vent to their outrage at the erasure and/or the dismissal of lesbian issues inside the women's movement, gay liberation, and the left. Distressed by their own marginality, these largely white, middle-class, urban, and college-educated activists also set out to wrestle the category 'lesbian' away from dominant discourses that equated homosexuality with sin, sickness, and criminality. In so doing, they urged an appeal to lesbian-feminist pride, visibility, and strength in numbers. In 1971, poet Judy Grahn testified to this strength: 'How they came into the world, the women-loving women, came in three by three, and four by four, the women-loving women, came in ten by ten, and ten by ten again, until there were more than you could count.'[2]

In effect, 'coming out' emblemized one's willingness to identify publicly as a lesbian in the context of a collective lesbian-feminist movement for social change. This movement signified a critique of the conservative, assimilationist respectability sought by members of the U.S.-based Daughters of Bilitis (DOB) and similar homophile associations that sprang up in the 1950s and 1960s.[3] Too, lesbian-feminist organizing 1970s-style meant the rupture of ties to what were understood as regressive butch/femme roles indigenous to gay bar culture. And it meant dissociation from (and growing judgment of) the enclaves of gay women who participated in sports leagues and work-related cliques, who lived and socialized in suburban neighbourhoods, private cottages, and trailer parks, some of whom were married, all of whom were thought to rely on codes of secrecy that 'the closet' secured.[4]

Indeed, for women who identified as feminists *and* as lesbians, coming out made the personal political in a direct, immediate way. Riddled with risks, this was not a process, as Toronto activist Chris Bearchell attests, that all lesbians were able or willing to undertake: 'As women we have so much to lose if we come out. We may have children. We usually have lower paying jobs. And we almost always have less chance for advancement and financial stability than do men, regardless of their sexual orientation ... These facts are part of our oppression. Lesbian invisibility and lesbian isolation are mutually reinforcing.'[5] Because lesbian and gay oppression rests on the possibility of always remaining hidden, refusing to obey the rules marked an especially aggressive break with heterosexual hegemony. For self-proclaimed lesbian feminists, the fight against state and social forces that organized their lived invisibility and persecution, came first.

It was the power of print that communicated the necessity and exuberance of coming out to geographically dispersed constituencies. Lesbian-feminist writings were published in periodicals whose titles captured the audacious recklessness of separatism: *The Furies* (Washington, DC), *Lesbian Tide* (Los Angeles), *Lavender Woman* (Chicago), *Lesbian Connection* (Ann Arbor), Collective Lesbian International Terrors (CLIT) statements (New York),[6] *Bad Apple Dyke* (New York), *Sinister Wisdom* (Des Moines), and *Amazon Quarterly* (West Sommerville, Mass.). Collections like *Lesbian/Woman* (1972), *Sappho Was a Right-On Woman* (1972), *Lesbian Nation* (1973), and *Lesbianism and the Women's Movement* (reprinted essays from *The Furies*, 1975) were among the first nonfiction 'bibles.' And lesbian-authored articles were included in early American feminist anthologies: *Women in Sexist Society* (1971), *Notes on Women's Liberation* (1969, 1970, 1971), *Sisterhood Is Powerful* (1970), *Women's Liberation: Blueprint for the Future* (1971), and *Radical Feminism* (1973).[7] All of these American texts were available at the Toronto Women's Bookstore.

Not only tangible testaments to the 'we are everywhere' proclamation, the publications offered a place to begin, however haltingly, to theorize lesbian oppression and the relationship of lesbianism to both women's and gay (men's) liberation. In 1972, Furies member Charlotte Bunch postulated that 'woman-identified lesbianism is more than a sexual preference, it is a political choice.'[8] And the ever-irreverent Jill Johnston quipped: 'Feminism at heart is a massive complaint. Lesbianism is the solution.'[9] Bursts of long-suppressed anger and passion touched off a series of axioms: 'lesbians live what feminists theorize about,' 'lesbians are the women's movement's natural leaders,' 'lesbians are the revolutionary vanguard of the women's movement,' 'lesbianism is the very antithesis of the male power struggle,' and 'lesbians are the most liberated women.' To those who believed in this powerful, essentialist discourse, 'lesbian + feminist' became the quintessential, uncontested symbol of protest against male domination and inhibitive sex/gender roles. It also became the ideological heartbeat of a new and potent identity-based politics.

By the mid-1970s, inspirational waves of lesbian-feminist thought and activity had rippled over the United States and spilled across the U.S./Canada border. Gradually and unevenly, with myriad regional specificities, lesbian-feminist cultural and political activity emerged in Halifax, Montréal, Ottawa, London, Guelph, Waterloo, Winnipeg, Regina, Saskatoon, Calgary, Edmonton, Vancouver, and Victoria.[10] Not all developments were created autonomously of other radical movements; some lesbian feminists, like those in the British Columbia Federation of Women (BCFW), worked in solidarity with straight feminists, while others maintained close affiliation to gay liberation and the independent left. In small cities and towns, out of necessity, lesbian feminists worked with gay men to develop social/cultural networks and community-based newsletters.[11]

Lesbian 'movers and shakers' were trained in the tradition of feminist self-reliance and collectivism already present in early women's liberationist rhetoric. Throughout the early-to-mid 1970s, the most well-organized expressions of grass-roots feminism in Toronto (and most other large centres) embodied the conceptual framework of gender separatism. A whole matrix of non-profit services, institutions, and political/cultural organizations were launched by women and for women, many of whom were lesbians: consciousness-raising groups, rallies and demonstrations, publishing houses and periodicals, therapy and counselling groups, health clinics, women's centres, women's studies courses, shelters and rape crisis centres, women's self-defence, women's caucuses in unions, artists' and coffeehouse collectives.

Significantly influenced by American literature, trips to the United States, and their own first-hand experience, some Canadian lesbian feminists began to feel that the introduction of lesbian-specific resources seemed natural, if not overdue. Straight feminists could not ignore the momentum of this argument. Dorothy E. Smith remembers that there were straight feminists who felt that lesbianism was the only authentic sexuality and politics.[12] Published in *The Other Woman* newspaper in 1973, Susan's query betrays a mishmash of curiosity, yearning, and angst: 'I can see lesbian feminism as a progressive answer theoretically. Every heterosexual woman in the movement wonders if it is not the most complete way of seeing things ... as one who has chosen a heterosexual love relationship, I have often wondered if this does represent a cop-out, a susceptability to the old traps and a rejection of myself and my sisters. In other words, have I simply not been strong enough to clear the last obstacle?'[13] In Toronto, before the emergence of the Lesbian Organization of Toronto (LOOT) in November 1976, overlapping circles of feminists founded a smattering of lesbian-centred projects. The term 'movement' was not yet in full usage, nor was it especially appropriate in view of the sheer lack of bodies and womanpower. The impetus driving most of the original efforts was the desire to make space for the safe exploration of one's lesbianism and one's relationship to a 'lesbian-feminist community,' however loosely conceived.

LESBIAN RAP GROUPS

To ease the often tumultuous, wrenching process of coming out, rap groups, drop-ins, and peer counselling sessions (rooted in principles of feminist consciousness raising) operated to articulate and consolidate lesbian-feminist identity. In 1970, a lesbian rap group (and then later a lesbian collective) formed in connection to, yet distinct from, the Toronto Women's Liberation Movement group. By late 1972, lesbian drop-ins and rap groups were held on alternate Friday evenings at A Woman's Place – a 'politically non-aligned' centre on Dupont Street.[14] An announcement in *The Other Woman* for the rap group read as follows: 'a place for lesbian women and women confused about their sexuality to meet other lesbian sisters in a casual non-ghettoized atmosphere. We will be trying to organize this as an alternative to the bars, or CHAT, so we're open for suggestions.'[15]

As mentioned in chapter 1, straight and lesbian feminists at A Woman's Place did not always coexist peacefully. None the less, lesbians who did go stood their ground and succeeded in carving out valuable territory for themselves. A former staff member of A Woman's Place, Phil Masters, registered this observation: 'It was almost all white and middle-class, most were in their twenties, some professional women. It was not all lesbians, although we used to watch the crops coming out in the fall: people went in there and within two months, 80 per cent of them were out.'

Women gained access to early samples of (American) lesbian fiction and non-fiction housed in the tiny corner of A Woman's Place occupied by Lettuce Out Books.[16] Phil Masters remembers reading the essay 'Woman-Identified Woman' and feeling envy for the Radicalesbians who '[had] their politics together and who acted their politics and were being so clear.'

LESBIAN PUBLISHING

From the start, many lesbians realized that they could not trust others to press for the legitimacy of lesbian-feminist issues within a broad feminist program. Notably, there is no mention of lesbianism in the early collections of Canadian women's movement writings – *Mother Was Not a Person* (1972) and *Women in Canada* (1977) – with the exception of one short piece in *Women Unite!* (1972).[17] In the mainstream press during this period, the pervasive non-coverage of lesbianism is only sporadically interrupted by brief, sensationalized accounts in the custom of *Time* magazine's smear of Kate Millett's bisexuality in 1970.[18] Headlines in the 1970s read: 'Alcoholism and Homosexuality Degraded Lee Bryant's Life for 10 years Until Her Conversion to Christianity' (1970), 'Three Women Claim Police Abused Them in Garage' (1974), 'Lesbians Win Custody Case Provided They Live Apart' (1973), 'Female Soldiers Wed and Shock U.S. Army' (1973), 'Lesbianism "Rampant"' [in Kingston's Prison for Women] (1973), and 'My Lesbian Lover Threatened to Kill Me' (1977).[19]

In a rare and surprising moment of mainstream media attention to lesbianism in Toronto – one that likely evoked disgust in some readers and curiosity, if not excitement, in others – an editorial writer for the *Toronto Sun* sounded the alarm bell: 'Women's lib is now in danger of being dominated by Marxist lesbians which is a scary thought. This business of women refusing to deal with men at all, constitutes rampant discrimination. The Woman's Place on Dupont is a headquarters for anti-male plots. There are mean-minded broads there. In the U.S. we've got such lethal anti-male organizations as SCUM, Redstockings and Witch, etc. Even NOW is fighting primarily for lesbian rights ... One interpretation of lib extremism is that it might be a biological phenomenon caused by overpopulation. For example, rats when overcrowded kill the opposite sex and refuse to breed.'[20] Though they relied heavily on American stories and analysis available through fledgling women's bookstores, subscriptions, and reprints in Canadian journals, by the early seventies some Canadian lesbian feminists began to produce their own material. The premier issue of Toronto's *The Other Woman* newspaper (Spring, 1972) created a scandal because, as Pat Leslie recalls, it contained more than one article of interest to lesbians. Leslie was discouraged: 'We were constantly hitting our heads against brick walls because we were not acceptable.' An amalgamation of two feminist newspapers – *Bellyfull* and *Velvet Fist* – *The Other Woman* was put together at the outset by a collective of five lesbians who insisted on the regular inclusion of lesbian-feminist content. *Long Time Coming*, English Canada's first lesbian-feminist periodical, was launched in February 1973 by Montréal Gay Women (originally the women's committee of Gay McGill). And Edmonton Lesbian Feminists (ELF) turned out a 'Lesbian Issue' of the feminist newspaper *On Our Way* in May 1974.[21]

LESBIAN CONFERENCES

In the early-to-mid 1970s, conferences provided lesbian feminists with an immediate and emotionally satisfying way of communicating, face to face, in the flesh. In late June 1973, a group of Toronto lesbians with connections to A Woman's Place organized a one-day 'Gay Women's Festival,' held at the YWCA on McGill Street. As Pat Leslie recalls, 'We wanted to get lesbians together to talk about being lesbians. We were thinking small.' By their deliberate use of the terms 'gay women' and 'festival,' organizers also intended to de-emphasize the event's political and academic character as a way of bridging the gap between 'feminist' and 'non-feminist' lesbians.

Following the festival, a debate unfolded on the 'Letters Page' of *The Other Woman*. Foreshadowing a central dilemma that would plague organizing initiatives in the late 1970s, one voice (signed 'Guthrie,' from Vancouver) emphasized the need for a 'narrower base' from which 'lesbian feminists' might formulate 'immediate and future goals and tactics.'[22] Responding to Guthrie, an (unidentified) conference organizer understood the purpose of the conference quite differently. She summed up her own position by paraphrasing the words of another participant: 'It was the first time I had seen such a great number of women meet in Toronto because they were lesbians, not in someone's house, not in a social situation, but expressing in order to exchange ideas, experience and information with a view to action.'[23] To this woman, appealing to a 'small clique of lesbian feminists who already know each other' at the expense of forging a broad bond 'with all our sisters in offices, schools, bars, homes' seemed like a dangerous path to follow.[24] Notwithstanding this main tension, energy generated by the rap groups, the drop-ins, and the June festival carried over to spawn the best-selling 'Lesbian Issue' of *The Other Woman* that fall, and a series of lesbian-specific projects over the next several years.

THE BRUNSWICK FOUR

On the evening of 5 January 1974, four lesbian feminists – Adrienne Potts, Pat Murphy, Heather Byers (a.k.a. Heather Elizabeth), and Sue Wells – went to the downtown Brunswick Tavern for a few beers. During the intermission of amateur night, two of the four brash, irrepressible 'killer dykes' mounted the stage to belt out a lusty rendition of 'I Enjoy Being a Dyke' (to the melody of the *South Pacific* classic 'I Enjoy Being a Girl').[25] In spite of the surprisingly warm response from the largely straight male clientele, the manager (Albert Nightingale) pulled the plug on the sound system halfway through their performance and later demanded that they leave the bar. When the women refused, they were forcibly removed by eight armed policemen (who were responding to a call about 'a lesbian riot'), thrown into a paddy wagon, detained for several hours at 14 Division, and subjected to verbal and physical intimidation. Upon release, the women went back to the tavern to locate witnesses, whereupon three of the four were promptly arrested and charged with creating a public disturbance – hence the 'Brunswick Four (minus one).'

Enraged by their experience of such profound antiwoman and antilesbian harassment, the 'Brunswick Four (minus one)' sought to publicize their case through networks of human-rights activists, lesbians, feminists, and gay liberationists. In *The Other Woman, Long Time Coming,* and *The Body Politic*, stories of bodily abuse (torn ligaments, bruising, punches to the back of the head, twisted arms) and verbal taunts such as 'You fucking hosebag, I bet you drive a tugboat' and 'Did you ever put your finger in a dike?' elicited shock and horror, though to many streetwise bar lesbians, and many more gay men, the scenario was routine rather than extraordinary.[26] The stories demanded of activists an organized, coordinated response. According to Pat Murphy, 'It was a good time in the community: a Defense Committee was struck, there were fund-raising dances, the courtroom was packed everyday with women ... It pulled women together for a while and it got the message out that you could be out any night of the week and something like this could happen.'

In May 1974, the trial and the legal defence led by high-profile feminist lawyer Judy LaMarsh (who waived all fees) catapulted lesbianism into the public realm. All three of Toronto's mass-circulation newspapers covered the story, and the words 'lesbian feminist' appear in all of the accounts.[27] In the end, Pat and Heather were acquitted and Adrienne was handed a suspended sentence and three months' probation.[28] However, to many lesbian feminists the case signified more of a beginning than an ending. Not only did lesbianism constitute newsworthy copy in ways it never had before, thus bringing (one piece of) lesbian reality to the general public, it extended and deepened feminist understanding of a sexist and heterosexist justice system. Most important, in the context of the women's movement, it marked a significant moment in the struggle for lesbian visibility, in the formation and expansion of lesbian community, and in the need to recognize the intersections of lesbianism and feminism.

THE AMAZON WORKSHOP

While the Brunswick Four strategized and campaigned, the spring of 1974 heralded a number of other developments in lesbian-feminist organizing. Having outgrown A Woman's Place (which itself was reforming and relocating), a group of predominantly lesbian-run and -utilized services moved in and collectively set up shop on Kensington Avenue under the umbrella Amazon Workshop. Women's Self-Defense, Amazon Press, and Toronto Women's Bookstore (formerly Lettuce Out Books) officially opened for business on 15 June 1974. Among the first formal services put in place by lesbian feminists for the benefit of lesbians *and* straight feminists, they offered lesbians (in particular) employment outside of straight, pink-collar work for 'The Man.' In fact, enterprising young lesbians were able to create projects for themselves and others primarily through the financial support of LIP (Local Initiatives Program) and OFY (Opportunity for Youth) grants.[29] Again, the visibility of lesbians within the women's movement and the consolidation of community were enhanced through these ventures. Moreover, their successes underlined the need for and viability of lesbian self-help initiatives, at the same time that they prefigured the institutionalization of this trend.

CLEMENTYNE'S CAFÉ

In November 1974, four women (including two from the Brunswick Four) got together and decided Toronto women needed a café. A cousin to the short-lived Labyris Collective,[30] 'Clementyne's,' as Eve Zaremba recalls, 'was conceived as an idea on Seaton Street' – one of the first, and most public, lesbian-feminist communal households (and formerly the headquarters of the Maoist sect Red Morning). The women involved found a space for the café, at 342 Jarvis Street; they signed a two-year lease and canvassed 150 women for $50 donations. Heather Elizabeth, Holly Devor, Pat Murphy, Chris Lawrence, Eve Zaremba, and others formed work-crews to renovate the 'magnificent, but ramshackle' three-storey Victorian 'castle.' As reported in *The Other Woman*, Clementyne's was to be a 'restaurant in the daytime, [with] lots of exciting events in the evenings (poetry, theatre, music, discussions),' and would be licensed one night every weekend 'for starters.'[31] However, in the spring of 1975, the collective's application for transforming a residential space into a commercial venture was rejected by city councillors on the grounds that it contravened a newly instituted municipal zoning by-law aimed at quashing massage parlours. Introduced as a strategy to 'clean up' waves of sex and crime purportedly overtaking the Yonge Street neighbourhood, the legislation named Jarvis Street as part of this zone, hence trapping Clementyne's in its teeth.[32]

In response to the stinging defeat, Phil Masters, editor of the *Women's Information Centre Newsletter* and supporter of the Clementyne's collective, outlined the virtues of a 'recreational and cultural centre for Toronto women' and demanded a by-law exemption. In so doing, she unwittingly pitted good/moral lesbian feminists against bad/immoral sex-trade workers who worked 'the sin strip,' thus betraying the chasm separating these two groups of women, which deepened as the decade wore on. Masters stated: 'The by-law was intended to restrict the growth of body-rub parlours – an admirable idea. But Clementyne's has no intention of turning into a body rub parlour. It intends to be a place where women can relax, talk, enjoy music, eat, hold meetings. Nothing exploitative or immoral about it. Clementyne's needs your support to get City Council to change its mind and allow Clementyne's to open. Everyone can help by writing to Mayor Crombie, Aldermen Heap and Sparrow, expressing support for Clementyne's.'[33] Denied a liquor licence, hence the operating capital necessary to ensure the café's solvency, Clementyne's foundered and the idea was subsequently shelved. In Long Time Coming, a reporter confirmed that 'energies are at their lowest.'[34] And yet in the late spring of 1975, 342 Jarvis Street became home to a number of feminist organizations and businesses (run largely by lesbians): The Other Woman newspaper, Wages for Housework and Wages Due Lesbians, Women's Information Centre (WIC), Women's Artmobile, the Cora Mobile (a travelling women's centre and bookstore), Tomorrow's Eve (theatre), Innervisions (video), an informal lesbian rap group, and Heather Elizabeth's barber shop. These services (several of which later formed the short-lived Toronto Women's Network) loosely constituted the Toronto Women's Building. Clearly a centre with some public profile, all six offices were broken into on 17 June 1975. Members of the centre speculated that the RCMP was responsible for the vandalism and the theft of mailing lists; they also linked the invasion to earlier antifeminist incidents of police surveillance and harassment.[35] As Pat Leslie mused, 'there was a sense that we should feel privileged that we were a threat to the state and that we were dangerous enough for them to break into the house to see what was there.'

In the late fall of 1975, energy at 342 Jarvis Street began to run low and government grants dried up. Among the last organizations to leave the building, the WIC folded and became the bond of association for the Women's Credit Union – several of whose staff had been active in both A Woman's Place and Clementyne's. In the tradition of the Seaton Street and Carlton Street communal households, four lesbians moved in to 342 Jarvis Street, and the infamous lesbian-feminist residence became the site of many informal gatherings. As Pat Murphy recalls, 'It was overwhelming when we moved in. We had very big parties there; we used to talk about how wonderful this would be as a lesbian centre. We had a feast at solstice and Heather, who loved to cook, baked a salmon and about 30 women came for dinner.

The more this happened, the more it dawned on people that this could really be a place.'

THREE OF CUPS COFFEEHOUSE

With the abandonment of the Clementyne's dream café, another circle of lesbian-feminist friends – Dougall Haggart, Artemis (Kathy McHugh), and Paulette Marchetti – decided to form a coffeehouse collective. Billed as an 'alternative space for all women' that was 'not a bar' and 'not a cruising ground,' the Three of Cups Coffeehouse opened at Scadding Court community centre on 26 December 1975. Interviewed for *The Other Woman*, Artemis stated, 'We're a feminist collective, but we don't want to be a political forum as much as a place where people are encouraged to come and just relax.'[36] Upon reflection, Marie Zemask contended, 'I thought [women] should have a place together, no matter what your political flux. And, I thought such a place should be about rest and rehab when you're in danger of burning out.'[37] Phoning for information from Hamilton, Rosemary Barnes remembers, 'We were told the Three of Cups was a *women's* coffeehouse, and we decided we would go anyway – there might be some lesbians hanging out. And to our delight, when we arrived we saw that virtually all the women were lesbians.'

The significance of Three of Cups is explored in the pages of *Long Time Coming*: 'The name of the coffeehouse is taken from a card in the Tarot deck. The Three of Cups card pictures three women in flowing, colourful robes dancing in a circle, raising goblets filled with the wine of life, fruits and garlands at their feet.'[38] Excited by elements of a new feminist spiritualism, collective members promoted vegetarian food, non-alcoholic beverages, and the practice of alternative dance forms. Dougall Haggart still maintains that 'dancing disco is a travesty of what dancing should be – a ritual, a linking of more than one person ... the circle.'[39]

From the beginning, the 'very art expression-oriented' forums at Three of Cups, which moved around from churches to community centres to the living room of 342 Jarvis Street, provided women musicians, filmmakers, poets, and writers with a stage. Before LOOT's residency at 342 Jarvis in February 1977, the list of local performers included Jude Angione, Judy Abrahms, Adrienne Potts, April Kassirer and Carol Rowe, Beverly Glenn Copeland, Rita MacNeil, Sara Ellen Dunlop, Alexa De Weil, Gillean Chase, and Gwen Hauser. American musicians like Alix Dobkin, Meg Christian, Teresa Trull, and BeBe K'Roche also made appearances, and the albums of Olivia recording stars Meg Christian, Cris Williamson, Holly Near, Margie Adam, and Kay Gardner were worn thin from overplay. To quote Ann Kado, a lesbian feminist and a Mohawk, 'Women's music made me feel good inside, it gave me a sense of warmth knowing that I wasn't the only one feeling this way. It made me feel good on the inside so that it didn't matter who was putting me down.' 'It was the sort of thing,' Natalie LaRoche adds, 'that went beyond entertainment to create community and give it strength by its very nature, by its very ability to draw women into something that inspired and gave energy to other women.'

Though straight feminists were never openly discouraged from attending, and a number of the performers were straight, they were greatly outnumbered. Naomi Brooks recalls: 'I took one straight woman and she was floored – she felt like she was the only straight woman there, and she was really freaked out about that.' Not all heterosexual feminists felt this way. Dorothy E. Smith remembers attending the coffee-house with a group of mostly straight women and she thought that it was wonderful.[40]

POTLUCK SUPPER GROUP

In the late spring of 1976, several women who were having trouble meeting women at the Three of Cups or the CHAT Thursday night dances, and who were not connected to 342 Jarvis Street or the bar scene, decided to form a lesbian potluck supper group. Every second or third week, remembers Nancy Adamson, the group would rotate to another woman's house. According to Lorna Weir: 'We ate dinner, we talked, it had no political character. Lesbians were simply meeting each other, having a good time. I liked that we were all lesbians. I liked the easiness of it, no formal agenda. There was no point at which we all sat down and agreed to discuss one subject. It was lesbians getting to know each other. I figured out by this time that I wanted a lover and this was a way of finding one.'

GAY WOMEN UNLIMITED

About the same time that the potluck supper group formed, Gay Women Unlimlited (GWU) used the CHAT newsletter, *Backchat*, to announce their intention to 'provide a meeting place and a warm social atmosphere in which gay women can help each other.'[41] In the tradition of informal lesbian social and cultural gatherings, Gay Women Unlimited offered an 'alternative to dances and clubs' through biweekly meetings at the CHAT centre. Promotional material with a strong self-help emphasis read as follows: 'If you're lonely, new in town, or just coming out and don't know where to turn, we'd like to see you on Monday night because we understand what you're feeling and we've all been where you are now and we can help.'[42] Invited to 'come and be part of the sisterhood,' gay women were then encouraged to partake in discussions (led by guest speakers), coming out seminars, poetry evenings, and by the summer of 1976, a 'lesbian moms group.'[43]

WAGES DUE LESBIANS

With a focus on political intervention rather than on the provision of culture, self-help, or services, Wages Due Lesbians (or Wages Due) was formed in 1975.[44] A subgroup of the international organization Wages for Housework and, specifically, its Toronto chapter, Wages Due attempted to formulate a class analysis based on an understanding of women's unpaid domestic labour that a priori included lesbians. Spokesperson Ellen Agger argued the organization's position at a rally on the University of Toronto campus in March of 1976: 'As lesbians often without the income of a husband, we are dependent on government benefits or our second jobs for money – jobs have been threatened by [Family Allowance, unemployment and social service] cutbacks ... women are being forced to depend much more on a man's wages ... all the independence from men that we have fought for as lesbian women is under attack. The only solution is economic independence for all women ... and this means to be paid for all the housework we already do in our homes and in our paid jobs. As lesbians, we want wages for housework so we are no longer forced to hide our lesbianism.'[45] Imaginative, forceful, and charismatic, Wages Due leaders linked the invisibility and closetry of most lesbians to the enslaving material conditions of their lives. With considerable panache and defiance, they pledged: 'We and millions more of us will be Coming Out with wages for housework.'[46] In *The Other Woman*, Ellen Woodsworth elaborated: 'The fight for wages for housework brings together women who are married and who are single; heterosexual and lesbian; young and old; and of every race and nationality. We are all going to fight until we get back all the money that we have worked for.'[47]

However, known for its sectarian leftist ideology, disruptive tactics, and, according to Gay Bell, a 'military leadership that was not going to be rocked or shared,' Wages Due was seen as closed (if not hostile) to new social, cultural, and political initiatives. Only a very small number of lesbian feminists were involved throughout the organization's tumultuous three-year history. As Phil Masters notes, 'There was no quicker way to have a nervous breakdown than to join that group. They were always purging people and destroying their lives.' And Naomi Brooks adds, 'Wages Due were really pushing it ... I thought to myself, wait a minute, I'm not doing housework for a boy (laughter). It seemed too far-fetched and a lot of women reacted the same way I did.' To Cate Smith, 'They were going for pie in the sky, and we needed people out there shooting for the moon, but at the time I thought they were crazy.' Later, in March 1978, following the lead of organizations in several American cities, members of Wages Due directed their energies at the formation of the Lesbian Mothers Defense Fund (LMDF). Set up to give pre-legal advice and information on custody battles in Canada and the United States, as well as referrals to lawyers, financial assistance, and peer counselling, LMDF provided countless women with support over the course of its remarkable nine-year existence. It announced its official closure in 1987.[48]

To summarize, in Toronto between 1970 and the first half of 1976, small friendship circles of largely young, white, middle-class lesbian feminists set out to create social and support-oriented settings wherein they could explore the precious opportunity to come out and invent themselves anew. Some of these settings included straight women and/ or gay men. Others were predominantly, if not exclusively, lesbian. Whether the founders realized it or not, their efforts were rooted in, and profoundly indebted to, earlier 'uptown' and 'downtown' gay and lesbian networks, particularly the public bar culture of the 1940s, 1950s, and 1960s. However, an almost complete lack of knowledge of previous lesbian subcultures, compounded by often outright rejection of what little was known, rendered impossible the building of bridges to bind and fortify 'old' and 'new' generations. In ways consistent with the observations of historians Joan Nestle and Lillian Faderman, the primary cleavage was class-based. From the early 1970s on, the vision of building safe, independent women-identified projects was played out against, or rather in opposition to, the largely working-class gay women's bar scene. In contrast to bar culture, the projects that lesbian feminists established served as critical (and for many, introductory) sites of training in feminist thought and practice. Furthermore, they offered participants a chance to explore and consolidate their own public, personal/political lesbian identity in the context of a lesbian-feminist community-in-formation.

In the early-to-mid 1970s, stirred by their experiences of betrayal, judgment, and dismissal inside the women's movement, gay liberation, and the left described in chapter 1, newly politicized lesbians sought to stake out countercultural territory for their dual primary identities as women and as lesbians. Emerging lesbian-feminist ideology did influence members of other progressive movements during this period. Yet, as subsequent chapters will show, lesbian feminists tended to be less interested in engaging directly with other radicals than they were in differentiating themselves and their own initiatives from all non-lesbians and non-feminists.

Importantly, the alternative institutions that were founded, coordinated, and staffed by lesbian feminists in the early-to-mid 1970s were officially open to all women, and were not referred to as *lesbian spaces*: the word 'lesbian' did not appear in their names. None the less, by 1975, the category 'lesbian feminist' had a wide, general currency as a descriptor of any woman who claimed the double identity of lesbian + feminist. Because emphasis was on the cultivation of social, cultural, and self-help services, there was little engagement in political debates in ways that would have revealed the multiple meanings of 'lesbian feminist' and its less-than-coherent character at this time. However, ideological and strategic differences related to the fight against gender and sexual oppression would surface as the 1970s rolled on. Indeed, as subsequent chapters bring into view, a particular definition of 'lesbian feminist' came to assume a certain, though not uncontested, hegemony.

Before 1976, Toronto lesbian feminists tended to concentrate on developing the confidence and skills to meet their own immediate personal and social needs and the needs of their community. Theorizing lesbian oppression, building a political analysis and a set of strategies, and conceptualizing this work in relation to a broad national or international lesbian-feminist movement were not yet imperative. There were few alliances forged between the patchwork of nascent lesbian-feminist projects and interconnected social movements in the city and elsewhere. Beyond the handful of irregularly produced publications, there were few formal links between lesbian-feminist organizations across the country other than friendships formed through cross-country travel. Two weekend (predominantly anglophone) lesbian conferences in Montréal in 1974 and 1975, and a national conference of women's centres in Thunder Bay in 1975, offered much-needed venues for contacts and the exchange of information.[49]

Within the broader context of the mid-to-late 1970s, the Arab oil embargo and the growing rate of inflation set conditions for a creeping conservatism in political, economic, and social affairs. A North American recession motivated an intensified struggle concerning wage and price controls and state spending. Against this backdrop, a new moral climate of social relations was shaped, and sexual and moral issues became key rallying points in the conservative agenda. In Toronto, right-wing constituencies were beginning to coalesce and flex their political muscle in response to the continued 'liberalization' of gender and sexual norms inherited from the 1960s. Given the sanctity of 'the family' as the right's ideological cornerstone, the mounting visibility of gay men and lesbians was perceived as both objectionable and cause for counter-attack. Paul Fromm, writing for the Edmund Burke Society newsletter, *Straight Talk*, exclaimed in his diatribe 'Your Family, Their Target' that 'there have always been homosexuals and lesbians. A healthy society tries to restrict such deviates.'[50] As early as 1972, through a rash of bombings and public interventions, the Western Guard, a forerunner to the League Against Homosexuals, began to make its antigay and antilesbian presence felt. In 1974 in Milton, a city outside of Toronto, fundamentalist minister Ken Campbell formed Halton Renaissance (later, Renaissance International), which was to become one of the fiercest opponents of gay/lesbian liberation and feminism in the country.

Located in the contradictory moment of organized state, police, and economic repression and the budding culture of feminist, left, and gay resistance, young, mostly white and middle-class lesbian feminists endeavoured to establish a room, or rooms, of their own. It is this constellation of small projects run by and primarily for lesbian feminists, coupled with the gradual increase in the number of out lesbians, that laid the foundation for the Lesbian Organization of Toronto in the fall of 1976.

3

'Family of Woman We've Begun': Envisioning Lesbian Nation[1]

Course it ain't quite that simple, so I better explain, just why you've got to ride on the lesbian train. 'Cause if you wait for the man to straighten out your head, you'll all be a waiting, then you'll all be dead.
Alix Dobkin, 1975[2]

In October 1976, the Lesbian Organization of Ottawa Now (LOON) sponsored the third National Lesbian conference. Held in Ottawa on the grounds of the University of Ottawa, the three-day gathering attracted over three hundred and fifty lesbians (plus some bisexuals and a handful of lesbian-positive heterosexuals) – by far the largest assembly ever convened in the country. The motto 'Together We Can Move Mountains' greeted participants upon entering the conference space, and served all weekend-long as an informal call to action. A testament to the expanding, maturing character of lesbian-feminist organizing since the early 1970s, the deepening drive to constitute 'an autonomous lesbian movement' was formalized in a unanimous vote to found a national affiliation of lesbian-feminist organizations. *Lesbian Canada Lesbienne* – the newly conceived bilingual communications organ – would serve to coordinate activities among the five designated regions.[3] Writing of her 'love affair with the National Lesbian Movement,' Halifax resident Ann Fulton announced: 'We have something going for us that most don't – we're dykes! We're strong and proud. If we can just grow to understand each other, we'll have a bond unlike that of any other group in the country. I personally cannot think of anything which could make me happier. It brings tears to my eyes, and warms me nearly as much as a real live woman ... A few days before the next conference, I foresee every dyke in the land dropping whatever she is doing, and going immediately to Cape Breton Island. When we have all arrived there, the waters of the Atlantic Ocean are going to open before us, and we will march to the Isle of Lesbos, and there we will have the greatest conference ever. And there is no stopping a movement with potential like that.'[4]

The excitement at the prospect of lesbians coming out into their own, both culturally and politically, at local and national levels, was infectious. At the Ottawa conference, lesbians announced that they were angry at the role of (often invisible) handmaiden to the women's movement and gay (men's) liberation. This anger, combined with the pure magic of 'wimmin's energy,' formed the backdrop against which Toronto lesbian feminists Eve Zaremba and Marcia McVea circulated an open letter.[5] Mindful of the irony of 'having travelled 300 miles to interest lesbians in a Toronto-based venture by and for lesbians,' Eve and Marcia, coworkers at the Women's Credit Union, identified the 'problem of community': 'Crucial to the spirit of community are resources available: in Toronto, there is Nellie's, *The Other Woman* newspaper, Amazon Press, the Women's Bookstore, Women's Credit Union – all based on the ethic "do for thyselves what man will not" – and despite all these we do not have the cohesion that a place of our own and more open communication could provide ... To foster and support ventures that will bring us together is essential, so that we can experience and share our strength.'[6] Zaremba and McVea were familiar with the web of women-run feminist services and businesses already in place, and the brief history of lesbian drop-ins, rap groups, coffeehouses, potluck supper groups, and communal households (some of which were still in operation). They were also unhappy with the loose, disorganized state of lesbian-feminist activity in Toronto. Similarly disconcerted and impatient, Joyce Rock publicized her concerns in the June 1976 issue of *The Body Politic*. Flushed with exasperation, she asked, 'Where are the lesbians in this city? What are they doing? Why don't they collect themselves at the Grads [a lesbian bar] or the [Three of Cups] coffeehouse with constant activity in constant numbers? The women of the Three of Cups are not machines, but need OUR input, OUR ideas, OUR bodies as audience.'[7] Rock's observation was not uncommon. The feeling that the community was always on the verge of going up in a puff of smoke was connected to the ongoing struggle to build up lesbian-feminist culture from scarce resources. At times, merely maintaining the few projects that did exist seemed like a monumental task.

Zaremba and McVea wanted their plea to serve as a lightning rod for the establishment of *what did not yet exist*. As Zaremba recalls, 'We believed lesbians qua lesbians should have a place and should have a voice and a way of meeting from the social to the political. The energy was there to build something as lesbians.' That the energy was also, and fundamentally, feminist energy was a pivotal assumption and one upon which the open letter, and the desire behind it, rested. Clearly, a move to test the waters and gauge support for an autonomous lesbian-feminist venture came from a vision of a galvanized, re-energized lesbian community. As well, it suggested the very existence of a community of women-identified women, no matter how small and dispersed, that was eager and prepared to translate the vision into reality. That such an intervention happened at a conference in Ottawa – a seemingly unlikely venue – underscored the absence of a lesbian-feminist space in Toronto within which such ideas could have been introduced, debated, and acted upon.

As in other communities across the country and in the United States, relations between Toronto feminists – straight and lesbian – had been strained since the late 1960s. The early-to-mid 1970s marked the eruption of several heated skirmishes and feelings of discontent and mistrust. Lesbians continued to work in almost all aspects of organized, grass-roots feminism, as well as in branches of gay liberation and the left, often silently and with little recognition. Lesbian caucuses had formed inside several gay men's groups like the Gay Alliance Toward Equality (GATE), though the number of lesbians attracted to coalition work with gay liberationists remained consistently low.

Lesbian feminists began to assert a thorough-going critique of gay-male politics and style at two conferences in 1976: 'The Not So Invisible Woman: Lesbian Perspectives in the Gay Movement,' a Kingston conference sponsored by the Queen's Homophile Association and held in May 1976, and the fourth annual National Gay Rights Coalition conference, 'Many Faces, One Focus,' held in Toronto in September 1976. Here, 'the sexism and liberalism of gay men' only reinforced the feelings that most politically active lesbians already harboured. While a lesbian caucus formed near the end of the Toronto conference, members were tired of the struggle to be heard and understood: 'Why make a priority of working with gay men who pay lip service to feminism and capitalize on hedonism?'[8] At the caucus meeting, suggestions for 'lesbian liberation' ranged from starting businesses that would make money for and hire only women to public actions around lesbian rights, to the formation of an anticapitalist lesbian movement. In spite of these disparate conceptions, most women shared the desire to convene in the hope of realizing a vision of lesbian-feminist culture, community, and politics independent of other movement demands or commitments. 'It was like a culmination,' says Zaremba. 'Everyone was getting fed up at the same time.'

Though the women's movement was not dead, contrary to post-International Women's Year proclamations in the mainstream press,[9] political activism in the grass-roots, multi-issue tradition of Toronto Women's Liberation, Toronto Women's Caucus, and Toronto New Feminists was at a low ebb.[10] In Toronto, there was no Ontario women's liberation umbrella organization like the British Columbia Federation of Women and its Lesbian Caucus within which to pressure for the inclusion of lesbian demands and policies.[11] This absence was compounded by (a) the historically strained and increasingly aggravated tensions between Toronto lesbians, gay men, and heterosexual feminists, and (b) the heavy influence of imported American lesbian separatist ideology and practice.

In their September/October issue, distributed immediately before the Ottawa Lesbian Conference in the fall of 1976, collective members of *The Other Woman* newspaper printed an editorial under the headline 'Lesbian Autonomy or Cooptation?' Referencing the climate of escalating lesbian disillusionment, and anticipating the havoc from fractures the women's movement could ill afford, they warned: 'The gay/straight split in the U.S. women's movement has neither group talking to each other. We do not want to replicate this pattern in the Canadian women's movement. We agree with the Lesbian Caucus of the British Columbia Federation of Women that lesbianism must be understood in the context of women's oppression. Feminists and lesbians need not be divided around the issue of sexual orientation as we can find common ground in our struggle for the liberation of women. The concerns of lesbians should be the concern of all women, straight or gay.'[12] Rooted in the integrationist rhetoric of 'sisterhood,' *The Other Woman's* position could not (or refused to) acknowledge the gathering momentum of autonomous lesbian activism in Ontario and elsewhere, especially since the spring of 1976. Not only were lesbian-only groups springing up in Ontario cities like Kingston, London, Kitchener, Guelph, and Ottawa, but 1976 conferences in Kingston, Bolton, and Toronto, and the first annual Michigan Womyn's Music Festival in August, provided forums for the emergence and coalescence of largely white, middle-class lesbian-feminist energy. At the time of LOOT's emergence, lesbian organizations across the country included the Edmonton Lesbian Feminists, the Lesbian Caucus of British Columbia Federation of Women (BCFW), the Lesbian Caucus of Saskatoon Women's Liberation, APPLE (Atlantic Provinces Political Lesbians for Equality) in Halifax, Gay Women at McGill, and the Montréal Lesbian Organization. Regular lesbian drop-ins took place in Calgary and Winnipeg, at the Vancouver Women's Bookstore, the Halifax Women's Centre, Saskatoon's Gay Community Centre, and the Victoria Women's Centre.

In Toronto, there was a definite sense that, although fragmented, the actual number of lesbians who were out, around, and interested was greater than ever before. Indeed, Zaremba and McVea's open letter to 'Toronto Lesbian Feminists' at once reflected personal knowledge of such women and presupposed a wider constituency beyond the perimeter of their own social and political circles. There was an audience, a potential base of support waiting to be tapped – a scenario that had no historical equivalent. Harkening back to homophile organizing in the 1950s, American lesbians Del Martin and Phyllis Lyon remember: 'So desperate were we for members in the early days of the Daughters of Bilitis that we coddled, nursed and practically hand-fed every woman who expressed the least interest. We had them over for dinner ... some moved in on us for days and weeks at a time.'[13] Even in the early 1970s, signs of lesbian-feminist organizing in Toronto were weak. 'Between 1970 and '72,' remembers Holly Devor, 'finding another lesbian feminist was like a miracle. I had to go all the way to Vancouver to find one, and what a thrill. It was a total thrill.'

By the mid-seventies, in the context of mounting enthusiasm for methodical, decisive attention to specifically lesbian questions and issues, however variously defined, 'seize the time' was a maxim ripe for material expression.[14] As Chris Bearchell notes, 'For too long I saw lesbian energy sustain the women's movement and did not see any corresponding energy sustaining lesbians. I wasn't prepared to do that anymore.'[15] 'Lesbian feminism,' says Lorna Weir, 'was about taking feminism and shaking it up ... It was exceedingly vengeful: "You straight feminists, you think you're so fucking superior" – "Well, we'll show you!"' Bristling with 'the rage of all women condensed to the point of explosion,' Toronto lesbian feminists appeared ready to strike out alone.[16]

Given the separatist undercurrent that ran through earlier Toronto feminist and lesbian initiatives, the desire for 'a place of our own' embodied a perfectly logical extension and elaboration of this tendency. Swollen with betrayal, anger, and lesbian pride, the current seemed ready to burst through to the surface. Whether or not it would feed an expanding pool of ideas, resources, and bodies and, ultimately, a veritable 'national lesbian movement' was unclear in late 1976 and early 1977. A glance across the vast geography of Canada revealed the uncertain footing of emergent, local lesbian-only groups, the untimely demise of *Lesbian Canada Lesbienne* after one issue, and a smattering of mixed lesbian/gay organizations dependent on shared facilities, resources, and memberships in small communities. In the United States, the direction of lesbian feminism and an autonomous lesbian movement – a once vehemently argued objective – now seemed indefinite. By 1975, the zeitgeist of lesbian activism embodied in the Radicalesbians, the Furies, and CLIT best captured in their manifestos had faded in major U.S. centres of political ferment. And yet in Canadian cities like Toronto, talk and debate about the 'almost dream-like' possibilities of lesbian-feminist organizing was just heating up.

LESBIANS IGNITE: STRIKING A MATCH, FANNING THE FLAMES

Toronto lesbian feminists met on 17 October 1976 at the CHAT office on Church Street. Advertising for the meeting was done by word of mouth. The exhilaration generated at the Ottawa conference was carried back to Toronto and hastily communicated to friends, acquaintances, and co-workers. Most of the women I interviewed remember the electricity snapping in the air the night of the first meeting: a room full of lesbians, groupings of those who knew each other, but most of whom were meeting and 'laying eyes on each other' for the first time. On edge, full of expectations, these women still marvel at the sweetness of this historic occasion. Fiona Rattray's memory of the event is sharp and detailed:

I'd been in a room of fifty faggots with their energy and it wasn't my energy. So, I remember going there and climbing the stairs to the second floor and [the room] seemed to be the size of a football stadium. It was this cavern full of women and it seemed to me there were about 30, but maybe the number was closer to 50 or 60 ... it seemed uncountable. Everybody was older than I was – I was 18 or 19. Of course, I might have been a tough little dyke, but I didn't consider myself to be very politically articulate and here were all these articulate, gorgeous, older women sitting in this room and I couldn't believe it. I couldn't even open my mouth to speak, there was all this lesbian energy. I remember seeing Susan Cole and thinking, wow, what an attractive, charming woman. There were women there who were talking about putting together a lesbian centre and the most I did was vote 'Yes, that was a good idea' (laughter) because I didn't know if I would make a political misstep if I opened my mouth. This was very feminist politics that these women were talking and I was coming from gay liberation politics.

Those who attended the planning meetings were keen to focus on the collective harnessing of 'lesbian drive.' After dividing up telephone lists of prospective participants in this still fuzzily defined venture and planning a series of meetings, a task force was struck at the founding meeting on 7 November 1976. The women represented many of the already established pockets of lesbian, feminist, gay, and left activity. Despite the immediately evident lack of consensus on the scope and direction of the project, the support for something stamped 'Lesbian' was categorical. In fact, as several women argued, the powerful premise of wanting to organize around something that they were interested in, that they knew something about, and that they felt they had a right to suggested significant mobilizing capacity.

Supportive of the plan, yet confused about where it would lead, women like CHAT board member Tin Lowes recalls her niggling feeling of unease towards the women-only gathering. She did not make public her suspicion that ceding leadership to lesbian feminists who were 'too political' would only magnify divisions already fracturing the lesbian community. Unhappily caught between her desire for the continued growth and expansion of her own mixed gay/lesbian organization and the super-charged enthusiasm of a new generation of activists, she and other CHAT women quietly sat back.

The most pressing needs outlined by women who attended the fall meetings and spoke out were better communication among lesbian feminists, a place to meet, and a base for political action. A reporter for *The Other Woman* summed up the substance of the discussions: 'The group hopes to serve as a bridge to unify various existing groups who can provide services to the lesbian community. Representatives of groups spoke of the need for more energy in their projects and the isolation they all felt in trying to do work in a city the size of Toronto. Women at the meetings expressed support and offered time and energy and connections to bolster sagging projects. The group also hopes to meet some of the social, political and counselling needs of Toronto's lesbian community.'[17] At the very least, most women agreed, a physical space would raise the profile of lesbians in the city and make it possible for women to come out of the closet in the company of other lesbians without fear of reprisal. Interviewed for *The Body Politic*, Rosemary Barnes stated, 'At first there was some talk about working for a second women's centre, but it soon became clear that what we wanted was a lesbian centre.'[18] Neither the rotation of organizations like the Three of Cups Coffeehouse to different spaces scattered across the downtown area, nor the shared rental of space with other community organizations promised quite the same reward as 'a place of our own.'

While members of the task force elected to meet every week and busy themselves with locating a space to house the newly named Lesbian Organization of Toronto (LOOT), general meetings (attended by anywhere from twenty to forty women) were held every two weeks. By the end of November the formerly and notoriously lesbian household, 342 Jarvis Street, became unexpectedly available and members of LOOT scrambled to sign the lease. From those first euphoric moments on, treasurer Rosemary Barnes remembers 'having heart attacks that my credit rating might be wrecked because we wouldn't have enough money to pay all the bills.' Nancy Adamson recalls that the whole initiative marked a very special development: 'The LOOT house gave us the sense that we could go off and be lesbians on our own. There was a real need to make a safe place in the world, and 342 Jarvis was a tangible expression of "this can happen." A lot of us had fantasies of going to live off the land and we incorporated that into being lesbians downtown.'

In the spirit of defiant lesbian-feminist connectionism, LOOT, together with *The Other Woman* newspaper and the Three of Cups Coffeehouse, officially moved in, on 1 February 1977, to occupy what Pat Murphy called the three-storey 'shabby, dilapidated but glorious castle.' A popular spin-off from the monthly provincial Wintario Lottery, LotoLesbian was instituted and money from ticket sales paid the rent, utilities, and the costs of supplies (which by March 1977 included the printing and mailing of the *LOOT Newsletter*). At the end of three months of coordination, planning, and fund-raising, finally ensconced in their new 'digs,' the groups jointly celebrated the opening of the first lesbian-feminist centre in Canada.[19]

PERSONAL AND POLITICAL BIOGRAPHIES: FIT FOR THE TASK?

Most of the women attracted to the dream of building a lesbian centre did not grow up in Toronto, and few had been in the city for more than five years before LOOT's formation. Whether, like Naomi Brooks, Sue Genge, and Marg Moores, they came to study, get a job, or seek out adventure, they found that downtown Toronto opened up a world of experience and opportunity unimaginable in the places they had called 'home' as young girls. According to Marg Moores, 'LOOT was kind of dark and run down and the couches were threadbare and there was a church pew. [At the beginning] I felt like I was from a small town and Toronto was this big puzzling city. The idea that all these women would rent a house and not live in it was kind of odd, and I thought having a business in a house was also strange and weird, but I was interested in the life of being a lesbian.'

For American-born Ruth Dworin, Nancy Adamson, Rosemary Barnes, and Judith Bennett, crossing the Canada/U.S. border offered not a novel, big-city adventure as much as the freedom to begin a new life unfettered by old baggage. For others, like Chris Bearchell, Nia Cordingley, Fiona Rattray, and Pam Godfrey, leaving a small(er) community or suburb (and the watchful, disapproving eye of parents, friends, and relatives) to enter into the frenzy of metropolitan life was a deliberate, conscious step towards coming out and establishing roots. Pat Hugh, born in Guyana, expelled from the convent at fifteen for kissing a female classmate, and later involved in a 'dicey relationship with an older married woman whose husband started to suspect,' left for Canada and promptly came out. Ann Kado, a former resident of a Windsor reform school for girls, and later, in the early 1970s, an active member of the American Indian Movement, moved back to the Toronto of her childhood, this time looking for a home to come out into. She recalls that 'most of the men in the Native movement were radicals and feminists and they gave support, but not the kind of support I needed at the time. Most of the Native lesbians around were far worse alcoholics than I was and they drank to hide. I needed to identify who I was and what I was. I thought I was a lesbian, but I needed to be sure.'

The time-tested phenomenon of migration to large, urban lesbian and gay subcultures is one that American theorist Gayle Rubin contends is steeped in longing and urgency: 'We must find our way into those social spaces where we can meet partners, find friends, get validation, and participate in community life which does not presuppose that we are straight.'[20] A stock theme of 1950s lesbian pulp fiction, 'picking up and moving out' signalled a character's decision to rupture familiar, habitual patterns of daily life. Laura, the hero of Ann Bannon's *I Am a Woman*, flees the malaise of the midwest to discover her 'true lesbian identity' in New York's Greenwich Village, where, as pulp novelist David George Kin claimed, 'the lost and the hopeless elbowed each other in search of success and satanic depravity.'[21] Themes of exile and journeying are also threaded through contemporary lesbian fiction: *Rubyfruit Jungle* by Rita Mae Brown (1973), *Shedding* by Verena Stefan (1978), *Anna's Country* by Elizabeth Lang (1981), and Carol Anne Douglas's *To the Cleveland Station* (1982), among others.[22] Writing for *The Body Politic* in 1979, LOOT member Lorna Weir reflected on her own quest: 'Coming out as a lesbian reinforced the necessity of breaking with my childhood: I took the geographical course and moved to another city, thus conveniently cutting out connection with straight friends and my previous sexual identity ... An altogether common way of coming out: flight is often a splendid solution to an existential predicament.'[23] Women attracted to LOOT possessed little history of lesbian-feminist activity in the city.[24] 'Starting from scratch' betrayed not only this lack of knowledge exacerbated by unfamiliarity with Toronto and its political/cultural traditions, but the brand-newness of lesbian feminism. With very few exceptions, these women had not been out as lesbians to themselves or others for more than two or three years. As Lorna Weir recalls, 'With everybody in that developmental phase, virtually at once, without the benefit of women who had done it ten or twenty years ago ... it was explosive.' Like every social movement before it, from Black civil rights to the new left to the women's movement, members were rarely fully versed in histories of activism. Poorly kept, difficult-to-find, and sometimes non-existent records, combined with chronically underdeveloped methods of educating fledgling activists, contributed to the phenomenon of disconnection.[25]

In the case of LOOT, discontinuity with past lesbian and feminist projects was magnified by the 1975–6 exodus of lesbian feminists to the west coast, that is, Vancouver, Victoria, and the Gulf islands. The leaders in charge of A Woman's Place, *The Other Woman*, Amazon Workshop, the Bare Breast Brigade, Three of Cups Coffeehouse, and Seaton House, as well as the Brunswick Four, 'escaped' Toronto and took their expertise, street smarts, and chutzpah with them.[26] Tales of their outrageous, high-profile pursuits had already become the staple fare of Toronto's legendary lesbian folklore. And yet despite the losses, the women drawn to LOOT and 342 Jarvis Street brought with them their own rich personal and political histories and experiences. Collectively, they constituted Toronto's swelling 'second wave' of lesbian-feminist organizing.

The approximately ten-member task force and those others most closely involved in the work of planning LOOT were predominantly white women in their twenties (with a handful of women either under twenty or over thirty) who had some college or university education. In late sixties fashion, almost all the women eschewed full-time work for 'The Man.'[27] Instead, they tended to rely on a combination of income-generating sources – part-time work, self-employment, social assistance, student loans (or grants), and/or unemployment insurance. Located in positions of relative marginality in relation to the capitalist marketplace, by 1976 these women had managed to gain political and social skills from work as activists in a range of grass-roots social movements. The breadth and depth of their expertise covered these areas: direct action (organizing and participating in demonstrations and 'zaps'; administration (fund-raising; accounting; booking halls, performers, and equipment); education (public speaking, drafting briefs and grant applications); publishing (newsletters, press releases, newspapers, and leaflets); and counselling (leading coming out and rap groups, answering crisis calls, providing information and referrals).

Clearly, the standard formula of time-plus-energy-plus-youth, mixed with indignation at societal injustices, in part made possible both the intellectual and practical work of plotting change. In addition to their skills, the women I interviewed told me how past experience as community organizers or service providers had taught them self-confidence, consciousness of oppression, a sense of their own capabilities, and the power of working together. With few exceptions, they were not raised in political households. Moreover, rarely encouraged to view themselves as subjects capable of making a difference, they often found the beginnings of their own pro-lesbian political education both surprising and empowering. In a society that fears change, red-baits collective organizing, propagates a fierce brand of conformist individualism, and identifies the government and elected representatives as the only legitimate agents of change, stepping out of line, as many lesbian feminists (and countless other radicals) discovered, was no small feat.

In the early 1970s, Pat Murphy, Chris Fox, Mary Axten, and Linda Jain were among the only lesbian members of the Community Homophile Association of Toronto (CHAT). A little later, women like Chris Bearchell, Konnie Reich, Fiona Rattray, and Naomi Brooks were active in such gay-liberationist groups as the Gay Alliance Toward Equality (GATE), the John Damien Defense Committee, *The Body Politic* newspaper, Gay Youth Toronto, the Coalition for Gay Rights in Ontario (CGRO), and the Gay Offensive Collective (GOC).

Pat Leslie, Eve Zaremba, Marcia McVea, Chris Lawrence, Darlene Lawson, and Phil Masters, among others, stretched politically and socially in the women's liberation movement. The organizations and services in which they participated included *The Other Woman* newspaper, the Three of Cups Coffeehouse, the Women's Credit Union, the Abortion Caravan, the YWCA, Women's Referral and Education Centre, A Woman's Place (later Women's Information Centre), Nellie's, and the Rape Crisis Centre. Rosemary Barnes, Ruth Dworin, Amy Gottlieb, Judith Bennett, and Nancy Adamson were among the newly arrived Americans. They brought with them knowledge and skills gained through the student movement, civil-rights work, the women's movement, and, to a minor extent, lesbian-feminist politics.

By 1975/6, Naomi Brooks, Natalie LaRoche, Gay Bell, Amy Gottlieb, and Sue Genge had begun to raise the question of sexual politics as a legitimate political concern in the context of Toronto's independent left: the Young Socialists, the Revolutionary Marxist Group, the League for Socialist Action, and, later, the Revolutionary Workers League.[28] At York University, Lorna Weir and Mariana Valverde were studying Marx and other left intellectuals. Maureen Fitzgerald was exercising her skills as an editor and publisher inside the Canadian Women's Educational Press, a socialist-feminist organization. Strike support and union organizing, underground publishing, abortion and the Morgentaler campaign, antiwar protest, and Québec nationalism were areas of grass-roots activism familiar to many of the lesbians attracted to LOOT, whether they were part of the organized left or not.

Consistent with the redefined and expanded feminist notion of 'political activity,' numerous poets, actors, writers, and musicians were eager to stretch their cultural/political talents at 342 Jarvis Street: among them, Beverly Glenn Copeland, Carol (C.T.) Rowe and April Kassirer, Gwen Hauser, Lynne Fernie, Charlene Sheard, Keltie Creed, and the indomitable Sara Ellen Dunlop – co-owner of the Music Room and the Melody Room on Yonge Street in the mid-1960s, singer, and founder of Mama Quilla I.

In effect, the women excited by the prospect of a lesbian-feminist centre held different yet overlapping analyses of power and domination. Without long, drawn-out histories of mistrust or hostility engendered by clashes and infighting, this diversity was initially viewed as enriching rather than problematic. 'Because the whole project was so risky, there was a respect for people's differences,' says Chris Bearchell. 'We were trying to do something we had virtually given up trying to do in the women's movement.' And Naomi Brooks muses, 'Now, looking back, the idea of me – a revolutionary socialist, and Pat Murphy – a homophile activist, being in the same room and working on the same thing is mind-blowing. And there were lots of women like Pat and me.' Since all of the women who came to invest a piece of themselves in LOOT identified as lesbians, it was felt that this commonality, significantly anchored by their commitment to 'feminism,' would lend any venture a potency uncharacteristic of past organizing efforts. As Pat Leslie attests, 'We couldn't even begin to discuss differences until we saw that we could look in a room and see that we were all lesbians and acknowledge that fact.'

Oppressed as women in a patriarchal world, lesbians argued that, as lesbians, they were marginalized by people and institutions saturated with heterosexual bias.[29] This double oppression alone differentiated them, they insisted, from their straight sisters and gay brothers, and underpinned the push for a united lesbian-feminist front. They did not foresee the personal and political discord between and among LOOT women that would precipitate the hardening of distinct ideological camps.

Constructing a new organization and, ultimately, a new movement did not transpire independently of the broader context of 1970s radicalism. And yet LOOT lesbians could not count on strong, consistent support from other social-change movements. Eve Zaremba claims, 'We were hidden in the women's movement and we were tertiary, not even secondary in the gay movement which has always been a men's movement.' To some lesbian feminists, Toronto's grass-roots left seemed even more harsh and dismissive of sexual politics. A member of the Young Socialists, later the League for Socialist Action (LSA), Naomi Brooks recalls the refrain of her left comrades: 'Oh, those crazy girls, you're just getting into personal and spiritual stuff. You're going to be forgetting the working-class.' And as Natalie LaRoche adds, the concept of lesbian liberation was not embraced eagerly by other radicals: 'The left was where some of us thought we were involved in prefigurative struggles, but they thought we were supporting 'life/ stylist' communities. They did not fully understand the significance of building those kind of communities where you could organize from and defend yourselves from and get healed from as well as go out and fight the world. Straight women too said this is just lifestyle politics. They didn't understand the implications of not being able to be out at your workplace, or the fear of losing kids.' In actuality, few women had ever experienced the opportunity to launch and bring to fruition a lesbian-specific project. Swept up in the euphoria of organizing *as lesbian feminists*, 'with the world our lesbian oyster,' Susan Cole contends that the popular maxim 'feminism is the theory and lesbianism is the practice' embodied 'the chauvinism we needed to get an assertive, empowered thing going.' The promise of celebrating love for women as it had never been celebrated before aroused considerable, even lustful, anticipation. As Naomi Brooks recollects, 'Bread and roses said a lot about LOOT – we wanted the bread, we wanted the basics but we also wanted the good stuff, the roses, the stuff we couldn't get anywhere else.' Rosemary Barnes recalls, 'We all fantasized that this place was going to be *the place* where emotional support, affection and unconditional acceptance would be guaranteed.' 'In the larger social world which hates our sexual preference,' says Lorna Weir, 'it was very common to say, Yes, I'm completely all right and be utterly uncritical and cavalier. It was a time of vast euphoria.'

To those lesbians in particular for whom oppression based on sexual difference had been lived through isolation, fear, secrecy, lies, physical, and/or emotional pain, the expectations for healing and growth were enormous. Several older lesbians were aware that the multiple dimensions of oppression did not magically disappear upon coming out. As Eve Zaremba remembers it, 'There was a tendency to totally dismiss the past because that's the only way we could deal with the new. But there's a nagging part of you back there. Self-hatred is how we put it back then – coming to know as a lesbian that something is wrong with you.' According to Natalie LaRoche: 'Just as Marx says that the whole is greater than the sum of its parts, the founding of LOOT felt like an experiment in a prefigurative kind of community. A lot of us were very damaged, hurt people, and we wanted to serve our own selves and create a healthy community.'

SOMEWHERE OVER THE RAINBOW ...

Brash and courageous, LOOT's lesbian-feminist vision resonated with the fresh idealism characteristic of so many radical social movements.[30]

Yearning for 'a new world whose material foundations have not yet been laid' inspired hope rather than despair; history, it seemed, could be transformed by the purity of acts of will.[31] Fundamental to the ideological armoury of popular movements, as U.S. feminist Annie Popkin avows, was the conviction that lived social struggle contained in embryo the forms of a future revolutionary society.[32] It simply was a matter of wrestling the unsatisfactory present into line with this utopian future.

Elements holding popular social movements together revolve around a sense of shared oppression and the commitment to collective modes of resistance. Yet even then, as historian Barbara Taylor has argued, these bonds are almost never enough: 'Political visions are fragile – they appear and are lost again ... The history of all progressive movements is littered with such half-remembered hopes, with dreams that have failed.'[33] Not prepared to buckle under to pessimism, in his 1972 essay 'Refugees from Amerika,' gay-liberationist Carl Wittman states, 'To be a free territory, we must govern ourselves, set up our own institutions, defend ourselves, and use our own energies to improve our lives.'[34]

As part of the hunger to imagine a Lesbian Nation into being, lesbian speculative fiction in the 1970s offered an inspirational mythology for what French author Monique Wittig calls 'lesbian peoples.' From the Red Dykes of Wittig and Zweig's *Lesbian Peoples* (1976), who endeavour to realize a lesbian utopia on tropical islands, to a place devoid of men where all women are lovers in Bertha Harris's *Lover* (1976), to Joanna Russ's planet of women in *The Female Man* (1975), to the spiritual society of hill women in Sally Gearhart's *The Wanderground* (1978), the ideal lesbian-feminist program for social organization was dreamed into materiality.[35]

To the founders of the Lesbian Organization of Toronto, access to a spacious, centrally located building – a concrete testament to lesbian-feminist energy and will – constituted one piece of a collective redefinition. 'It was the middle of winter,' says Fiona Rattray, 'but LOOT was this lush spring growth and I gravitated to it immediately.' The spirit that inhered in coming together as lesbians was contagious. Gay Bell perfectly captures the momentum: 'I had the definite feeling that every woman in the world is going to catch on to lesbianism and is going to come out. Maybe only 10 per cent of women would remain steadfastly heterosexual, but basically every woman is going to get the hang of it. Just like everyone is going to start smoking dope and they're going to realize it's stupid to shoot people and we're not going to have war anymore and human beings are going to change – everyone is going to realize that lesbianism makes complete sense and that the patriarchy will just dissolve.' As far as writers for mass-circulation magazines were concerned, the seventies marked a sharp departure from the artefacts of the sixties: underground newspapers, communes, participatory democracy, group sex, Consciousness III, acid heads, and rock festivals. 'The seventies so far,' according to Philip Marchand of *Maclean's*, 'have been marked by a remembrance of conservatism past, even in the way we see rebellion. All this makes the sixties look like a street rumble between decades.' In effect, he continued, the old psychic themes of anger, collectivism, the desire to relate, free love, ecology, risks, conspiracy as paranoia, and sedition had become acutely anachronistic in the 'earn, baby earn' decade of the seventies. Instead, apathy, individualism, personal salvation, positions of power, gold stocks, securities, and the 'hope to cope' reigned supreme.[36]

In striking contrast to the observations of Marchand and fellow cultural pundits, for neither lesbian nor straight feminists did the 1970s herald the death of insurgency and the quiet, ordered practice of conservative values. Rebellion signified neither a dirty word nor the doomed passion of a preceding generation. The optimism of 1970s activists not yet frustrated, jaded, or burnt out by a recognition of the long and laborious process of social change coloured the view of Naomi Brooks. She reminisces: 'The revolution was around the corner. It was going to happen at any moment. We were on the crest of a wave. We felt we had these ideas that no one had ever had before. Lesbians were going to take over the world – we had the truth and the light and the only way ... I mean, the incredible arrogance. I wish I knew then as much as I thought I did.'

Revolutionary slogans like 'smash the state' and 'seize state power' did not attend to the organization of gender and sexuality – the very sites of struggle that women's liberationists, most notably lesbian feminists, sought to problematize. Indeed, for women attracted to lesbian organizing, becoming the authorities of their own lives, wresting control away from sexologists, psychiatrists, doctors, teachers, clergy, judges, journalists, landlords, and parents first demanded a consciousness of their lived realities as lesbians and feminists. Theorist Shane Phelan argues that 'the cost to people of growing up hearing that they or others like them are sick, warped, in need of a good fuck, or otherwise defective, is a cost that can be seen only when one makes the judgment that these things are not true.'[37] Recognition of what Dorothy E. Smith has identified as the 'line of fault' or disjuncture between everyday lesbian experience and the mainstream social categories, institutions, and images deployed to regulate that experience constitutes the first step on the path towards self-empowerment.[38]

No longer prepared to bear the brunt of the costs of 'deviance' alone, in hiding, lesbians who attended LOOT organizational meetings began to look to themselves and to each other for meaning. 'We were grappling with issues that were so large,' says Cate Smith, 'and each of us carried a part of the struggle. Individually it would have been fragmented ... together we had a chance of having the whole picture of what was going on.'

OPEN THE UMBRELLA, BUT NOT INSIDE A BAR

A formal description of the Lesbian Organization of Toronto appeared in the first *LOOT Newsletter*, dated March 1977: 'LOOT is an umbrella organization for lesbians. It serves social, recreational, personal, cultural, political and educational purposes for the women involved. Mostly, it simply allows a lesbian to meet and get together with other lesbians who share her interests. All lesbians are welcome. To help make decisions about LOOT, you just have to come to meetings. We do not exclude anyone on the basis of her race, religion, politics, economic status, occupation or degree of openness.'[39] The metaphor of the 'umbrella' was used deliberately to highlight LOOT's inclusive approach to the Toronto lesbian-feminist community. Rosemary Barnes remembers the similarities to the Community Homophile Association in the early seventies: 'Like CHAT, it was going to be everything to everybody.' From the start, the mandate of the organization was to appeal to all lesbians. As advertised in the *LOOT Newsletter* in 1977, 'The organization is new and can become whatever you want to make it. Remember, *you are LOOT*, so come and get involved!' (emphasis in original).[40] Chris Bearchell stresses the push to publicize LOOT's whereabouts: 'For our first Open House, we drew a picture of the building on a nice blue leaflet. It had 342 Jarvis written right on it and we put it up in laundromats and health food stores. We had hundreds of people to that first event and it was more outward-looking than anything that had gone before. There was hemming and hawing – "what if we get somebody hostile, what if a man tries to come in ... " but we just said, "Fuck it!" We want to tell women we're here and we want them to come to the house.' The umbrella also symbolized the accommodation of differences between individuals and groups that the planners anticipated, given their appeal to such a wide spectrum of women. In 1956, the invitation to 'all women regardless of race, religion or ethnic background' was made by the Daughters of Bilitis (DOB) – the first lesbian political organization in the United States.[41]

Convinced of the need to recast the traditional linkage of the term 'organization' with politics, LOOT task-force members took pains to emphasize opportunities for socializing, recreation, and self-help. At the same time, gracing LOOT's introductory promotional pamphlet was a quote from American lesbian activist Rita Mae Brown: 'Becoming a Lesbian does not make you instantly pure, perpetually happy and devotedly revolutionary. But once you have taken your life in your own hands, you will find you are no longer alone ... you will be part of that surge forward and you will leave your fingerprints on the shape of things to come.'[42]

LOOT's political edge was unmistakable, though its mandate was vaguely defined. Task-force members were united in what they didn't want: a lesbian bar. At the Montreal lesbian conference in 1974, bars were labelled 'pretty oppressive places' and workshop participants (including several future LOOT members) brainstormed 'alternatives' to 'overpriced drinks, cover charges, the petty rules of male owners and managers, and the cruising type of atmosphere.'[43] Hardly unique to LOOT, and as with the Daughters of Bilitis twenty years earlier, the desire to build a lesbian organization that did not resemble a bar was hinged to a critique of gay women who made bar culture central to their lives. Lesbian-feminist contributors to the Boston women's health manual *Our Bodies, Our Selves* warned, 'The bar becomes a hustling scene, full of pimps and drug dealers, as well as straight men with straight women who come to get their voyeuristic rocks off on watching us.'[44]

In 1973, Adrienne Potts and Lydia Gross reconsidered the troubled relationship of 'lesbian feminists to bar women.' In *The Other Woman's* 'Lesbian Issue,' they wrote: 'Our arrogance and self-righteousness at the state of things really doesn't belong BETWEEN us and our lesbian sisters, no matter how involved in perpetuating a destructive system they may be ... Let's save our snottiness for the man. We can afford to be nice to our sisters ... (this doesn't mean we stop disagreeing with their actions and start indulging their acceptance of the status quo, we just learn less cruel ways of disagreeing and better ways of changing minds.)'[45] More than three years later, the once thinly veiled condescension seems to have matured and concomitantly dampened any overtures to 'sisterhood' and openness to dialogue. Because, as Pam Godfrey noted, 'the Bluejay bar would never take posters or leaflets so we'd put them up in the bathroom and they'd rip them down,' many lesbian feminists were tired of being told they were 'ruining it for everyone.' Naomi Brooks's memory of the tension is consistent with the recollections of others involved in planning LOOT and 342 Jarvis Street: 'We made attempts but it was like, "Well if they can't see what we're talking about and the rightness of our ways, then fuck them" ... We had no sympathy, tolerance or understanding for where [bar women] were coming from at all. We were full of our politics. They had their own way of life, and we were very much a challenge to it. They were politically very conservative; they wanted to own homes and go on trips. You'd meet in the john and that was about it.'

Reaching out to and making welcome those women who found and sustained community, lovers, and family in the local bars was not a primary feature of the largely white, middle-class lesbian-feminist program. Dina, a working-class lesbian, came out to herself and 'her people' through bar culture in the early 1960s. She was offended and angered by what she saw as the narrow, self-serving vision of lesbian feminists: 'They'd go on about 'those lonely bar types,' and I used to think, "Fuck, I was doing it before you were born, bitch." Somehow it wasn't okay to be over in a bar drinking and being that unruly and that ferocious and fighting. But there was no way we were going to apologize to other lesbians. We had to live with shit from the "hets" in terms of housing and jobs and kids. I thought, "I've been out there in the trenches getting rocks thrown at me, blackmailed, attempted murder on my life, losing my army career, losing income, losing my home." Somehow, none of this mattered to them.' Whereas the first meeting of the Lesbian Caucus of the BCFW took place at the Ms. Club, a downtown Vancouver lesbian bar, there was virtually no history of communication between 'political' and 'non-political' lesbians in Toronto.[46] And with no precedent upon which to build communication and understanding, the stalemate persisted. As LOOT regular Rachel stated candidly, 'I would never have gone to a bar. If the alternative was going to a bar, I'd still be married. I never would have made it in the bar scene – the tough dykes and the fear and the homophobia.' Resigned to living 'worlds apart,' their only common ground was one of mutual distrust. As Phil Masters and many others saw it: '[Bar women] wanted the bar to be a place where closeted lesbians who worked in offices could come and hang out and dance but not have political trouble-making ... There were so few of us back then that you felt betrayed by women who weren't supporting you and your feminist analysis of the world. There was so little space for us and our voice was so small we needed as much support as we could get. If there was a bunch of dykes out there and they just wanted to have fun and not understand and play into old stereotyped patterns, it could mean death to the movement ... didn't they see what would happen if they didn't care?' Again, the fragility of lesbian feminism is evinced through the perception of scarcity – scarce resources, scarce bodies – which in turn magnified feelings of urgency, impatience, and frustration. To lesbian feminists for whom coming out publicly in as many contexts as possible was a significant measure of one's courage and commitment to lesbian liberation, the 'non-feminism' of bar lesbians was an unsettling affront. To lesbian militants, 'playing it safe' meant maintaining a stake in the status quo. Now, in retrospect, Natalie LaRoche notes, 'We [lesbian feminists] were privileged: we could come out during the daylight, and they could not.'

COMING OUT IN/TO COMMUNITY

Despite differing needs, expectations, and personal/political histories, most of the women present at the LOOT founding meetings shared a common belief: based on the sheer strength of conviction, the process of establishing a physical space – one into which women could come out en masse – would signify a definitive break with the legacy of lesbian invisibility. No longer confined to seedy, male-operated bars in run-down hotels, the uncomfortable edges of feminist, gay, and left groups, or dusty corners of the closet, they found that the profile of lesbian-feminist existence was raised both inside and outside the organization through 'the LOOT house.' In fact, LOOT's very emergence was predicated on the realization that it was impossible to organize *as lesbians* without being out. Notwithstanding the pledge to honour multiple degrees of openness, queries such as who is out, how long has she been out, how far is she out, to whom and in what contexts is she out, and so on constituted key elements of lesbian-feminist discourse.

One year before LOOT's formation, Charlene D. used *The Other Woman* newspaper to air her view that there could be no personal safety in lesbian invisibility: 'You will be hassled and you will bleed a little each time, but we must support each other ... Are we going to let society closet our feelings forever? Do you enjoy not being able to be touched or kissed in public? Or is fear your leader instead of love? Society has forced us into ghettoes. The only time we are really "gay" is at the Saturday night bars, if we can afford them. Can you afford to live this way? What I am saying, in fact, is Come out all the way out!'[47]

Without denying that the cultural, psychological, emotional, and material repercussions of coming out may be experienced differently by lesbians and gay men, former LOOT member Mariana Valverde asserted, 'Coming out is a key concept for lesbian politics as well as gay male politics. It arises out of our own lives, it names our experience, and it gives others a sense of what it might be like to discover – and fight against – one's oppression as a lesbian.'[48]

To cite Eve Zaremba, 'Coming out is about struggling with identity and seeing if one identity fits you better than another. So you try it on, and I remember the newness was like being a teenager, being very young, except that we weren't teenagers anymore.' Similarly, for Gay Bell, who 'couldn't come out' until she was 31 because she 'never met any lesbians,' when she did, she 'came out like a kid, and had all sorts of kid-like idealisms.' Referring to the 'activist' (as opposed to the 'secretive') lesbians she interviewed for her study of lesbian identities in the mid-1970s, American sociologist Barbara Ponse contends that 'their open stance is ultimately directed at other lesbians in efforts to promote solidarity and to provide support for other women in the coming out process. The net effect of such politically motivated, purposive disclosure is an intensified commitment to lesbian identity and lesbianism as an alternate life-style.'[49]

As British feminist Wendy Clark suggests, 'When one's identity is secret and stigmatized it takes on a particular and vital significance to the participants.'[50] Monster and outlaw, as writer Bertha Harris put it, the lesbian feminist seeks proof of her own existence in the absence of a shared birth heritage.[51] Coming-out workshops were run at lesbian conferences held in Toronto in 1973, Montréal in 1974 and 1975, and Kingston and Ottawa in 1976. Telling 'coming out stories' was (and is) a time-honoured practice, and the chief matter of lesbian oral culture. American writers Julia Penelope Stanley and Susan Wolfe assert that 'coming out stories are the foundation of our lives as Lesbians, as real to ourselves; as such, our sharing of them defines us as participants in Lesbian culture, as members of a community.'[52]

By the late 1970s, the published collections of first-person narratives or autobiographical accounts (in various forms, from interviews to journal entries to poetry) offered readers the possibility of alternative, liberatory subject-positions in ways most often associated with fiction. 'Exuberant and unabashed political propaganda,' to quote critic Bonnie Zimmerman,[53] popular (American) titles included: *The New Lesbians* (1977), *We're Here: Conversations with Lesbian Women* (1977), *Women Who Love Women* (1977), *Word Is Out: Stories of Some of Our Lives* (1978), and *The Coming Out Stories* (1980). Personal testimony was also central to *The Ladder* in the 1950s and 1960s, and to the non-fiction classics *Lesbian/Woman* (1972) and *Sappho Was a Right-On Woman* (1972). And articles like 'A Rite of Passage,' 'Come out – all the way!,' 'Linda's Story,' 'Thoughts on Becoming,' 'Coming Out at Seventeen,' and 'The First Dance' became the regular copy of English Canadian publications: *Long Time Coming*, *The Other Woman*, *The Pedestal*, the *LOOT Newsletter*, and *The Body Politic*. In the counter-texts that fictionalize the lesbian rite of passage, insistence on naturalness and normality is achieved through strong protagonists: the archetypal lesbian hero Molly Bolt in Rita Mae Brown's *Rubyfruit Jungle* (1972), Su in June Arnold's *Sister Gin* (1975), and Inez Riverfingers in Elana Nachmann's *Riverfinger Women* (1974).[54]

To its founders, the Lesbian Organization of Toronto would make possible the solid, systematic institutionalization of this powerful 'coming out' tradition. Harnessing energy powered by what Amy Gottlieb thought seemed like 'thousands of conversions to lesbianism by the mid-70s' promised not only an end to speechlessness, but the expansion of a still amorphous lesbian-feminist community. To quote Vancouver activist Sara Diamond, 'The *political choice* is in deciding to come out vs. staying in the closet. It's in deciding to fight for the right to be who we are.'[55] 'Coming home to lesbianism,' 'discovering my true identity,' and 'finally ending the search for self' are all statements made by women I interviewed that underscore the experienced *essentiality* of their lesbian-feminist identity. As Judith Quinlan put it, 'Being a lesbian requires vision, courage and pig-headed stupidity in about equal parts ... Being a lesbian means exploring a void, it means deep mining for an identity in the pit of female invisibility.'[56] In stark contrast to the historic equation of lesbianism with sin, sickness, deviance, and perversion, the relief and the pride in giving voice to woman identification demanded a reformulated definition – one fashioned from the standpoint of lesbian feminists themselves.

As Rosemary Barnes exclaims, 'There were no bounds to the high of coming out, that synergy.' Hence, a politics rooted firmly in the articulation of personal experience. Writing for *The Pedestal* (Vancouver) in 1975, Judi Morton argued, 'If in my job or my social life, I choose not to restrict my contact with other lesbians, I must constantly deal with abuse, ignorance or aggression. The line to political identity is very short from here.'[57] LOOT organizers would later discover that the translation of individual acts of self-identification into public, political modes of collective resistance is neither automatic nor easy.[58] But in the early days of hope and idealism, the lavender lesbian sky was the limit; coming out in great numbers, with wild abandon, was *the* key strategy. Indeed, as American writer Alice Echols avows, 'Coming out, which [the Furies] maintained involved breaking the final tie to male privilege, became a way to separate the serious revolutionaries from the dilettantes and the dabblers.'[59]

LESBIAN VISIBILITY AND THE PARADOX OF CLOSETRY

Though lesbian visibility was identified as pivotal to the health and growth of a new movement and a necessary precondition for cultural and political activism, many lesbians harboured the very real, tangible fear of being out. As women and as lesbians, those attracted to building a lesbian-feminist organization were keenly aware of the potential repercussions of coming out: loss of jobs, family ties, friends, child custody; harassment in the workplace, on the streets, in the media, at the hands of medical practitioners and other figures of authority. Thus, coming out, recalls Mariana Valverde, was not simply 'a question of screwing up your courage to tell X or Y about your "true" identity.'[60] For most lesbians, taking the long road to embracing the dreaded word 'lesbian,' with all its bends and bumps, proved to be a much more complicated process. Though as activists they participated (in varying degrees) in the shared creation of a lesbian reality, they were continually faced with mediating the break between this reality and the unchanged heterosexism and homophobia of institutions.

Notwithstanding the 'moral imperative' to come out that Valverde has identified,[61] because not all LOOT members (including task force members) were out equally, it was seen as neither possible nor desirable to demand open lesbian identification under *all* circumstances. To protect members from unwanted exposure, the mailing list was kept under lock and key in suburban Etobicoke and never publicly circulated. The use of pseudonyms in print (for instance, the *LOOT Newsletter*) or 'first names only' was general practice, and mainstream news photographers were not permitted entrance to 342 Jarvis Street. As a group of seasoned lesbian activists in Vancouver maintained, 'There is a big difference between being out to 50 or even 500 other lesbians and being out to a heterosexist and homophobic world. Many of us can't be that public, many of us won't, certainly most of us aren't.'[62] According to Marg Moores, 'People were even nervous coming in the door [at 342 Jarvis Street] thinking there was a camera on them from across the street or the phone was being tapped ... We were worried about being found out, but not too worried to stop going.' Gay Bell's level of anxiety was not atypical: 'I remember having arguments with Pat Leslie because she wanted to collect everything [almanacs, diaries, photos] for the archives and I said, Pat, for fuck sakes, the cops just have to walk into those archives and there's a bunch of dead ducks sitting there.'

LOOT task-force members did not distribute a press release to mainstream media organs announcing the opening of 342 Jarvis Street. Nor did they seek out interviews with industry journalists as free publicity for their organization. Yet the decision to spurn the mass media was not solely informed by the fact that, to quote Susan Cole, 'many of us were damn scared.' Notorious for both sensationalizing and misrepresenting grass-roots feminism and gay liberation (read: male homosexuality), the press could not be trusted, argued several of LOOT's more experienced organizers.[63] Hardly unique to lesbians, feminists, or gay men, suspicion of the media had a long history in virtually all progressive social movements. Rather than engage with untrustworthy reporters trained in the business of gathering facts and manufacturing news, members of alternative organizations invariably sought to create their own communication networks. News of LOOT's emergence was carried in *The Body Politic*, *The Other Woman*, and the *LOOT Newsletter*, and picked up by a number of small lesbian and feminist publications across the country.

Despite the prevailing disdain for all commercial media outlets, not everyone compelled by lesbian-feminist activism was convinced that such an approach was in LOOT's best interests. Throughout the midseventies, Chris Bearchell polished and honed media skills as chair of the John Damien Defense Committee and as a producer of 'This Show May Be Offensive to Heterosexuals,' a gay and lesbian television series. Beginning in 1976, she penned a 'Dykes' column for *The Body Politic*, and in the paper's November 1977 issue, she wrote:

While asserting ourselves in our own sympathetic media may make us a more cohesive community, it is not enough. We must have a higher profile in the ugly, amorphous mess of the straight establishment press and broadcast media. We must, as much as possible, set our own terms when we deal with them. We have to counteract centuries of invisibility. We have to respond to their every slight, however slight it may seem. The lesbian image is not going to change until we decide to change it. And we must. There are many more lesbians 'out there' than any of us realize, and the contact these women will have with their own community depends on that community's efforts to break through their isolation. It is the truth about us – our real faces, the reality of our lives – that the mass media fear so much. That truth is a powerful weapon. We should use it.[64]

Despite Bearchell's brave call for a revamped relationship to mainstream print and broadcasting, a mere handful of lesbians were prepared to crack what radicals of all stripes referred to as the media's 'conspiracy of silence.' Only later would members realize the implications of uneven degrees of outness for the excecution of strategies internal and external to the Lesbian Organization of Toronto.

EARLY MOMENTS IN ANTI-PERMISSIVE MORAL POLICING

The mid-to-late 1970s was not an easy time for lesbians to be out in Toronto or anywhere else in the country. Beyond the doorstep of 342 Jarvis Street, on the larger political scene, antihomosexual fervour was gaining momentum. A reassertion of the dominance of heterosexual gender relations became the mandate of organizations like Positive Parents, Renaissance, the Western Guard, and the Edmund Burke Society. The hostility of judges and lawyers towards lesbian mothers, especially 'political activists,' in child-custody cases, revealed the state as a formidable institution of social and sexual control.[65] Throughout this period, gay men in particular became the targets of stepped-up state regulation: hundreds were arrested and charged by police in bar and bath raids in Montréal, Ottawa, and Vancouver, and in washroom and park entrapments in smaller communities like Orillia and Owen Sound. On the heels of the firing of jockey John Damien from the

Ontario Racing Commission 'for being a faggot,' and the dismissal of gay teaching assistant Doug Wilson from the University of Saskatchewan in 1975, Barbara Thornborrow and Gloria Cameron were expelled in early 1977 from the Canadian Armed Forces for being lesbians.[66] Despite the lobbying efforts of groups like the John Damien Defense Committee, GATE, and CGRO, by 1976 lesbians and gay men had no legal protection from discrimation in either the Ontario Human Rights Code or the Canadian Human Rights Act.[67]

Overall, the spotlight was on lesbian and gay communities, and many Toronto lesbians were not prepared to be caught in its roving, penetrating glare. Whether they identified as feminists or not, for countless numbers of lesbians and gay women who lived in and around Toronto, the risks of merely learning the address of LOOT were great, and the price of exposure extremely high. Rocking the heterosexual boat amidst the stirring of a soon-to-be well-organized, well-financed conservative backlash, without the concerted endorsement of non-lesbian organizers in other social movements, was seen by some as reckless, if not foolhardy. Still, those women committed to LOOT's invention repeatedly echoed their original pledge 'to be all things to all lesbians.' At their first Open House in March 1977, they vowed to translate this pledge into practice.

PART TWO

4

The politics of lesbian-feminist life/style

In the late 1960s and early 1970s, in large urban centres across North America and Britain, largely white, middle-class women's liberationists attacked the mainstream fashion and beauty industries, which were in the business of reinforcing the construction of gender differences between women and men and capitalizing on women's subordination.[1] The disruption of beauty contests, the exposure of sexist images in mass-circulation women's magazines and pornography, and the symbolic trashing of feminine artifice were tactics used to expose patriarchal and capitalist discourse.[2] In contrast to liberal feminists who continued to have a stake in 'dressing for corporate success,' grassroots feminist activists championed the 'natural' face scrubbed clean of make-up and the 'natural' body minus all binding outer and undergarments. Perfume, deodorants, hair-removal products, makeup, bras, girdles, nylons, high heels, tight skirts and dresses – the trappings of a woman-hating culture – were publicly repudiated.

Into this context of angry rule-breaking, self-proclaimed lesbian feminists began to insinuate their own distinctive politics of everyday life. Members of LOOT sought to attain their personal/political potential by exploiting what they perceived to be a fundamental contradiction within the women's movement: heterosexual feminists, however radical, retained a measure of investment in both appearing attractive to men and in servicing men emotionally, physically, and sexually. The heterosexual feminists that I interviewed roundly disagree with this statement; they were quick to detail all the ways in which they too adopted life/style codes that opposed standard feminine and heterosexual modes of relating to men. However, keen to differentiate themselves from heterosexual women, most lesbian feminists argued that straight feminists could not be trusted to set and reinforce radical community norms. The majority of lesbian feminists I interviewed believed that though many heterosexual sisters made efforts to disobey patriarchal directives, they didn't push at life/style conventions hard enough, deep enough, or passionately enough. Lorna Weir remembers that 'straight feminists were not dressing as badly or as consistently awfully as lesbians, and straight feminists had a greater stylistic range and variation.'

To the dismay of most lesbian feminists I interviewed, gay men towards whom they might lean for support were either busily perfecting misogyny through camp and drag, roaming the bars decked out in hyper-sexualized 'Village People' gear, losing themselves in super-masculine, disco 'clone' appeal.[3] To most LOOT-goers, 'bar dykes,' specifically the femmes, yielded unthinkingly to the antiwoman trappings of make-up, hair dye, skirts, high heels, perfume, lipstick, and a submissive demeanour. Only a non-compromising, non-consumerist, and aggressive lesbian-feminist life/style program would liberate the 'real' woman and the 'real' feminist. Borrowing from the antimaterialist and anti-artifice platforms of the grass-roots left, hippie culture, and the women's and peace movements, blending in the pro-racial and cultural pride of civil-rights activists, lesbian feminists sought to devise their own distinguishing forms of cultural currency.[4]

Despite the diverse personal and political histories and locations of LOOT founders, a shared community life promised a transcendence of internal differences. The fractures that began to surface along radical-feminist, separatist, socialist, and gay-liberationist lines could be smoothed over in a collective desire to build on a new-found sense of security and 'amazonian' strength. LOOT-goers were convinced that non-conformity to emergent lesbian-feminist codes invited assimilation into an oppressive, antiwoman, and antilesbian culture. Rather, 'creating an appearance' concretized the bold, defiant assertion of lesbian-feminist visibility.

As early as 1972, Phyllis Lyon and Del Martin wrote, 'If you look like every other woman on the street how in the world are you going to find other lesbians, or, more to the point, how are they going to find you?'[5] Reflecting on her experience of coming out in 1976, former LOOT member Rosemary Barnes says, 'Contact with other lesbians gives a woman permission to dress differently, talk differently and adopt a new personal style ... restricted feminine behaviours are regarded in a critical light, and independent activity on the part of women is encouraged, even required by the community.'[6]

Codes were communicated through visual and printed descriptions in U.S. feminist and lesbian newspapers, and in books ordered by the Toronto Women's Bookstore from women-run presses like Diana (Baltimore), Daughters, Inc. (Plainfield, Vermont), and Naiad (Reno, Nevada).[7] Before it folded in the spring of 1977, Toronto's *The Other Woman* newspaper reprinted American essays and reviews of lesbian literature (fiction and non-fiction) that contained references to uniquely lesbian style and language. The centrespread of the fifth-anniversary issue of *The Other Woman* (January/February 1977) offered a smorgasbord of photographs that conveyed the commitment to lesbian life/style held by the editorial collective members. The monthly *LOOT Newsletter*, *The Body Politic*, *Long Time Coming* (Montreal), *The Pedestal* (Vancouver), *Lesbian Canada Lesbienne* (Halifax), and local newsletters all presented a wealth of visual and printed commentary.[8] In Toronto, thirteen half-hour instalments of 'Gay News and Views' and six episodes of the program 'This Show May Be Offensive to Heterosexuals' were broadcast through the fall of 1977 on three cable television stations.[9] In contrast, as announced in *Maclean's* magazine in 1975, 'The new T.V. line-up includes shows that return to the old values: 'The Waltons,' 'Apple's Way,' and 'Little House on the Prairie.'[10]

The roots of the alternative communication ventures ran deep into the ground of homophile organizing in the 1950s and 1960s.[41] During this period, publications like the *ASK Newsletter* (Vancouver), *ONE* (San Francisco), *The Ladder* (San Francisco), the *Mattachine Review* (Los Angeles), *Vector* (San Francisco), and *Gay* and *Two* (Toronto) often provided the only reliable sources of information on gay and lesbian life from a standpoint that undermined sexological, psychiatric, and religious accounts of homosexual deviance and sickness.[11] Like these earlier communication vehicles, 1970s lesbian 'survival material' presented a wellspring of rich clues to au courant lesbian-feminist identity, life/style, and community formation. As LOOT member Gay Bell exclaimed in 1979, 'We read lesbian; therefore we are lesbian.'[12]

Lesbian-authored print and visual texts were concerned not only to instruct competence in the norms, ideas, and strategies of a movement; they worked to organize a system of communication and to coordinate relations among activists.[13] Networks were built, discussions were fostered, and lesbian feminists became knowable to themselves and to each other across diverse geographical settings, on both sides of the Canada/U.S. border, *through texts*. In other words, these materials provided an oppositional textual or discursive organization for emerging lesbian-feminist subjectivity and activism. Notions of 'correctness' became standardized through textually mediated counter-discourse that yoked the multiple local sites of white, middle-class lesbian-feminist activity to the broad ideals of an autonomous lesbian movement.

In the mid-to-late 1970s, attending conferences, folk festivals, and concerts featuring American lesbian writers and musicians in Toronto, Winnipeg, Vancouver, Montréal, and Halifax made possible contact with sophisticated principles of 'dyke style.' In Toronto, Alix Dobkin, Meg Christian, Kay Gardner, the Berkeley Women's Music Collective, and others performed at Three of Cups Coffeehouse events (between 1975 and 1978) and at concerts arranged by Sappho Sound beginning in 1978.[14]

New York–based lesbian author Jill Johnston travelled to Toronto to promote her ground-breaking text, *Lesbian Nation* (1973), and later became the focus of the film *Jill Johnston: October 1975*, by Toronto film-makers Kay Armatage and Lydia Wazano. Some LOOT lesbians had been introduced to authors Rita Mae Brown, Ti-Grace Atkinson, and Kate Millett in *Some American Feminists*, a 1977 National Film Board production. Charlotte Bunch was invited to speak at a LOOT Sunday brunch in November 1977. Californian filmmaker Barbara Hammer often appeared in her own highly experimental, provocative lesbian films.[15] How these superstar role models talked, how they moved, what they wrote, sang, and made images about, what they wore, all provided a vast reservoir of cultural and political capital to Toronto lesbians eager to come out and confirm membership in a much wider lesbian movement.

'A' IS FOR AMAZON: ESTABLISHING THE PARTICULARS OF STYLE

The best of 1970s lesbian-feminist style was conceived of in opposition to both shadowy and sharp images of lesbian oppression: the pitiful, tortured, masculine lesbian of the 1920s and 1930s, best portrayed in Radclyffe Hall's *The Well of Loneliness* (1928); pre-Depression Harlem's Black 'bulldagger'; the alcoholic, predatory pervert in pulp novels and Hollywood films like *The Children's Hour* (1962), *The Fox* (1963), and *The Killing of Sister George* (1968); the middle-class, respectability-seeking homophiles of the 1950s; the role-playing butches and femmes who frequented downtown Toronto's Cameo Club and the Bluejay in the 1970s; and the closeted 'gay ladies' featured in *Chatelaine* magazine's 'Gay Women: A Minority Report' (1977)[16]

Lesbian-feminist fashion 1970s-style turned around the daily worn, hallowed uniform of short hair (preferably cut at LOOT by Pat, Karen, or Erving), hairy legs and armpits, flannel shirt, blue jeans, and work-boots – all borrowed heavily from butch sexuality and very similar to 1970s urban-gay male style, but not acknowledged as such. Several women took pride in their ability to grow a beard or a moustache. 'In full costume,' says Natalie LaRoche, 'we were heavy-looking dykes – gorgeous, beautiful and larger than life.' Long-time activist Holly Devor recalls the fundamental principle of lesbian-feminist style: 'The goal was to make yourself so unfeminine, so unattractive that no man would find you a sexual turn-on. No man. Zero. To have wanted to wear dresses, it was crazy. The expression was, "you have a prick in your head and you've got to get it out" ... Having denied femininity, the only thing left was to ape masculinity, but we didn't see it that way back then: it was about wearing comfortable clothes and choosing not to be a sex object. If we made ourselves unattractive to each other in the process, nobody talked about it.'

Mainstream journalists tended to report on a glaringly different trend. As *Maclean's* contributor Philip Marchand observed, 'The no-makeup naturalness of the sixties has been replaced by all manner of cosmetics for both men and women. Fashion has lost its political and artistic meanings and has become what it used to be – the garment trade.' In addition, he commented blithely, 'Bras are back. In 1967 there were 796,292 bras shipped to outlets in Canada and in 1973 the figure more than doubled.'[17]

Downtown lesbian feminists zestfully flaunted their bra-free departures from such 'establishment rubbish.' Buttons pinned proudly to a second-hand vest announced defiant political platforms and the exuberance of coming out: 'lesbians ignite,' 'lesbians are everywhere,' 'a woman without a man is like a fish without a bicycle,' 'don't die wondering,' 'how dare you presume I'm straight,' and 'castration for the nation.' On occasion, as a way of stripping the female breast of its signification as a western, male sexual fetish, buttons were pinned to form-fitting T-shirts emblazoned with the LOOT logo.[18] Most of the time, however, concealing breasts beneath baggy plaid shirts and sweatshirts (also splattered with political slogans) or behind vests and blazers was considered natural; binding breasts with bandages (to achieve a more butch look) before going to a local gay bar, hooking them into a bra before a day in the secretarial pool, or squeezing them into a tight bubble top before a night on 'the track' was unnatural.

The informal mandating of blue jeans at LOOT was taken for granted; the official outlawing of jeans and loose shirt-tails inside lesbian bars (often enforced by straight male managers and owners) was an objectionable affront to most LOOT members. One contributor to *The Other Woman* newspaper spelled it out: 'The Bluejay has done it again by ejecting feminists for being too dykey. The bar's clothing rules are macho and their thinking is reactionary. Going by appearances is oppressive.'[19] Not a faithful bar patron, LOOT-goer Eve Zaremba recalls: 'You had to have nice slacks and they wanted to keep that in [the code] in order to keep us out ... there was a real longing for respectability and we [the politicos] were not it. Some of us were barred for life – that was the big joke.' 'I went to the Bluejay once,' says Gay Bell, 'and it was very strange. I remember saying to the drummer, "It's great that you're all women," and she just sort of looked at me all sarcastic and negative.' Out-fitted in her 'lumberjill fatigues,' Fiona Rattray remembers being thrown down the stairs and out the door by the male bouncer of JoJo's, a downtown lesbian bar. 'Dressing up in clunky platform shoes and velvet jackets like those apolitical dykes' to gain entrance to mixed gay/lesbian disco bars (the Quest and the Carriage House) was pooh-poohed as expensive 'display and spectacle' that most lesbian feminists couldn't afford and refused to condone.

Hidden at the end of alleyways or in hard-to-find basements, poorly lit, open only on weekends, periodically inspected by the police, and simply 'not nice places to drop into or hang out in,' lesbian bars held little charm for most LOOT-goers. Into 'rock 'n' roll and bluejeans,' Susan Cole recalls being 'completely freaked out by butches and femmes at the Cameo Club who were dancing the polka to Tony Orlando and Dawn's 'Tie a Yellow Ribbon 'Round the Old Oak Tree.' Acutely conscious of the chasm separating two fundamentally different lesbian cultures in the late 1970s, LOOT regular Val Edwards reported: 'Most community lesbians don't have anything to do with the bar scene, and those of us who do think that with enough exposure to our profound political insights and liberating alternative lifestyles, the bar dykes will throw off their wide belts, polyester knits and disco music and start listening to Teresa Trull or Holly Near.'[20]

In 1967, researchers Simon and Gagnon noted how norms, argot, and various kinds of social activity reinforced the experience of identity and collectivity for individual lesbians and male homosexuals.[21] For public lesbians in the 1970s, part of 'right-on' attitude was exuding 'cool': travelling in groups; playing pool; reading the right literature; going to the right events, dances, coffee-houses, picnics; being seen in the right places at the right times in the right company. Smoking dope and drinking alcohol was 'in' (though both were officially banned from 342 Jarvis Street and, as Pat Leslie said, 'there was lots of paranoia about the police and being busted'). Stoned and high on 'the hippie drugs,' it was easy to run around being bold and outrageous. Writing LESBIAN MONEY on dollar bills, swearing, and using insiders' language – faggot, het, dyke, gomer, Amazon, goddess, Lavender Menace (a favourite drink), and so on – were other ways of cultivating an abrasive toughness.[73] To honour matriarchal traditions, some lesbian feminists, like Artemis, assumed the names of Greek goddesses. Others, like Heather Elizabeth, dropped their surnames completely in order to rupture a patrilineal tie. Not all of these customs, rituals, and innovations were the exclusive property of lesbians: straight and bisexual feminists practised their own variations of dissent from patriarchal and capitalist life/style conventions.

At summer music festivals – Michigan Womyn's Music Festival (started in 1976) and the National Women's Music Festival in Champagne, Illinois (started in 1973) – vanloads of Toronto lesbians crossed the Canada/U.S. border.[23] To Val Edwards, 'Michigan ... [was] the grand culmination of a year's frustrated dream for a women's world: sisterhood was more than a meaningless cliché.'[24] Once at the festival, they were tempted to buy cherished Olivia record albums (a much-vaunted antidote to 'cock rock'), woman-identified silver jewellery, buttons, T-shirts, publications, albums, and other goods from under the Merchant's Tent. Displays of goods stamped 'Lesbian' were also a prominent feature of regional and national lesbian conferences. The sale of attitude intrinsic to each commodity (particularly the wearable ones) appealed to lesbian consumers. To sound engineer Ruth Dworin, 'The stuff sold was modest in quality and quantity; it was amateurish, but it was like taking home a souvenir of a whole city of women you had helped create. In later years, it was like going to the lesbian shopping mall.'

An inventory of 1970s lesbian-feminist life/style is richly detailed in the 1980 film *Labyris Rising*. A deliberate, feisty send-up of the urban-gay male style captured by Kenneth Anger in *Scorpio Rising* (1974), this lesbian cult classic was shot on location at 342 Jarvis Street and the Fly By Night Lounge by former LOOT members Margaret Moores and Almerinda Travassos.[25] The half-hour Super 8 film is full of clues: the double-headed axe (labrys) or cunt beads on a chain, the famous maxim 'woman-identified woman' embroidered on the back of blue jeans, pinky rings, interlocking women's symbols, pink triangles, and suspenders. While reading the Washington, DC-based feminist journal *off our backs*, the protagonist drags deeply on her marijuana joint and drifts off to remember scenes from the Michigan festival to the music of Be Be K'Roche, Heather Bishop, Joan Armatrading, and Janis Joplin.[26] Repeated shots of women pulling on heavy boots punctuate the film and lend it an almost war-like, military character.

The drive to lace up sensible shoes or boots and don clothes that facilitated quick and easy movement was also informed by heightened feminist consciousness of the need for safety from male violence.[27] Especially vulnerable to attack for parading butch or masculine style, boisterous, ass-kicking lesbians argued that they had a stake in actively defending themselves against sexist and heterosexist harassment and assault. Short, cropped hair meant a rapist had less to grab on to. A column in the 1973 'Lesbian Issue' of *The Other Woman* advised all dykes to 'learn to spit, learn to punch, learn to be insulting and sound like you mean it.'[28] Chilled by accounts of beatings and police violence told by the Brunswick Four and, later, by women like Chris Bearchell, Konnie Reich, Fiona Rattray, and Nia Cordingley, many lesbians took up the offensive.[29] The mushrooming of women-only self-defence classes in the early-to-mid 1970s (often taught by lesbians at A Woman's Place and, later, Amazon Workshop) introduced many women to concepts of personal, physical strength, as well as the power of fighting back. To former Wen-Do learner Gay Bell, wearing clothes and footwear that signalled 'I'm no pushover,' or 'I ain't nobody's baby,' both inside and outside the classroom, seemed only natural. Gone were the days of discretion and 'drag.'

Not only a utilitarian, androgynous, and (relatively) cheap lesbian billboard, the standard uniform also served to unite lesbians under the illusion of shared class membership. Former LOOT member and gay-liberationist Fiona Rattray talks about the attempts lesbians made to undermine capitalism through style: 'Women around LOOT were mostly middle-class, but it was hard to tell because it was 'politically in' to be downwardly mobile. You'd just get into a blue collar job and live as cheaply as you could. Today, I would say that lesbians in general are into being trendy, upwardly mobile and acquiring houses, but at that point it was the exact opposite: money and capitalism and patriarchy all went together and that was evil and bad. And the way women were dressing – if you walked into 342 Jarvis, you'd think everyone was coming from a working-class background because you're all wearing jeans and flannel and sneakers or boots, and that gave you a shared façade. Of course everyone had their own little attitudes that would leak out and you'd discover them.' In the early 1970s, women like Robin Morgan and Kathleen Barry in the United States argued that class was a male-defined category irrelevant to women's experience of oppression.[30] And Rita Mae Brown described 'race and class barriers' as 'latter day diseases sprung from sexism.'[31] However, at the downtown Toronto Daughters of Bolton conference in December 1976, class differences among lesbians proved to be a thorny, charged, and fracturing subject of debate. Working-class lesbians attacked the hypocrisy of middle-class lesbian and straight feminists who were adept at 'dressing beneath [their] class and renouncing the obvious symbols of material accumulation.'[32] In a searing commentary published by *The Other Woman* newspaper a month before its demise, Pat Leslie added that 'never wearing the right clothes or speaking the right way leads you to believe that you don't stand a chance anyway, so why bother.'[33] As Phil Masters remembers the conference, 'It was yelling and threats and one person saying middle-class people talk and working-class people use violence. People were scared. We were all supposed to be sisters together and here were women saying that working-class people beat people up. It was so scary it shut us up for a while. It was the realization that we weren't all oppressed equally.'

Working-class lesbians didn't want to be downwardly mobile because, as Pat Leslie continues, 'we were already down there and had no choice.' And yet despite the early, tentative critiques (also voiced inside the left and the women's movement) of the romanticization of poverty and self-proletarianization acted out (in part) through style, the official opening of LOOT on 1 February 1977 trumpeted the togetherness of lesbian feminists, at long last. The language of commonality was used almost immediately (and desperately, some argued) to displace the divisive feelings of bitterness, defensiveness, guilt, and anguish that had erupted at the Bolton conference.

If attitudes did 'leak out' at or around LOOT, they were more often ignored or (sheepishly) capped than explored. As Amy Gottlieb re-

members, lesbians (and non-lesbian feminists) were more comfortable
discussing class at an individual level: 'I'm middle-class and I'm bad,
you're working-class and you're good, so I have to give to you. It was
a warped recognition of class inequality whereby a middle- or upper-
class woman would elect to give up the *trappings* of privilege, without
giving up privilege itself.'[34] To Dina, a working-class lesbian who was
turned on to feminism by a lover in 1978, such behaviour was per-
plexing: 'Some of our sisters who came from rich families said to those
families, "I don't want your money, I'm going to live here in this hole
and I'm going to wear work boots and I'm going to look like I paint
barns and I'm going to drive this shit box of a car and I'm going to
love it." I thought, man, that was pretty fucking weird. Being poor
for so long and striving for every cent, I couldn't understand it.' Looking back, Eve Zaremba sees the ethos of downward mobility and the
practices it encompassed as a form of 'reverse snobbery.' Still, Gottlieb
argues that there was 'a radical component to our discussions about
class – it wasn't just guilt. But we weren't able to figure out strategies
around how to organize and who to reach.'

Occasionally, as Cate Smith recalls, 'camaraderie in minor economic
hardship' was acted out through organized rent parties. And, for cultural events, there were attempts to introduce ticket prices geared to
income (the 'sliding scale' philosophy) and exchanges where one could
do a work shift in lieu of buying a ticket. Yet, as several working-
class lesbians maintained, they always seemed to end up doing the
work shifts and the 'shit work.' Donna Marchand remembers that,
'for a LOOT brunch or dinner, it was the working-class dykes who
did the shopping and the cleanup. The others would say, "We'll organize it, we'll do the books, we understand the books, my father
is an accountant." Well, my father was a cook on the railroad.'

Very few LOOT regulars worked for pay full time. In fact, defying
the 9:00 am to 5:00 pm drudgery of underpaid, undervalued work
for The Man was a source of considerable pride. According to 'the
line,' feminists who held straight jobs and thus sold out community
principles were less reliable and simply could not be counted on. In
the style of the late sixties and early seventies counterculture, dropping
out and going into 'uncareers' was not only common among those
women interested in birthing a lesbian-feminist centre, it was de
rigueur.

In part, most lesbian feminists wanted to take jobs where they could
be out. Typesetting part-time at the gay publishing company Pink Type

and working for feminist services like the Women's Referral and Education Centre, the Women's Credit Union, the Rape Crisis Centre, or Nellie's Hostel made possible a less closeted work life. Participants in an informal economy, some women chose to give massage, cut hair, or do illustrations, handwriting analysis, or carpentry. Some women drove for lesbian-managed courier services and moving companies. Susan Sturman and Alex Maas started up a feminist printing press and design company (Superbia). Ruth Dworin (plus eight other original collective members) founded a feminist music production company (Sappho Sound).

Over the course of LOOT's existence, and as an extension of earlier feminist ventures like Amazon Press and Times Change (a women's employment service), a series of businesses operated out of 342 Jarvis Street, including Sappho Sound and Superbia Press. LOOT was also used by several enterprising young lesbians as a forum for carpentry, auto and bicycle repair/maintenance classes, and income-tax workshops. Indeed, many of the ideas for today's lesbian commercial and cultural network – among them, the music production company Womynly Way – were first conceived at 342 Jarvis Street.

Feminists like Rosemary Barnes, who was also the LOOT treasurer, argued for the need to realize economic security independent of The Man. She recalled: 'We had to figure out what kind of businesses we could organize or offer to the world that were consistent with our own world view ... Sappho Sound, a restaurant, and the Women's Credit Union were consistent with that ... something that made our survival more secure in society. If we didn't have businesses for ourselves and we depended on other people for jobs and we had to do jobs and support systems that we didn't like, we were in a precarious situation.'[35] Yet not everyone was equally enthusiastic about the prospect of applying the entrepreneurial spirit to the creation of feminist/lesbian-run businesses. In fact, the trend that took hold among some North American feminists in the 1970s 'to better meet lesbian needs under capitalism' was met by others with alarm. And this tension would prove increasingly thorny into the 1980s. Borrowing from the analysis of American feminists Brooke Williams and Hannah Darby, Pat Leslie warned readers of *The Other Woman*: 'Working in a "feminist" business becomes pseudo-movement busywork, and energy which could be devoted to political action is sidetracked into the work of owning, operating and keeping afloat an enterprise. These individual solutions are being mistakenly construed as solutions for all women, but are really a way of running away from the political realities of women's oppression.'[36]

For LOOT lesbians, many of whom were moved by the late 1960s anti-establishment credo, opting out of capitalism also meant pulling on faded jeans and a T-shirt in the morning instead of a crisp linen or polyester suit and panty hose. One all-purpose protective suit of armour sufficed (and, in its plainness, had little mass-marketing appeal). Other popular actions included buying second-hand clothes and furniture at a LOOT 'redistribution event,' stealing the occasional loaf of bread (for kicks), hiding or downplaying aspects of material privilege, *choosing* to apply for welfare, and *choosing* to drop out of school.[37] Several LOOT members described to me the delight they and others took in appearing as if they were receiving Unemployment Insurance (and thus 'screwing the state'), even if they weren't. Each of the graduate students among LOOT regulars remembers her efforts to downplay investment in the academy – a position consistent with both the prevailing anti-intellectualism and the more general trend towards advancing a declassed, neutralized collectivity. And though a number of women like Susan Cole did have straight jobs, the consensus, according to Phil Masters, was that 'everyone did just enough to get by.'

SETTING UP HOUSE AND SETTLING IN

Communal living, as many lesbian feminists discovered in the mid-to-late 1970s was the most convenient and cheapest way of concentrating lesbian cultural resources and fostering attitude, downward mobility, and lesbian-feminist education and consciousness. Not an original enterprise, communal living has a long and rich history. Like the nineteenth- and early-twentieth-century utopian socialist societies in England, Germany, and the United States, communal households opposed the individualizing regime of capitalist private property, and they flourished in both urban and rural settings during the civil-rights, left, women's, and gay movements of the 1960s.[38] Such households were lauded as models for an alternative social order. Ritually and practically, according to critic Colin Webster, '[they] anticipate the paradise that will come after the old "demonic reality" has passed away.'[39]

In Toronto, enclaves of collective housing sprang out of this hoped-for paradise. In the late 1960s, Rochdale College and the Yorkville 'Village' neighbourhood (the infamous dens of sex, drugs, and rock 'n' roll) were the favoured hang-outs of anti-establishment students,

writers, poets, musicians, community activists, and Vietnam draft re-
sisters.[40] Alongside the gradual emergence of food and child-care co-
ops, free schools, drop-in centres, alternative media, and artists' collectives, communal living made manifest the utopian vision of a de-
centralized, egalitarian community free of the stain of competitiveness,
hierarchy, and atomization. Several LOOT members, some of whom
had lived as hippies and had been influenced by principles of anarchism, environmentalism, and the peace movement, were keen to translate priorities of free love, self-sufficiency, and collectivism into an
explicitly lesbian context. To those who didn't have much disposable
income (or who did, yet were uncomfortable with displaying wealth)
and who were smitten with the concept of 'wimmin-only' space, communal living promised the perfect interweaving of personal and political ideals.[41]

In the context of an increasingly institutionalized urban cooperative
housing movement in the 1970s, lesbians secured group households
as a double-edged tactic to counter rising rent costs *and* to concentrate
lesbian cultural (and political) resources. These households also stood
as (relatively) safe strongholds against the abusive actions of homophobic landowners.[42] Unlike the emergence of a gay-male residential
and commercial district (the roots of which stretched back to the
1940s), physical testaments to urban lesbian life were geographically
dispersed. None the less, a sense of community was fostered by knowing where lesbian feminists lived, whether they were close friends or
not. Households on Garden Avenue, Clinton Street, Walker Avenue,
Spruce Street, Gerard Street East, and Palmerston Boulevard were
some of the most visible headquarters or hotbeds of lesbian feminism.
McPhail Home for Women, operated by the YWCA, became an enclave
of largely working-class, young lesbians, many of whom, like Lilith
Finkler and Cynthia Wright, were involved with LOOT. Ann Kado
lived at Stop 158, a hostel for young women that was run largely
by lesbian workers. The Bain Co-op was also a place where pockets
of lesbians lived in close proximity to one another. And the third floor
of 342 Jarvis Street (the 'penthouse suite' above the offices of LOOT
and *The Other Woman* newspaper) offered the hustle and bustle of family
life to several lesbians: first Artemis, and then Pat Hugh, one of the
only Black lesbians who took an active role in LOOT.

The most purely crystallized form of self-sufficiency and freedom
from male culture was the lesbian-owned and -run rural commune.[43]
Though a more popular strategy in the United States than in Canada,

'living with lesbians' in the country, growing food, doing manual labour, basking with wimmin in the 'sunlight and sweet air' is eulogized by singer/songwriter Alix Dobkin on her second album.[44] 'Back-to-the-landers' like members of the Collective Lesbian International Terrors (CLIT) in the United States proclaimed, 'Within fifty years, lesbian separatism will have land-based societies around the world if we collectivize female property and resources into a unified network.'[45] In Toronto in 1978, the lesbian collective WORLD (women-only rural land development) and supporters held a benefit for Amazon Acres, a farm set up in British Columbia by several former Garden Avenue residents. And within two years, fed up with 'the garbage of the city,' Pat Murphy, Linda Jain, and several other former LOOT members moved to a collective farm north of Toronto.

Symbolically, and in reality, the communal household represented a refuge, a haven from the grind of invisibility, ridicule, and misunderstanding that lesbian feminists faced beyond their front doorstep. At Garden Avenue, Gay Bell remembers that 'no men were allowed because they spoiled the energy.' A lesbian-feminist household, including 342 Jarvis Street, became a moment-by-moment testing ground for experimentation with new ideas, new relationships, new vocabulary, new style, new ways of viewing the world, new ways of being with women as sisters and lovers. Such a place signified 'home' to those lesbians who were separated geographically and/or emotionally from biological family members. Here, feelings of laughter, love, lust, sadness, rejection, betrayal, hurt, jealousy, anger, stress, and disappointment arose and were processed in the context of (often intense) friendships.

Friendships, many of which dated back to A Woman's Place, the lesbian potluck dinner group, GATE, or Three of Cups Coffeehouse, were strengthened; old circles of friends were often broken or simply forgotten. On 'The Back Page' of *The Body Politic*, Lorna Weir summed up the course chosen by many 'young, tender dykes' like herself: 'Until I felt strong in being a lesbian I simply wasn't in a position to face struggling with my straight friends' sexual politics (or lack thereof) and probable homophobia.'[46] 'It was so nice,' says Virginia Adamson, 'to have a lesbian friend who would carry you around in a kerchief in her pocket for awhile.' Not only did disclosures of personal ups and downs offer the possibility of gaining and giving support, but they contributed to the semi-public character of lesbian living, in direct contrast to increasingly privatized, heterosexual nuclear-family arrangements.

Collective houses also provided settings for the pursuit of intimate relationships, both sexual and non-sexual (see chapter 5). Several women I interviewed recounted stories of entering collective houses as celibate feminists and then coming out as lesbians through sexual relations with housemates (or with women who were billeted from out of town). As Rachel says, 'So many women were finding themselves, finding a community, looking around for partners and finding partners.' In a number of instances, women were introduced (and informally recruited) to the particular political stance of their lovers through sexual encounters. And, not unlike the practice of 'dressing down and dykey,' for some lesbian feminists sex felt like a medium through which class differences (however crudely acknowledged) could be transcended, or at least smudged (in contrast to Gillean Chase's early warning, 'It takes more than a clitoris to stimulate class identification').[47]

Key elements of egalitarian process and consensus decision making enacted in political organizing at LOOT (see chapters 7 and 8) were often first learned and applied to household tasks of preparing food (preferably bought at the local co-op), clean-up, maintenance, and laundry. Not to be taken lightly, the pledge 'to share cooking, cleaning and common spaces' (in 'vegetarian, smoke-free comfort') was a customary feature of 'womyn's' co-op housing ads in the LOOT Newsletter. At the Clinton Street house, women had a joint bank account and they used a 'group journal' to facilitate daily communication among residents. They also shared a car, which was not, as Naomi Brooks recollects, at all unusual: 'If you had a vehicle, it was at the service of the community; it wasn't really yours. You paid for all the gas and repairs, but you didn't feel like you owned it.'[48] Undergirding all of these innovations was the strong belief, held over from the 1960s counterculture, in sharing and distributing power fairly.

Gossip, a primary source of household entertainment, was routinely swapped around the kitchen table: who was straight ('and should be avoided'), who was bisexual ('and couldn't be trusted'), who was coming out ('and needed support'), what army surplus store had the best deal on Kodiak boots, what rooms were free in what household, and so on. American fiction writer Jan Clausen defines gossip as 'one of life's staple pleasures, small reward for all the pains. Besides, it's so useful, helping as it does to delimit the boundaries of peer groups, enforce community standards, strengthen self-definition in a blurred, ambiguous, often hostile world ... In lesbian feminist communities, [it is] an irresistible form of entertainment.'[49]

In another favourite ritual, a time-tested staple of direct-action politics, housemates often planned 'zaps' together. In the tradition of the Brunswick Four, completely spontaneous or hastily planned zaps carried off by LOOT lesbians involved singing Alix Dobkin's 'A is for Amazon' in a doughnut shop on Queen Street or Meg Christian's 'Leaping Lesbians' in a neighbourhood laundromat.[50] To Cate Smith, these were moments of great fun: 'We had a group identity, we were like a herd, never going anywhere by ourselves. We'd go carousing, kissing in public, invading shops and rescuing women who were being harassed by men.' In a culture that perpetrates what poet Adrienne Rich calls 'the dangerous and painful condition of lesbian invisibility,' it was felt that no other rambunctious, risk-taking action could guarantee visibility, however fleeting, in quite the same way.[51] Organizing zaps and sharing gossip, rent, utilities, grocery bills, books, newspapers, music, poetry, clothing, posters, buttons, recipes, cats, lovers, and political ideology became part and parcel of life in downtown lesbian-feminist households.

'Womyn-only' households rarely lasted more than a year, and the instability was in large part due to the eruption of bitter personal/ political conflicts. In ways that did not depart from countercultural living in the 1960s, as critic Todd Gitlin notes, 'breaking down lines of property and hierarchy, establishing order – that irresistible bogey – while avoiding lines of traditional authority, was a perpetual battle.'[52] Moreover, for lesbian feminists, negotiating the expectation for limitless affection, on the one hand, and a warrior-like independence, on the other, was enormous, and often resulted in anxiety, bitterness, and frustration. As Susan Cole remembers it, 'The ego investment we had in the need to be liked, the need to belong, was intense because there was more going on than politics: it was your life.' Expressions of weakness, vulnerability, and uncertainty sometimes felt luxurious (if not mutinous) inside households, inside 342 Jarvis Street, and inside a community that seemed altogether too fragile, under siege, and impermanent. To some, the ubiquitous task of dismantling patriarchy and the institution of heterosexuality was burdened by an excess of responsibility. And yet, despite the personal disagreements, confusions, and conflicts that periodically wracked household dynamics and friendship circles, 'professional lesbians' struggled to enact the terms of their own idyllic vision of a 'future in the making.'

ACCOMMODATING DIFFERENCE WITHIN THE LESBIAN-FEMINIST FRAME

For out and proud downtown 'dyke warriors,' compromise meant a dilution of the white, middle-class feminist politics certified by standard dyke life/style. To quote Marg Moores, 'We were pretty pure about what we were doing at the time; it was a way to be powerful, and to do that you had to reject a lot of your life.' It was feminist theorist Ti-Grace Atkinson who once exclaimed: 'It is this full commitment, against any and all personal considerations, that constitutes the political significance of lesbianism.'[53] However, it would be simplistic to argue that every lesbian feminist connected to LOOT, and to lesbian feminism more broadly, subscribed to community standards with faithful religiosity all of the time.

Several LOOT-goers (who also happened to be informal leaders, like Amy Gottlieb) hung on to their long hair at minimal cost to their overall standing within the organization and outside of it. Similarly, several high-profile couples lived together away from the intensity and entanglements of communal living. The desire to live alone, shared by several working-class lesbians who were 'all too familiar with overcrowding,' was viewed by most LOOT dykes as odd, if not downright selfish.

Minor exceptions were made and rules were somewhat relaxed at LOOT-sponsored New Year's Eve dances, some concerts, and the occasional Three of Cups Coffeehouse. Here, one could spot a pair of tuxedo pants, a smart new tie, a leather vest or a new pair of jeans, cuff links, or a slinky blue rayon shirt. A group of lesbian feminists (some of whom lived communally on Walker Avenue) typically wore peasant skirts, cheesecloth tunics, and Birkenstock sandals, and were routinely referred to by the work-booted and flannel dykes as 'the airy fairy, granola-types into herbs, drawing pictures and expressing themselves,' or the 'flowy seaweeds into spirituality.'[54] Not incidentally, they were taken less seriously as political actors by certain LOOT 'heavies.'

Ann Kado, one of the only Native lesbians to consider herself a LOOT regular, wore Native jewellery and wrapped her long black hair in ties – a traditional Ojibwa warrior custom. In the context of growing awareness among progressive people of the intensifying agitation by Native peoples for self-determination across Canada in the 1970s, this departure from the dominant lesbian-feminist style was accepted by many LOOT members, and even stirred envy in some.[55] In recognition of the revolutionary character of First Nations struggles, a number of non-Native LOOT members donned beads, head and wrist bands, quills, silver, and turquoise.

Several Jewish lesbians were LOOT members from the start. But they rarely brought discussion or practice of Jewish culture to 342 Jarvis Street. Not restricted to LOOT, awareness of anti-Semitism and knowledge of the ongoing Jewish struggle for pride and identity were negligible among non-Jewish lesbians and members of progressive movements more broadly. Ruth Dworin says, 'I came out of a culture that values assertiveness. I didn't need assertiveness training, but when I spoke up in and around LOOT in the seventies, I was branded as pushy. Part of it was cast as my overtly middle-class power through language, but part of it was a covert anti-Semitism.' For the most part, recognition of Jewish oppression did not extend beyond wearing the Star of David as a gesture of solidarity. At LOOT, drop-ins held every Friday night disqualified those Jewish lesbians who observed Shabbat. In December 1978, lesbians were invited to the LOOT house 'to enjoy a traditional Christmas dinner, complete with turkey, tree trimming, carol singing and egg nog.'[56] Three years after LOOT's opening, Lilith (formerly Evelyn) wrote an exposé outlining her dilemma, and, to her dismay, it was published in the 'opinion' column of the newsletter. She asked: 'Am I a dykey kike or a kikey dyke?': 'Explaining my Jewishness to Gentile Lesbians has remained difficult. My friends celebrated Christmas and wanted to decorate the house that we share. I was upset. I had given up all religious observance because I felt it was totally oppressive. Was "Christmas" somehow different because it was part of mainstream culture? How do I deal with celebrations in the lesbian community? Christmas, Easter, Thanksgiving are not my holidays. My New Year is in September ... And yet to divide womyn because of a male-identified religion, Judaism?'[57] In the 1960s, organized religion was subjected to renewed attack from the left as an 'opiate of the masses,' and from the women's movement as anti-woman, patriarchal brainwashing. Early gay liberationists exposed the deeply anti-homosexual assumptions embedded in most religious literature and teachings. In the spirit of this criticism, LOOT lesbians almost uniformly divested themselves of what they considered to be the tyranny of religious traditions and customs. Though Toronto's

Metropolitan Community Church (MCC) drew large numbers of gay men and (fewer) women to its services, few lesbian feminists expressed interest in this institution. And most were openly disdainful of 'churching' – a same-gender marriage ceremony performed by the MCC's gay minister. Similarly, none of the LOOT regulars that I interviewed attended the meetings of Dignity – 'an organization of gay and concerned Catholics' founded in 1974 by members of the Our Lady of Lourdes church and located in the gay-male ghetto.

To fill their need for spiritual nourishment, a small number of LOOT lesbians invested in crystals, Tarot cards, and I Ching (most often purchased at U.S. womyn's music festivals) and celebrated summer and winter solstices. Travelling to the States and reading largely U.S.-based literature also encouraged a handful of Toronto lesbians to experiment with forms of feminist spirituality and bodywork – witchcraft, massage therapy, and Wicca, among others.[58]

THE EXCLUSION OF NON-CONFORMING LESBIANS

At the best of times, plugging into outlets stamped Lesbian was neither a smooth, nor an anxiety-free, undertaking. For lesbians who were interested in fitting in, getting it wrong carried a sometimes hefty price. Former LOOT treasurer Rosemary Barnes reflects on departure from LOOT-style correctness: 'The fall from grace occurs when the woman discovers that the approval of other lesbians is not unaffected by her choice of activities or opinions. Many women are surprised and very angry when they find that they are expected either to dress, talk and act in accordance with certain rules, or to face being ignored or disapproved of.'[59] With time and emotional investment at a premium in all grass-roots, progressive organizations, women with full-time paid work, women who did not live downtown, and women who could not (or would not) make LOOT and the lesbian-feminist community 'home' were never fully abreast of the trends.[60]

Those who were terrified of exposure, arrest, job loss, or the loss of child custody were not prepared to oufit themselves daily and parade about recklessly in garb that was identifiably lesbian (or feminist). Lacking money to travel to American music festivals and lacking access to local cultural capital or connections inside lesbian co-ops also organized one's relationship to prevailing life/style imperatives. For example, because they 'couldn't live their whole lives at LOOT, even if they wanted to,' Deb Stinson and several others felt the painful incongruity of 'blossoming among all these lesbians' and then 'falling twice as hard outside the built walls of LOOT's utopia.'

Lesbians with young children did not have hours to devote to consolidating friendships or planning lesbian cultural and political events. Moreover, attachment to children in a climate that was neither openly child-positive nor especially respectful of connections (however tenuous) to boys and men made lesbian mothers less desirable recruits to the lesbian-feminist fold. Not unique to Toronto lesbian organizing, similar debates about children were erupting in most urban lesbian-feminist communities across the country and in the United States.[61] Dina, a lesbian mother, recalls, 'If you had a boy child, you were supposed to get rid of him. No one cared that ours had been the bat boy for our all-female baseball team or that he chummed with the girls. That didn't count.' As LOOT regular Amy Gottlieb explains, 'Complaints that LOOT did not include lesbian mothers were due to the dominant sense of what lesbianism was about at the time – you didn't do what heterosexual women did: you didn't sleep with men; you weren't dependent on men, and you didn't have their kids ... If a woman did have kids, that was her problem.' A formal child-care policy was never established at LOOT, and women did not bring children to meetings. The absence of such a policy was likely most debilitating for working-class lesbian mothers. The couple of mothers who did visit 342 Jarvis Street never assumed that the costs of babysitting would be collectively absorbed. Infrequently, they were given money from the profits made at a paid event if they asked for it.[62]

Though it is difficult to say how general this feeling was, the heterosexual and bisexual feminists I interviewed commonly felt resentment over the political legitimacy that LOOT lesbians seemed to reap upon donning plaid shirts, work boots, and labyrises full-time, moving into high-profile womyn-only households, and hanging out at 342 Jarvis Street. The apparent shift away from devising strategies and tactics of political action and movement-building to focus on personal identity and a 'morally good' living was both confusing and immobilizing. Some straight and bisexual women felt stymied by the guilt they harboured (and were made to harbour) for 'selling out.' If upending the misery of patriarchal fashion could be cornered by bona fide lesbian feminists, then nothing any non-lesbian feminist wore (no matter how radical her efforts) really made a difference. And if lesbian feminists decided that living downtown in a collective 'gomer-free' zone was the most correct arrangement, then living with a man (or with another woman in suburbia) was sure to incite dyke ire.

Lesbian-feminist disapproval was not reserved for women who were attached to men either through an adult relationship or through off-spring. In the late 1970s, a seventeen-year-old Japanese-Canadian, Midi Onodera, came out as a lesbian in the context of Toronto's underground punk movement. Aggressive, angry, and questioning, musicians like Siouxsie Sioux, Polystyrene, Lydia Lunch, and the Bush Tetras became her role models, not 'the feminist darlings' of Olivia Records. Encountering lesbian feminists for the first time at a LOOT-sponsored event was traumatic. And though Onodera remains uncertain about the extent to which racism further complicated the meeting, she is not prepared to rule it out: 'Back then it was strange to see any mohawks [haircuts] on the streets, let alone an Asian woman with bleached hair. I deliberately exaggerated the fact that I was different – ever-changing hair colour, leather, metal, black. I walked into a room of flannel shirts, work boots and P.C. [politically correct] politics, and I was viewed with distaste and distrust. Punk, these feminists claimed, reinforced the subservient position of women, catered to violence against women, and glorified the sexual objectification of women. And my being Asian likely pushed us even further apart.'[63]

Wearing clothes that allegedly confirmed one's status as a sexual object also spelled trouble. As sporadic LOOT-goer Mary Axten attests, 'My first trip to LOOT was really offputting. I was with my lover of seven years who was an absolutely beautiful Woman-woman – she was into Miss Clairol: she was a blonde, wore make-up, had beautiful clothes and that was all important to her; I didn't give a hoot. Well, talk about trashed! She couldn't get her foot in the door; they were jumping all over her because looking like that meant (a) she was less of a lesbian and (b) she couldn't possibly be doing it for anybody but men. And I thought to myself, what am I doing here? To hell with it!'

Though there was no official upper-age limit at LOOT, older lesbians like Mary Axten rarely felt at ease in the company of 'the young turks,' most of whom were under thirty. As Virginia Adamson admits, 'I had no sense of how older lesbians had struggled. Now I know how hard it is to stay lesbian and stay functioning in the community, but back then, they were just old women to me.' Deb Stinson, a weekend regular who drove 100 kilometres from Hamilton, remembers bringing her lover, who was thirty-one years older than she was, to a LOOT drop-in: 'There was no one there who [my lover] could relate to; in fact, a number of people looked at her, and it was like, "What are you doing here?" We ended up having a big fight. She said, "Everyone is forty years younger than I am, and no one wants to talk to me anyhow."' Similarly, not all teenaged lesbians felt comfortable at LOOT. Lilith Finkler remembers wanting to start up a lesbian-feminist youth group and being subtly discouraged on the grounds that 'young dykes were considered "jail bait"': they were under the 'legal' age for both alcohol consumption (eighteen) and sex (twenty-one). Not only would the advertised gathering of young lesbians purportedly 'make the place unsafe for older lesbians,' Finkler was told that it might even serve to 'close LOOT down.'

Spoken recognition of disability-related issues at LOOT was almost non-existent. None of the women I interviewed talked of meeting the needs of disabled lesbians in the 1970s, though they remember that the LOOT building was not physically accessible to all women. Sharon Stone, a disabled lesbian and former LOOT member, has since written that she was not the only disabled lesbian at LOOT – there were several others who had disabilities that were not usually apparent and that they did not talk about. It is, therefore, possible that disabled lesbians did not view LOOT as a safe place.[64]

Two women who visited 342 Jarvis Street in knit pant-suits after a hard day of typing at the office quickly vacated the premises upon meeting the gaze of arrogant young dykes clad in plaid and denim. Dina, a working-class lesbian and one of the founders of the original Cameo Club on Howard Park Drive in Toronto's west end, was introduced to LOOT in 1978 through her feminist lover. Now in her late forties, she reminisces: 'I had never owned a pair of jeans until I met Marlene so we went off to the market to buy a pair and that was a big deal. I said to my girlfriend, "you want me to wear them out? In public?" You had to dress down at LOOT – all the women looked like they were ready to paint a barn. I thought to myself, I was in the army and I had to wear a uniform, I was a femme at home and I had to wear a uniform, and now these assholes have a uniform and it's not even pretty. I can't wear my polyester, I can't wear my lipstick, I can't wear my eye make-up, I had to exchange my purse for a knapsack, and I'm thinking, this is feminism?' As a matter of course, overt traces of heterosexual 'passing' were disparaged by LOOT regulars. As sociologist Barbara Ponse describes, 'passing entails a variety of strategies by the lesbian, including attentiveness to the details of speech, affect, dress, and demeanor and sometimes, the construction of a 'straight front' in concert with male accomplices.'[65] Using straight signs to pass was, it was believed, something that uninitiated, unenlightened, and homophobic gay women did to conveniently preserve the very invisibility that young, white lesbian feminists decried. Indeed, all energy devoted to beautifying oneself for men's pleasure or making up for 'male-identified' fringe culture like punk was considered to be bad energy. Arguing against the admission of male-to-female lesbian-identified transsexuals to 342 Jarvis Street (see chapter 5), several LOOT members underscored the offensive, caricatured femininity exhibited by these 'masquerading men.' Lesbians in the sex-trade industry, like Gwendolyn, felt belittled because her costumes were somehow read as proof of her deep-seated allegiance to heterosexuality. 'We were the people of paint,' says Gwendolyn. 'Any girl from Filmore's or the Stage 212 (strip clubs) stood out because she wore a whole lot of make-up and no dyke ever talked to you. They were all in their cliques.'

In the minds of many LOOT-goers, deviation from lesbian-feminist style codes only saluted the very power of patriarchal modes of self-presentation that they were fighting so resolutely to redress. As Pat Murphy claims, 'We had no time for clothes or cover that lied about who we were.' And yet, ironically, what did matter to many woman-identified women was the full-time, raw toughness, bravado, and 'no bullshit' style of the working-class bar butch minus the knife, the tattoo, the dildo, and the 'passive femme wife.'

RIDING THE SAFE SEA OF WOMEN IN STYLE AND IN GOOD COMPANY

Consistent with the growing emphasis in grass-roots feminism on personal experience as *the* basis for analysis and political practice, 'dressing down and dykey' in the company of 'true sisters' granted LOOT-goers an immediate and concrete sense of creating social change. Eager to confirm and validate their outlawed identity, many LOOT members saw their style codes and collective living as the ideal means to channel two mighty resources – lesbian anger and energy. The axis of lesbian-feminist everyday life – 342 Jarvis Street or 'the LOOT bunker' – gave the dream shape in bricks and mortar. In effect, what was more personal (or more political) than what one wore, how one lived, and with whom? The ambition central to social movements in the late sixties and early seventies – 'to found a new age in the ashes of the old' – was dusted off, polished up, and reinvigorated in the late 1970s, lesbian feminist-style.[66] Despite Joreen's early critique that a woman's life was not the political property of the women's movement, no aspect of lesbian-feminist living escaped scrutiny.[67]

In what was neither a private nor a neutral affair, members of the Lesbian Organization of Toronto argued that elements of lesbian life/style positively served to distinguish lesbian feminists from heterosexual sisters, gay brothers, and non-feminist lesbians. Certainly, not being concentrated in residential or commercial enclaves, lesbian-feminist life lacked the highly visible features of either the Yorkville Village hippie culture in the sixties or the gay-male culture of the 'Yonge and Wellesley fruit belt' in the seventies. Nor was lesbianism the focus of mass-media attention. However, for lesbian activists, announcing their personal/political difference to one another, to other progressive politicos, and, on occasion, to upholders of the status quo *through life/style* not only made lesbian existence distinct, it also made possible the constitution of an urban 'amazon acres' in which they could exert control. It was in this world of cultural/political supports and institutions like LOOT that a sense of 'minority-group identity' furthered by separatist tendencies began to emerge and take root.

Naturally, it was presumed, behind the political correctness of denim, flannel, woman-identified signifiers, communal living, and LOOT membership, that one could find the 'real lesbian' and the 'real feminist.' Lesbians who capitulated to the codes were rewarded, at least in principle, in status and a way out of painful isolation. On offer was a sense of moral worth denied them in a culture that decreed them obscene. Though not always fully comfortable with the mantle of what Jan Clausen calls 'a walking revolutionary project,' LOOT regulars repeatedly reminded themselves and each other of the cowardice of others.[67] Thinking back, Cate Smith is reminded that 'people saw things as very much black or white. There was a right way and a wrong way to be a lesbian, and if you were not the right kind of lesbian, you were held up to ridicule.'

By branding non-conformists 'male-identified,' 'good' dykes were able to stake out high moral ground proudly defended in the name of lesbian autonomy. Many LOOT members described to me the feeling of liberation that accompanied their lived independence from men and male values. In effect, proximity to contaminating maleness was the elemental yardstick against which lesbian and feminist mettle was measured. Those who were openly disdainful of, or oblivious to, the life/style requirements predicated on separation from The Man did not hinge their identities on lesbian-feminist approval.

Several women I interviewed who were not LOOT regulars confessed that they were never completely sure, or didn't care to know, what constituted 'ultra dyke hipness' and what did not. Others who loved women, who were interested in LOOT-styled lesbian feminism and may have considered themselves feminists, yet who did not meet the requirements, suffered the sting of exclusion. Reflecting on 1970s lesbian-feminist organizing in Los Angeles, McCoy and Hicks conclude that 'being outcast from the community was a very painful price to pay for those unfortunates labeled "liberal" or "politically incorrect", and it became a political and personal tragedy that affected far too many lives.'[68]

On occasion, a straight or bisexual feminist, an older lesbian, a punk dyke, a gay bar-goer, a lesbian mother, a lesbian transsexual, or a sex-trade worker passed through LOOT and wider lesbian-feminist circles, but almost never stayed. Without the clothes and comportment emblematic of right-on lesbian identity, misfits were often the objects of criticism. Moreover, they rarely possessed the will or the strength in numbers to contest conventions. The initial, tentative challenges that a smattering of working-class lesbians posed to 'slumming' and to the organization of class differences that investment in a 'declassed collectivity' varnished over were almost fully eclipsed. Significantly, this eclipse coincided with the disintegration and virtual collapse of the revolutionary left by the late 1970s as well as the persistent disengagement of most lesbians from the intellectual and practical work of class struggle. At most, well-meaning though largely ineffectual attempts were made by middle-class lesbians to deal with the niggling, little understood 'problem of class.'

By the same token, LOOT's white majority was largely indifferent to, or simply unaware of, the ways in which dress and conduct were mediated by racial and ethnic differences, though this myopia was by no means unique to lesbian feminists during this period. More pointedly, fearing dilution and loss of 'home,' LOOT faithfuls tended to pose the vision of a purely lesbian community, culture, and shared political identity *against* recognition and respect for other bases or contexts of oppression.

Clearly, gender and sexual sameness did not guarantee equal access to resources needed to secure captial-L lesbian attitude, dress, and conduct. Nor was a desire for these particular resources universally shared. A middle-class lesbian who 'only flirted with feminism in the 70s,' Caroline Schaillee remembers women who hung out at 342 Jarvis Street by 'their energy and body language, which was very male. I was fearful, and all I saw when I saw them was this striving, aggressive energy. It was too fanatical, too aggressive. I thought they were using the same models and the same tools as the oppressor.

In spite of the lofty, fresh vision of openness and inclusion publicized by LOOT founders from the start, the reality suggests a different story. The intention was not to restrict or limit the organization's membership in any way; erasure of all traces of power, hierarchy, and competition was the golden rule of feminist and lesbian organizing. Yet membership composition had always been a source of tension within the women's movement. And lesbian organizing was no different. As Nancy Adamson mused, 'I remember sitting there one night thinking, here we were, we wanted women to come, we wanted lesbians to come, and how could that not be welcoming? It wasn't till much later that I realized that those words and that desire do not make a group open just because you want it to be.' Eve Zaremba remembers the impatience: 'We wanted people to come to us. We had gone through what they were going through and we were here, so why can't they make it? We felt that we had arrived. Of course we hadn't, and we had all been brand-new once. But we weren't in first grade anymore, we were in second.'

Gay sociologist Kenneth Plummer notes that 'the process of identity formation may control, restrict and inhibit but at once, offers comfort, security and assuredness.'[69] LOOT's pro-woman, pro-lesbian, and antimale norms narrowed its membership parameters and restricted access to insiders. And yet even within the bounds of conformity, a number of lesbian feminists intimated that there was neither smooth nor seamless (nor even fully conscious) observance of community standards all of the time – hence their insistence that norms were not conspiratorially devised but loosely invented as they went along. Eruptive transgressions included: dabbling in long hair, wrap-around skirts, red meat, bras, leather, living alone, saying NO to committee work, and secretly coveting disco diva Donna Summer and Toronto-based rock star Carol Pope and her band, Rough Trade.

Departures from the (apparent) hegemony of life/style not only suggest unstable and sometimes contradictory features of the rules, but a certain flexibility or latitude in their interpretation that undermined the presumed fixity and solidity of lesbian-feminist identity. In these moments of instability, the degree of elasticity of the rules *and* their overriding moral regulatory character is revealed. Today, unsure of the extent to which they concertedly pushed for or pulled against these rules, or even how they may have reconciled this tension, many former

LOOT members concede that flouting the imaginary line demarcating 'in' or 'out' meant the possibility of dire consequences. Here, the concept of 'difference' rested uneasily on tongues and in minds. Looking back over the years of feminist organizing from her own standpoint as a British activist, Wendy Clark observes, 'Any differences within our ranks become either those that must be conformed with (that is, similarities) or they stay as differences, uncomfortable and problematic.'[70]

In sum, for the predominantly white, young, middle-class lesbians who maintained an ideological and political investment in building Lesbian Nation, following life/style guides, however hazily known, facilitated entry into LOOT and the larger community in which it was embedded. LOOT-goers of all political stripes sought affirmation in the guise of an almost totalizing sameness all the while that they paradoxically trumpeted the particularities of 'lesbian-feminist difference.' Endeavouring to differentiate lesbian feminists from straight feminists, gay men, bar dykes, and all non-lesbians, LOOT members asserted the radical specificity of lesbian feminism through what Judith Butler might call the self-disclosing, repetitive performance of life/style imperatives.[72] In effect, reinvesting the feminist dictum 'the personal is political' with bold, lesbian-specific faith served as a potent 'gravitational point' for a newly forming feminist constituency.[73] I argue that life/style standards also played a pivotal role in the shift from homophobic definitions of lesbianism to what Katie King has called 'feminism's magical sign of liberation.'[74] Similarly, in chapter 5, examining the sexual standards upheld at LOOT affords us another glimpse into the construction of empancipatory lesbian-feminist identity and community formation in the 1970s.

5

Mining lesbian-feminist sexual discourse and practice

I love to see you in the low-light, love
and touch your secret weakness with my fire
Let's burn together all through the night
I'm just a dream child of desire.
Cris Williamson, 1975[1]

In the late 1960s in Canada, the United States, Britain, and parts of Western Europe, women's liberationists began to define sexual freedom from the standpoint of their own experience, on their own terms.[2] As early as 1967, women members of the Student Union for Peace Action (SUPA) charged that 'woman is the object, man is the subject. Women are screwed, men do the screwing.'[3] A member of Toronto Women's Liberation stated, 'What is conspicuously absent, is the notion of the woman as sexual subject whose body yearns to receive pleasure as well as give it.'[4] Contrary to the Victorian classification of sexual behaviour by 'experts' in the fields of medicine, psychiatry, and psychology as the private, natural, and unchanging property of individuals, feminists argued that sexuality, like other aspects of women's (and men's) lives, is social, and hence a matter of political debate and struggle.

In the late 1960s, feminist demands for contraceptive information and abortion on demand challenged the Canadian criminal code and were publicized through the Abortion Caravan that crossed the country in 1970.[5] Pockets of outspoken, white, middle-class women seized the moment to recast publicly the terms of female (hetero)sexual subjectivity, both practically and discursively: the elimination of the madonna/whore dichotomy, the liberation of masturbation, the reclamation of clitoral orgasm, and, for some, the celebration of celibacy.[6] They were cynical about a 'sexual revolution' that seemed to ensure more exploitative male access to female bodies. In her widely read essay 'Sexual Politics: A Manifesto for the Revolution,' Kate Millett stalwartly maintained that feminism would catalyse (bi)sexual freedom and 'the end of enforced, perverse heterosexuality.'[7]

In the mid-1970s, while *Chatelaine* magazine announced (to its one million Canadian readers) the explosion of 'healthy and permissible' heterosex in a period of 'cool experimentation,'[8] Canadian radical and socialist feminists alike processed the dissatisfactions and confusions characteristic of their past sexual experiences. As Myrna Kostash lamented in the November 1974 issue of *Maclean's* magazine, 'There didn't seem to be very many men around who were willing and able to go the long, arduous and introspective journey with you toward joyful lovemaking.'[9]

All across North America, feminists, both straight and lesbian, established antiviolence support services. In Toronto, with the financial support of federal government grants – Opportunity for Youth (OFY) and the Local Initiatives Program (LIP) – the Rape Crisis Centre (1974) and Women's Counselling Referral and Education Centre (WCREC) were founded to provide information and counselling for survivors of sexual assault and abuse. Both Interval House and Nellie's – emergency hostels for battered and homeless women – opened in 1974.

In the spirit of renewed antiviolence activism that was sweeping the states of California and New York, the Toronto chapter of Women Against Violence Against Women (WAVAW) was founded by several LOOT lesbians and friends in November 1977. The *Snuff* film, in which a woman was purportedly killed in the sexual-climax scene, was first screened at Cinema 2000 on Yonge Street on 5 November 1977 – the same day on which the National Protest against Rape was held – and it provided the catalyst for WAVAW's formation.[10] Lesbian feminists made up the backbone of this antiviolence activism as volunteers and paid staff.[11]

The women I interviewed recall that, in this climate of rage, it was virtually impossible for lesbian, bisexual, or heterosexual feminists to claim the right to sexual pleasure. In the absence of an empowering female erotic heritage, burdened by the vestigial Victorian reduction of (white, middle-class) women's sexuality to passionlessness combined with Christian notions of women's bodies as impurity and evil incarnate, most feminists lived with sexual fear, inhibition, and guilt.

According to former LOOT member Natalie LaRoche, 'Women can't even talk about their own slippery, their own sexuality, so why would lesbians? We've been taught that our bodies are dirty and our cunts stink.' Several lesbians I interviewed underscored their own struggle to come to terms with child sexual abuse perpetrated against them by adult heterosexual men.[12] As LOOT regular Lilith Finkler contends, 'You're looking at one out of three being an incest survivor and one out of two by the age of thirty being a rape survivor. Many of us lesbians are survivors of sexual violence.' The desire to disrupt both overt and more subtle patterns of heterosexual subjugation in their sexual and emotional relations with women was strongly felt, though not easily articulated.

DIFFERENTIATING LESBIAN SEX FROM HETERO/BI SEX

To lesbian feminists at LOOT, sex wasn't something to be sequestered in bar culture and private, closeted relationships; it became an integral feature of their *political* identity and another measure of their 'correctness.' Extending the feminist maxim, the personal is political, LOOT members argued that 'being a lesbian isn't an on-again off-again sexual pastime, it's a full-time belief,' or a world-view, or a whole mode of loving and relating, or a primary intensity between women.[13] As LOOT regular Gay Bell observed in *The Body Politic*, 'We know our lives are not comprised of just our sexuality, but do others know that?'[14] By embracing the construct 'woman loving women,' LOOT-goers activated a shift away from genital sex. In so doing, they hoped to neutralize the sensationalism of highly sexualized images of lesbians in pulp novels and popular heterosexual pornography. They also intended to counter the tendency among some heterosexual feminists to define lesbianism as primarily a *sexual* phenomenon and to dismiss it on this basis. Indeed, sex between women – the thing that made lesbianism 'queer' and 'perverse' – became the thing that lesbian feminists were initially likely to de-emphasize.

Strategically, by accentuating not only the spiritual power of the 'erotic' available to all women, but the pure political virtue of woman-identification, lesbian activists directed attention away from the sexual taint of lesbianism.[15] According to several women I interviewed, once lesbianism was redefined as *the* political choice, lesbian sex was afforded considerable moral valence. American critic B. Ruby Rich has observed that 'in the 1970s, the sexual frontier moved from the vagina to the clitoris as decisively as the art world moved from Paris to New York after World War II. The shift was connected, often dramatically, to assaults on heterosexuality itself and the emergence of the "political lesbian."[16]

In harmony with the feminist credo, the personal is political, lesbians argued that loving women, not fucking them, was a logical extension of their commitment to the eradication of women's oppression. They were aware that lots of women had sex with or were attracted to women yet did not name themselves as lesbian; however, this was exactly the kind of separation between practice and identity that LOOT members scorned.

Bent on reconciling sex with dominant lesbian-feminist ideology in ways that were consistent with life/style requirements, most LOOT lesbians sought to differentiate lesbianism, and lesbian sex specifically, from everything male, both heterosexual and gay. Not merely distinct, lesbian sex had to be seen or understood to be *the* superior form of sex. Writing in the late 1970s, lesbian novelist and essayist Jane Rule comments, 'The onus is on the lesbian to prove to heterosexual women and men that her experience is essentially better, if it is to be accepted at all.'[17] The following statistic from *The Advocate*, a glossy gay-male magazine from Los Angeles, was reprinted in the July 1977 *LOOT Newsletter*. It was wedged between announcements for the annual National Gay Rights Coalition meeting and a meeting of the Ad Hoc Anti–Anita Bryant coalition: 'Two American studies on female sexuality found that of two groups of women, 162 lesbians and 100 randomly selected women, only 18% of the random sample almost always experienced orgasm during lovemaking as opposed to 87% of the lesbians surveyed.'[18]

By the late 1970s, male sexuality had become increasingly portrayed as the embodiment of coercion, violence, and aggression by radical-feminist leaders in Toronto's antiviolence movement. Condemnation of heterosexual feminists who 'collaborated with men – the enemy' as traitors to the cause naturally followed. Though American lesbian Anne Koedt had published early warning signals not to reject straight women on the basis of their 'unliberated sex life,' the political privileging of lesbian sexual relations present in most American lesbian writings during this period had considerable appeal for a large contingent of LOOT regulars.[19] Lesbian contributors to the instantly popular and widely distributed health manual *Our Bodies, Our Selves* insisted that 'relationships with men in this society have a built-in power imbalance, and few of us who have explored the possibility of relationships with women would choose again to start with that handicap.'[20] As lesbian separatist singer/songwriter Alix Dobkin so succinctly stated, 'Men have the whole world to stick it in.'[21]

Lesbian diva and former Furies collective member Rita Mae Brown summarized the lesbian-feminist position: 'If you can't find it in yourself to love another woman, and that includes physical love, then how can you truly say you care about women's liberation?'[22] Levelling one of her most caustic, unforgiving indictments, Brown minced no words: 'Straight women are confused by men, don't put women first. They betray lesbians and in its deepest form, they betray their own selves. You can't build a strong movement if our sisters are out there fucking with the oppressor.'[23]

Former LOOT member Lorna Weir reflects on the political privileging of sexual difference used by lesbians to define correct feminism. She recalls that 'the suspicion of heterosexual desire remained a constant feature among lesbian feminists whose underlying theoretical position would periodically lead them to cast doubt upon the feminism of their heterosexual sisters, the assumption being that sexual preference was a political choice on the same plane as a decision to boycott California lettuce.'[24] Though the vast majority of LOOT members had been active heterosexuals, and a number had been married before coming out into the women's movement, most expressed discontent with, or dismissed out-of-hand, their heterosexual past. Whole chunks of personal history became submerged under the desire to create distance between the discomfort of heterosexual memories and the promise of something not yet fully known.

At LOOT, certain elements of sex, like other elements of life/style, were never officially deemed more or less feminist than any others. However, several women I interviewed recall how heterosexual desire was invalidated and rendered a liability. Rosemary Barnes told me: 'We felt that we'd rejected the family, rejected marriage and that we didn't have to take very seriously the women who were still hooked into that. So we hit them over the head with heterosexual privilege which didn't help them very much.'

In a piece prepared for the 1973 'Lesbian Issue' of *The Other Woman*, contributors wrote: 'Energies spent on men may give women a false sense of security, but in the final analysis only serve to delay the destruction of the system.'[25] This and similar separatist statements not only provoked tremendous guilt in heterosexual feminists, but, as

Varda Burstyn attests, it made a critical examination of the politics of heterosexuality almost impossible. In the September 1976 issue of *The Other Woman*, Hari Matta (a pseudonym) spoke out against what she perceived to be a serious double standard: 'Lesbian women may criticize heterosexual women for being co-opted, male-dominated, not committed enough, but counter-criticisms (such as gay women are repressing their sexuality because of unresolved fears of men) are absolutely taboo. There is no real discussion of women's sexuality going on anymore in the women's movement for fear it might actually lead somewhere and threaten the present status quo.'[26]

In the 1987 collection *Who's On Top?*, Dinah Forbes notes that 'today, ten years later, many heterosexual feminists still feel silenced, unable within the movement to analyse or talk about the role of men in their lives.'[27] Even celibacy, a practice consciously embraced by many feminists (both lesbian and straight) in the early 1970s, carried a male referent. Like bisexuality, it signalled fence-sitting.

The danger of an erotic liaison with a woman who self-identified as bisexual was a much talked-about subject among Toronto lesbian feminists. Commonly held positions centred on the emotional risk of being open to a bisexual only to have her capitulate to the competing demands of a male lover. Trying lesbianism on, like one would a new pair of shoes, 'pretending that lesbian sex was far out, sharp and hip,' was seen by most LOOT members as an affront to the (already fragile) program of woman-identification. An experimental 'sex-but-no-commitment-policy' was not only seen as an offensive male trip; it was also a source of much lesbian heartbreak, grief, and anger.[28]

On political grounds, as a lesbian-feminist rule, bisexual women were cast off as untrustworthy because they slept with men. In the eyes of the most outspoken lesbian feminists, refusal or reluctance to leap over the fence into the 'final frontier' meant an automatic weakening of commitment to the feminist project. Bisexuality was a transitional stage through which women passed to a higher stage of mutuality and equality. Like their heterosexual sisters, bisexual feminists (or the ones who spoke out) found this sexual prescriptivism repugnant. In an unsigned article printed in the July 1975 issue of *Long Time Coming* (Montréal), the author critiques the 'holier than thou' attitude of most lesbians, who feel they are better women and better feminists than are bisexuals.[29] And in an early *Broadside* article, Lilith, a former member of LOOT, gave voice to her fear of banishment from her own community: 'I felt confused, unsure and afraid to approach other lesbians with my own personal truths. After all, as a lesbian, I had not wanted to hear about other women's straight experiences. And a dyke gone "het" is just ten times worse. I was a traitor to my cause. I was fearful of others discovering my political inconsistencies and personal confusions.'[30]

HE AIN'T MY BROTHER: A LESBIAN CRITIQUE OF GAY MEN'S SEX

At LOOT, and among lesbian feminists more generally, a rejection of male sexuality extended beyond its heterosexual expression. Gay-male sexuality, particularly the eroticization and increasing commercialization of sex in urban gay-male communities, emerged as a focus of lesbian-feminist criticism in the early 1970s. In the 'Lesbian Issue' of *The Other Woman*, Rowena Hunnisett challenged her lesbian and feminist readers to imagine 'a more sexist game than the on-the-make game of gay men hunting for sexual prey.'[31] In the same issue, reprinted from a speech she delivered at Toronto's Gay Pride Week in August 1973, Adrienne Potts informed her 95 per cent gay-male audience that 'you're not my brothers as long as you keep struggling for the freedom to cruise and trick in High Park.'[32] In *The Other Woman* in 1974, Gillean Chase complained, 'It is not accidental that male organizations for gays provide travelogues about where to get laid from town to town – an index of places to go for possible sexual adventures. It is not accidental that *The Body Politic* prints pictures of pretty boys and personal ads for "desirable" companionship.'[33]

By the late 1970s, in the context of mounting visibility of gay-male sex and the attendant escalation of state sexual regulation (see chapter 7), most activist lesbians were perplexed by, and even scornful of, what they understood to be 'anonymous,' 'penis-fixated,' 'casual,' and 'public' sex practised by gay men.[34] To the majority of LOOT members, the worst forms of heterosexual power imbalance, objectification, and insensitivity were intrinsic to gay-male sexual activities. Though she identified as an active supporter of gay liberation, former LOOT member Gay Bell had her own limits: 'I used to typeset *The Body Politic* and I used to go crazy typesetting their want ads in terms of describing what big dicks they wanted, which used to gross me out because I felt it was okay to sense the sexuality between men but to describe it verbally I found difficult to deal with. I used to sit at the typewriter and holler and scream and yell and the guys would go, "Gay is typesetting the want ads again."'

In her article 'Stranger in Paradise' (reprinted in *The Body Politic* in 1976),

Rita Mae Brown sums up her visit to a gay-men's bathhouse: 'To those of us forced to live beneath our abilities politically, sexually, socially, artistically and economically, sexual submission carries no hidden shudder of delight.'[35] As LOOT-goer Deb Stinson recollects, 'It seemed like [gay men's] liberation was centred around their right to fuck, and not even their right to fuck equals, but their right to fuck whoever they want, whenever they want, as many as they want, and there was no way I could bring that to bear on anything in my experience.' And Pat Hugh adds, 'I didn't stick my vagina in a hole in the wall in Woolworth's washroom. I got to know the women I had sex with and I knew them after we stopped having sex.' Most LOOT members agreed that gay-male sexual practices, rather than being liberatory, ensnared practitioners in the same oppressive roles of power/powerlessness from which lesbians were so valiantly striving to flee.[36]

Scanning the classified advertisements in issues of *The Body Politic* from the late 1970s (where I found two or three lesbian ads for every three or four pages of gay-men's ads), I found two highly representative ads placed by (white) gay men for the purposes of soliciting sex:

Toronto: Slim attractive smooth-skinned 27, 5'8', 130 lbs. Seeks young top male(s) dominatrix for exper. in B/C, D/C, W/M, S/M. You must be under 30, good-looking, exciting, sensual, clean and honest. Home and assistance offered to pretty youth under 25. Lasting relationship possible if serious and sincere and the crème de la crème. Photo a must.

Slave 27 smooth good shape and figure slim, very well-built docile and experienced into full servitude and humiliation especially VA SPKING WS DS Service BC no pain no marks please.[37]

LOOT-goers Chris Bearchell and Konnie Reich were involved in gay-liberation politics, and they remembered the envy they felt years ago towards the richness of gay-male sexual possibilities. Comprising a tiny minority, these women were drawn to the complex dynamics of dominance and submission, lust and fantasy that were played out in some segments of the gay-male community. They also learned about the danger of state sexual regulation in the form of censorship, bath and bar raids, and police harassment and entrapment. These women were also among the first to condemn the commercialism and the overt racism that had entered into the mass production and consumption of gay-male sexual style by the late 1970s and early 1980s.[38]

Despite evidence of a gay-positive lesbian sexual fringe, most activist lesbians throughout the 1970s remained highly uncomfortable with what they saw as unabashed sexual objectification practised by gay men. Indeed, this level of discomfort was often reflected in, and magnified by, the antagonism many lesbian feminists felt towards the sexism and misogyny encountered in coalition work with gay men.

LESBIAN SEXUALITY'S ELEVATED MORAL VALENCE

In the late 1970s, LOOT lesbians inhabited the general feminist arena of sexual pessimism in a 'country that has no language.'[39] Many found themselves grappling with the historically constituted absences of language and imagery to describe the joys and terrors of same-gender sex. Lesbian historians writing in the 1970s used the language of romanticism to describe the homoerotic relations between white, middle-class women in the nineteenth and early-twentieth centuries. Owing to the historical records themselves and to what Martha Vicinus calls the 'presentist' desire of researchers to downplay the sexual dimension of female same-gender relations, sex is either underexplored or denied altogether in these accounts in favour of romance in friendship, diffuse affectionality, and emotional and spiritual fulfilment.[40] Interestingly, the particulars of sex itself are overshadowed by similar ideological emphasis placed on the romantic, egalitarian character of lesbian-feminist relations in the 1970s.

Like most women during this period, whether lesbian, feminist, or neither, LOOT members were most comfortable speaking about sex in veiled references, innuendos, and metaphors. As Nancy Adamson remembers, 'We were all very new at being lesbians and we were very unsure about what it meant to be a lesbian, like working out our sexuality and how to express and combine it with our feminist ideas.' Before the 1979 Bi-National lesbian conference in Toronto, sexuality panels were organized for the Montréal lesbian conferences in 1974 and 1975, and the Ottawa conferences in 1976 and 1978. However, except for attention to the ups and downs of relationships, the joy of masturbation, and the tentative comment recorded in a 1976 Workshop Report that 'perhaps we need to be unashamed of enjoying lesbian erotica,'[41] former LOOT members don't recall sexually explicit discussions.

When questioned about their experience of LOOT as a sexual space, the majority of former members invariably hesitated, and then emphasized the vast amounts of erotic energy in the air. Seen by some as a panacea for female sexual (economic and political) malaise, lesbian loving relationships were infused with an organic, almost magical potential by Judith Quinlan, who wrote, 'Whenever we try to make our love grow outside the mind-binding institutions of marriage, monogamy and sado-masochistic ritual, we are whirling into a life-loving vortex that will eventually level the towers of patriarchal babble.'[42] Still, graphic sex talk was not completely tabooed; a heavy accent on 'lesbian feminist prudery' overlooks early attempts to match pleasure with woman identification.[43] 'Inarticulate,' to use Marilyn Frye's term, yet eager to invent words and images in the almost total absence of circulating lesbian sexual culture, natural (that is, dildo-free) and egalitarian representations of lesbian sex dominated.[44] The 'Love Poems' of Adrienne Rich (1978) and Pat Parker (1978) and the lyrics of 'The Changer and the Changed' (1975) and of 'The Ways a Woman Can Be' by Teresa Trull (1976) celebrate the joys of women-loving, the need for warmth and comfort, and the 'easing of pain.'[45]

Dusting off, polishing up, and twisting around the powerful ideology of (heterosexual) romance to meet a distinctly lesbian-feminist purpose was a tried and true tactic. In the late 1950s, pulp novelist Ann Bannon depicted lesbian love as 'near perfection between women,' 'clean, beautiful,' and based on an 'instinctive understanding that surpasses words.'[46] In the 1970s, early issues of *The Other Woman* contained a number of variations on this theme; for instance, 'Heterosexual women only know one way of relating sexually. But loving women is a gentle, sensual thing and it's not something confined to genitals. It involves our whole selves.'[47] In 1973, Holly Devor wrote: 'A woman knows best the desires, pace, mood of another woman and is best able to satisfy her. Frigidity among lesbians is almost unheard of. Long lasting, gentle and satisfying sexuality is the norm.'[48] In 1973, a contributor to *The Other Woman* claimed, 'Lesbianism is not a sexual perversion: it has nothing to do with sex. It is not another way to "do it." It is touching and rubbing and cuddling and fondness. It is holding and rocking and kissing and licking. Its only goal is closeness and pleasure. It does not exist for the Big Orgasm. It exists for feeling nice ... It's like loving yourself.'[49]

Not restricted to Toronto, the local production of sexual discourse was continually penetrated by the wider discourse that extended beyond it. Illustrative of the articulation between local and extra-local discourses, one dedicated fan prepared this review of a downtown 'wimmin-only' screening of Californian Barbara Hammer's lesbian erotic films for the *LOOT Newsletter*: '"Dyketactics," her 1974 film, shows the ritual, tactile love between women with a depth and tenderness unknowable by men. The film "Women I Love" brings woman and nature into one, comparing the exploration of a woman with the intense explorations of various vegetables or fruits, or flow and ebb of the sea. Hosts of daffodils are symbolic of the strength, yet beautiful fragility of woman-love, as are butterflies or dew-wet glistening webs.'[50]

Asked to describe her memory of lesbian sexual practice in the late 1970s, former resident of 342 Jarvis Street Holly Devor muses: 'It was supposed to be *au naturel*. God gave you hands, hands were okay; God gave you a tongue, that's okay. God did not give you leather or a dildo, so you're not supposed to use that stuff. We were celebrating women's bodies and womanliness. You could suck tit till you were blue in the face – that was great. You could smear blood all over you, put your face in someone's bleeding cunt – that was fine because that's your woman's body. But anything that looked like men or the whole hetero trip was not acceptable.'

Among the only mainstream news coverage of LOOT was the article 'Lesbians Shouldn't Be Isolated' by Michele Landsberg in the *Toronto Star* in 1979. Here, one lesbian feminist quoted by columnist Landsberg states, 'We're in uncharted waters ... We're trying to forge relationships that aren't based on power but on mutual love and nurturing. Men are conditioned to take, emotionally, but women are conditioned to give.'[51] And in 1981, in a Coalition for Gay Rights in Ontario brief to the Ontario legislature, Rosemary Barnes, a former member of LOOT, describes her vision of lesbian sex: 'The three most important things in lesbian lovemaking are mouth, hands and eyes – in that order. Oh yeah, breasts, legs and fingers and arms and ears. Anything that makes caressing, whispering, stroking breasts, running fingers through her hair, nuzzling, more fun. I like wrestling for hours – playing on the plateaus, scaling new heights. And taking bubblebaths after if there is time.'[52]

American lesbian writer Jan Zita Grover suggests that the heavy reliance on floral, ocean, and mountain metaphors revealed 'as much a language of genteel displacements, of feints, as a language in search of the ineffable.'[53] Described glowingly in mostly diffuse, allegorical terms, lesbian feminism was championed as one of the few places where one could hope to find post-revolutionary love in pre-revolutionary times. And, apparently, there was no shortage of opportunity, hence no collectively acknowledged need or desire to actively solicit love (or sex) through paid advertising. Notwithstanding the very important exception of sex-trade workers, there was almost no tradition of either lesbian or straight women advertising for sexual partners (regardless of the nature of the publication). In one of the smattering of lesbian classified ads to appear in *The Body Politic* in the late 1970s, one woman courageously appealed to modesty and moderation: 'Toronto: Youthful looking feminist, university student, age 39, studying sociology and psychology. Non-smoking, light drinking Aquarius who likes reading, ballet, classical music, dining, walking, discussion, quiet times. Uncloseted. Not into role playing. Occasionally attends a gay coffee house. Honest, gentle, affectionate nature. Have many friends, seeking a comfortable, loving, possibly permanent emotional, intellectual and physical lesbian relationship.'[54] Ideological codes of power-free mutuality and romance served to organize the realm of lesbian desire in reaction to what *The Other Woman* named as the 'dictatorship of genital sexuality.'[55] In print, lesbian-feminist lovemaking seemed idyllic and superior, the pinnacle of exchange that was egalitarian, mutually pleasurable, and, perhaps most important, honest. The authors of *The Joy of Lesbian Sex* painted lesbian sexuality as 'the interface of mind, body and spirit. It is equal because women together are equals and vehemence against the lesbian is vehemence against democracy.'[56] The belief was, to quote Naomi Brooks, that 'all wives were prostitutes, but between women, it was like this miracle was going to happen, and any sexual problem a lesbian had was a leftover from her male relationship.'

LESBIAN RELATIONSHIPS: NON-MONOGAMY RULES IN THEORY

According to my narrators, relationships with more than one lover promised a disruption to patterns of old-fashioned, emotionally immature, and often embittered heterosexual coupledom. Rooted in the 'free love' and 'if it feels good, do it' discourse of the 1960s and early 1970s, these new configurations also intended the integration of left, feminist, and counter-cultural anticapitalist ideals of communal living and consensus decision making. In the early 1970s, several women who were active in Toronto's Revolutionary Marxist Group had sex with women but did not define themselves as lesbians. To cite Sue Genge, '*Not* sleeping with women was buying into the old structures of monogamy and the nuclear family,' and sleeping with women was 'a point of analysis: it had political meaning.' For feminist adventurers, both straight and lesbian, as long as the alternative, non-monogamous arrangements did not involve raunchy, recreational sex free of emotional commitment, they were perceived, even encouraged, as right-on. Indeed, by the early 1970s, many people were living in a variety of family arrangements, out of every imaginable blend between necessity and choice.

For lesbian feminists specifically, concurrent relations with several lovers, or non-monogamy, signified (at least in theory) the acme of a sexually liberated self and, by extension, a sexually liberated community.[57] Unlike the primary and secondary relationships many gay men constructed, a number of LOOT lesbians trumpeted the pursuit of several primary relationships at once. However, former LOOT member Fiona Rattray described to me the hazards of sleeping around: 'At this point I was into sleeping with nearly every woman that came along, that was part of the way I connected into the community – I slept with women and then became friends with them, which not everyone was doing. I know I got a lot of "attitude" about the fact that I liked to be so sexual: the message was that I was a slut and a sleaze sleeping my way around town, and that I was frittering away energy that could have been used to change the world over night.'

On the topic of multiple relationships, Chris Bearchell adds: 'You didn't just have non-monogamy by going to a LOOT committee and drawing a name from the hat. You had to find each other.' At the Ontario Lesbian Conference in Ottawa in 1978, in response to the monogamy–versus–non-monogamy workshop, one participant wrote, 'Non-monogamy is a luxury reserved for women living in larger cities, since anywhere else it's hard to find anyone, let alone multiple relationships.'[58] While some downtown lesbian feminists struggled to come to grips with the 'incestuous swapping of lovers,' others felt tormented by the question of whether it was really possible to have a happy triangle. One woman claims that the only reason non-monogamy worked for her was because she was unemployed for a year and thus had the time and energy necessary to devote to two lovers. She also had the support, if not the urging, of a community of like-minded activists.

Living and loving up to community expectations was often easier said than done. Writing for The Body Politic in 1976, Kate Middleton burst the bubble of unconditional lesbian sexual bliss: 'Too often, as lesbians, we accept the fact that lesbianism is somewhat like sexual nirvana. Everyone is cool (meaning hot). In the land of dykes, making love is always satisfying, sleeping with men is less rewarding, and we all get it on with great regularity. If we could breed, we'd propagate at a rate alarming to rabbits and other fuzzy creatures. Well, frankly speaking, we're fooling ourselves ... As lesbians, we are not immediately the perfect sexual creatures we're made out to be. We have hang ups and frustrations too ... Once we realize our weaknesses we can start to improve upon them.'[59] According to several women I've interviewed, the assumption that lesbian sex (in the context of one or more relationships) was universally desirable, easy to get, always satisfying, and problem-free seemed more mythological than real. Ruth Dworin says, 'I had to be the world's best lover, the world's best companion and the world's best everything because the myth said, "Once a woman tries 'it' with another woman, she'll never go back to men," and I felt like I kept letting down the club.' Speaking of sex at LOOT, Chris Bearchell recalls that 'women were meeting behind their lovers' backs, having arguments about furtive glances across the room, and it was the same kind of dynamic that you would have found in any lesbian bar at the time. I don't remember knife fights or fist fights, but there were nonmonogamy, monogamy, promiscuity and jealousy issues in the air a lot of the time.'

Overall, there was little room for open discussion of sexual anxiety, power differentials, fear, and ambivalence among lesbians who identified as feminists.[60] Several women recounted to me their own valiant efforts to match the antipossessiveness line in spite of their deep-down desire for a long-term, monogamous relationship. And the 1980s issue of physical and psychological abuse within lesbian relationships was not a subject of conversation or analysis in the 1970s. Crossing over between the communities of bar women and lesbian feminists, Dina discerned that 'women hanging out at LOOT and Mama Quilla II [the rock and roll band] were saying that the bar dykes used to beat the shit out of each other, and I get in with this group [of lesbian feminists] and I think, "You just fucked her head so desperately and you think that's okay?" I would much rather have a punch in my face so at least I'd know I just got fucked.'

THE INTERNAL STRETCHING OF LESBIAN SEXUAL DISCOURSE

Evidence of occasional rule bending, and even breaking, suggests that the sexually correct codes defined by lesbian feminists were less stable than the ideology prescribed. At the idyllic site of the Michigan Womyn's Music Festival, temporarily free from exhausting, daily work shifts, amidst 3000 almost-nude festi-goers, 1500 kilometres from home, Canadian lesbian feminists often had relatively anonymous sex (the details of which they did not often reveal once home, unless the sex signalled the beginning of a long-distance relationship). And several former members of LOOT told me stories of having clandestine sex on the couch in the office following a meeting and in one of the bedrooms in the upstairs apartment at 342 Jarvis Street.

On Friday nights at the drop-in, a handful of lesbians regularly shed their shirts and danced bare-breasted. Access to alcohol and dope at most lesbian and feminist events lubricated the social and the sexual. At candle-lit coffee-houses, dyked out in full regalia, lesbians read sex into and between the lines of music like Margie Adam's 'Sleazy' (1976), Gwen Avery's 'Sugar Mama' (1977), Heather Bishop's rerecording of Bessie Smith's 'Prove It On Me Blues,' and 'Kahlua Mama' by Be Be K'Roche (1974).[61] Music producer and LOOT member Ruth Dworin remembers, with a grin, that the line 'takin' me to your secret, letting me know, taking me in, letting it all go' in Cris Williamson's recording of 'Sweet Woman' (1975) left little to the lesbian erotic imagination. In fact, Ruth avows, 'There must have been hundreds upon thousands of women who were seduced to "Dream Child" [on the same album].'

When asked to reflect on the existence of sexually explicit lesbian literature and imagery, LOOT members remarked that there was very little to choose from. There was one lesbian art show at 342 Jarvis Street, where there were some examples of eroticism. Deb Stinson remembers one painting of a 'huge open flower-like thing that was a labia all done in shades of pink.' In her 1978 made-for-LOOT bibliography, Lorna Weir recommends *What Lesbians Do*, a 'soft-pedalled sex manual' by Godiva (1975); 'the joyous approaches to lesbian lovemaking' in *Loving Women*, by the Nomadic Sisters (1976); and 'the nonpornographic, finely-illustrated' *Liberating Masturbation*, by Betty Dodson (1974).[62] In their interviews, several women also mentioned Tee Corrinne's *Cunt Coloring Book* (1977), *The Joy of Lesbian Sex* (1977), the 'Sexuality Issue' of *Amazon Quarterly* (March 1975), and Samois's *What Colour Is Your Handkerchief? A Lesbian S/M Reader* (1979).[63] Of the titles listed above, all were available at Glad Day Bookshop, while only one (*Liberating Masturbation*) was habitually stocked and sold at the Toronto Women's Bookstore.

Thus, though not always readily available, the sex-related texts that did circulate were well-thumbed, often passed, with giggles, from woman to woman. But rarely was the (sometimes controversial) content of the resources discussed or debated among lesbian readers/viewers. As Lynne Fernie says, most lesbians felt 'too embarrassed to talk about something that was supposed to be so natural.' Whether lesbians fantasized (and admitted it) or not, sexual fantasy was matter-of-factly pooh-poohed as male crap. Furthermore, American activist Paula Webster recalls: 'We feared contradicting what we said we wanted and began to lie or tell only half-truths, keeping secrets that might reveal our deviance to members of our movement, community or preference group ... The sexual domain in general had become less taboo but some wishes, some thoughts, some acts and some partners were as off-limits as before.'[64]

SHORING UP LOOT'S SEXUAL ORTHODOXY

Notwithstanding the odd departure from community standards, the fact that lesbians who openly flaunted their sexuality encountered disapproval, no matter how subtle, attests to the power of such standards. One did not dress for sex, because the art of costumed sexual seduction was so overdetermined by the objectifying 'male gaze' as to render it virtually irrecoverable. Nor did the staged removal of clothes – a popular and long-standing arousal technique – jibe with notions of an organic, even instinctive, sexual exchange. Keen to defuse the wrath stirred up by lesbian dancer Margaret Dwight Spore's impromptu performance at the 1976 Ottawa Lesbian Conference, Gay Bell assured readers of *The Other Woman* that stripping is not about sex or desire; it's about creative energy. 'As for being turned on, that is a hang up which genitally oriented male sexuality has foisted on us. Stripping does not have to create a blaze in the loins, but it is rather more significant when it releases the power of our own creativity by eliminating what is not essential (clothes in a warm space).'[65]

In 1979, three years after she performed a striptease at the Ottawa Lesbian Conference, Babba Yaga (a.k.a. Margaret Dwight Spore) conducted a sexuality workshop and performed another strip act at 342 Jarvis Street. Amy Gottlieb remembers that the response by LOOT members to the strip was mixed. For herself, she felt that 'this was the thing that could draw in more women, not to see skin necessarily, but to appeal to a diversity of women who had varying approaches to sex and sexuality.' However, most LOOT lesbians were influenced by the feminist analysis that shaped and was shaped by the climate of intensifying antiviolence and antipornography activism: the spectacle of striptease objectifies and exploits women. Meanwhile, at downtown clubs like the Bluejay, the Studio Two, and the Pussycat Club, women (some of whom were lesbians) occasionally stripped for a 'rowdy, sex-starved lesbian clientele.' One evening of striptease at the Bluejay in the mid-1970s is recalled by Konnie Reich this way: 'They locked the doors so women couldn't get out and the cops couldn't get in (they only had a club licence and were vulnerable to harassment from the cops). And what I remember about the audience reaction was a great deal of exuberant, macho, disgusting behaviour from women, butches really, hooting and pounding the stage and grabbing at the dancer ... stuff that would not be tolerated or accepted in a heterosexual strip club situation. But this kind of thing we had never had available to us as lesbians. This was the first time it was in our environment, on our terms, directed at us, and most of us didn't know how to handle it. It was pure starvation.' At LOOT, unorthodox sexual habits were judged almost uniformly as male-identified and antifeminist. (Male-identification in this context, unlike its early equation with a lack of consciousness of women's oppression, signified a conscious allegiance to men.) Not only was promiscuity without love derided, but the active pursuit of cross-generational lesbian sex spelled disaster. Among lesbian feminists, this form of sex was not talked about freely and openly. Singer Meg Christian's 'Ode to a Gym Teacher' (with the popular substitutes of tawny owl, camp counsellor, or sports coach) validates the 'crush' a young girl has on an older woman and the creative tactics she uses to express the infatuation:

> I sang her songs by Johnny Mathis
> I gave her everything
> A new chain for her whistle
> And some daisies in the spring
> Some suggestive poems for Christmas
> by Miss Edna Millay
> And a lacy, lacy, lacy card for Valentine's day.[66]

A tribute to feelings many young girls experienced yet hid or denied for fear of rebuke, the tune offered positive affirmation to both lesbian youth and to those older LOOT-goers who remembered schoolgirl crushes. A staple selection at coffee-houses, potlucks, and informal gatherings, 'Ode' is still talked about by many of the women I interviewed with much enthusiasm and laughter. At the same time, the song operated to elevate the crush to a safe, almost spiritual plane – the 'girl who sticks to teacher like a leaf sticks to a tree' *may* grow up to be gay. The possibly sexual character of same-gender, cross-generational relations is not celebrated, let alone entertained. Thus, for some listeners, most notably the young dyke who benefited from a sexually active adolescence, the lyrics did not go far enough.

Several other lesbians ran the risk of being branded male-identified or antifeminist for unconventional sexual practices. A smattering of lesbians who were turned on by Joan Bridi Miller's article on sado-masochism (s/m) in *Gay Community News* (1976), Pat Califia's late 1970s columns in the *Advocate*, and Samois's *What Color Is Your Handkerchief? A Lesbian S/M Sexuality Reader* (1979) wrestled with new concepts and images around the kitchen table.[67] The debates that began to percolate – the terms of which were set by white American lesbians – appealed to a number of Toronto activists.[68] By the early 1980s, Sue Golding, Gillian Rogerson, Ryan Hotchkiss, Val Scott, Lee Lyons, and other sex radicals/militants and biker-women had begun to articulate a distinctive pro-sex feminism that positively foreshadowed the coalescence of lesbians, sex workers, transvestites, gay men, transsexuals, and transgendered people under the 'queer' banner in the 1990s.[69]

Remembering the late 1970s, Chris Bearchell and Konnie Reich note that they experimented with vibrators and dildos, s/m (fisting in particular), home-made lesbian porn, cruising, and picking up women they didn't know.[70] Among these gay liberationists the indictments 'slut' and 'sleaze' were tossed around as positive terms of endearment (even badges of honour). To women like Chris, Konnie, and others, shedding the shame of lesbian sexual desire and contesting the void of an erotic heritage meant speaking the truly unspeakable. This was not a legacy faced exclusively by lesbians: American feminist Ellen Willis contends that 'it's precisely sex as an aggressive, unladylike activity, an expression of violent and unpretty emotion, an exercise of erotic power, and a specifically genital experience that has been taboo for women.'[71]

Openly talking about the use of dildoes was especially incorrect in the 1970s. In the following exchange between popular Montréal columnist Amy Vanderdyke and advice-seeker 'Willing But Nervous,' the 'correct' lesbian-feminist position is transparently couched in humour:

Q: I have a friend who wants us to get it on with an artificial love-making device. Is it unhealthy to use these? She says her gestalt group recommends that if it feels good, do it.

A: There has been an assault of devices for love battering on the market, but this is the first time I've heard of Gestalt with a battery. Do what you want, but I think it's time we got 'back to the hand.'[72]

Vancouver lesbian Jan Brown recalls the penetration taboo: 'With the exception of a menstrual sponge, entering a vagina with anything, even a finger, was what men did to us. Penetration represented the kind of inherently oppressive sex we were trying to leave behind. Well-read girls knew that fucking was a vestige of the hetero-patriarchal power structure. Women, we all knew, came by clitoral not vaginal stimulation.'[73]

In 1975, Chris Fox, a frequent contributor to the gay journal *The Body Politic*, reviewed *Loving Women* – 'the first book of lesbian love-making' – for the feminist journal *The Other Woman*, and suffered criticism from her lesbian-feminist readers. Ironically, *Loving Women* was one of five titles to be denied entry to Canada, and to Glad Day Bookshop specifically, in 1980 by Canadian customs officials on the grounds that it was 'immoral or indecent.'[74] In her review, Fox not only called for the (heretical) launch of a 'porn page' in *The Other Woman*, but she confessed: 'Dildos reminded me of years of thinking I was sick; the concept of lesbian love as inferior to and imitative of hetero love; dildos were the essence of 'unnaturalness.' The dildo, anathema to the "liberated" lesbian. Demystification is a wonderful thing.'[75]

By the late 1970s, there are signs that a number of 'card-carrying' lesbian feminists were prepared publicly to poke holes in the edifice of correct lesbian sexual discourse. The June 1979 issue of the *LOOT Newsletter* marked the appearance of a 'fun' column written by the two notorious satirists 'Bulldyke and Butchford' (who later renamed the LOOT Newsletter *Lavender Sheets* in April 1980, three issues before it folded). In the same issue, a tongue-in-cheek 'Sluts' Rights' commentary written pseudonymously by Ann Cognita was published 'despite the better judgement of the editorial staff.'[76] And in the final issue of *Lavender Sheets*, an agitated 'exhibitionist' seeks advice from the 'Dear Lezzy' columnist: 'Ever since Michigan [Womyn's Music Festival] ... I've gone sort of hog-wild ... Whenever womyn gather I want to take off all my clothes and dance wildly and attract attention and stuff ... What if I get arrested? What would my family say?!'[77]

In September 1979, Mariana Valverde, LOOT-goer and collective member of *The Body Politic*, admitted to readers of her column that, 'deep down somewhere, far beneath the very correct lesbian feminist that my friends know, there is a very, very young, very "femme" girl who just wants to get fucked, in any and every way.'[78] Winnipeg-born lesbian comic Robin Tyler performed at the Bi-National lesbian conference in Toronto in May 1979, and made her début at the Michigan Womyn's Music Festival that August. The formerly 'asexual feminist who now uses sex appeal on stage,' Tyler delivered lines like, '[The cop] threw me into handcuffs – which is how I got into bondage – and took me to jail for female impersonation.'[79] And in an interview with LOOT member Val Edwards, Tyler confessed that through humour she hoped 'to make it okay to be butch.'[80]

However, throughout the three-and-a-half years of LOOT's existence, righteous notions of a correct sexuality fundamentally separated lesbian politicos from gay women who were not LOOT faithfuls. Like the clash in vision and life/style politics, not only did this separation manifest in physical distance and a mutual wariness, for lesbian feminists it meant dissociation from the historically specific sexual organization of language, codes, and styles that the 'unenlightened' accomplished on their own terms. American historian Joan Nestle recalls that, in the heart of the lesbian-feminist 1970s, 'whole communities of women disappeared ... because those were the women who looked like men. Or the women who looked like whores.'[81] Though the sex-based schisms between lesbians seem far less acute in the context of Toronto and other Canadian cities, in part owing to smaller numbers, I have uncovered some evidence to support Nestle's contention.

LES ÉTRANGÈRES: BUTCHES AND FEMMES

In *The Body Politic* in 1976, American lesbians Fran Koski and Maida Tilchin warned, 'If we want to forget the bars and the butches, then we are white-washing our history as oppressively as the straights have rewritten it for us.'[82] And yet at LOOT (as in earlier lesbian and feminist collectives), butches, femmes, and working-class bar dykes (and, in different ways, suburban gay women) were routinely spurned for being falsely conscious heterosexual mimics, wedded to exploitative role-playing.[83] Writing for *The Body Politic* in the late 1970s, LOOT-goer Lorna Weir concluded that '"femme" behaviour is just as much a caricature of women as "butch", and deeply apolitical.'[84] To long-time activist Pat Murphy, 'The bar butch meant male, breast-binding, the boss, the ego that always had to be stroked. They were the ones who gave lesbians a bad name. Now I look back and see that butches were alienated in the process. Their stories could not be heard.'

Curiously, the butch/femme codes that some lesbians at LOOT embodied, rather than being explored, were continually being scrambled and pulled apart. 'We refused to admit we were playing out butch and femme roles because we felt we had transcended all that through our politics,' according to Naomi Brooks. Natalie LaRoche's memory of this refusal is sharp: 'Everywhere I looked at LOOT I saw lesbian couples, one more butchy woman and one more femmey woman, which I had to ignore because *it didn't exist*. What I did come to notice, but didn't have language for till years later, was an antifemme attitude, in that femme style and the more femmey types of jobs and values are devalued in our community. So the cooking, the crafts, the counseling, the volunteer work is never recognized, but the hard labour, the technical work, the repair work, is butch-work, which is not only recognized, but it's usually paid. At LOOT, the more butch you looked, the more butch you talked, the more power was ascribed to you, except if you *really* looked like a man. Because I was more femmey, which was less valued, LOOT contributed to that part of my oppression.'[85] Split off from the rich history of lesbian bar culture in the 1940s, 1950s, and 1960s, lesbians who came out in the 1970s could neither understand nor accept the political character of earlier struggles to claim and defend public space. In *The Other Woman*, Gillean Chase insisted, 'Gay clubs are not political places. They are sexual places. So it is not surprising to see both men and women into game playing, cock or cunt teasing.'[86] Though a few lesbian feminists were intrigued by the sophisticated rules of bar culture, much-travelled stories of twisted jealousy, territoriality, and violence confirmed what most LOOT-goers suspected about the Mafia-run, drug-soaked underworld of bars portrayed in the mass media, pulp novels, and tabloids.

Two snarling Dobermann pinschers held in check by a bouncer at the door to the Bluejay was not a particularly inviting sight. And infrequent visits to the local bars commonly yielded accounts like Ann Kado's of 'big women in three-piece suits and ties who were ready to pound your face in if you so much as opened your mouth, let alone ask their "little woman" to dance.' As former LOOT member Nancy Adamson observed, 'There was a lot of angst [among lesbians] about sexuality, so women who had taken on roles and were comfortable in them were a threat because they suggested there might be other ways of looking at this question ... It was easier for us to say, "These poor women, they just don't understand."'

SEX-TRADE WORKERS

A sexual politics that was deeply antimale and rooted in middle-class experience also divided LOOT-goers from lesbian prostitutes and other sex-trade workers (dancers, strippers, porn actors, masseuses). Mary Axten remembers that in the 1960s, prostitutes used to go to the Melody Room, a gay after-hours club on Church Street in Toronto, to be with their lovers after working a long night. Lorna Weir remembers a prostitute coming to an International Women's Day Committee (IWDC) meeting in 1979. Capturing the historical moment, she quips, 'How to paralyse sixty strong feminists? Throw one hooker who insists on hookers' rights as a demand of International Women's Day into one of our meetings.' It wasn't until the late 1970s and early 1980s that sex-trade workers began to organize by and for themselves: BEAVER (Better End to All Vicious Erotic Repression) and, later, CABE (Canadian Association of Burlesque Entertainers) were among the first formally constituted organizations.[87]

The absence of discussion of prostitutes' rights (and the absence of prostitutes themselves in feminist circles) was not unique to lesbian organizing – ambivalence and confusion on this question had hobbled feminist organizing for years.[88] The Toronto Wages for Housework Committee, a feminist organization that was attempting to link prostitutes and homemakers together by comparing the exploitative conditions of their work, condemned the oppressive treatment of women in the sex trade. Despite the committed efforts of Wages for Housework, the dominant feminist tendency in the mid-to-late 1970s was to view sex workers as powerless victims of untramelled male lust. Lilith Finkler recalls that WAVAW voted against a request made by several young prostitutes to organize a joint educational forum in 1978. Looking back to the late 1970s, Gwendolyn, a local dancer and part-time prostitute, traces the exclusion of sex workers to early lesbian and feminist credo: 'According to "the line," working girls fucked gomers for money and made other women vulnerable to abuse and violence. Feminist dykes believed that all women like me really needed was protection from men and male sex, and until I got it, or got out altogether, I wasn't welcome.' Gwendolyn then recounted a story about the feminist management at the downtown Fly By Night, a lesbian bar tucked in behind her workplace – the Stage 212 strip club. She said: 'I wanted to put up a poster for CABE – it was a benefit at the Dream Factory. They didn't include me. They asked me to leave while they had a discussion about whether to put it up. There were as many as 10 dykes around. They didn't include me in their process. When they asked me back to the circle, they'd all dispersed except for one or two. They said, "Okay, you can put it up because you're a woman and this is a woman's bar, but we can't support it because it's violence against women and it's sexist."' Largely unaware of the implications of their actions for sex workers, feminists (both radical and socialist) descended on the downtown sex district to protest 'the promotion of death as a sexual turn-on' at Cinema 2000. Months later, LOOT regular Gay Bell recognized the danger of this feminist descent, yet, ambivalent about the ethics of selling sex, she (and feminists in general) could offer sex workers no concrete support: 'We do not want our efforts to stop the *Snuff* film to be co-opted into a clean-up campaign in the interests of big business and the bourgeois morality which is very hard on the women and gays who survive on Yonge Street (albeit in a sex-money way).'[89]

MALE-TO-FEMALE LESBIAN TRANSSEXUALS

Faithful to the widely read CLIT statement (1975, 1976) and in anticipation of the polemics formulated by American radical feminists Janice Raymond and Mary Daly, male-to-female lesbian-identified transsexuals were also deemed undesirable invaders of lesbian-feminist space.[90] The fear of infiltration, whether by the state (government agents, the police, the RCMP) or other possible informants, was familiar to almost all members of radical social movements. In the specific case of LOOT, a formal request to join the organization was made by a male-to-female lesbian transsexual in 1978. During informal discussion that ensued over the next several months, the 'sex-change he-creature' who 'dared identify himself as a woman and a lesbian' was denounced almost uniformly as an inauthentic impostor.[91] Poisoned by a residual heterosexuality, 'he' would only separate lesbians from each other and wreak havoc within the organization and the larger community.

One of the most outspoken architect of LOOT's anti-transsexual policy was Pat Murphy. One of the oldest LOOT members, respected for her experience and her wisdom, she was especially known for her charisma and her persuasive style. Trained as a psychiatric nurse, suspicious of 'quick fix' sexual surgery and its role in 'the future non-existence of women,' Pat was also concerned with what she saw as a high post-surgery suicide rate among transsexuals. Moreover, 'as a feminist,' she argued (and still argues), that 'lesbian transsexualism is a helluva long way around, through self-mutilation, to heterosexual privilege and ultimately to more access to women, as a male.'[92] Susan Cole echoed Pat's position: 'It was about giving men who had the power to choose, the choice to choose more power.' And Phil Masters agreed: 'A woman's voice was almost never heard as a woman's voice – it was always filtered through men's voices. So here a guy comes along saying "I'm going to be a girl now and speak for girls." And we thought, "No you're not." A person cannot just join the colonized by fiat.'

Few LOOT-goers had ever met a transsexual, so to most of them the debate had a somewhat abstract character. None the less, there was no mistaking the fiery, emotional tenor of the discussions. Having attended the LOOT meeting in October 1978 at which a vote was planned, Lilith Finkler described to me her personal predicament: 'My best friend's lover was a transsexual and we went to this meeting at LOOT about transsexuals and I'm sitting there going, "Oh boy, they're talking about Sherry and whether or not she's going to be accepted." Now, I'm really upset and embarrassed because I was not true to my friend at that meeting. I was really pressured by group politics and I just felt like all these people were giving me the bottom line, which was, "If you're changed from a man to a woman you're still a man," and I went along with it. At subsequent meetings they had posters up that said, "Women born women only" and there was this big transsexual scare where they went around hunting down transsexuals.'

Only one of the eighteen lesbian feminists present during the final LOOT debate voted to permit lesbian transsexuals official entry to 342 Jarvis Street. Though not present for the vote, Mary Axten, one of the first women to join the Community Homophile Association of Toronto (CHAT) in 1971, and a gay woman since the 1950s, was furious upon receiving news of the verdict. She said, 'I remember I could have gone and hammered those little suckers [at LOOT] into the woodwork a couple of times and made them listen to some sense. There they were, bitterly complaining about being oppressed, "Nobody loves me," and turning their backs on people who need warmth and companionship. In this entire world, who is more lonely than a lesbian transsexual?'

LOOT received one letter from a lesbian who could not attend the meeting at which the vote was held. She wrote: 'The only way we have of identifying a fellow lesbian is her word that she is a lesbian. A self-identified lesbian transsexual is a *bona fide* lesbian [emphasis in original]. LOOT should accept the transsexual and laud her "heroic struggle" to become a lesbian.'[93] Disturbed by the fever and tension spurred by the debate, Pat Hugh, the upstairs tenant at 342 Jarvis Street, refused to participate. Several weeks following the vote, she exploded with anger at the paranoia that persisted: 'A young androgynous-looking friend of mine who was just coming out came to a LOOT Sunday meeting. In the hallway, before she even got to the living room, this woman accosted her and said, "I think you're this transsexual and your kind is not welcome here." Well this poor woman just ran out of the house and immediately got involved with a man. She's out again, thank god, you know, thank god.'

Virtually all LOOT members were adamant that if transsexuals needed community support, they should create their own independent organizations.[94] Because it was inconceivable for a male-to-female transsexual to 'know the essence of being a woman,' it was entirely inappropriate for 'him' to seek comfort at LOOT or in any other lesbian-feminist group. Scrawled on the LOOT graffiti board was the barbed query, 'So what makes a woman – a castrated penis or a life of male oppression?'[95] In order to protect the integrity of women's space, all traces of maleness, whether visible or not, had to be purged. Legislating the exclusion of lesbian-identified transsexuals seemed like a perfectly reasonable, logical response.[96]

THE PUSH AND PULL AGAINST THE ODDS

In the mid-to-late 1970s in Toronto, lesbian feminists felt caught between a mainstream culture that either ignored or oversexualized their existence, a women's movement and left organizations mostly content to preserve the invisibility of lesbians, and a gay-liberation movement that tended to equate political lesbianism with asexual puritanism. Reacting to these perceptions, LOOT-goers argued that antipatriarchal lesbian love was not antisex; it was precious, liberating, and joyous in all its diffuse and fluid dimensions. In the midst of the legitimation of male sexual violence in mainstream culture (exposed by groups like WAVAW and the Rape Crisis Centre), love between women bloomed against all odds.

At and around LOOT, largely white, middle-class lesbian activists combated the patriarchal equation of 'lesbian' with sexual perversion, child molestation, and an unnatural appetite for sex. Making love with another woman in the context of a feminist commitment to 'sisterhood' was understood by virtually all the women I interviewed as a political act. Ironically, though the practice of sex itself was rarely discussed openly, lesbian feminists grappled with questions of whom they slept with, how many women they had (or wanted to have) relationships with, what kind of lesbian love they valorized, and how they wanted sex represented, if at all. Sometimes such talk was serious business; other times it was a source of ribald humour.

In the minds of many lesbian feminists, the prospect of overcoming sexual fear and shame resided in woman-to-woman relationships. Buoyed by Rita Mae Brown's declaration 'An army of lovers cannot fail,' they felt that the *real* sexual/political revolution was imminent. Certainly, similar claims to sexual democracy were made by some heterosexuals and gay men in the 1960s and early 1970s. However, by the late 1970s, weighed against the explicit lesbian-feminist claim to truly revolutionary erotic relations between equals, all other forms of sexual expression seemed diminished. In other words, if mutually respectful, egalitarian, and power-free relations could be enacted through sex between women, then a particular kind of sex was advantaged. As demonstrated above, the implications of such powerful ideological messages for LOOT's membership – who came, who stayed, and who didn't – were significant.

By the turn of the decade, tentative challenges were being waged to seemingly hegemonic lesbian sexual standards in small, tentative ways. Not unlike challenges posed to lesbian-feminist life/style conventions, departures from essentialized antimale discourse on sex suggest vying definitions or rival discourses of correctness. In effect, the terrain of sex appears much more messy and uneven than the neatness I originally suspected I would find. In light of my research, the description of 1970s lesbian feminism by scholars like Phelan, Faderman, and Echols as redolent of desexualized romanticism seems overstated. I would argue that elements of this grand narrative were strong among organized lesbians, and were in keeping with influential feminist attention to male violence and female victimization. Some LOOT members disclosed to me their memories of having to hide or deny any sexually unorthodox tendencies. But the occasional blurrings of good/bad distinctions and the existence of contradictions and ambiguities alongside ideological alignment beg the question of instability.[97] In other words, attention to life/style and sex-related departures from the dominant orthodoxy serves to loosen our analytic grip on lesbian feminism as a coherent, stable category of meaning and experience.

PART THREE

6

LOOT's structure and program: Politics redefined

Members of the Lesbian Organization of Toronto quickly sought to establish a formal structure to meet the needs articulated by their constituency. The task force (later the co-ordinating committee) attempted to introduce an infrastructure and principles of decision making that drew heavily on earlier experiments in feminist collectivism. From the late 1960s on, grass-roots feminist activists struggled to build radically different organizational forms and processes in opposition, and in reaction, to patriarchal conventions of hierarchy, leadership, and élitism.[1] Following the lead of these brave alternatives, and closely linked to the feminist ideology of 'the personal is political' and sisterhood (with a distinctly lesbian face), LOOT members committed themselves to the ideals of consensus decision making, power sharing, and equality among members. Deeply suspicious of the top-down bureaucratic, male-dominated forms of organizing intrinsic to traditional political parties and tightly structured organizations with rigid leaderships, they grappled with strategies to ensure women's empowerment. Naomi Brooks summarizes LOOT's philosophy: 'We were trying out a new vision of how to work together, and each of us was there as ourselves. We weren't there to represent another organization, and we rarely went into the communities as representatives of LOOT. LOOT was nonhierarchical, non-patriarchal. We wouldn't take votes saying, "We should support this." It was like "We have to respond to this." There weren't membership cards ... if you were at the Sunday brunch meetings you had a voice. The first year of the Not So Amazon lesbian baseball league, we almost took consensus over whether a pitch was a strike or a ball; you'd play ball at LOOT and it was very much that style of ball.' From the start, not everyone who came to 342 Jarvis

Street was comfortable with LOOT's overtly political focus. Task-force member Darlene Lawson complained, 'Feminists around here have been told not to be so high profile. And what does that say if we need a lesbian feminist perspective?'[2] In effect, the political-versus-'non-political' tension was one that had long separated lesbians who identified as feminists and non-feminist clusters of professional 'gay ladies' and bar-going lesbians – the very women whom LOOT members had trouble attracting to the organization.[3] Yet, as underscored in preceding chapters, few if any initiatives served to bridge the yawning gap between these communities. Writing in the late 1970s, American lesbian feminists Barbara Gittings and Kay Tobin maintained that 'the majority of lesbians who come around to any gay group are not looking for analysis or warfare or reconstruction ... They want to meet and mix with other gay women in the legitimate pursuit of friendship and love.'[4]

Realizing that political work was perhaps the least likely source of potential connection, LOOT-goers hoped, at first, that a highly organized social scene would appeal to the bar crowd. Friday nights, women got together at LOOT drop-ins, where they exchanged coming-out stories over beer and popcorn. The LOOT lending library carried a diverse collection of fiction and non-fiction. The annual LOOT Open House, Dyke-O, the Lesbian Bingo, pot-luck dinners, Sunday brunches, card playing, board games, movie screenings, and dances were also integral socializing practices at 342 Jarvis Street. Gay Days – the first large-scale Gala Jubilee and the precursor to the annual Lesbian and Gay Pride Day – was a week-long festival planned by a mixed lesbian/gay group, Liberated Energy, and held in August 1978. Several LOOT members participated in organizing the Gay Days' booths and a fair at Queen's Park, a large dance in the evening, and a Sunday picnic on Hanlan's Point.

The LOOT dances, most of which were held at St Paul's United Church on Avenue Road, quickly established a firm reputation for success. According to Phil Masters, 'It wasn't a trickle of change. One dance would have 100 people and the next would have 180 and then the next, 320. It was like there was no space, you couldn't move. It was an explosion.' On the sports scene, at sporadic intervals, baseball, basketball, and volleyball games/tournaments were introduced and coordinated by a couple of LOOT members. With its original core of four LOOT regulars, the Amazon Motorcycle Club – allegedly the first group of lesbian-feminist bikers in North America – was formed in 1978.

Clearly, the social components of LOOT, and of 342 Jarvis Street more generally, were successful in drawing women to the organization and introducing lesbians to each other in a relaxed social context. Non-confrontational and personally validating, the activities offered women the opportunity to come out and get involved. But despite these efforts, bar-goers rarely attended LOOT-sponsored events. Without activist histories and fearful of, or uninterested in, organized lesbian feminism, bar-goers had little faith in their own or anyone else's ability to change the system. Not only did they question the relevance of feminism to their lives, they resisted feminist assumptions that they were, as Deb Stinson put it, 'falsely conscious dupes of the patriarchy.' Stinson asserts: 'It was a total negation of what we [bar dykes]were doing because the books they were reading, we didn't read. The thoughts they were thinking, we weren't thinking. We weren't out to change the system, we were out to make our place in it. We knew our place in the big picture, we knew where the boundaries were, we knew what was allowed and what wasn't, so changing it would have left us with nothing. We had fought for our place. We'd been going along all these years and there hadn't been any changes. And they were out there with their feminist ideals, but the ideals weren't based in the realities we were living. We could better our jobs, become a union rep, get a cottage up north, and all that existed within the larger framework. The political dykes were talking about changing this larger framework.' Several LOOT members that I interviewed spoke of their frustration with what they perceived as the intransigence of 'apolitical' gay women. According to Eve Zaremba and others, bad attitude saturated statements like 'Don't tell me you're one of those boring political women' or 'My life is just fine. Nobody hassles me about being gay. If you go around looking for trouble, you get it.' Pat Leslie recalls the assumptions about lesbian political culture held by women who were either antagonistic or indifferent towards the LOOT project: 'Political dykes talk politics. We don't know how to have a good time, we can't enjoy a beer at the bar, we can't play a game of pool, we're uptight, we'd rather be yelling stuff on the street. Being political threatened some lesbians because it demanded something of them.'

Clearly, the relationship of lesbians to the women's movement, and to political activity more generally, was and still is complicated and many-levelled. In part, the vast majority of lesbians in the 1970s deployed common-sense survival mechanisms to mediate their fears of disclosure – a reality that is very much intact in the 1990s. Rather than grapple with being a politico, disrupting their carefully established routines, and endangering their jobs, children, friends, and so on, they set about devising a set of non-confrontational coping strategies. Not unique to women who love women, the practice of disengagement from political culture (broadly defined) is a feature of generalized disillusionment with politics in Western liberal-democratic societies. Former members of the Lesbian Caucus of the BCFW Nym Hughes, Yvonne Johnson, and Yvette Perrault contend that, 'given the level of societal discouragement of any political activity and the specific fear that lesbians face in identifying publicly as lesbians, it seems amazing that any lesbians are politically active at all.'[5]

Notwithstanding the multiple barriers to activism, the intensity and abundance of feminist energy at LOOT made possible a rich range of initiatives. In 1977, during the first few months of LOOT's existence, a number of committees were put in place to facilitate the planning and execution of multiple activities: peer support and one-on-one telephone counselling, social events, a monthly newsletter, a coming-out rap group, Amethyst – a support group for addicted lesbians, bi-weekly general-membership meetings, and the coordination of the organization itself, including the LOOT budget. Consciousness-raising groups, through which feminists in the late 1960s theorized their oppression and solidified their collectivity, were not formally instituted at LOOT. Instead, the focus was on ensuring that LOOT members had access to services and to each other in a safe, supportive context. Immediately gratifying and pre-eminently political acts, the provision and consumption of lesbian-centred resources reinforced feelings of pride, self-esteem, and commitment to community building. Indeed, such initiatives signified that the very notion of what constituted 'politics' was under contestation.

At one point, the *LOOT Newsletter* was entirely written, designed, typeset, pasted up, and printed 'in house,' and mailed out to four hundred subscribers (at its peak circulation). As Amy Gottlieb recalls, 'It wasn't seen as a vehicle for organizing; it was seen as a way of keeping in touch with women. I don't think LOOT was ever clear about what to politically organize around in order to use the newsletter in that way.' Still, to Gottlieb and others, its very existence was political in reconceptualized feminist terms, and it made a significant difference to its readers. Rachel remarked: 'It was the first of its kind. I felt a sense of pride that we could do this, that we could put this thing out and that we were building this network and building this community and so [the newsletter] was tangible evidence of what we were doing. I planned my whole month by it.'

What follows is a capsule of the contents of a typical LOOT news-letter – November 1977: announcements for Charlotte Bunch's up-coming visit to 342 Jarvis Street; a lecture series sponsored by the Women's Fund Raising Coalition; the formation of LOOT's Media Committee and Sappho Sound – the music-production collective; the launch of the women's poetry salon; the unveiling of the LOOT library; calls for participation in theatre, gay television, and the LOOT drive to winterize the house; reports from the LOOT task force and the counselling collective; a LOOT financial update; a film review of *In the Best Interests of Children* (reprinted from *Kinesis*); and the dates of LOOT's next general meeting, the GATE dance, the LOOT potluck dinner, the Hallowe'en costume party, the upcoming Three of Cups concert featuring Meg Christian and Teresa Trull, and the WAVAW leafleting action.

Peer counselling via the telephone was often the first service that any lesbian or gay organization established. A staple feature of wom-en's drop-ins, shelters, and rape crisis centres, the hot-line connected women in need of advice, emergency care, and information. Since the early 1970s, lesbians had called the CHAT crisis line and, later, the Toronto Area Gays (TAG) phone-line in search of support, as well as news of bars, coming-out groups, political demonstrations, pickets, dances, picnics, and so on. In 1977, a lesbian-only line was seen by LOOT members as a necessary and long-overdue addition to the tra-dition of grass-roots feminist self-help organizing. Rosemary Barnes, a telephone counsellor and psychologist-in-training, took calls on the LOOT phone-line a couple of evenings a week. In an interview, she told me: 'Our phone number was listed in the phone book and over the years, thousands of women called up looking for information and advice. Some were terrified to leave their own homes, some callers were unhappily married, others were young kids. Men would call up and masturbate on the line, or irate boyfriends would contact us look-ing for their girlfriends. Women who called would often show up in droves at the drop-ins.'

The Counseling Collective – one of the most significant and long-standing components of LOOT – provided women, many of whom were just coming out, with referrals to feminist therapists at the Wom-en's Counselling, Referral and Education Centre (WCREC). As well, several collective members who were trained as facilitators at WCREC offered information on upcoming events, legal and medical advice, and small, supportive group settings wherein women were encouraged to 'let their hair down.' Writing for *The Body Politic* in May 1977, Ilona Laney stated: 'LOOT hopes these services will help lesbian women who want to end their isolation and to communicate freely with other lesbians.'[6] As Naomi Brooks recalls, before the sophisticated developments in feminist psychoanalysis of the 1980s, counselling was not about working through layers and depths of internalized homophobia: 'We didn't have the skills. It was simply about, "Can I help you? Can I give you information?" When someone asked, "What should I do, I'm desperate to meet women and my mother just threw a pot of beans at my head," we'd invite her down to LOOT.'

The LOOT task force met weekly, handled the finances, brought issues and policy proposals to the general membership on the last Sunday of every month, and oversaw the operations of all committees. Without access to any form of state funding, the organization was forever dependent on time and energy devoted to fund raising. Loto-Lesbian, a 50/50 draw, became a staple method of quick financing, and was necessarily supplemented by membership fees, as well as the sale of beer at events, T-shirts, dance tickets, and a multitude of other creative cash-generating schemes.

For many LOOT-goers, the immediate and practical provision and consumption of services either coexisted with, or were supplanted by, the desire to explore and develop myriad aspects of 'wimmin's culture.' To Ruth Dworin, 'Making culture is a way of shaping how people perceive the world and it's a powerful and relatively painless consciousness-raising tool.' Dworin and others perceived the making of lesbian-feminist culture as a political intervention rather than a set of activities independent of politics. Creative expression became another avenue for the integration of feminist principles: skills-sharing; a belief in the importance of non-hierarchical, collective process – that is, the eradication of barriers between artists and spectators; and an emphasis on personal growth.

At 342 Jarvis Street, performing and/or supporting the performances of lesbian playwrights, actors, poets, writers, filmmakers, and musicians (often through Three of Cups events) became an ongoing attraction. Alexa De Weil, Gwen Hauser, and Betsy Warland read their poetry in the living-room. Members of the all-lesbian band Mama Quilla II practised in the basement next to the house printing press.[7]

Cate Smith remembers when Winnipeg-born Heather Bishop sang lesbian lyrics (straight lyrics were forbidden) and entertained five women
in the living-room of the LOOT house. Folk artists Beverly Glenn
Copeland and Vancouver-born Ferron also played at 342 Jarvis Street,
and Sappho Sound arranged for American musicians like Isquieda and
Teresa Trull to travel north. Ruth Dworin has vivid memories of co-
founding Sappho Sound, the lesbian-feminist sound-production company: 'I did sound crews at women's music festivals all summer. I
wanted to do sound in Toronto and a group of us fell into producing
concerts. It was nuts-o. There were nine collective members, nine
names on the bank loan. We lost money on two of our first major
shows. We deejayed LOOT dances, a series of coffee-houses in the
summer of 1979, we did Mama Quilla's first performance at 519
Church Street and we produced sound for Gay Days in August of
1978.'

Classical musicians April Kassirer and C.T. (Carol) Rowe played at
LOOT brunches and evening concerts and were invited to perform
on the afternoon stage at the Michigan Womyn's Music Festival in
August 1978. To Natalie LaRoche, the brunches were divine: 'I always
believed in the importance of bringing culture into the revolution, like
building a culture of resistance. Sunday afternoons, we'd have these
crêpes with champagne and orange juice and a concert of women's
chamber music and there'd be tables in this ancient Victorian house
with real tablecloths. I thought I'd died and gone to heaven.'

In the fall of 1977, The Dyke Brigade (whose members were all
LOOT regulars) helped to create the thirteen-week television series
'This Show May Be Offensive to Heterosexuals.' Between 1977 and
1980, 342 Jarvis Street became a favoured site of collectively produced
theatre and performance art: 'I Feel Guilty,' 'Amazon Acres,' and 'The
Cupettes.' Atthis Theatre, a lesbian and feminist theatre collective, was
founded by LOOT member Keltie Creed in the spring of 1979. The
company's 'maiden performance' was 'A Late Snow' by Jane Chambers
– 'the first all-women, practically almost all-lesbian play published thus
far.'[8]

Though enthusiastically executed and received, not all the lesbian
and feminist culture workshopped at 342 Jarvis Street was of superior
quality and merit. According to Eve Zaremba, 'It was all very simple,
simplistic even, and mostly poor quality, but back then, we were so
thirsty for anything to do with our lives, we didn't care. We were
very uncritical. You couldn't say anything bad. If a woman wrote it,

it was good, which is a terrible way of looking at things because it ain't so and you never get better that way.' Still, many took advantage of opportunities to build confidence, take risks, and test out new, original ideas. Actor Gay Bell enjoyed her theatrical start at LOOT: 'I was supported as a performance artist and I developed a community, which for an artist in a marginal medium is crucial. Without that I don't think I could have done it. I was able to develop a sense of not being an individual artist living in a garret that might produce something of worth a hundred years from now. I learned that I was an artist as an expresser of my community and as a person who could help other lesbians develop their expression.'

To lesbian feminists who had never acted on a stage, written a poem, held a camera, led a coming-out workshop, or danced bare-breasted at a drop-in, the possibilities seemed boundless, exhilarating, unfamiliar, and self-affirming. In the September 1977 issue of the *LOOT Newsletter*, Gay Bell eulogized the Michigan Womyn's Music Festival and the passion it evoked: 'It seems that once women decide to put their energy into women-oriented projects their creativity is immediate and infinite ... There's a new album called 'Lesbian Concentrate' and that's what it felt like. What else would make several hundred women soaked from the weekend sit in the dark under a canopy in the pouring rain, the splash of water being emptied from the roof a rhythm to our giggles and our own solidarity and joy?'[9]

Importantly, impulses to excavate creative potential were not unique to the lesbian community. By the mid-1970s, the women's movement had generated an explosion of attempts to integrate largely white, middle-class feminist ideology and politics with subversive modes of cultural expression. The yield: experimental and disruptive interventions in visual arts, performance, theatre, dance, music, film and video, and literature. As well, there was the always financially precarious institution of feminist performance and exhibition spaces, bookstores, libraries, festivals, workshops, conferences, presses, and periodicals like *Fireweed: A Women's Literary and Cultural Journal*.

In the gay-male community, in addition to the work of individual artists like filmmaker Richard Benner, video artist Colin Campbell, female impersonator Craig Russell, and poet Michael Lynch, a small number of important cultural institutions were founded, such as the Gay Offensive Collective (1977), the 'Our Image' literary supplement to *The Body Politic* (1976), the Sisters of Perpetual Indulgence (1977), and the Buddies in Bad Times Theatre (1978). Among the most vibrant, popular testaments to gay men's social and cultural life were the Radical Faeries; the leather/motorcycle clubs, such as, Spearhead (1969), Lanyards (1974), and Trident (1975); drag performances at the Club Manatee, David's, and the Carriage House; and sports leagues, such as, the Judy Garland Memorial Bowling League (1974) and the Cabbagetown Group Softball League (1977).

In addition to contributing generally to this counter-cultural efflorescence, a number of lesbian feminists were keen to experiment with more traditional modes of political action such as lobbying, education, letter writing, demonstrations, and coalition building. Yet few LOOT regulars were prepared to indulge fully in the physical, emotional, and intellectual demands and sacrifices intrinsic to front-line, direct action. Assuming the role of up-front political activist necessitated a certain degree of outness and comfort with a public profile. In February 1978, a year after LOOT's opening, task-force member Susan Cole articulated a central dilemma: 'The only way we can have political power is if we are all out of the closet and because of our oppression, we are not all out of the closet to make a movement happen ... In terms of expanding the lesbian network, I don't think LOOT is really going to grow if there are not more women who are going to come out publicly. At the same time, I do not want to be a public lesbian ... I think it's bad that I feel this way, but I am not interested in having the first thing somebody says about me is that I am a lesbian.' Sharply, painfully aware of her own and others' implication in perpetuating lesbian invisibility, Cole continued: 'It's the deep contradiction that keeps us down: we don't put our bodies on the line in demonstrations, never mind getting people to speak publicly and do public education. We have trouble being on marches or on the streets. The last one I went to, I had my dark glasses and runners on, it was summer. Winter is different, you've got hats and scarves to cover you up.'[10]

Today, Pat Leslie maintains that 'everything LOOT did was against the law.' The possibility of police raids and charges being laid for selling liquor at 342 Jarvis Street, pandering to minors, or possession of illegal drugs remained a constant threat. At one LOOT-sponsored dance, Natalie LaRoche was arrested by a plainclothes officer for selling beer illegally five minutes after the liquor licence expired. Not only fearful of a criminal record, but of losing jobs, alienating family members and friends, and being the target of public ridicule and abuse, LOOT-goers often found themselves caught between the need for self-protection and the bold, unbridled desire to agitate for lesbian and feminist liberation. For many, vocal political protest was terrifying. Having been an out, politically ardent dyke since 1973, Chris Bearchell was disheartened by what she viewed as trepidation and half-measures. In 1978, she stated: 'It's really a bummer to be one of the only two people called upon to speak as a lesbian 90 per cent of the time. I would really like to be number three. We can count the out public lesbians on two hands.'[11] In 1982, reflecting on their own experiences, Lorna Weir and Eve Zaremba wrote: 'One of the characteristics of dykes is that they are relatively easy to politicize – a process of becoming aware, angry and sensitive to a whole range of issues – and hard to organize. Just try putting out a leaflet or keeping a group together.'[12]

Without minimizing the innumerable obstacles to direct-action politics, most LOOT-goers were intrigued by, and committed to, the prospect of making effective and real change. From the start, they underlined the danger of sinking into what Pat Leslie termed 'cultural feminism.'[13] Writing for *The Other Woman* in 1975, Leslie avowed: 'We know the importance of relating the cultural side of feminism to our political strategies as this is our best weapon, but feminism is not just reading poems or playing the flute ... We are looking inward and being narrow when we take pleasure in celebrating womanhood to the exclusion of all else.'[14]

In January 1977, *The Other Woman* announced that LOOT would have a political interest group and that Toronto lesbian feminists would benefit from planning local political action.[15] For the first time in the short history of feminist, gay, and lesbian activism in Toronto, experimentation with naming a distinctly lesbian-feminist politics and practice seemed not only possible, but compelling. As documented in chapter 1, lesbian projects in the early-to-mid 1970s were founded almost entirely on the need to break down isolation and to give and receive practical support in social settings. Pivotal sites of education, politicization, and the formation of lesbian-feminist subjectivity and community, their primary purpose was an inward focus on safety, security, and self-help – a necessary and arguably political step on the path to confrontation with a hostile world.

At LOOT in early 1977, what a public, outward-focused, lesbian-feminist political praxis would look like, how it would play out, whom it would touch, and in what direction it might go were questions that had no historical precedents. To quote Eve Zaremba, 'There wasn't a lesbian politic that people plugged into, there, already made. We were making it.' In a letter to the LOOT membership date July 1977, Gay Bell identified 'the need to deal with important political dilemmas, i.e., the meanings of lesbian separatism, feminist anarchism, feminist socialism, lesbian feminism and feminist spirituality.'[16] And yet in spite of the bubbling ferment and a new sense of confidence embodied by a handful of seasoned activists, the political committee sputtered, fizzled, and was dormant throughout LOOT's first year. In the light of the diverse political and personal histories of the women attracted to LOOT and the reluctance of many to assume a fully out, public profile, cohesion proved slippery and elusive. Moreover, given that most members believed that 'everything LOOT did was political,' it is conceivable that a committee devoted to politics seemed redundant.[17] It was enough, Fiona Rattray and others argued, that the house existed, that it offered a viable feminist alternative to the bars, and that all lesbians could come and be themselves without fear of censure or rebuke.

From the start, LOOT members had difficulty identifying the particulars of a lesbian politic and its differentiation from feminist or gay discourse and practice. As Lorna Weir recalls, 'There was nothing in the [American] literature, for example, in *The Furies* or *Sappho Was a Right-On Woman*, that gave us guidance on a politic that would help to mobilize lesbians.' Unlike the slate of lesbian rights (such as access to jobs, housing, services, and child custody) prepared by the Lesbian Caucus of the BCFW in 1974–5, LOOT members did not strike a basis of unity or a clearly formulated statement of political purpose and goals. In the absence of a solid agenda, LOOT members found themselves groping tentatively towards some notion of lesbian-feminist politics that might guide their efforts.

The uncertainty of LOOT's future mandate is clearly captured in the December 1976 / January 1977 issue of the newsletter: 'We now have 280 women's names on the mailing list. Questions are being asked: do we want to open a restaurant/disco, do we want to buy a house, do we want to develop into a lesbian political centre for all of Ontario or Canada, do we want to have a newspaper instead of a newsletter?'[18] In February 1978, almost a year after LOOT's first open house, task-force member Brenda Lang emphasized, 'LOOT is not a social club for the pregnant women of Windsor. It is a place where it is really important to everybody who goes there. It is a way of life. It is a necessary thing, plus the fact that there is a smattering of lesbian feminist politics.'[19] Several months later, a summary of

LOOT's accomplishments was published in the newsletter: 'LOOT has grown in leaps and bounds in the past year ... Our efforts are continually being rewarded: fantastic turn-outs at events like Amateur Nite; warm, gratifying drop-ins, an ever-increasing mailing list, and a great response to our poster contest. Most importantly, LOOT has come to represent hope for many women who have not yet come out as lesbians ... Through us women can cast aside their despair to gain the happiness and peace of mind that we all deserve.'[20]

Because concepts of heterosexism and compulsory heterosexuality were only beginning to circulate, it was difficult, if not impossible, to develop a full understanding of lesbian oppression. The lack of concrete, action-oriented projects frustrated a number of prominent LOOT members. At a task-force meeting in the spring of 1978, Pat Leslie claimed: 'The biggest mistake we've made is neglecting the political and educational needs of our community. We accuse the faggots of all kinds of things, but at least they are organizing and we're not.'[21] Reported with pride in the May 1978 issue of the LOOT Newsletter is the statement: 'We are the most visible and diversified organization in Toronto.'[22] However, the only political leadership that LOOT members exercised during the organization's first year was the formation of Women Against Violence Against Women – an anti-violence and antipornography group with a dominant but largely invisible lesbian membership and no lesbianspecific policies. It was not until late 1978 that an ad hoc committee of LOOT members and non-LOOT lesbian activists (from the International Women's Day Committee) combined forces to organize the Bi-National Lesbian Conference in May 1979 on the campus of the University of Toronto.

LINING UP ON SIDE OR BEING SILENT

Without a coherent set of political offensives fashioned within the organization, LOOT members shifted their attention to external political crises. Pressured to take a stand on a succession of developments arising beyond their own doorstep, LOOT members made some decisions with ease; others proved more knotty. Among the fruits of consensus, between 1977 and 1980 they endorsed the Wages Due Lesbians picket of the Supreme Court of Ontario in protest of the unjust treatment of lesbian mothers in child-custody cases. And though not lesbian-specific events, they co-sponsored, in the fall of 1977, a workshop on Women and Alcohol, a public screening of the film *In the Best Interests of Children* and the 'Evolving Woman' lecture series (featuring Florence Kennedy, Phyllis Chesler, and Kate Millett). LOOT representatives signed petitions protesting budget cuts to Nellie's Hostel, the Rape Crisis Centre, and WCREC; they drafted a letter in support of the York University Staff Association strike; and they attended the annual conference of the National Gay Rights Coalition.[23]

Over the course of LOOT's three-year existence, individual members took part in many other political campaigns and initiatives, but infrequently as official LOOT spokeswomen. Given the vast array of concerns raised at monthly general meetings where policies were formulated and passed, the actual number of decisions made and actions taken was small. Amy Gottlieb remembers her own hunger for a sense of satisfaction – something that always seemed just out of reach: 'We never had enough time and we didn't take enough time to really talk about things. Sunday meetings we'd be discussing absolutely everything at once. It was chaos. I always felt I wanted more – more women to be there, more things to happen.'

Even for experienced and skilled activists like Gottlieb, it was difficult to sustain energy, focus, and passion for political work when the gains were so paltry. As one contributor to the November 1977 issue of the *LOOT Newsletter* warned, lesbians were tired: 'So many of us have felt burnout in the past that by now we should have learned to eliminate that burnout feeling from our experience. We should know when we are overextending ourselves, spreading ourselves too thin and simply giving too much energy for too long ... Unless we get some new input and new woman-power, we will stretch ourselves to the limit and take our places among the casualties of the women's movement.'[24]

Familiar to most grass-roots feminist groups, and to LOOT in particular, was the persistent quandary of how to integrate new members into decision-making and task-sharing processes. The belief and hope that all LOOT-goers possessed equal knowledge of feminism, and equal skills and commitment foundered in the face of a radically divergent reality. Shared understanding and experience of feminist praxis could not be presupposed. Unlike the Gay Alliance for Equality (GATE) or the Community Homophile Association (CHAT), there was no education committee struck at LOOT that could have been responsible for both intra-organizational learning and outreach-oriented teaching. Hence, as Eve Zaremba claims, the uneven field made up of differently skilled and differently abled players continually militated against the continuity of process and the accomplishment of tasks: 'If you're open to everybody, the common denominator is that you do nothing, or you focus on whatever happens to be the priority of the group that evening, and it depends on whoever shows up ... The people who were there would be what would happen. Because new women were always coming in to LOOT, it was hard to take something from A to Z, or even half way through the alphabet. Then people get discouraged and say, "Fuck it."'

Debate on contentious issues was commonly marred by internal bickering, a lack of time to organize and present thoughts, and reigning confusion as to what avenues to pursue. Yet not necessarily a negative state of affairs, the confusion also signified an open-ended, unstructured casting about and searching for meaning and direction in the absence of finished blueprints. The overarching theoretical and practical commitment to collective process – no leadership, rotation of administrative tasks, agreement by consensus, and emphasis on personal experience – marked a deliberate attempt to include all lesbians, especially those with little history of political activism. As Judith Bennett outlined in 1978: 'The process of a collective is not a hierarchy; we don't have offices, we don't have a president or a vice-president, there aren't chairmen, there aren't fixed leaders, it changes from time to time ... At LOOT we operate as a group of collectives.'[25] In contrast to their experiences of the silencing, oppressive operations of highly structured, male-dominated groups, LOOT members felt embraced and enabled by the collective model.

However, as was the case for innumerable feminist grass-roots organizations, the 'tyranny of structurelessness' operated to disorganize the focus and the function of the group itself.[26] Recalling her own experiences in the 1970s with the Bread and Roses collective in Boston, Meredith Tax notes, 'Instead of developing strategies, we had fantasies of the future society. In these fantasies, nobody had power; everything was shared or dispersed.'[27] Ruth Dworin recalls, 'There was the myth that women, especially lesbians, were better at working things out, that we'd been spared the corruption of power because we hadn't had it and therefore could learn different ways of operating.' During the course of our interview, seasoned gay liberationist Mary Axten asked me, 'What is a camel?' And before I could respond, she replied, 'A horse designed by a collective.' Years later, most LOOT members recall their frustration with the slow, cumbersome pace of collectively engineered work. They commented on how present-day collectives are still plagued by vexing questions of leadership, power sharing, and structure.[28]

Schisms within the LOOT membership were often suppressed and conflict was avoided during meetings so as to protect the illusion of one happy family. According to Nancy Adamson, 'we held ourselves hostage to our fear of conflict without understanding what was happening.' Rosemary Barnes replays the operative dynamic: 'I learned that disagreement could speedily progress to what appeared to be painful accusation, so I glued my mouth shut and kept my ears open until I could spot what triggered an attack.'[29]

Though the promise of embodied, democratic process and procedures prevailed, the limitations of the consensus model were neither fully discoverable nor contestable from inside positions of intense ideological investment. Those who spoke the loudest, the longest, and with the most regularity were able to exert pressure and influence without being formally accountable for their behaviour. Rather than serve as forums for open discussion and exploration of issues, meetings were often used to publicize positions determined in advance of the meeting proper, in consultation with friends and housemates. Here, the power of friendship circles consolidated through the practice of communal living was evinced in the context of Sunday general meetings. As Adamson recounts: 'It seemed people were already lined up and you had to line up or be silent and then it was very hard to raise questions or to say 'I don't know what I think.' It was like you should arrive knowing and you argued for your position and you attempted to convince those poor misguided people who disagreed with you.' Ruth Dworin echoes Adamson's observation: 'People didn't listen to each other in those meetings. They were into grandstanding and speaking and having themselves heard. There was not a lot of constructive dialogue.'

Referring to the women's movement in general, sociologist and long-time activist Dorothy E. Smith has noted that 'what was politely called dialogue, was generally furious, hurtful, angry and mean conversation, rows, silences.'[30] As it happened repeatedly across the Canadian feminist landscape, dissenters from the dominant line either remained silent or they were trounced and guilt-tripped. 'Trashed' one too many times, a number of LOOT-goers who held positions across the political spectrum gradually withdrew from the fold.[31] To those who stayed and endured, feelings of intimidation, stupidity, and inadequacy were not uncommon. As Ann Kado states: 'Most of the time I spent sitting back trying to figure out what they meant by their 24-letter words. I felt very uneasy and I'd have to turn to a friend for translation. It was all gibberish as far as I was concerned. Every time I turned around or said something I was in constant fear I was going to be politically incorrect. Whatever meeting it was, I had to sit there and concentrate hard and by the time the meeting ended, I'd have such a headache.'

Fiona Rattray shared a similar sense of unease in the midst of the 'power-house' women at LOOT: 'I was always afraid of saying the wrong thing at the wrong time. It took a long time to realize that making a mistake is like snot hanging out of your nose – you wipe it off, you go on with your life. But we were all so caught up in what was politically correct. The tyranny was ironic but no one was prepared to admit it was happening.' Without losing sight of the limitations and pressures of feminist collective process, positions on a number of political questions were eventually determined in LOOT general meetings. These positions, examined in the next two chapters, testify to a particular consistency whether they were recognized as official LOOT policy or not.

7

Coalition politics: Lesbian feminists meet gay liberationists

Our enemies they wish we'd live in silence
They fear us so they often turn to violence
We'll never let them force compliance
Our rights are what we'll have
We will never know our places
We will always be outrageous
We have seen the last of cages
We'll fight until we are free.
Michael Riordan and Heather Ramsay, 1977[1]

In January 1977, district councillors in Dade County, Florida, passed an ordinance that prohibited discrimination on the basis of affectional or sexual preference in areas of housing, employment, and services. A landmark victory for gay and lesbian activists, the decision was appealed and overturned in June 1977. Anita Bryant – former Miss America and reigning promoter of Florida orange juice – became the quintessential symbol of rising antigay and antilesbian forces across North America. Bryant's 'Save Our Children' campaign, coordinated and financed by fundamentalist Christian organizations, was intended to exploit the dominant discursive equation of homosexuality and child molestation. Pledging to continue the crusade against homosexuals and their 'perverse, abominable and dangerous' lifestyle, Bryant set out to galvanize anti-homosexual forces in Minneapolis, San Antonio, and San Francisco.

The first major defeat in the struggle for gay and lesbian civil rights in the United States, the Dade County case unfolded in the context of a mobilizing American New Right. Signs of emerging moral conservatism were evinced in reinvigorated organizing and rhetoric that was explicitly anti-abortion, anti–Equal Rights Amendment, anti-affirmative action, antipornography, and pro-family. Consistent with the shift of gender and sexual issues to the political centre in the mid-1970s, the Dade County ruling inaugurated a new wave of violence, state persecution, and legal initiatives directed against minority sexual populations and the commercial sex industry.[2] At the same time, deepening gender/sexual repression was not separable from the larger political and economic climate of escalating inflation, anti-union and pro–Ku Klux Klan organizing, mounting unemployment, and the imminence of economic recession.

As news of the Dade County defeat spread across the U.S./Canada border, organizing efforts in opposition to Bryant's anti-homosexual crusade were launched in most large Canadian cities.[3] For a period of almost one year, mainstream media coverage of the crusade prompted vociferous public debate over homosexuality and homophobia.[4] Former LOOT member and gay liberationist Chris Bearchell commented: 'Anita Bryant did [gays and lesbians] a big favour. She broke the gay story in the mainstream press. If they wanted to cover her, they had to cover us, and she was big news.' The scope and tenor of the stories and letters printed in the *Toronto Sun*, *Toronto Star*, *Globe and Mail*, and religious papers like the *Catholic Register* reveal deep-seated antigay and antilesbian hostilities.[5] *Toronto Sun* columnist Claire Hoy described homosexuals as 'morally bankrupt,' 'perverse,' and 'sick,' and then warned his readers of 'the need to protect children from their clawing hands and demented aspirations.' Building directly on the 'Save Our Children' gospel, Hoy exclaimed: '[Homosexuals] want society to condone and institutionalize their disgusting activity so they can then reach out into the schools and twist young minds into thinking they can somehow get fulfillment from this nefarious lifestyle.'[6]

In Toronto, the Ad Hoc Coalition to Stop Anita Bryant was formed in June 1977, coordinated by the Coalition for Gay Rights in Ontario and composed of members from GATE, the John Damien Defense Committee, the Metropolitan Community Church, and CHAT.[7] Representatives from the Revolutionary Marxist Group, the League for Socialist Action and Wages Due Lesbians also attended meetings. A small, loose contingent of LOOT members decided to join the coalition. Convinced of the pressing need to combat Bryant's 'hysterical hate campaign' and its backing by religious and New Right strategists, Chris Bearchell, Fiona Rattray, and several other gay-liberationist members of LOOT plunged themselves into protest work (but not as official LOOT representatives until January 1978).[8] Though keenly aware of the limitations of the cosmetic ideal of gay and lesbian unity, they attended meetings, drafted and distributed leaflets, and helped to plan two summer-time demonstrations. They were also encouraged by the release of the *Life Together* report issued by the Ontario Human Rights Commission in July which, in response to a five-year lobby by largely gay-male activists, recommended the immediate inclusion of sexual orientation in the provincial human-rights code.[9]

As reported in *The Body Politic* and the *Militant*, on 25 June 1977 300 gay men, lesbians, and supporters marched in and out of bars chanting 'Out of the bars, into the streets, gay liberation now,' and on 22 July 700 attended a rally outside city hall.[10] Together, these two public actions signified an unparalleled surge in the history of post-Stonewall gay and lesbian organizing in Toronto. The summer also marked the eruption of national actions across Canada. The National Gay Rights Coalition passed a highly publicized motion calling on the federal government to prevent Anita Bryant's entry into Canada. Splashed across posters, the headline 'Stop Fooling Yourself – Civil Rights Are Your Concern' reminded Toronto gays and lesbians of the need for protection against discrimination in housing, employment, and services. Significantly, it secured legislative reform as *the* key focus of gay-liberationist energy.

Anita Bryant's invitation to Toronto in January 1978 by Reverend Ken Campbell of the People's Church sparked an intensified need for local, organized protest. Campbell's Renaissance International, the Fishers of Men, the Faith Baptist Church, and the Edmund Burke Society began to mobilize in support of Bryant. For lesbians and gay men, the question of derailing the 'Save Our Children' crusade became much more than one of solidarity with American brothers and sisters. *The Body Politic* reported that the Bryant campaign promised 'seed money' to any Canadian group wanting to organize in opposition to gay-rights legislation.[11] Dormant for a year, the LOOT political committee began convening in January and sent representatives to meetings of the Ad Hoc Committee to Stop Anita Bryant.[12]

A mass rally and dance at the St Lawrence Market on 14 January 1978 attracted over 1000 gay men, lesbians, and friends.[13] The following day, five hundred protesters braved arctic conditions to set up a picket line outside of the People's Church in Willowdale while Bryant was inside leading Sunday morning prayers.[14] To Chris Bearchell,

'Anita Bryant was the most visible manifestation of the Right inter-
fering in our community at that time.' As Naomi Brooks recalls, 'It
was clear she wanted to get all of us; it was a Hitler kind of crusade.'
And as Gay Bell reminisces, 'It's hard to recreate what it felt like.
It was very emotional. It was shocking to have someone with that
kind of profile in the media making remarks about our core being.'

It was also significant, argues Bearchell, that speakers at the rallies
made explicit the connections between 'outrageous homophobia' and
the denial of custody rights to lesbian mothers, the deportation of
Jamaican domestic workers, and recent government attacks on social
spending and job security. Rallying mottoes printed out on chant sheets
– 'Gays, Women, Children Unite! Same Struggle, Same Fight,' 'Gays,
Women, All Workers Unite! Same Enemy, Same Fight,' and 'Lesbian
Liberation Now!' – illustrate self-conscious efforts to forge links be-
tween oppressions. Among the feminist organizations in attendance
were Times Change (women's employment service), Nellie's Hostel,
Toronto Women's Hostel, the March 8th Coalition, Women's Credit
Union, WCREC, the Women's Educational Press, and WAVAW.

LOOT members tended to disagree on the meaning of the Bryant
crusade and on an appropriate set of responses. As Gay Bell recalls,
'At LOOT, there was considerable cold-shouldering and disapproval
for being involved in gay male politics. To me, it always felt like walking
along a razor blade.' Radical feminists and separatists, in conjunction
with members of Wages Due Lesbians, were more concerned to elu-
cidate the differences between lesbians and gay men in defiance of
what Pat Murphy saw as 'common-sense efforts to lump us all together.' They maintained that Anita Bryant's campaign was not directly
about them – it was largely about gay-male sexual practice, and pedophilia in particular, which was, in their view, *neither* a lesbian nor
a feminist issue.

Even though lesbian and straight feminists had argued since the early
1970s that almost all sexual abuse of children is done by heterosexual
men, the LOOT membership (with few exceptions) condemned the
increasingly public, 'exotic' character of (some) gay men's penchant for
man-boy love (see the next section). In particular, they were disturbed
by what they viewed as the exploitative character of adult/child sexual
relations. Consequently, as described in chapter 5, the long-standing
disenchantment of LOOT members with highly visible and articulate
gay-male sexual culture resurfaced. Some LOOT task-force members
maintained that a focus on pedophilia invited the organized wrath of

moral conservatives and, in so doing, jeopardized lesbian and gay struggles for legal protection from discrimination and for liberation more broadly defined.

Frustrated and angered by earlier, unhappy confrontations with gay men's sexism, if not overt antifeminism, many radical feminists and separatists were leery of, and in some cases, virulently opposed to, yet another attempt to construct an alliance. Even when political interests appeared to coincide, collaboration was more easily argued in talk than executed in practice. Indeed, from the standpoint of the majority of LOOT-goers, the first signs of organized anti-Bryant protest were hardly reassuring. As Pat Murphy, Susan Cole, and others recall, the 'ugly, blatantly misogynist' tactics deployed by gay-male activists (and borrowed, in part, from the tradition of gay men's drag and camp) could not be countenanced. Murphy argued, 'It was the same old thing – burn the witch! My heart broke when I'd see [Bryant] with a pie in her face. It hurt me to see her like that.' From the printing of buttons and T-shirts that proclaimed 'Anita Sucks Oranges,' 'Squeeze Anita Out,' and 'Anita Dear, Cram It,' to the delivery of antiwoman speeches and the burning of the Miss Orange Juice Queen in effigy, LOOT members disparaged all initiatives that they felt smacked of woman-hatred.

Many LOOT-goers were influenced by the criticisms made by some American feminists. At a June 1977 rally of women who had separated from the Gay Pride and anti-Bryant demonstration in New York, lesbian poet Adrienne Rich charged that 'Anita was equated with Hitler, or viciously lampooned in terms of her female anatomy by gay men ... The woman-hating tone of large sections of the marches reasserted to us that we could not find real "brotherly" solidarity in the gay movement.'[15] Speaking of gay men who participated in the Toronto anti-Bryant protests, Susan Cole lashed out: '"Cunt," "Bitch," they fumed as they marched down the street. I and others got the sense that Anita Bryant was being used as a convenient target for what was plainly unadulterated woman-hating. For my part, it didn't matter a damn whether it was the fundamentalists who were willing to serve her up as sacrifice or whether it was the boys venting their anger at womankind. It was all the patriarchy to me.'

Aware that Bryant was implicated in discourse and practices that produced gay and lesbian oppression, the majority of LOOT members none the less felt that she was coerced – the puppet of a powerful though mostly invisible male-dominated regime.[16] Thus, they tended not to hold her entirely responsibile and blameworthy because she was a woman whose *alleged* or *apparent* power to direct and accomplish antigay and antilesbian violence was, Murphy, Cole, and others insisted, illusory.[17] The essentialism of notions of women's natural superiority and universal victimization undergirded and gave shape to feelings of protectiveness harboured by most LOOT members *and* straight radical feminists. Indeed, this was a position that carried serious consequences for the depth and breadth of LOOT's commitment to counterattack.

Importantly, however, not all lesbians agreed with the dominant interpretation advanced by most LOOT-goers. Betty, an older gay woman who came out through A Woman's Place but was not a LOOT regular, contended: 'I was so happy when [Anita Bryant] got the pie in the face. I was sorry I didn't do it. I thought it was great. And with the effigy, I would have liked to have been with the boys lighting the first match.' Deb Stinson, a working-class lesbian who had one foot in bar culture and the other in lesbian feminism, explained her position: 'It didn't matter to me that most LOOT women thought that all women were precious. Anita Bryant was fucking me over and that was the bottom line. Being a woman did not excuse her behaviour.' Even within the regular LOOT membership, there was a certain measure of dissent. As Gay Bell asserted: 'The effigy didn't bother me. I also liked the Sisters of Perpetual Indulgence. I don't feel that women are holy and I had no trouble criticizing right-wing women. In fact, it's important to satirize them.' Yet there were few opportunities at LOOT to facilitate a wide-ranging airing of competing analyses.

One meeting of the revived political committee was held at 342 Jarvis Street in early January. Though a number of LOOT members joined coalition committees, instructed gay men on the inappropriateness of 'burn the bitch' tactics, and provided a speaker for the 14 January rally, the organization itself did not assume a position of full, public leadership. This did not mean that lesbian feminists felt distanced from, or uninspired by, the anti-Bryant crusade. Many of the women I interviewed remember the hundreds of angry lesbian feminists present at the January demonstrations and the exuberance engendered by such historically unmatched visibility. However, the lack of leadership, from start to finish, reflected the lack of consensus among LOOT members. Clearly, the ubiquitous desire to devise some semblance of unity among lesbian feminists, however tenuous, was more important than the triumph of one ideological position over another.

Concomitantly, the same fear of conflict that operated internally to thwart the resolution of contentious issues within LOOT, combined with the tentative grasp of new, anti-heterosexist discourse, meant that there was viritually no critical treatment of the anti-Bryant campaign in the *LOOT Newsletter*.[18] Nor was critical commentary carried in other Canadian lesbian or feminist periodicals. Given the potential power of print to educate and mobilize constituencies, this absence was disenabling.

Members of LOOT's task force convened in late January 1978 to evaluate their participation in the coalition and to contemplate their future actions. The dialogue reproduced in part below (originally taped in February 1978) displays a degree of discord that extended beyond Bryant's crusade to the broader question of LOOT's emphasis and priorities.[19] It reflects the residual reluctance of several LOOT leaders to place anti-Bryant activism atop the organization's agenda:

Chris Bearchell: We have been political but we have not taken responsibility for anything yet. Anita Bryant is coming back to town in April and the feminist and lesbian element really manipulated and, in a sense, led the last action against Bryant. But LOOT didn't initiate that action – we effectively took it over and led it. The next time we should not bother waiting for others to initiate it but do it ourselves.

Judith Bennett: I think that might be laying a guilt trip on us. It's too destructive. We can't get too overtly political or we will kill ourselves. We are just not strong. When we took over their organized thing last time, let's face it, we fucked it up ... and we don't have it together enough to organize one when we fucked it up before.

Chris Bearchell: If we don't have a response to Bryant it will be interpreted that there is more support for her than there is. We tried to make it clear last time to the women in the world that Bryant was not just a homophobic evangelical asshole but also the thin edge of the wedge of the anti-feminist forces from the States. We really didn't get that across. Whatever the media deliberately buries is probably the most important part of it and they buried the feminist response to Bryant. I don't feel like we can let them get away with that.

Brenda Lang: I feel that we dramatize her campaign ... and feed her with something to hit us with ... I'd prefer to put that energy into something that's going to get us going rather than hold us back because we're always involved with that and not involved with fulfilling our own needs.

Judith Bennett: Yes, I think that also by ignoring her we can pay attention to other needs in our community, and people will suffer if those aren't paid attention to. It's a matter of priorities.

Chris Bearchell: She puts people back into the closet in droves. It's not an exaggeration when the gay movement says she's responsible for deaths in the States – that happened, and I would feel like I was turning my back on that if I didn't do something ... I think it's possible to sustain the things we need for our community and be able to respond when we feel like we're being offended like that.

Caught up in their own ambivalence towards working with gay men, frustrated by their inability to arrive at consensus, and divided on the objectives of the organization, LOOT members did not mount a unified response to the 'Save Our Children' campaign. Divisions within the membership surfaced along broad radical-feminist and socialist-feminist lines. And with almost no history or experience of mediating different political positions within lesbian activism, compromise proved problematic. At the same time, it became clear that gay-male activists were resistant to, if not threatened by, the prospect of sharing leadership with, or ceding leadership to, lesbian feminists.[20] As Amy Gottlieb recalls, 'Gay men, in their typical way, weren't open to lesbians being represented as much as we needed to be represented. But still, gay men couldn't ignore LOOT members.'

According to Fiona Rattray, 'Mostly LOOT's work consisted of marching in the streets, "gaycotting" orange juice and occasional letter writing.' But overall, the absence of bodies needed to accomplish the work impeded a vigorous, offensive program of action. To quote Natalie LaRoche: 'I don't think the demos or rallies raised the profile of LOOT. They raised the visibility of lesbians, and LOOT was there, LOOT was strongly there, but it was invisible largely because a lot of people were so scared of being out. I repressed the fear, but there were a lot of people who were just terrified.'

From the beginning, lesbian feminists acknowledged the danger of the 'Save Our Children' campaign.[21] However, they were also aware that a civil-rights strategy was insufficient to combat the sexual *and* gender oppression experienced by lesbians, hence their endorsement of legal reform as a politically smart yet insufficient priority.[22] The majority of LOOT members believed that reform offered gay men the right to the same status and privileges accorded straight men.[23] Additionally, they resisted traditional forms of organizing and decision making adopted by gay-male coalition leaders (for instance, single-issue, mass-action lobbying and an elected executive). Conceptualizing themselves alongside gay men as a 'sexual minority' had definite appeal for LOOT members, particularly as a strategy to garner short-term political gains. Yet for those who were keen to define and defend a lesbian-feminist identity that was distinct from gay maleness, such a strategy was singularly incomplete.

By January 1978, a handful of LOOT representatives did work closely with the coalition and they succeeded in challenging some aspects of gay men's behaviour, such as, sexist language and hierarchical process. Radical feminists tended to dispute the utility of converging lesbian and gay-male communities, and yet they could not easily ignore the sequence of developments that placed gay men and lesbians not only under public scrutiny, but also under siege.

MEN LOVING BOYS LOVING MEN: THE SPECTRE OF PEDOPHILIA

In early August of 1977, Toronto's mainstream media reported that Emanuel Jaques, a 12-year-old Portuguese shoe-shine boy, was murdered on the rooftop of a Yonge Street massage parlour by a 'homosexual mob.'[24] 'The victim of a lengthy homosexual orgy,' Jaques became a touchstone for the same 'Maple Leaf Mini-Bryants' who had earlier voiced their opposition to the inclusion of sexual-orientation protection in the provincial Human Rights Code. Demonized as folk devils, the entire community of gay men was held openly accountable for the crime. Though lesbians were not explicitly named in the attack, gay liberationists like Chris Bearchell and Konnie Reich recall that the smear campaign represented 'the thin edge of the wedge.' To Bearchell, 'The media always buried lesbians under the gay-male referent – homosexual. But we knew that when they came for the perverts, we would not be spared.'

Outraged by the Jaques killing, Toronto's Portuguese community demonstrated on the streets and vented their fury at the ugly and senseless crime. Influenced by dominant media accounts, many carried cards that read: 'stamp out gays,' 'kill the homosexuals,' 'hang the perverts,' 'bring back capital punishment,' and 'clean up Yonge Street.'[25]

As criminologist Yvonne Chi-Ying Ng argues, 'The relationship between homosexual behaviour, pedophilia and murderous acts became
a cluster of images that cemented in the public mind.'[26]

On 21 November 1977, *The Body Politic* mailed out issue no. 39 to
subscribers and bookstores. The issue contained the article 'Men Loving Boys Loving Men' by Gerald Hannon – the third in a series of
three on this theme.[27] Written from the standpoint of a boy-lover himself, the tone and content of the spread suggested competing desires
to confess, educate, and provoke. In five consecutive columns leading
up to and following the publication of issue no. 39, Claire Hoy of
the *Toronto Sun* vilified 'radical homosexuals' and their 'rag,' *The Body
Politic*.[28] Referring to homosexuals as 'filthy garbage' and 'child rapers,'
he called for immediate police action against the newspaper. The office
of *The Body Politic* was raided by the Metropolitan Toronto Police and
the Ontario Provincial Police on 30 December 1977.[29] Charged under
the Criminal Code with using the mails for the purpose of transmitting
and delivering obscene, indecent, immoral, and scurrilous material
(Section 169) and with possession for the purpose of distribution (Section 159), the paper's collective members mobilized. They hired a lawyer, formed the Free *The Body Politic* Defense Fund (composed of five
gay men and five lesbians), and brought a list of demands to anti–Anita
Bryant rallies.

By early January 1978, Toronto's gay and lesbian communities were
reeling from the chaos induced by a remarkably dense historical and
political conjuncture: the onset of the Jaques murder trial; Anita Bryant's impending visit; the legal, political, and financial defence of *The
Body Politic*; and the official hearings at the Ontario legislature on
sexual-orientation legislation scheduled for February. In the midst of
this penetrating public focus on homosexuality and the ensuing scram-
ble of gay liberationists to take charge, most lesbian feminists were
busy with WAVAW and with plans for an International Women's Day
celebration. A small collection of LOOT members, many of whom had
participated in the Stop Anita Bryant Coalition in the summer of 1977,
argued that *The Body Politic* must be defended and that LOOT needed
to take a strong, principled stand against state censorship and police
and media harassment. Not all lesbian feminists agreed with this argument and disputes arose concerning LOOT's priorities.

A meeting of LOOT's newly resurrected political committee held
in early January 1978 to discuss the 'Men Loving Boys Loving Men'
crisis signalled one of few conscious attempts made to generate analysis

and to formulate and implement policy. Though the debate unleashed fundamental disagreement on multiple levels, most lesbian feminists agreed that the bad timing of the article could have been prevented. Published when it was, they argued, it endangered the civil-rights campaign that seemed to be gaining momentum. Bluntly told, void of nuance, the sensationalist account worked to feed and reinforce the myth of the homosexual child molester, hence providing right-wing organizers with fuel for their 'pro-family,' anti-homosexual backlash. In fact, some LOOT members and a handful of outspoken gay men believed that the exposé confirmed their own and the general public's worst fears about homosexuals and served to grease the wheels of Anita Bryant's powerful 'Save Our Children' machine.[30]

Many LOOT members felt that the portrayal of men loving boys tested and ultimately broke the already strained back of joint lesbian/gay activism. Uttered in the context of WAVAW's recent formation and a refocused, antiviolence feminism, the statement initially formulated during anti-Bryant organizing – 'pedophilia is neither a lesbian nor a feminist issue' – was recapitulated with a renewed, steely confidence. During the debate at LOOT in January 1978, Darlene Lawson made her perspective clear: 'Believe me, to most of the people I've talked to, LOOT should not be associated with condoning pedophilia. It could be argued that *The Body Politic* boys brought the bust on themselves ... So if we're going to talk about the rights of lesbians and LOOT, maybe we shouldn't take a position at all on this thing.'[31]

Spokeswomen for the newly formed Lesbian Mothers Defense Fund (LMDF) were among the most vigorous and persuasive critics of cross-generational sex. Positioning themselves as moral guardians and recasting maternal feminist rhetoric of the nineteenth century, they argued for the 'innocence' of children. Francie Wyland exhorted: '[We] are outraged at *The Body Politic*'s glorification of child molestation by homosexual men ... Articles like "Men Loving Boys" give Anita Bryant more ammunition by misrepresenting what our struggle is about.'[32] An ardent supporter of the LMDF, Winnipeg-born lesbian-feminist comic Robin Tyler was quoted in *The Body Politic*, saying the article 'was inopportune, tacky, poorly researched and written. Pedophilia is not our issue. Children are in a one-down socio-economic position. Seducing them is simply not right.'[33]

Disturbed, even outraged, by homophobic *Toronto Sun* columnist Claire Hoy, some lesbian feminists were none the less quick to point out that his tirades against 'gutter queens,' 'the limp-wristed set,' and 'militant homosexuals' referred to gay men. It was no secret, Susan Cole and others avowed, that *The Body Politic* was a 'boys' paper,' with 'pathetically minuscule lesbian content' and no solid commitment to the specificities of lesbian and feminist liberation. As Darlene Lawson wryly suggested: 'Would it really destroy the lesbian movement in this community or this country if *The Body Politic* was not operating?'[34] Indeed, some LOOT leaders continued, *The Body Politic* had courted the wrath of police and politicians for years. So, they concluded, if it had not been this particular sex-related scandal, it would have been something else that had little or nothing to do with women, lesbian or straight. Former collective member of *The Body Politic* Ed Jackson remembers his dismay at the intensely negative criticism of 'Men Loving Boys' voiced by many lesbian feminists (and, not insignificantly, some gay men). However, he is quick to note the almost non-existent gender-mixed infrastructure within lesbian and gay political organizing during this period that may have furnished a context for productive dialogue.

Most of all, though aggravated by the ill-timed release of the article and the exaggerated reminder of the newspaper's androcentrism, LOOT-goers experienced a sense of rage that cut across their ideological differences. A long-time member of the Revolutionary Marxist Group (later the Revolutionary Workers League), Amy Gottlieb recalls that 'there was a general feeling that it was awful and terrible and how could men do this to boys and there must be something wrong with these men and they're really beyond the pale, and no wonder we didn't want to have anything to do with them. I know for myself, I was pretty outraged at the time.'

At LOOT general meetings and in several public forums following the raid, members spoke out against the sexual, economic, physical, and emotional inequalities between gay men and young boys. In their interviews with me, they remembered being furious with the romanticization of adult/youth love and the exploitation of the power wielded by adult males over children, particularly young girls. Former psychiatric nurse and youth counsellor Pat Murphy was a high-profile, vocal critic: '[Gay men] didn't see the relationship between power and sexuality ... They'd have sexual relationships with a young kid that they'd taken to McDonald's for a hamburger and they'd say he's all willing and he likes it ... It was all romantic sexuality that was to their own advantage. It's like paying five bucks at McDonald's for an all-day blow job.' A teacher at an alternative elementary school, Ruth Dworin recalls that she had a hard time with pedophiles: 'My students and I ran into Dick (a pseudonym) on the street car and he was wearing a GATE button. He made a pass at one of my 7-year-olds. I wanted to strangle him. It was totally inappropriate. I wanted my students to meet a real, live gay man, but this was not the kind of education I wanted to give them.'

Disallowing the 'Men Loving Boys' article as a 'celebration of sex,'[35] many lesbian feminists railed against the lack of power and privilege of young boys. Not only, they argued, did Gerald Hannon's standpoint assure a foregrounding of adult-male sexual desire, it secured the erasure of meaning/s that the boys themselves attached to cross-generational sexual encounters. A year after the first printing of the article, Lorna Weir considered its shortcomings in a review essay for *The Body Politic*: 'It would have been hard for the *men* not to define the boys in terms of the adult needs they fulfilled. Of course, this really isn't so different from the way men define women for men's needs, as floosies or nursemaids or saints, depending on the needs of the moment. But if men involved with boys see them as the embodiment of lost innocence, or as sensual creatures completely unencumbered by adult guilt, then they're failing to deal with them as whole, complex human beings with needs of their own.'[36]

In the context of LOOT general meetings and one scheduled debate at 342 Jarvis Street in January 1978, almost all LOOT members agreed that the content of 'Men Loving Boys Loving Men' was troublesome. However, there was no unified position on the nature and form of a politically effective response beyond the feminist critique of inequality. Whereas the inclusion of sexual-orientation protection in the Human Rights Code was supported unanimously by lesbian feminists as a principal though partial objective of gay/lesbian liberation, there was no agreement on the role of the state vis-à-vis 'obscene' materials and 'age of consent' laws.

Lesbian feminists of all political stripes condemned the police seizure of twelve shipping cartons full of materials from *The Body Politic* office (including lists of subscribers) and the laying of charges against Pink Triangle Press. Recognizing the assault – the depth and severity of which were unknown to lesbian institutions – they were shaken by such a vulgar display of injustice. And yet different interpretations held by LOOT members on the role of the state evoked different assessments of the appropriate response. Only two months earlier, a band of radical feminists from LOOT and WAVAW descended upon Mayor Crombie's office demanding the closure of the *Snuff* film at

Cinema 2000 and aligning themselves with the 'Clean Up Yonge Street' campaign and, inadvertently, against sex workers in ways that recalled their efforts to circumvent the anti–massage parlour by-law in 1975 (see chapter 2). In a letter to *The Body Politic* in 1978, Pat Leslie cautioned against support for state censorship laws that 'could conceivably be used against us.'[37] And yet, at the same time, Eve Zaremba, Susan Cole, and other joint members of WAVAW and LOOT began to argue for the necessary involvement of the state (via the Criminal Code, customs regulations, and censor boards) to legislate against 'pornographic material' that, according to Zaremba, not only 'taught the hatred of women,' but also 'promoted child abuse.'[38] In concert with feminist antiporn organizations in the United States that also formed in late 1977, Zaremba, Cole, and others began a call for state-adminstered penalties against the owners of the commercial pornography industry – 'the purveyors of violence against women' – a call that foreshadowed the infamous Minneapolis Ordinance designed by antipornography crusaders Catharine MacKinnon and Andrea Dworkin in 1983.[39]

Darlene Lawson avowed during the January 1978 debate on *The Body Politic* that enlisting state agents to censor such 'damaging' accounts as 'Men Loving Boys Loving Men' was not only conceivable, but it was a justified strategy.[40] Ironically, it was one that also appealed to right-wing lobbyists. Only weeks earlier, Claire Hoy had demanded the repeal of two small Ontario arts grants awarded to *The Body Politic* on the grounds that 'our taxes are helping to promote the abuse of children' (a demand that anticipated Jesse Helms's homophobic assault on the National Endowment of the Arts in 1990 and *Toronto Sun* columnist Christina Blizzard's attack on the 'flagrant misuse of state funds' by the AIDS Committee of Toronto in 1992 and the Toronto-based Inside/Out lesbian and gay film/video collective in 1993).[41]

AGE OF CONSENT LAWS: THE DILEMMA OF PROTECTION

Though opposed to the criminalization of homosexual sex under the age of twenty-one, the majority of LOOT members were more concerned with how the abolition of age-of-consent laws – a central plank of the National Gay Rights Coalition's platform – would eliminate all judicial measures to prohibit the sexual violation of heterosexual girls and women.[42] A number of LOOT members told me of the pain, humiliation, and fear of unwanted, forced sexual relations with adult heterosexual men. It was often these women, along with the advocates of lesbian mothers, whose angry, impassioned accounts were first and foremost heard and taken seriously at LOOT. Other women added the knowledge that they had gained from work with battered women and children in hostels, rape crisis centres, counselling centres, prisons, and psychiatric hospitals. And refusing to confine discussion of violence to straight men, Pat Murphy and friends retold tales of 'gay men fucking little boys in the basement of the CHAT centre.' Out of these overlapping stories, analysis of women's and children's sexual exploitation by men began to emerge as the dominant feminist discourse at LOOT, WAVAW, the Rape Crisis Centre, and a number of other feminist organizations in the city.[43]

Many LOOT-goers (and straight feminists) were suspicious of claims to consensual sex, whether straight or gay. As stated by Susan Cole, 'Gay men were interested in eliminating age-of-consent laws so that they could find many, many dozen more holes into which they could plug their penises.' Cole and others were not encouraged by the stories that some gay men, as teenagers, delighted in the sexual education they sought and received from older men, or that virtually all boys, as males, are taught to view themselves as sexual subjects. That intergenerational sex among males often entailed a positive and genuinely different experience from intergenerational heterosex was not a tradition with which women, lesbian or straight, identified. In effect, once issues of de facto male sexual power were linked with sexual abuse, there was little room for oppositional narratives.[44]

Working with children as a child-care or day-care worker, a teacher, a youth counsellor, or a girl-guide leader, a lesbian often struggled to hide her sexuality for fear of losing her job. Adult lesbians, most LOOT members contended, were lovers of adult woman-identified women – they were not child molesters, nor did they sexually desire children. As Amy Gottlieb recalls, 'There was a need to say we were really different and, by implication, we wouldn't do *this* with young girls.' Only one narrator mentioned having had sex with an older woman, while two women told me about the sex they had experienced with underage female partners. Perhaps a compulsion to disengage from the messiness of one's past in the service of a politically consistent present prevented others from disclosing similiar acts. Even the lesbian 'crush' popularized by singer/songwriter Meg Christian's 'Ode to a Gym Teacher' (1974) was eulogized in language reminiscent of nineteenth-century ennobling of same-gender romantic friendships.

Ultimately, notwithstanding Jane Rule's heretical wish 'to make adults easier to seduce,' breaking the cross-generational taboo was incongruent with 1970s right-on, reciprocal, relational love between adult, women-identified women.[45] Several years after LOOT's closure, Chris Bearchell remembered the pain of her own sexually active youth (which led her to involvement in youth liberation in Edmonton). In 1983, she wrote: 'There are lesbians doing time in Canada because they've been convicted of gross indecency, because their lovers are under twenty-one. There are lesbians who've opted for suicide rather than face that prospect. They deserve support, not silence.'[46]

Several young lesbians at LOOT called for the abolition of age-of-consent laws (in concert with organized gay liberation), but their call was either ignored or dismissed.[47] LOOT members elected to place a young person's right to protection from exploitation over and above what they perceived as a misguided libertarian emphasis on sexual freedom. There was also conflict among the membership regarding such issues as the calibration of age difference: for instance, What age limits (if any) are appropriate in determining when the impermissible becomes permissible? How do gay and lesbian youth who seek sex from adults make sense of this desire in view of unequal power relations based on age? Given the unpredictable playing out of seduction and the enormous complexity of adult/child sexual relations, can a young person really know what s/he is consenting to?

Consonant with bourgeois norms of propriety, members of LOOT seemed partial to century-old notions of childhood as the age of vulnerability to be guarded at all costs from adult corruption.[48] American theorist Gayle Rubin argues: 'The notion that sex per se is harmful to the young has been chiseled into extensive social and legal structures (i.e., statutory rape laws) designed to insulate minors from sexual knowledge and experience.'[49] In the absence of organized protest, the heterosexist bedrock of the law and the rootedness of age-of-consent rhetoric in the patriarchal definition of children as property remained in place. Cognizant of this tension, most LOOT members felt that securing some sort of legal protection for young girls was a necessary yet unsatisfactory pursuit.

A non-conforming voice at LOOT belonged to Evelyn (Lilith) Finkler. A teenager and one of the six young lesbians who introduced a pro-abolition position on age-of-consent law to the BiNational Lesbian Conference in 1979, she recalls her unpopular stance: 'I remember trying to talk about age of consent and how I found the law really oppressive and how it was important to encourage child sexuality. We don't immediately become sexual at the age of 18 or 21, and if one of the tenets of feminism was control over our own bodies, I thought, "Why can't that be extended to children?" I was sexually abused and I still felt that the age-of-consent laws were wrong. But women at LOOT didn't want to hear what I had to say because it was inconvenient.'

Lesbian feminists in several other organizations across the country established formal policy on age-of-consent laws, but there was no uniformity among them. In 1975, the Lesbian Caucus of the British Columbia Federation of Women (BCFW) stated: 'The present laws provide some protection against the sexual exploitation of young women. Abolition of age of consent laws would worsen the situation.'[50] Contrarily, Toronto's Lesbian Caucus of GATE took a position in favour of the abolition of age-of-consent laws, as did Gay Youth Toronto.[51] A delegate at the NGRC conference in 1975, Chris Bearchell reported: 'Two lesbians, age 16 and 18, felt that people over the age of 21 should base their decision on the recommendation of those under 21 – so, youth speaking for themselves ... No one under the age of 21 spoke in opposition to the abolition of age of consent laws.'[52]

Years later, reflecting on the broad question of sexual self-determination, Lorna Weir laments the lost opportunity to expand feminist discourse to include young women whose sexual agency is subject to both parental and state control: 'Age of consent was bred out of lesbian politics as a potential area of interest and debate and that struck me as manifestly untrue and shortsighted because of delinquency charges. Adolescent women, lesbian and straight, were paying a terrible price for being actively sexual. But then again, this was the era of jackboot lesbian feminism.' The need for a more creative, nuanced approach to the state's regulation of youth sexuality was outlined by Lisa at the LOOT task force meeting in the spring of 1978. Arguing that 'the age-of-consent laws do not articulate the nature of the oppression, and, in fact, are used against lesbian and gay people,' she asserted: 'There must be another way of defining rape or molestation under the law which recognizes the vulnerability of children to assault and violation, but doesn't preclude [their] right across the board to engage in non-coercive sexual involvement with adults.'[53] Had girlhood memories of lust for older women been an admissible subject of dialogue at LOOT, recognition of the disjuncture between practice and ideology may have opened up space for the formation of alternative strategies. Instead, lesbian feminists and supporters tended to apply an analysis of unequal power in adult/child heterosexual relations to adult/youth homosexual relations without considering how same-gender sex might fundamentally alter the dynamic.

DIVIDED LOYALTIES AND THE UNFAMILIARITY OF NEGOTIATION

Though the lines were not impermeable, political differences among LOOT members surfaced and structured debate on *The Body Politic* crisis. Not only did most radical feminists resist working with gay men; they identified the 'Men Loving Boys Loving Men' emergency as a gay men's struggle from which they would benefit little. Despite not being regular readers or contributors to *The Body Politic*, they resented not having been consulted before the decision to publish the controversial article. They were horrified by the raw, brutal OPP/Metro Police incursion; however, their ambivalence towards all forms of male sexuality led to both tacit and openly expressed support (along-side moral conservatives) for state regulation of male homosexual pornography and, by extension, all gay-male sexual expression. In effect, the slide from criticism of sexual practice and representation to support for state sexual censorship was riddled with flaws, not least of all the deflection away from the root causes of sexual and gender inequality in capitalist, racist, and patriarchal culture.

Those women who either felt closely aligned with or were sympathetic to the left tradition of gay-liberationist politics, most of whom also identified as socialists, were the first to critique the oppressive force of state sexual repression. By the late 1970s, Chris Bearchell, Konnie Reich, Sue Golding, Gillian Rodgerson, Anna Marie Smith, and others began to expose the contradictory character of state practices, that is, how the family-court system is set up to protect the adult male who molests his ten-year-old daughter at the same time that it warehouses sexually active, underage 'female delinquents' in reform schools and jails. They questioned the seizures of sexually explicit print materials like *Show Me! The Book of Children's Sexuality* and *The Joy of Lesbian Sex*, which were confiscated in the raid on *The Body Politic*. And they expressed agreement with Gayle Rubin's letter to *The Body Politic* wherein she cautioned against abandoning already vulnerable and stigmatized groups like boy-lovers, sadomasochists, and transsexuals to further attack and isolation.[54]

Unable to reach consensus, LOOT members never hammered out a formal statement and a set of strategies regarding *The Body Politic* crisis. In ways that parallel the Anita Bryant debate, discussion within the membership exposed the complexity of the issue. Stymied by the hardening of divided ideological loyalties and still wedded to the maintenance of organizational unity, LOOT never assumed a full leadership role, though the lesbian and feminist critique of adult men's power over children unsettled the sexual-libertarian posture of some gay men.

That yet another stalemate vexed the LOOT membership is reflective, in part, of an emerging radical versus socialist feminist split. Though lesbians occupied positions on both sides of the radical/socialist divide, most LOOT members, including the majority of the informal leaders, aligned themselves with the vision espoused by radical feminists, both lesbian and straight. In the two instances described above, the discord was characterized by the suspicion of, and unfamiliarity with, modes of compromise; competing estimations of the need to differentiate lesbian feminists from gay men; conflicting analyses of the role of the state; and, hence, divergent takes on the practice of coalition politics.[55]

Convinced that lesbianism was a basis for political activity, members of LOOT demonstrated a degree of political confidence, maturity, and voice unthinkable five years earlier. However, as they wrestled with allegiances to gay liberation and the (straight) women's movement *as lesbian feminists*, the presumed coherence of the category lesbian feminist itself came increasingly under strain.

8

Coalition politics: Lesbian feminists meet women's liberationists

this is how we tried to love,
and these are the forces they had ranged against us,
and these are the forces we had ranged within us,
within us and against us, against us and within us.
Adrienne Rich, 'Twenty-One Love Poems,' 1978[1]

In the late fall of 1977, at the suggestion of several women from the Revolutionary Workers League, a diverse group of Toronto feminists gathered to plan an International Women's Day (IWD) rally and demonstration for March 1978.[2] International Women's Day had been celebrated in Toronto on a much smaller scale in 1974 and during International Women's Year in 1975. However, in 1977, in the spirit of the International Women's Day for Peace and Social Progress first proposed at the 1910 Conference of Socialist Women in Copehagen, Toronto's newly constituted March 8th Coalition represented the first multi-issue, feminist action group in the city since the late 1960s.[3] Carolyn Egan, Varda Burstyn, Laura Sky, and other long-time activists envisioned IWD, led by the coalition, as an event inclusive of all women's experience with a primary commitment to reach women who were not yet politicized and who did not identify as feminists.[4] By mounting a powerful show of strength and unity, they sought to counteract mainstream-media claims that the Canadian women's movement was dead.

To reinvigorate the tradition of multi-issue organizing with the express goal of building an independent, mass women's movement, coalition members began to question the kinds of alliances and organizational forms required to make gains for women. Mindful of past efforts, they recognized that 'sisterhood is no longer enough' and that contradictions of class, race, and sexuality needed to be addressed both analytically and strategically.[5] Seeking solidarity with trade-union women was identified as a key objective.

Lesbians feminists, the majority of whom attended the meetings as joint representatives of LOOT and the newly formed Women Against Violence Against Women (WAVAW), entered the March 8th Coalition with feelings of apprehension bordering on suspicion. Since the early 1970s, collaboration with heterosexual and bisexual feminists had routinely ended in bitter feelings of mistrust. In 1978, radical-lesbian feminists at LOOT were especially irritated by the left orientation of the predominantly heterosexual leaders of the loosely knit coalition. Conversely, to the handful of socialist lesbians who felt stranded between the LOOT/WAVAW brand of radicalism and the heterosexism of most left feminists, the coalition promised a much-desired personal and political synthesis.

At one coalition meeting in February 1978, all those present agreed on the leadership of women and a women-only celebration/dance in the evening. On the issue of whether to encourage, allow, or discourage men from participating in the IWD march, pandemonium erupted.[6] After a bitter 'knock 'em down, drag 'em out fight,' a contingent of very vocal, angry women from WAVAW and LOOT – 'a third of the meeting and almost all the lesbians' stormed out, protesting the decision to permit men access to the march.[7] Lorna Weir recalls that 'the fur really flew at the meeting and the discussion was very vituperative.' Three years earlier, at the International Women's Year celebration, a small contingent of lesbian feminists had expressed their discontent with the presence of men at the events.[8] In 1978, the dominant feeling among the majority of women who departed was that, once again, straight women subverted the feminist movement by pressing for cooperation with other social movements that involved men. In 1979, WAVAW/LOOT again intervened in the March 8th Coaliton meetings to protest the involvement of men; again, they lost the vote after a much quieter debate.

Both years, most LOOT/WAVAW militants felt 'shafted' by feminists who wasted valuable organizing time, as Darlene Lawson said, 'making IWD attractive to men' and 'selling the day down the river.'[9] To Cate Smith, 'The history of IWD was a protest march and we felt that we couldn't march with our oppressors, men, as a protest.' Moreover, as Phil Masters has argued, 'Because of our location in the world, we as lesbians felt the need for autonomy.' Offended by the realization that 'the IWD action did not belong to women,' those who left the coalition declared their resolute refusal 'to let the men split us up.'[10] 'Losing *one* lesbian because the oppressor was invited to march,' recalls Pat Murphy, 'was one lesbian too many.' At a LOOT Task Force meeting in late February 1978, Murphy objected to what she viewed as the politically misguided and homophobic agenda of the coalition members: 'We can't even get together to have one big day all our own without causing freak out – one day of the year we've lost already. We can't say "no" to men one day of the year, on IWD. We couldn't say "no" without women turning on us and calling us bad names, calling us 'man-hating dyke separatists,' which is a helluva way to shut somebody up ... As a woman, I don't want to always have to say "yes." When we wanted to say "no" for one day, we got trashed as women by other women ... We're stronger if we can really say to each other that we can stand up alone without Daddy and without all that bull-shit.'[11] In a letter to the coalition, WAVAW spelled out their opposition: '[We] are not opposed to women uniting with men *when it is in our own interests to do so*. IWD, however, is a day reserved for women' (emphasis in original).[12] Disturbed by the 'leftist-styled demo' that employed the 'male standards' of a 'military exercise,' WAVAW/LOOT members equated March 8th organizing with male-identification and the inevitable dilution of 'autonomous feminist strength and energy.'[13]

Gay-male presence was not openly welcomed at IWD. However, it was the 'obvious influence of the male left' that was specially unnerving to LOOT/WAVAW objectors, several of whom, including Susan Cole and Darlene Lawson, were still 'recovering' from their own inauspicious experiences in the left. As one (unidentified) LOOT member argued at the time, 'Some women cannot do anything without men being present, which explains their weakness to manipulation from male-dominated, sectarian left groups.'[14] A co-founder of WAVAW, Eve Zaremba voiced her assessment of IWD at a LOOT Task Force meeting in March 1979, several weeks after the event: 'When we talk about IWD as a representation of the women's movement, I don't think it was ... A feminist perspective is one that puts women first, rather than unions first ... I didn't find IWD taking the feminist standpoint. The centre of things was somewhere else and women were used ... There were communists there, socialists there, the INCO people, a whole bunch of people with specialized interests it seemed to me, all the lobbies.'[15]

Zaremba publicized her complaints in the première issue of the radical-feminist monthly *Broadside* in May 1979. Incensed by the 'contaminating presence' of the left and the 'side-lining' of 'pure' feminist concerns, she rejected the concept of solidarity: 'This IWD was a dress rehearsal for May Day, another date on the left's calendar, indistinguishable from any other leftist event. The Rally lacked any feminist content, soft-pedalled women's liberation and was unconsciously coy on the subject of lesbians ... The women who let this happen should consider how they (and we) have been used and abused again in the name of some liberal idea of solidarity. Solidarity at this price is not solidarity at all, it's a sell-out.'[16]

The widening gap between radical feminists, almost all of whom were lesbians, and socialist feminists, a handful of whom were lesbians, was rooted in fundamental disagreements that extended beyond the question of men on the march. During her interview with me in 1990, Susan Cole reflected on the competing views: 'We were trying to articulate a politic of woman-centredness, woman-identification and they, the socialist feminists, were flipped out that the dykes didn't like men. They were threatened and unable to see what the political question really was. We told them they could have men on the curb doing child care. It wasn't that we didn't want to be with *the penis*. We thought that the best way to politically organize, the most effective thing for a nation to see, would be 7,000 women instead of 10,000 men and women. All they heard was, "Dykes don't like my husband." Some of them may have had some good pure working-class, class struggle politics, but I don't think that's what was going on. These women were not able to see that they, *THEY* had this problem with this guy. *WE* did not have the problem with this guy.' Socialist or 'anti-capitalist' feminists considered the vote to allow men on the IWD march, in both 1978 and 1979, a victory.[17] The few lesbian members of this majority faction were less satisfied with the outcome. As Natalie LaRoche argued, 'IWD had always been a workers' holiday to celebrate women workers. And as socialists and lesbians we wanted to keep it that way. But that didn't mean that we weren't torn and unhappy about the walk-out of our lesbian sisters.'

Meanwhile, radical feminists, lesbian and straight, regrouped. In defiance, they planned a women-only celebration on March 8th, 1978, three days before the official IWD rally and march. To Fiona Rattray, 'The alternative march, which was not a specifically lesbian event, came from extreme feelings of being cut off and isolated from the women's

movement and from lesbians who were closing doors in our faces.'
The poster 'Feminists Are Everywhere' was designed in honour of the
festivities.[18] Activities included a feast and gathering at the 519 Church
Street Community Centre, speeches, songs, and poems, followed by
a parade of two hundred to Convocation Hall at the University of
Toronto for a concert with performers Beverly Glenn Copeland and
Rita MacNeil. On the afternoon of the coalition-organized rally and
demonstration later that week, neither WAVAW nor LOOT members
marched under their respective banners. A small contingent of LOOT/
WAVAW leaders distributed leaflets outlining their criticism of IWD
priorities.

Following IWD in 1978, the International Women's Day Committee
(IWDC) was formed by an eclectic group of women who had political
roots in the left. That year, with IWDC at the helm of the March
8th Coalition, alliances were made with Organized Working Women
(OWW), Wives Supporting the INCO Strike in Sudbury (WSS), and
striking workers at the Fleck auto-parts plant and at York University's
staff association.[19] In addition, coalition members outlined their intention to reach out to immigrant women's groups, the reproductive-
rights movement, women's services, WAVAW, neighbourhood organizations, universities, high schools, and the lesbian community.

For some LOOT members, deciding to struggle inside the March
8th Coalition, and in the context of the fledgling IWDC, required a
reconceptualized, more expansive sense of struggle itself. As Naomi
Brooks described it, 'The more I was around women, the less I wanted
to be around men and male organizing. But I stayed in the March
8th Coalition because I thought we should be working with men.'
Having been a member of the mixed-gender Gay Days organizing committee in 1978,[20] Virginia Adamson began to equate alliance building
with hope for a more powerful challenge to multiple oppressions: 'We
were trying to figure out a way to be interdependent without com-
promising our identity. Sure, you can't disregard your own oppression
as lesbians, but you can't monopolize it either. [IWD organizing] was
a way we could begin to make link-ups with straight feminists, socialists, and gays.'

Taught by the female leaders/elders of her own Mohawk culture
that men and women were equal, Ann Kado rejected the desire of
radical (and the few separatist) lesbians 'to go outside the city, make
an independent city and make it work.' Instead, she argued, IWD was
a time 'to confront men in the city, in the world, build on their support
and attract the numbers that no small farm in the country ever could.'

During the IWD keynote address of March 1978, a call for 'lesbian rights' was highlighted alongside demands for control of women's bodies, universal, quality child care, and an end to cutbacks in social services, violence against women, and the deportation of Jamaican domestic workers. Collectively, the issues were placed in the larger framework of the economic crisis of the mid-to-late 1970s. According to former coalition members Egan, Gardner, and Persad, the reference to lesbians was not introduced without some internal ambivalence: 'The Coalition voted to take up this demand after discussion and some hesitancy on the part of a number of the participants ... [However] it did put sexuality on the political program of many organizations that might otherwise not have taken it up. The very fact that mixed organizations had to come to terms with its inclusion was a step forward.'[21]

Most LOOT members doubted the strength and sincerity of an IWD program that appeared to 'add on' the decidedly vague formulation of lesbian rights as an afterthought. At the LOOT 'Lesbian Feminist Strategy' meeting in March 1979, coalition member Gay Bell avowed, 'We were supposed to say, "Thank you for giving us this," and "Boy, we should be really thankful we had it there." I'm saying, we have to expect it.'[22] In both 1978 and 1979, lesbian feminists criticized the way in which a civil-rights approach to lesbianism revealed the coalition's liberal-individualistic approach to the terrain of sexual politics. By directing its inventory of anticapitalist and antipatriarchal demands at the state, the coalition reduced lesbian oppression to the rights of lesbian mothers in child-custody battles and the inclusion of anti-discrimination protection in the Ontario Human Rights Code. Without questions of women's sexuality and the varying manifestations of lesbian oppression being integrated into the larger set of demands, 'the lesbian question' floated, isolated and unanchored. Consequently, the prevailing complicity of straight feminists in heterosexist discourse and practice remained largely unexamined.

Inside the March 8th Coalition and IWDC, appraisals of lesbian activists were made based on a 'good lesbian (socialist)' versus a 'bad lesbian (radical/separatist)' dichotomy. A small contingent of socialist lesbian members of LOOT – women like Lorna Weir, Amy Gottlieb, Mariana Valverde, and Natalie LaRoche – did join the coalition and, later, IWDC. Yet throughout 1978 and 1979, they had difficulty seizing the occasion of IWD to formulate and clarify lesbian-specific political objectives beyond nebulous demands for lesbian visibility and lesbian rights. Gottlieb remembers, 'We had trouble being clear as lesbians about what we wanted.' In fact, as with the Stop Anita Bryant Coalition and the defence of *The Body Politic*, difficulties in teasing out the distinctive character of lesbian oppression meant that leadership and direction on questions of sexual politics within IWDC emerged slowly.

Puzzled by the difficulties of translating experiential knowledge of lesbian oppression into a set of action-oriented political projects, Kathy Arnup, a lesbian feminist member of IWDC, recalls the impasse: 'We always felt there must be something more to it than 'Lesbian Rights Now!' But what do you say? Greater lesbian visibility? An end to heterosexism? It's all very abstract. So lesbianism was not prominent enough on IWD, but it was also confusion on our part as to what it meant, how to articulate it and bring it forward in a way that went further than wearing a sign when we walked down the street.'

A number of homophobic incidents indicated to lesbian activists that heterosexual feminists had learned little on their own, which made the prospect of joint organizing seem unsafe. At a March 8th Coalition meeting in February 1979, a motion was introduced to remove lesbian rights and the decriminalization of abortion from the coalition's list of four major demands. The motion was finally defeated, but not before a heated discussion had transpired, much of which revolved around a concern for the respectability of the women's movement. That the erasure of references to lesbianism was raised at all delivered a painful shock to the few active lesbian-feminist members of the coalition. And news of the debate only confirmed the disenchantment of those already critical of the lip-service paid to lesbian issues inside the coalition and the larger women's movement. Furthermore, on the leaflets circulated to advertise IWD in 1979, LOOT was not credited with sponsorship of the all-women's dance.[23] Reminded of the omission of LOOT from the resource list printed in the *Everywoman's Almanac* in 1978, lesbian feminists were angered by yet another oversight.

In the late 1970s, the few members of the March 8th Coalition and IWDC who self-identified as lesbian feminists could not always be counted on to table and agitate for lesbian issues. 'Many lesbians in the women's movement,' argues Lorna Weir, 'did not politicize their lesbianism in any way, even where tactically possible.' Many LOOT members resented 'the lefty dykes' who, according to Pat Leslie, felt that they 'didn't have to go to LOOT to be a lesbian.' To Fiona Rattray and others, the practice of closetry was discouraging: 'Not all the lesbians in March 8th and IWDC were out and that pissed off a lot of us who were at LOOT. I think they felt that they would be heard more clearly if they didn't publicly identify as lesbians because the press was into saying all feminists were dykes. And us little rag-tag, obvious dykes were doing nothing for their media image.'

Building solidarity within and across movements that had little, if any, history of political partnership often proved to be a troublesome proposition. In the late 1970s, convinced of the usefulness of opening up the question of sexual orientation for wide-ranging discussion in local unions, Sue Genge acknowledged the homophobia among unionists.[24] A former steward in the Canadian Union of Public Employees (CUPE), a lesbian, and an IWDC member, Genge recollects that, 'for union women who had never thought about the issue, who had never met a lesbian, they didn't know how to deal with it or how to incorporate lesbian issues ... It was a clash of cultures.' Arja Lane, a key organizer of Wives Supporting the [INCO] Strike (WSS) in Sudbury, remembers travelling to Toronto to lead the IWD march in 1979: 'The march in Toronto showed how women's fight against oppression had grown to include lesbian mothers, punky dykes, pro-abortion groups and left activists. Some of the WSS women were horrified to be associated in public with such 'perverted, unchristian, communist hippies' ... Some thought it was "disgusting, family-destroying and boring."'[25]

On IWD in 1979, the subject of lesbianism was introduced to the 3000 people in attendance at the University of Toronto's Convocation Hall as a 'touchy issue.' Subsequently, a lesbian mother who was embroiled in a child-custody hearing appeared on stage with a pillowcase over her head and proceeded to speak, as Lorna Weir recalls, in a 'tiny, high-pitched voice' in an effort to safeguard her identity. Unfortunately, according to Weir (who was in part responsible for the hooded lesbian's appearance), 'She didn't stomp over to the microphone and give [male judges and lawyers] hell. She totally crumbled.' As Chris Bearchell later wrote in The Body Politic, '[Upon seeing the hood,] lesbians in that auditorium were confronted with an image of themselves as pathetic and invisible.'[26] To quote Virginia Adamson, 'It was a prototypical statement of our silence that brought up a lot of ire.'

By the end of IWD activities in March 1979, the tensions that separated radical-feminist members of LOOT and WAVAW and socialist-feminist members of the March 8th coalition and IWDC had reached a feverish, almost explosive, pitch. No escaping its ferocity, the 'men on the march' quarrel marked a particularly abrupt shift in lesbian-feminist political relations. Nancy Adamson observed: 'Before, where it seemed that we could disagree quite heatedly in a meeting, after it was over, it was over and we were still all lesbians together – the IWD debate changed us. Suddenly politics weren't in a meeting. They were your whole life, so the political decisions you made, how you voted, followed you outside of meetings.' In an ambitious attempt to resolve feelings of misunderstanding, mistrust, and bitterness harboured by feminists of all sexual orientations and political persuasions, representatives from LOOT, WAVAW, and IWDC met weekly for several months to plan an all-day community forum for late March 1979. Cleverly coined 'The Hetero-Mackerel Meets the Lavender Herring: A Fine Kettle of Fish,' the event was billed as an open discussion on the relationship between lesbianism and the women's movement. As Pat Leslie announced in the *LOOT Newsletter*, 'For too long, Toronto had been sharply divided on this question and all three groups felt the need to provide a forum in which a dialogue could finally begin.'[27]

LESBIANISM AND FEMINISM: A FINE KETTLE OF FISH

> I got WAVAW over here, IWDC over there, my heart belongs to LOOT, I don't know which to choose, I got women's movement blues. I got a man over here and a woman over there, I don't know which to choose, I'm so confused, I've got the bisexual women's blues.
> *Refrain:* Don't be denying the woman you've been eyeing.
> 'Personal Friends,' March 1979[28]

Intent on striking a light, humorous note, 'Personal Friends' – the small band of Fine Kettle organizers – opened the day with a short comic sketch. Three feminist contestants represented the three main currents in the women's movement: socialist, radical/lesbian, and liberal. In turn, each one was asked a series of staged, tongue-in-cheek questions in order that the host and the audience – WAVAW, IWDC, LOOT, and non-aligned feminists – might identify the 'real feminist.' According to hostess Lily Tomlin (a.k.a. Gay Bell), 'The real feminist is a woman who recognizes women are oppressed and battles the forces of oppression day and night, night and day at every turn and every straight.' As Pat Leslie recalls, 'We planned the skit so people would loosen up and not feel so tense. We wanted to make fun of ourselves and the problems we had that we were taking so seriously.' Full of sexual innuendo and playful barbs, the sketch lampooned feminist stereotypes in an effort to dispel the follies of political correctness, trashing, and labelling.

In response to a question about style, the socialist candidate replied: 'Dressing pretty is important for those of us who are organizing the proletariat. To help us identify with working women, we have to be uniform in our appearance, but it's important to keep your boots on so you can kick the pigs.' Asked how she first got involved in feminism, the lesbian/radical-feminist candidate responded: 'I was going to the circus to see Bozo the Clown and this woman sat down and put her hand on my knee and asked me if I wanted to join the women's movement.'

At the end of the ice-breaking entertainment, which included several sing-alongs, the spirit of unity and sisterhood was invoked when the hostess posed the final question, 'Will the real feminist please stand up?' and all three contestants leapt to their feet. Buoyed by feelings of hope and openness generated by the bravely satiric spectacle, Maureen Fitzgerald, a lesbian-feminist member of IWDC, explained the three aims of the forum to the 120 women assembled: 'First, to get together and talk, interpersonally. Second, to make a commitment to see us all working together in the women's movement in Toronto. And third, to see the whole issue of female sexuality, not just lesbian rights, but female sexuality and oppression of all of us as women, integrated into the discussion of the women's movement in Toronto.'

Respectful of the 'pain, anguish and gnashing of teeth in our own personal lives as lesbians and non-lesbians trying to work together,' Fitzgerald reminded the women in attendance that the event signified 'a start, not a finishing point.' Squashed into the downtown Niagara Centre on Wellington Street, Toronto's grass-roots feminist community had not gathered to take stock of movement tensions and future directions since the Bolton and Daughter of Bolton conferences in the mid-1970s. Apprehensive, keenly aware of the risks involved in coming together, and yet 'willing to experiment in good faith,' Margaret Moores remembers, 'We all wanted one big love-in.'

After a series of short presentations from LOOT, WAVAW, and IWDC spokeswomen, small groups were formed, and women were encouraged to discuss issues related to the topic of lesbianism and the women's movement. Almost immediately, the dialogue in each group degenerated into a bitter shouting match. As Lilith Finkler later wrote in *Broadside*, 'The Fine Kettle of Fish deteriorated rapidly into a session of angry declarations and anti-*man*-ifestos.'[29] Most objectionable to Fiona Rattray was the 'bastardization of feminist process': 'There was such a need for reconciliation between all the splits. There were great hopes that the day would heal the wounds, and, of course, you can't heal anything in one or two meetings. There were a lot of people standing on their soap boxes saying, "Well, you've done this to us," and others would say, "No, you haven't listened to us," so it became a stalemate.'

Ironically, almost no attention was paid in the small groups to forging a broad feminist commitment to eradicating heterosexist and homophobic discourse and practice – the main aim of the assembly. Instead, the radical feminist versus socialist feminist divisions that had emerged and structured debate during IWD organizing carried over to dictate the tone and substance of the Fine Kettle forum. The majority of LOOT and WAVAW members – almost all lesbians – lined up on the radical-feminist front. IWDC socialists – most of whom were heterosexual – were positioned, and positioned themselves, in opposition. Memories of confusion figure prominently in my interviews with Amy Gottlieb, Lorna Weir, Natalie LaRoche, Gay Bell, and several others who identified as lesbian socialists. Yet inhabiting this space of dislocation provided them with a certain insight into the deep ideological differences that substructed and gave shape to the talk.

A lesbian-feminist member of both LOOT and IWDC, Mariana Valverde exclaimed: 'It was the most appalling event I'd been to in my entire life. Some very nasty things were said about straight women and I didn't feel that the radical lesbians were saying these things because the women were straight but because they were socialists. People like Susan Cole seemed to believe that the only reason you were a socialist is because you like to hang out with men. It was as though lesbians were just radical feminists by nature.' Long-time socialist, co-founder of the Immigrant Women's Health Centre, and heterosexual member of IWDC, Carolyn Egan was deeply troubled by what unfolded: 'The meeting was a real débâcle. The woman-identified sectarianism of the radical feminists meant that there was a lot of anger towards socialism because that was the roadblock – socialism was what seemed to be "stopping women" from being able to be "real feminists." We didn't go in naively thinking it would be a tea party but we didn't think it would be the explosion of socialist-bashing that it was. It was all very disturbing.'

The connections women had to men, especially leftist men, offended radical feminists, both straight and lesbian. Hardly a secret to heterosexual and bisexual feminists, this antimale discourse, which was articulated along both antileft *and* anti-heterosexual lines, assumed a new level of dominance in the context of an explicitly political, mixed-feminist setting. Indeed, for a number of non-lesbians, meeting 'lesbian judges' eye to eye who were determined to ascertain whether a woman was a real feminist based on whom she slept with amounted to a devastating personal attack. A bisexual mother of a son, a trade unionist, and an IWDC member, Laura Sky has vivid, hurtful memories of being publicly pilloried: 'I remember overhearing lesbians from LOOT and WAVAW whisper "prick lover, prick lover" whenever I spoke. I was surprised at how much it hurt. I was surprised by my own anger and by the fucking impossibility of it all ... After the meeting was over, I just wanted to drive my car at top speed across a playing field, screaming my lungs out and hoping that I wouldn't hit any children.'

At the same time, many of the lesbians I interviewed were also quick to mention that the radical/socialist divide was complicated by the homophobia of some straight feminists. They stated that heterosexual and bisexual women were not simply innocent victims of a rabid, unchecked lesbian chauvinism. LOOT member Virginia Adamson witnessed a subtle dynamic, one that magnified tensions in insidious, unspoken ways: 'There had been a lot of dabbling in lesbianism among members of IWDC and some lesbians' hearts had been broken. It seems like a little thing, but it wasn't. It was political and it was there but it wasn't talked about.'

A number of straight feminists were 'caught putting their homophobic feet in their mouths' and then recoiling in guilt and defensiveness. According to Margaret Moores, 'The straight women were dishing it out – yeah, talk about homophobia. The more butchy women were attacked by straight feminists for aping men.' In addition, the majority of LOOT members felt that the male-dominated left's historic dismissal of issues of sexuality (including lesbian/gay rights and violence against women) had some bearing on the reluctance with which socialist feminists approached the terrain of sexuality. Indeed, acrimonious charges of male-identification were laid by members of each faction in a contest for the definition of feminist political and sexual correctness.

Though critical of the invisibility of lesbian feminists within IWDC and the March 8th Coalition, most politically active LOOT-goers were often unable or unwilling to assume a public stance *as out lesbians*. Troubled by this contradiction and somewhat intolerant of closetry, Chris Bearchell wrote in *The Body Politic* in 1979: 'No dyke has a right to be surprised, let alone angry if her straight sisters treat lesbianism as a "touchy issue" while she diligently hides her sexuality behind a cloak of feminism.'[30]

As with other debates that lesbian feminists at LOOT engaged in, there was virtually no reportage or analysis of the Fine Kettle affair in the lesbian, feminist, or gay press. Pat Leslie's comments in the April 1979 issue of the *LOOT Newsletter* were brief, descriptive, and emotionally guarded: 'Most women recognized that the brick walls dividing us are not knocked down in one day; there were still many disgruntled women who were disappointed in the lack of openness and ability to listen to others.'[31]

Almost fifteen years later, radical feminists like Susan Cole and Phil Masters have virtually no memory of the Fine Kettle of Fish event. Reflecting on her past experience, former IWDC member Kathy Arnup contends: 'I felt I was part of something that had turned really ugly and horrible and not knowing what to do, we all dragged off into our different camps.' A member of both LOOT and IWDC, Amy Gottlieb recalls the anguish of smashed expectations: 'I remember my anxiety, my anger, and the sinking feeling of being let down.' Before the community centre was evacuated that evening, signatures were collected for a follow-up meeting, but it never happened.

Throughout 1978 and 1979, the LOOT political committee met sporadically, though until organizing for the Bi-National Lesbian Conference began in late 1978 (see next section), there were no lesbian-specific political projects launched. Many LOOT members who also worked with WAVAW were busy instituting antiviolence measures and policy. In contrast to the confusion and frustration intrinsic to discussions of lesbian-feminist goals and strategies, the focus on (hetero)sexual danger provided the women who attended WAVAW meetings (first held at 342 Jarvis Street and then relocated owing to space constraints) with avenues for action. Images, especially the 'misogynistic hate propaganda' peddled in mass-market magazines like *Hustler* and *Penthouse*, and, later, 'snuff' films, repeatedly fuelled the fury of the largely white, college-educated membership.[32]

In early 1979, Political Lesbians of Toronto (PLOT) was formed by several LOOT members, the majority of whom identified as socialists, though because of scarce energy and an uncertain mandate, it folded almost immediately.[33] Lesbian feminists who were tired of negotiating gay men's sexism became increasingly alienated from the male-dominated National Gay Rights Coalition.[34] Only seventy women (with fewer than half from Toronto) attended the Ottawa Regional

Lesbian Conference in May 1978. Yet, contrary to the emphasis on movement building at the Bi-National Lesbian Conference in 1976, the focus of the 1978 conference was on 'personal growth' – coming out, lesbian relationships, and so on. One registrant observed in the *Body Politic*: 'Lesbian creativity is flowering within the lesbian feminist movement'; another is quoted as follows: 'Here I was crawling into this conference on my hands and knees from burn out, nails raw to the quick from hanging on to my sexual orientation in this heterosexist society, Anita [Bryant's] return trips to Canada, *The Body Politic* raid and I felt like I had arrived at a tea party – so little did the majority seem to realize the gravity of our situation.'[35] Following the conference, *Dyke Daily* – a proposed bimonthly provincial newsletter – was published, only to fold after one issue because of the 'negligible amount of material' received by the editor.[36]

In the late spring of 1979, following the Fine Kettle forum, IWDC introduced Lesbian Perspectives – a subgroup initiated by the organization's lesbian-feminist members, almost all of whom had gained personal and political experience at LOOT. At the time, no other group, including LOOT, was struggling to refine anti-heterosexist objectives; and in several instances, lesbian activists were withdrawing into the separatist safety of a 'hermetically sealed lavender bubble.'[37] In response to Eve Zaremba's blistering attack on IWD as a 'dress rehearsal for May Day' in the first issue of *Broadside* (May 1979), IWDC summarized their attempts to redress past mistakes: 'Since IWD, we have engaged in extensive self-criticism of our handling of lesbianism on March 8th, participated in the Fine Kettle of Fish, and are organizing an educational on lesbianism and feminism. We are one of the first feminist groups to deal with the oppression of lesbians in a highly public fashion; we are in the process of creating our own guidelines and first efforts have been seriously flawed. We've succeeded in discussing lesbian rights in certain schools, community groups, unions, where the issue has never been raised.'[38]

Certainly, these initiatives did not guarantee an instant, integrated understanding of sexual subordination as it related to *all women*, including lesbians; problems within the March 8th Coalition and IWDC persisted. Reflecting on the level of analysis, Lorna Weir suggested, 'For example, we didn't know what a socialist feminist perspective on age-of-consent laws would look like in the 1970s, and I'm not sure we do in the 90s either.' However, before the founding of Lesbians Against the Right (LAR) in 1981, Lesbian Perspectives was the only group to begin to make education, policy making, and outreach on lesbian issues a priority. Not coincidently, Lesbian Perspectives member Sue Genge was instrumental in pushing her union, the Ontario Division of the Canadian Union of Public Employees (CUPE), to include a sexual-orientation non-discrimination clause in their contract. Members of the lesbian caucus also set their sights on broadening the women's movement to include themselves as well as working-class women, trade unionists, immigrant women, 'third world' women, and progressive men (gay and straight).

'UNITED IN ARMED STRUGGLE': ORGANIZING BI-NATIONALLY

Magic Women of all our countries
It is our turn
To let us
Speak our love to each other.
Bi-National Lesbian Conference Program, 1979

In the fall of 1978, the energy that radical-feminist leaders of LOOT had initially brought to the organization, and to events like IWD, was being funnelled into WAVAW and the new journal, *Broadside, a Feminist Review*. Not interested in these ventures, and eager to experiment with an explicitly lesbian-feminist project, a group of eighteen to twenty lesbians, drawn largely from IWDC and the socialist membership of LOOT, formed the Bi-National Lesbian Conference organizing committee in November 1978. Throughout the winter and spring of 1979, the ad hoc committee, most of whom would later form the nucleus of IWDC's Lesbian Perspectives, scheduled meetings for 342 Jarvis Street. Though the conference was officially sponsored by LOOT, Sue Genge remembers the socialist lesbian line on the Bi-National event: 'Our concern was that LOOT was a social organization and those of us in the Revolutionary Workers League and IWDC wanted the Toronto conference on lesbians to be a political conference. So we went to LOOT and said, "How about this?" We wanted higher visibility for lesbians and more activity around lesbian issues.'

Not all LOOT members were uniformly enthusiastic about hosting the conference. With most of the political energy drained out of 342 Jarvis Street, those who were left, most of whom were not founding members, feared that the scarcity of lesbian political energy and resources would mean failure. According to Cate Smith, by early 1979 there was a feeling among 'the conservative and more socially oriented' members of LOOT that conference organizers were setting their sights far too high: 'There was the feeling at LOOT that we were either taking over or destroying LOOT, draining all its energy away and putting it into a short-term project. But the conference extended LOOT's lifespan as opposed to shortening it.' Despite internal disagreements over the priority of the conference, the organizing drive gave LOOT members a concrete focus and galvanized the membership, particularly in the months leading up to the event. Brimming with expectations, conference organizers articulated their vision of the event on the opening page of the program: 'It is our hope that this conference will provide us all with the opportunity to exchange experience and ideas, to share our culture, and form a common direction. This can be the beginning of a communication network to use in forming and strengthening a dykenamic movement.'[39]

Without state funding, the finance subcommittee miraculously generated over $14,000 via benefits like dances and concerts, the sale of advertising in the conference program, raffles, donations from local businesses and community groups, and the advance collection of conference registration fees. Keen to discourage 'eastern big-city imperialism,' organizers mailed out a detailed questionnaire to groups and individuals across Canada and Québec asking for input and feedback. An integral feature of the conference machinery, subcommittees were struck to oversee the agenda, publicity, billeting, food, transportation, entertainment and workshops. Though organizers had popularized the slogan 'What Do You Do With 1,000 Lesbians?/Que fait-on avec mille lesbiennes?' approximately four hundred women registered for the May 19–21 weekend. On the Saturday night at the banquet and theatre/music event, six hundred women danced wildly to Mama Quilla II and the Winnipeg band Equis.

All day Saturday and Sunday, workshops were held on the campus of the University of Toronto, at Hart House.[40] Simultaneous translation service was installed to facilitate communication with French-speaking lesbians, and the conference program was printed in both English and French. Reflective of the stated needs for discussion of personal, political, social, and cultural life, the range of topics covered in the thirty-five sessions was vast. Day One was devoted to 'our communities' and included sessions on 'coming out/staying in,' 'lesbians and welfare,' 'minority lesbians,' 'lesbians in prisons,' and 'coping with booze, dope and cigarettes.' Day Two focused on 'our movement' –

the different ideological currents among lesbian feminists and alliances with other movements such as the left, gay liberation, anarchism, and the women's movement. Day Three was set aside for a plenary panel and small discussion groups on lesbian-feminist strategies for organization and movement building. In addition, included among the thirteen skills-sharing workshops were bicycle and car repair, how to start a newspaper, and basic sound and lighting. And the list of fourteen cultural workshops included lesbian poetry, filmmaking, photography, body awareness, and theatre.

The issue-oriented workshops in particular ignited tremendous bursts of excitement, though as Naomi Brooks remembers, 'We'd have these big debates but then they'd end and you'd walk out of the room and the energy would be gone.' Notwithstanding the difficulties of sustaining a political focus and of developing a list of goals for the future – one of the organizing committee's principal objectives – the three-day extravaganza showcased the sophisticated level of organizing expertise reached by largely white, middle-class lesbian feminists, both individually and collectively. Overcoming internecine squabbles, stalemates, and doubts, they demonstrated to themselves and to other grass-roots activists, locally and nationally, that lesbians were capable of assuming leadership and successfully carrying out a complex project from start to finish.[41]

The impact of the conference on the broader culture was far less impressive, yet public exposure was not deemed a priority. Eager to protect the identities of their registrants and forever wary of mainstream media sensationalism, organizers vetoed the idea of a press conference; they chose not to issue a press release and they did not follow through on the proposed 'Dykes in the Street' demonstration (which was staged two years later at the Bi-National Conference in Vancouver). None the less, Brooks was astonished at the show of amazonian strength: 'There were just so many lesbians there and they were from all over the country and even some international women. Everyone was so high on this amazing energy and even women who would never have been caught dead at political events were hanging around the conference. We felt that we had built a national lesbian movement. This was it, it was happening.'

Virginia Adamson has only positive memories of the conference: '[It] was the only time that we felt that we were part of a national movement. We recognized the Québec question, our need for autonomy and the differences among us ... There was a confidence in the organizing that allowed for an amazing conference and a lot of different people to come from across the country and it was a joyous time.' For Nancy Adamson, the weekend event stirred up mixed emotions – the feeling of gratification and, paradoxically, the foreboding sense of impending closure: '[The conference] did leave me with a feeling of, "Look at us here, we're making change, we're doing something really important and there are a lot of us spread out across the country." There was a spirit there; we had all this confidence, this energy and commitment and then somehow it was gone. I remember being confused about that but I was part of it being gone because I was moving in a different direction myself.'

By the summer of 1979, LOOT was floundering in the wake of the Bi-National conference. An anonymous contributor to the June issue of the *LOOT Newsletter* wrote, 'In the absence of any regenerating energy, there has been a slow deterioration.'[42] In the prairie journal *After Stonewall*, Amy Gottlieb published the 'Lesbian Bill of Rights' – a clarion call first drafted at the conference's closing plenary panel and intended to refocus and re-ignite lesbian struggles. Though short on practical directives and long on fiery rhetoric, the passionately argued manifesto clearly reflects an unrestrained optimism: 'In the past decade, as many women came out, declaring themselves proud amazons, we have struggled to understand our oppression and unearth our potential to transform our lives. We have built communities and networks, attempting to create a supportive and growing atmosphere ... We have taken a collective stride into the future. Let's let our militance and imagination lead us forward, always hoping that we will be respected for who we are – women-loving women. We will march together and with others, with strength and dignity, toward a new day.'[43] In spite of Gottlieb's inspiring vision, deepened by her perception of the power in allying with 'others' (named in the article as gay liberation, the women's movement, and organized labour), LOOT was not destined to play a role in this future vision. Following the conference, the Toronto centre was unable to benefit from either the rush of enthusiasm or the show of new faces. Disheartened by the turn of events, inveterate activist Pat Leslie submitted, 'Without a political movement, a lesbian culture is useless. So where is our movement now? It is not to be found at LOOT.'[44] Conceived at the conference as a regionally rotating vehicle to spark debate on the future of Canadian lesbian organizing, *Lesbian/lesbienne* – 'the national newsmagazine of the lesbian movement' – folded after four issues.

Exhausted from the long, bitterly cold winter, Anita Bryant and *The Body Politic* crisis, the 'men on IWD' debacle and the Fine Kettle of Fish, women left the city, started up or joined other projects, or withdrew from formal activism altogether. A number of radical-feminist leaders from LOOT and the now-defunct WAVAW redirected their energy to a host of diverse ventures: the formation of the Feminist Party of Canada, the publication of *Broadside*, and the establishment of the Fly By Night – 'a bar catering to women.'[45]

Once the conference ended, there was no other project put in place to harness and focus the energy stirred up by its success. The intensity that had marked the first two years of LOOT's existence had virtually disappeared. With LOOT members increasingly leaving to found other projects and to enter and influence the larger public arena *as lesbian feminists*, LOOT itself began to suffer under the burden of reduced energy, bodies, and commitment. Never again able to recapture the spirit that had inspired its creation, the organization limped along for one last year before closing its doors on 1 May 1980.

To many of the women I interviewed, LOOT's demise marked the end of a political era. Conceived at a time when virtually all feminist grass-roots groups and services were single-issue and state-funded, LOOT represented a brave attempt to re-activate multi-issue organizing in the late 1960s tradition of the Toronto Women's Liberation Movement (TWLM) and the Toronto Women's Caucus (TWC). Paradoxically, however, the very ground that initially nourished lesbian strength and self-determination gave way to widening ideological fissures, the gradual redirection of energy away from LOOT, and, eventually, the organization's demise. While the collective push to host the Bi-National Lesbian Conference in May 1979 temporarily galvanized the increasingly balkanized LOOT membership, by the fall of 1979, the organization's end was in view.

PART FOUR

9

LOOT's closure: An evaluation

I've often thought that the contradictions inherent in trying to be a prefigurative organization in capitalist, heterosexist pig society are so great that
you're bound to break up and disagree. Partly it comes from trying to build
on destruction. We go to lesbian and gay organizations for support because
we've been so destroyed as individuals and we need to be able to fight back.[1]

In September 1979, the headline of the *LOOT Newsletter* read, 'We have
an empty house.' Warning bells had been clanging since the summer;
by the fall of 1979, virtually all of LOOT's original founders had left
the organization, now 'a decaying mass of rubble ... , seemingly abandoned for the Fly By Night [bar].'[2] In the summer of 1979, Butchford
and Bulldyke – columnists for the revamped LOOT newsletter, *Lesbian
Perspective* – began using humour to poke fun at heretofore rarely challenged maxims of proper lesbian-feminist living as a way of expanding
the organization's appeal. They announced the formation of 'Politi-
coholics Anonymous' for those who 'suffer from the activist disease,'
and they irreverently satirized the food at the Michigan Womyn's
Music Festival: 'The eats rate a full 10 on the P.C. scale. I didn't know
that salt was politically incorrect until I noticed there wasn't any. In
fact, the food was so P.C. that some womyn were P.I. and P.O.'d (pigged
out).'[3] Those who were convinced of LOOT's value called two public
meetings in October 1979 to investigate 'the lack of a relevant political
perspective' and LOOT's 'failure to involve the community.'[4] Before
the meetings, a notice in the October newsletter appealed to the
membership to solve the riddle of divided loyalties: 'Toronto is not
Armpit, New Jersey. It is a big city which should be able to support
a lesbian group. How do we solve the problem of: political lesbians

staying away from LOOT because it is not "political" enough and /
or other lesbians finding their support at the women's bar?'[5]

In the months to follow, strongly worded statements in the newsletter were aimed at pressing, even frightening, current and former
LOOT-goers into responsible, immediate action. Sharon Stone expressed acute dismay at the prospect of shutting down a service so
fundamental to LOOT's existence: 'Our phone-line is slipping ... We
cannot let it. It is unthinkable that a womyn may be forced to call Toronto Area Gays (TAG) because no lesbians want to answer her questions. What happened to sisterhood? And separatists, how can you
so easily let a womyn turn to males for help? I hope this situation
angers you. I don't want you to find our plight touching and hope
that someone does something. I want you to be moved enough to
volunteer at least an hour a month yourself. Because if you don't
do it, who will?'[6]

Afraid that their newsletter was on the brink of collapse, several
LOOT members reminded readers that 'things taken for granted eventually disappear. It is the only lesbian publication we know of in Canada.'[7] The newsletter, phone-line, and drop-ins continued in a scaled-
down capacity through the winter of 1979/80 and the spring of 1980;
the passion and hope that had once inspired lesbian-feminist activism
at LOOT were gone. Despite all salvage operations, on 1 May 1980
the last of the furniture and files were moved out and the doors of
342 Jarvis Street were closed. The daily outpouring of energy required
to react to internal and external political crises, coupled with the faithful provision of an enormous amount of social, cultural, and political
activity, took its toll on the core group, which rarely numbered more
than fifteen. Refusing to let LOOT die completely, a couple of members
relocated the phone-line in the WRCEC office, where calls were taken
until the mid-1980s.

Reasons given by former members for LOOT's demise were varied,
and feelings ranged from sadness to loss to relief. Comments printed
in the May 1980 newsletter included: 'It really pisses me off. Last year
we had a lesbian conference and 600 women turned up. Where the
hell is everybody?' and 'What's everybody getting sentimental about?
All you need to do is take a couple of pictures, keep them on file
and find a new place.'[8] In earlier issues of the newsletter, there was
speculation that once women came out and established contacts and
friends through LOOT, the organization lost its function. According
to one unnamed woman, 'cliqueishness' made it almost impossible to

penetrate the LOOT circle. Maureen wrote, 'I think there is a lack of trust and bonding as indicated by recent past events like Fine Kettle of Fish where womyn refused to communicate.'[9] Others blamed the Fly By Night: 'LOOT cannot compete with the bar and wall to wall womyn.'[10] In November 1979, yet another unsigned commentary was published in the newsletter: 'LOOT was supposed to be everyone's home three years ago. Yet intolerance and different political outlooks and, in some cases, lack of them, created painful alienation and an element of bitterness. The lack of communication and the gap between ideology and application was and still is glaring.'[11]

Clearly, the factors contributing to the organization's demise were multiple and complex. Yet even with a collective commitment to consider options, it would have been difficult to act on constructive self-criticism when almost no one was prepared to take the risk of signing an article or speaking out and making their views publicly known. In actuality, unable or unwilling to effect radical changes within the organization, and turned off by the burdensome responsibility, those women still loyal to LOOT began to retreat. To Rosemary Barnes and others who had invested huge chunks of their lives in LOOT's well-being, 'It was like being in love for the first time and realizing, "Oh my god, it's not working, my god it's the end of the world."'

Months after 342 Jarvis Street was vacated, a critical account of LOOT's closure and the 'disintegration of the lesbian community' was published in *Broadside*.[12] Former editor of the *LOOT Newsletter*, Val Edwards connected the organization's 'failure' to the fragmented backgrounds of LOOT-goers, and the political differences that plagued the membership. Having concluded that 'lesbian feminists have nothing in common,' 'the movement is a "paper tiger,"' and the community is dying a slow death, Edwards goaded her readers to respond: 'Have we found, or can we find, that special something that makes us truly different from homosexual men and heterosexual women, that aspect of our lesbianism that transcends us as individuals? Have we anything to say to the world as lesbians qua lesbians, rather than as gay liberationists and feminists? Or are we simply a maze of intersecting social circles, void of any real political or cultural content?'[13]

Contrary to Edwards's cynicism, the series of responses that were printed in *Broadside* pursued a considerably more hopeful tack. As Judith Quinlan put it, '[I] have come to accept the "lesbian community" as the many-headed Hydra sprouting new life every time an old limb withers.' She continued: 'It is this ability – to send out shoots when the above-ground portion of the plant is trampled on – that characterizes the lesbian movement ... Our network – our links with our sisters and foremothers – transcends the monolithic institutions of the patriarchy. We are spinning webs, not building pyramids.'[14]

Over ten years later, the women I interviewed reflected on their understandings of why the organization folded when it did and how they felt about its loss. Much less bitter than Edwards, they tended to be philosophical about 'the old LOOT days.' Naomi Brooks stated that, after three years, 'We just got older.' According to Margaret Moores, 'I was sad, but it was a relief that people were being honest about saying "No, I can't do it anymore." That was good.' Fiona Rattray speculated, 'Things arise as they're needed. There was a big need for an alternative to the bars, so LOOT happened. When it closed, it was awful and painful and gut-wrenching, but that's the way it had to go.' As Eve Zaremba saw it, 'No organization can satisfy everyone, yet the need is there, the pressure is there and the expectation is there. So it falls down because of inflated expectations.' Most women pinpointed the combination of locked ideological horns and lost organizational drive and focus. And a number of them highlighted the need to reassess their commitment to outer-directed activism. Brooks noted, 'After the [Bi-National] conference people started thinking about what their priorities were and doing more for themselves instead of for the movement ... It was a real regrouping kind of time.'

Curiously, though money to cover LOOT's expenses was always scarce, in the end, a financial crisis did not precipitate the organization's close. Former treasurer Rosemary Barnes provides her analysis: 'When I left, there was a big fat bank account but the house was almost empty. People were leaving the task force and other groups weren't being replaced – it was pretty clear that the original vision – this umbrella being a place for everyone – wasn't working. And there wasn't another vision to replace it that excited people in the same way. We were not in the situation of lots of ideas and energy and no money. There was money left, but the energy had gone in different directions.'

To Phil Masters, LOOT's demise was painful, but not unexpected: 'When LOOT closed, it was like the Women's Credit Union closing, and A Woman's Place. It's so hard to keep anything going; anything that is so marginal in this society is living off adrenalin with no other kind of support and once that is dissipated, how does a feminist group survive?' In the early 1970s, numerous women-run services and organizations were spawned by A Woman's Place, for instance, the Women's Bookstore, Nellie's, Women's Self-Defense, the Amazon Workshop, and, arguably, LOOT itself. Years later Eve Zaremba recalls, 'LOOT was a ball of fire and it threw sparks that took off.' To Gay Bell, 'When LOOT died, it wasn't like the lesbian community stopped; it was that we reformed, or formed in different ways, like atoms moving in a different formation.'

Upon LOOT's close, in addition to *Broadside*, the Feminist Party of Canada, and the Fly By Night lounge, lesbian feminists became involved in the All Girls Hit and Miss Leather Marching Band, Mama Quilla II, anti-nuclear theatre, the direct action-oriented Women Against Nuclear Technology (WANT), Political Lesbians United Against the Media (PLUM),[15] the Right to Privacy Committee (established after the police raid in December 1978 on The Barracks, a gay men's bathhouse), and the municipal campaigns of gay politician George Hislop and gay-positive mayor John Sewell. By 1981, several former LOOT-goers were immersed in Gays and Lesbians Against the Right Everywhere (GLARE), Lesbians Against the Right (LAR),[16] the Gay Community Council, Gay Community Appeal, Gay Counseling Centre, the Lesbian and Gay History Group, Take Back the Night organizing, and the committee that lobbied to introduce lesbian/gay-positive curriculum into Toronto schools, among other feminist, lesbian, and gay projects.

Ten years after LOOT's official closure, I asked the women I interviewed what they had learned from their experiences at LOOT, and what impact organizing had had on them as women, as lesbians, and as feminist community organizers in the mid-to-late 1970s. What follows is a cross-section of their responses.

Rachel: LOOT was an institution – it was the first openly lesbian building in Canada. It felt like we really lost something. The connections with the women I met at LOOT have stayed on, they have become family. But LOOT was the focus of a lot of good times, a lot of growing, an important place in my life. Without LOOT I don't know if I'd be who and what I am today.

Donna Marchand: Locally, I felt part of a movement. I was around people who were really making things happen. You couldn't go to 342 Jarvis Street and not get the sense that something was cooking, that we were crossing boundaries. What struck me was the ability to laugh through all kinds of adversity.

Natalie LaRoche: I acquired my lesbian identity and pride. I learned what it's like to live in a special society. We felt we were very special, we took care of each other, we loved each other, we had adventures with each other, we slept with each other, we ate with each other, we plotted with each other, we organized with each other. It was very intense and very hopeful. I lived my politics and we got to see tangibly what kind of organizing worked and what didn't. The world was our political workshop. Many of us are making our livings from what we learned in the seventies – the skills of the theatre, printing, teaching, writing, editing, community organizing, counselling. And those skills continue to count.

Pat Hugh: I grew up in Guyana where 'lesbian' wasn't even discussed; there was no language. So, it felt good that I lived at LOOT and went to LOOT picnics and we all walked under the LOOT banner and hung out and people were aware that we were all lesbians. It felt like a family. But when I moved out, and LOOT closed the following month, it was time for an apartment of my own. Thirty women had keys to my front door and it was time for a key of my own.

Amy Gottlieb: I learned how to be a lesbian and feel more comfortable about it. I learned how to embrace it as an identity, socially and as a political lesbian. I learned more political organizing skills inside the RMG [Revolutionary Marxist Group], but LOOT gave me a sense of what some of the issues were for me and for other lesbians. It really reinforced the fact that I had chosen something I felt comfortable with, and that I was proud of, and that I had a community of support. Over such a short period of time, I grew an incredible amount.

Ann Kado: I learned strength, identity, how to be myself. I look at the older lesbians and I say, 'Thanks,' because if it wasn't for them, I probably wouldn't be alive today, and I'm grateful for that ... I couldn't run to the Native community. If I ran, I always ran to the lesbian and women's community. It was a family, I could feel it. If they wanted to fight, fine, what family doesn't have fights? But socially, when we weren't talking politics, when we were just out to have a fun time, there was that family feeling. Here I could actually relax and feel like I was a somebody.

Lilith Finkler: I learned to be proud as a lesbian, which is ironic because so many of the women were in the closet, but what I learned was lesbian pride. I came from a traditional Jewish family where you're supposed to get married and have babies, so to make peace with who I was, that was really wonderful.

Nancy Adamson: For all the political differences and the dress code and the fact that we were very judgmental of each other, there was also a sense of being there for people, helping people through the hard times of coming out to family, at work, breaking up with lovers, learning how to stay in a small community with those women that you have political fights or ended relationships with. I think we really struggled to make lesbian feminism mean something in our everyday lives. Sometimes we succeeded and sometimes we didn't. I remember the successes more, the sense of community, of belonging somewhere, of beginning to learn about political organizing.

Gay Bell: LOOT gave me a strong sense of community which still remains. LOOT doesn't have to continue in its bricks and its cement to have had its effect. It was a crucial locus of our development as a community in Toronto, in Canada and in the world. Just the fact that we're doing interviews about it reinforces its reality. I don't think it disappears any more than for Latin American people who do resistance movements and have a very strong strategy and attachment to the memory of people who have been murdered or disappeared. For them that is the way they organize. For us, the development and history and continuity of our community is the way that we organize. I can feel that when I'm depressed, when there's trouble at my work, there is a lesbian community, though there's no particular place I can go and find everyone sitting there. I still have that image, and LOOT has given me that image, that anchor and a sense of worth and value in myself and with my friends and other community members. And it works very strongly against the invisibility which is the nature of our oppression.

PUTTING TOGETHER A HOME WHERE THE LESBIAN BODY CAN LIVE

As the above meditations attest, over the course of LOOT's existence, the majority of its members benefited significantly from their multifaceted relationships to the organization and to the process of constructing a public, predominantly white, middle-class lesbian-feminist discourse and practice. This process of elaborating lesbian subject positions and forming a community had a particular, highly specified, and meaningful character. In creating and nurturing woman-identified life/style and sexual norms, self-help services, cultural and social events, support-based networks, and political interventions, LOOT faithfuls sought to institutionalize their desire for visibility and autonomy in ways that emphasized their distinctness from straight feminists, gay men, the left, and all non-feminist lesbians/gay women.

Weary of faint-heartedness they strove to establish a sense of pride in who they were and in the revolutionary vision they aimed to realize.

Occasions like concerts, drop-ins, peer counselling, theatre, and dances made possible the discovery of what it actually meant to 'be' a lesbian and 'do' lesbianism in an active, self-consciously feminist and celebratory manner. As Val Edwards wrote in *Broadside*, 'Our greatest moments were surely the women-only coffeehouses, brunches and dances where we felt that thrill of making the lesbian house we created come alive, or of taking over a church hall and making it our own, if only for a night.'[17] Principal sites of entertainment, these phenomena were successful and sustaining elements of a maturing lesbian community because they were, in large part, politically and ideologically non-controversial. In other words, they offered women in and around LOOT a taste of unified sisterhood in ways that internal, fractious political debates and decision making did not. Indeed, extensions of the social/cultural tradition of rap groups, potlucks, and coffee-houses in the early 1970s, they enabled identification with emergent lesbian-feminist culture in safe, supportive contexts.

Caught up in the urgency and intensity of cultivating pride upon departing the closet, LOOT-goers found themselves inventing alternative modes of feminist thinking, dressing, acting, speaking, relating, making love, producing culture, and doing politics, lesbianly. Essential to each of these constitutive processes was a loyal devotion to the collective. Psychologists McCoy and Hicks have explored the power of lesbian nation building in Los Angeles in the 1970s: 'To many women, "the community" became an entity with a life of its own ... it held the power to pass judgement, and as a new-found home for the homeless, it took on a mighty significance. It seems little wonder that many lesbians in despair look toward the community for magical fulfillment of expectations, dreams, and hopes which have previously been thwarted by patriarchal culture.'[18]

LOOT became the downtown Toronto headquarters of largely white, middle-class lesbian-feminist activism in the late 1970s. The birth of LOOT and the sheer increase in numbers of out lesbian feminists meant that political dykes no longer had to fight for a voice inside either mixed gay/lesbian groups like Community Homophile Association of Toronto or straight feminist organizations like Toronto Women's Liberation Movement. And as Naomi Brooks notes, 'We discovered that we might have something to say to each other outside the bar scene.' To women who had largely cut themselves off from the past, from their biological families, and from the outside world, 342 Jarvis Street represented a home – a social and emotional refuge. Indeed, it promised a training centre specializing in the initiation and acceptance of newly declared lesbian feminists, where the social, recreational, educational, sexual, cultural, and political needs of *all lesbians* would be met. LOOT also promised a break from the history of seedy, Mafia-controlled, and straight-owned bars, as well as from the closetry of private house parties and relationships.

That a social and service-focused organization eventually won out over the desire of a smaller minority of LOOT members to establish a militant, more traditional political formation tells us much about the immediate needs expressed by many largely white, middle-class lesbians during this period. For the first time in their lives, access to a lesbian-feminist haven where they could talk, dance, meet lovers and friends, perform, read, and just hang out became synonymous with nourishment and safety. Former LOOT-goers remember the exhilaration they felt in coming out to themselves and to each other through 342 Jarvis Street. According to Rosemary Barnes, 'LOOT became an important personal base for relationships with women that have continued for years, including with Nancy, my lover.'

In the brief, published analyses of LOOT, there is some dispute over the scope of the organization's accomplishments. Sociologists John Cleveland and Sharon Stone have both referred to LOOT as a social-service centre, and in my interviews a number of former LOOT members echoed this assessment.[19] Yet, to Natalie LaRoche, this is inaccurate: 'LOOT was an experiment in a prefigurative kind of a community. We tried to run it democratically, we tried to have lots of input, we tried to make a space for everybody. LOOT was a collective creation and that makes it more than just a service. We were serving our own selves and creating a healthy community.'

In the spirit and practice of making a Lesbian Nation, members of LOOT executed a tremendous amount of brash, original, and inspiring work. To Naomi Brooks, 'We had a common dream: We would be everything to everyone, and we did it. For a long time, everything really radically, politically feminist came out of LOOT in one way or another for a couple of years.' For the majority of lesbian feminists I've interviewed, the intensity and volume of empowering 'dyke energy' generated during this period has yet to be matched. At the same time, some of them revealed that this intensity was also marked by feelings of bitterness, anger, and disappointment – feelings that still linger today.

Compelled to mine for lesbian identity in the pit of female invisibility, LOOT-goers searched for meaning in ways that reinforced their collective uniqueness.[20] Almost everyone I interviewed associated the decade with the positive process of integrating lesbianism and feminism into all aspects of one's life and learning to take pride in lesbian identity. The psychological damage of living as 'deviants' seemed so much easier to overcome at LOOT, at least superficially, as Lorna Weir notes: 'Lesbians in the coming-out process are heavily marked by homophobia, and being members of the larger social world that hates our sexual preference, it was common initially to say, "Yes, I'm completely alright," and be utterly cavalier about it.'

All LOOT-going lesbians fiercely defended the need for a politicized, visible constituency unafraid of 'kicking up shit.' They were aware that bourgeois, suburban gay women and working-class bar dykes commonly associated lesbian feminism with the surrender of identity, personal taste, and privacy. Yet, rather than giving up and ultimately, giving in to oppressive forces, LOOT members were trying to live an ideal future into an inhospitable, unreconstructed present – something that they felt those who did not give 'two rips about feminism' knew nothing about.[21] Refusing to sequester their new-found political/sexual identities in underground bar culture or privatized, closeted relationships, LOOT-goers transformed what it meant to *be* a full-time lesbian feminist. Indeed, the provision of an alternative to previous forms of lesbian social organization and the naming of the category *lesbian feminist* as a basis for cultural and political organizing are among LOOT's major achievements. On the heels of LOOT's demise, an unnamed contributor to *Broadside* acknowledged the debt owed those lesbian activists who pushed hard at conventions: 'It is the feminist lesbian community that lends support to the closet community by being political and visible, thereby creating an atmosphere for some future generations of lesbians in which all may express themselves openly and freely.'[22]

From the beginning, LOOT-goers shared a common desire to come out, to create a public lesbian-feminist discourse, and to make 342 Jarvis Street open and accessible to all lesbians. Yet even within the LOOT membership not everyone was out equally. With the exception of two or three members, LOOT regulars lived with the fear of dis-

closure and the repercussions of being on the front line. One contributor to *Broadside* in 1980 solemnly stated, 'Not everyone [can] wear
neon signs in our daily life ... This community takes great risks individually and collectively by being visible in an oppressive society
where we have no legal protection and no legal recourse.'[23] In her
interview, Rachel noted: 'There were women at LOOT who remained
in the closet – the teachers, the professional women, and some
working-class women who were in managerial-type positions in chain
stores like Loblaws, middle managers who were starting to earn decent
salaries, who had worked a long time and weren't interested in jeop-
ardizing that.'

LOOT's umbrella design provided a pluralistic structure in an attempt to maximize and coordinate the impact of lesbian-feminist organizing while encouraging a diversity of people and projects. However, the umbrella only stretched so far and did not grow beyond a
certain point. Clashes ensued as lesbians sought to fulfil often very
divergent needs. Rosemary Barnes named the different psychological
bases of these competing desires: 'Some women felt the organization
was unfriendly, too political, and not supportive of women who were
coming out. Other women saw the organization as too social, wishy-
washy, or apolitical and mainly of value to women coming out. LOOT
disappointed women for two basically different reasons. For some
women, it was not the warm, friendly group that could satisfy expectations of nurturance, while for others, it was not the energetic,
assertive group that could satisfy interests in effective, independent
action.'[24]

Not only did these different perspectives make it difficult to keep
lesbian-feminists already at LOOT committed to the project of maintaining a viable lesbian feminist centre, but the organization was beset
with the ongoing dilemma of attracting new women. The problem of
restricted membership was not new: ten years earlier, Toronto Wom-
en's Liberation had struggled with trying to expand their largely white,
middle-class, Marxist membership and they were criticized for being
cliquish to the point that one woman felt like an 'uninvited guest at
an exclusive Revolutionary Women's Club.'[25] In the mid-1970s, feminist groups like the Rape Crisis Centre and the Daughters of Bolton
conference were the sites of purges and counterpurges over heterosexual privilege and class.

In the 1990s, looking back, most former LOOT-goers remember the
radical-feminist emphasis on gender/sexuality as the primary site of

women's subordination. They also point to the impossibility of transcending individual solutions without a collective consciousness of systemic inequalities rooted in relations of class, race, and ethnicity. Indeed, they vividly recall the power of concepts like 'Lesbian Nation' and 'Lesbians Ignite' to varnish over uncomfortable, if not intolerable, differences. Cognizant of LOOT's limitations, an anonymous contributor to the October/November 1980 issue of *Broadside* deduced that 'because of the great diversity among lesbians on feminist/class/racial/ethnic grounds, organizing such a community, visibly or invisibly, is a monumental task.'[26] In the eyes of Chris Bearchell, 'LOOT drew around itself a kind of base of support. Once it got that, the perspective of reaching out, of being that beacon, of making the bridge between women in the bars, of reaching into other communities and other classes really just became a theoretical desire, not a practical project ... And it was a largely white organization. In spite of whatever desire we had to be open and inclusive, just the fact of who started it and who was sustaining it had a lot to do with how comfortable women from other communities and experiences felt walking in and claiming it, though they were invited to.'

Less internal policing of 'right-on-ness,' more attention paid to the disjunctures between ideology and practice, and a broad acceptance of different, even competing, lesbian subject positions might have provided the basis for recruitment and outreach beyond LOOT's narrow constituency. That such a move never transpired tells us much about the psychological needs of a community whose very existence in the late 1970s was precarious and virtually invisible.

Even in the short history of lesbian-feminist organizing, the elaboration of an orthodox correctness and the narrowing of group borders was not a new phenomenon. Writing for *The Other Woman* in 1973, Adrienne Potts warned about lesbian-feminist 'arrogance and self-righteousness' as a barrier to reaching lesbians beyond the movement.[27] Vancouver activists Hughes, Johnson, and Perrault have admitted, 'we tend to create definitions of our own that are equally restrictive and generally untrue for the majority of dykes.'[28] Yet as American theorist Chela Sandoval argues, this dynamic is not unique to lesbian-feminist organizing: 'Even the most revolutionary communities come to prohibit their members' full participation; every marginalized group that has organized in opposition to the dominant order has imported [the] same desire to find, name, categorize and tame reality in a way that ultimately works to create marginalized positions within its own ranks.'[29]

Two-and-a-half years after LOOT's first open house, Ruth Dworin used the *LOOT Newsletter* to pose a difficult question to lesbian community members. She implored, 'How many women have become exiles from the women's movement because they were made to feel that their behaviour was "Politically Incorrect?"' Dworin continued: 'Lesbians and feminists in Canada and the U.S. are being attacked by extremely well-organized reactionary right-wing forces who seek to destroy us and our movement. It is very frightening to see similar political forces at work within our movement, dividing us and alienating many potential feminists.'[30]

Dworin's despair was shared by other activists disillusioned by rigidifying ideologies that increasingly factionalized social movements in the 1970s. In 1976, Chris Bearchell presciently alerted readers of *The Body Politic* to the limitations of a simplistic, identity-based lesbian chauvinism: 'The potential power of organized lesbianism does not lie in the (perhaps pleasant) daydream of converting all women to love for each other and then thumbing our collective nose at our then former oppressors – men.'[31] Writing in 1980, Val Edwards identified the need to return the phrases 'politically correct' and 'politically incorrect' to 'the intellectual cesspool from which they emerged.'[32] At the same time, British lesbian activist Sue Cartledge asked, 'Do we want a feminist analysis aimed at changing the world, or a code of right-on and right-off behaviours aimed at policing women?'[33]

As earlier chapters have documented, correct discourse and practice of white, middle-class lesbian-feminist life/style, sex, culture, and politics were not consciously, dictatorially instituted or mandated. Met with ambivalence, or, in some instances, downright defiance, the orthodoxy was neither coherently nor uniformly observed at all times, under all circumstances. In small but significant ways, right-on lines and the meanings attached to them were internally debated, contested, and reconstituted. Unlike the deep, internal fissures that scarred lesbian organizing in the United States, the precarious coexistence of gay-liberationist, socialist, radical, and separatist lesbians during LOOT's first two years bespeaks a much less monolithic lesbian feminism than that suggested by Faderman, Phelan, and others.[34] However, contrary to LOOT's pledge to welcome *all lesbians* without exception, a hegemonic discourse of correct-line-ism prevailed. Asked to address this discourse, Dworin was not the only critic. She claims that 'there were a lot of myths about what it was to be a good lesbian, from what you did in bed, to what you did in the streets to what you did in the community. There were a lot of myths about what the community of lesbians is – the "feminism is the theory and lesbianism is the practice" myth. The myth went: because we were all lesbians, we were more peaceful, more humane. Lesbian relationships were inherently better and more pure than hetero relationships. Women "naturally" understood each other better. Women in bed knew what each other wanted. There was a feeling of a natural superiority – women were better communicators, better at working things out. Collectivity was the politically correct lesbian way of organizing ... When those myths did not jibe with my reality, I always felt like I was the one who was fucked up.'[35] Initially, lesbians came to LOOT possessing differences in consciousness, degree of social conformity, and analysis of the roots of lesbian oppression; however, well-intentioned claims to openness, consensus, and diversity were quickly buried under the push for unity. By stressing the commonality of a true, if not transcendent, lesbian-feminist identity as a medium sufficient for the creation of a politics, a culture, and a community, other potential interests or fragments of identity often became less relevant to LOOT leaders.

Lesbian feminists themselves sometimes found the observance of community standards oppressive and often motivated by guilt and moralism. American writer Jan Clausen remembers, 'The lesbian feminist way of life I knew was very hard on women, yet we were not supposed to notice or complain about that fact. We were supposed to content ourselves with our elect status and the glory of our exhausting service.'[36] As outlined in chapter 6, the process characteristic of this service proved both liberating and exasperating, if not agonizing, to LOOT members.

Building on the tradition of feminist collectivism, LOOT offered women an environment where they could work, socialize, and develop strength, self-confidence, and skills. According to Mariana Valverde, 'We did believe that we had to invent everything. I don't want to romanticize it because I don't think we knew what we were doing. But we did feel we could make a difference.' Margaret Moores exclaimed, 'It was great because you could go in there with no experience at all and it was, "Okay, go ahead and do it." If you were enthusiastic and wanted to do it, you could. We made lots of mistakes, things that make you cringe now.' And as Gay Bell reminisces, 'For many of us, this was our first heavy-duty effort at organizing. We were pretty green, and though we might have been in the vanguard, we were very naïve.'

Internal to the LOOT membership, the articulation of lesbian-specific goals and the design of strategies to attain them were not easy tasks. Many of the women I interviewed stressed that there were few occasions to produce and implement analyses; the new left / feminist study group so pivotal to radicalization and the development of theory within groups like Toronto Women's Liberation in the late 1960s was not introduced at LOOT. Nor did members of LOOT make a priority of pro-active interventions in straight milieux through routine public educationals – a tactic that may have accelerated a certain sharpening of analysis and action. Moreover, as Amy Gottlieb has observed, the language and the theory that they needed to describe and formulate a set of pro-lesbian and anti-heterosexist goals were just emerging; hence, analytic tools were tentatively and only partially conceptualized.

As documented in chapters 6, 7, and 8, lesbian feminists of all political persuasions were befuddled by the matter of formalizing a lesbian-feminist strategy. Taken aback by her own realization, Susan Cole stated, 'You want me to tell you about my lesbian-feminist politics and now I realize that I don't have any, and never have had any lesbian politics.' Asked to reflect on this quandary, Eve Zaremba responded, 'There isn't one gut issue for lesbians. You get a family membership at the zoo and it says "husband and wife," so you chip away at heterosexism, but it's not the sort of thing that brings people out and storming the city.' Discouraged by the lack of lesbian-specific, public, and direct-action-oriented initiatives, at the end of LOOT's first year many LOOT members channelled their political energies to Women Against Violence Against Women (WAVAW) – 'the first attempt at a radical feminist political organization in Toronto.'[37]

Familiar with the slipperiness of 'the enemy' and the difficulty of activating an effective program to smash heterosexual privilege, LOOT members often experienced frustration. They exposed the heterosexist policies and practices of virtually every institution, from the media, the courts, and the school system to organized religion and the nuclear family; yet this knowledge did not easily translate into a determinate political content. Devising such conceptual jewels as heterosexism and the institution of heterosexuality were political acts of consciousness. However, the lack of a central locus of lesbian oppression made it difficult to concoct a comprehensive politics of lesbian-feminist organizing. LOOT-goers were convinced that legal protection against discrimination in housing, jobs, and child custody was only one arm of a necessarily more complex, counter-hegemonic mandate for change. In the face of the equally slippery concept of lesbian oppression, it is not surprising that largely cultural and domestic modes of right-on life/style, sexuality, and socializing were often substituted, or came to stand in for, more traditional forms of political struggle and action.

In the absence of direct-action-oriented, political projects generated internal to the organization, LOOT members attempted to forge a lesbian-feminist politic in response to political developments that arose in the context of the women's and gay men's movements. Again, as shown in previous chapters, articulating definitive lesbian-feminist reactions to political crises was accomplished dialectically *within and against* positions argued by gay-male activists and women's liberationists. Lorna Weir has suggested that 'all groups which mediate two movements have an extremely difficult role to play; the temptation exists to play one movement off against the other, thus preserving and confirming the superiority of the centre. Political purism is a vice to which groups with a foot in two or more movements are particularly prone.'[38]

Having identified men and patriarchal culture as *the* pivotal site of women's subordination, radical-feminist leaders at LOOT were suspicious of, if not wholly adverse to, broadening the struggle for a transformed world beyond their self-defined feminist community. Fearing the dissolution of an already fragile Lesbian Nation, they did not make a priority of cultivating alliances with anti-imperialist struggles, the trade-union movement, the fight for universal day care, or gay men's battle against sexual policing. To Virginia Adamson, sharing knowledge in the context of joint organizing was not easy: 'It was hard to teach straight women and gay men anything because we were still teaching ourselves.' Pat Leslie made a similar point: 'We were so busy building our own autonomy, community, whatever that meant to us, that we weren't bothered by the external events until it indirectly affected us, like "men loving boys" ... we were always playing out in our talks at LOOT a long scenario about a Lesbian Nation and how extreme we should go.'[39]

In part, the resistance of most LOOT-goers to coalition-based activism was rooted in the fear of co-optation and manipulation, if not a full-scale take-over at the hands of gay men and socialist feminists.

Notwithstanding the dissenting voices of several seasoned gay-liberationist lesbians, the majority of LOOT members feared absorption into a gay-male movement that they felt was unaccountable to lesbians and feminists. Exposure to gay men's sexism and their 'male-identified causes' from the late 1960s on repeatedly forced lesbian feminists to leave mixed-gender projects in anger and disgust. At LOOT, the most weighty statements made during in-house debates were supplied by lesbian feminists who knew or had worked with gay men and who had first-hand knowledge of gay-male 'sexual perversion and rampant misogyny.' Though the intensification of police violence in the 1980s and the emerging AIDS crisis propelled a bridging of some past gay/lesbian antagonisms, in the mid-to-late 1970s few lesbian feminists (or straight feminists) were attracted to what they perceived as the increasingly commercialized, 'cruising-oriented,' and self-interested subculture of gay brothers.

Some LOOT members participated alongside their straight sisters in abortion and child-care struggles, the union movement, anti-male violence organizing, anti-racist activism, and so on, but with varying degrees of apprehension and mistrust. Significantly, there were no lesbian equivalents to the bath raids or the state seizure of *The Body Politic* that might have united lesbian, bisexual, and straight feminists in anti-heterosexist struggle. As it was, the maxim 'feminism is the theory and lesbianism is the practice' illuminated the need to promote lesbian visibility, to establish lesbian institutions, and to develop an independent lesbian politic. At the same time, it operated to undermine and delegitimate the experiences of heterosexual and bisexual feminists and it militated against coalitions of lesbians and non-lesbian women, though the lesbian caucus of IWDC introduced in 1979 began to change this.

Heterosexual feminists were never officially banned from 342 Jarvis Street, yet neither were they openly welcomed. After interviewing five LOOT members, *Toronto Star* columnist Michele Landsberg was disturbed by the apparent gay/straight standoff. She wrote:

I began to see where the deep schism must come between radical lesbians and other feminists. They have worked out a critique of our society that is so massively rejecting ('The family is simply an economic noose, a trap for women and children') that there is almost no point of contact left. No wonder, then, that feminist groups dominated by lesbians seem to be skewed toward a tiresome, monotone militance. They must feel very little urge to reach out to the wider community which has already written them off. Heterosexual feminists, on the other hand, no matter how dissenting, still feel themselves linked to this country's public life. They seem to care much more about fighting for change in a way which doesn't burn bridges, doesn't isolate them from other women and doesn't alienate potential allies. I think both sides have a lot to say to one another: feminists have a duty to be alert to the economic and social vulnerabilty of lesbians, and radical lesbians have something to learn about constructive ways of change. It would be a shame if the conversation were strangled by embarrassment and mutual wariness.[40]

Asked to recall their feelings about the article – the only account of LOOT to appear in the mainstream press – the women I interviewed expressed unanimous dissatisfaction with Landsberg's commentary. They resented her oversimplification of complex, long-standing tensions between lesbian and straight feminists and they found her unsolicited advice that 'lesbians shouldn't be so isolated' both irksome and patronizing. Landsberg's homophobic discomfort with 'the shabby downtown headquarters of LOOT' and with her lesbian informants was particularly objectionable to them. Not only did she admit that 'it was time to confront my squeamishness,' but she stated that the women were 'anxious to explain themselves,' as if, Rachel pointed out, lesbianism once again required explanation.

Casting back ten years, Amy Gottlieb remembers her community's need to recognize and defend the fragility of what they had created in the face of adversity. She said, 'There were issues of confidentiality and security and the two sort of melded together to form a way in which we were building ourselves up and steeling ourselves against the external environment, for good reasons.' To LOOT regulars, any facile, impatient calls to reconcile gay/straight differences and to assume a higher public profile were premature and neglected to honour the desire lesbian feminists had to be heard and be taken seriously *on their own terms*.

Suspicion and miscommunication persisted through the 1970s between many straight and lesbian feminists, though as argued in chapter 8, the conflicts were centred less on sexual preference and more on radical/socialist divisions – divisions that were also present within the LOOT membership. Without a full integration of gender and sexual politics into their program for social change, members of the revolutionary left had little hope of appealing to radical lesbians already hostile to their male-dominated perspective and constituency.[41] In an article for the anthology *Feminism and Political Economy*, Lorna Weir criticizes socialist feminists in the 1970s for ceding the terrain of sexual politics, that is, rape, violence against women, and pornography, to radical feminists, many of whom were lesbians.[42] She contends that the class reductionism inherited from the socialist tradition contributed to the reticence with which socialist feminists handled questions pertaining to sex.

Beginning in 1979, the lesbians who founded Lesbian Perspectives inside IWDC – almost all of whom were LOOT members – struggled hard to incorporate sexual politics into the larger socialist agenda. Yet the value of their interventions was not fully realized in the 1970s. Dorothy E. Smith elucidates the contradiction: 'It was possible for the women's movement to be profoundly influenced by lesbians, lesbian thinking, culture and politics, and at the same time, to repudiate building a political practice into which lesbian issues and issues of sexuality were fully integrated.'[43] None the less, the impact that lesbian feminists had on straight feminists and gay-male liberationists should not be underestimated. Former LOOT members know that their pioneering efforts served to heighten lesbian visibility in lesbian, feminist, gay, and left communities and, to a lesser extent, in mainstream society. As Rosemary Barnes views it: 'There's a strength that lesbianism brings to feminism in general in terms of having space for women and thinking about how we feel about society completely independently of relationships with men that I think sustains all parts of feminism. Almost any organization we can name is ultimately sustained by the fact that there are lesbians there.'

In 1979, Pat Leslie asserted that 'without the definition of ourselves as lesbians, without this house, both the gay movement and the women's movement in this city would lack strength.'[44] Major contributions to the women's movement include insisting on the importance of women-only spaces, bringing to public attention the pervasive ordinariness of male sexual violence against women, enunciating the need for a politics of anti-heterosexism, and helping to bring an end to the debilitating economism that limited the socialist-feminist presence inside IWDC, the RMG/RWL, and other revolutionary-left formations. In relation to gay liberation, members of LOOT brought the need for attention to the specificity of lesbian experience to the fore, as well as a critique of gay men's sexism and sexual libertarianism. By LOOT's end, a number of lesbian feminists had begun to champion the building of coalitions across all progressive constituencies.

As more and more LOOT members turned their attention away from LOOT outward, the need for the organization diminished. Having offered its founders and regular members a safe site within which to come out, LOOT's job of reconstructing the political and existential identities of lesbian feminists was complete. Once they felt comfortable functioning *as lesbians* in the world – a state nourished by the social, support-oriented, and cultural components spawned by LOOT – they no longer needed an organizational home. Moreover, as they discovered in the context of political debates, the commonalities they shared – the desire for greater lesbian visibility and an end to compulsory heterosexuality – were not enough to overcome the ideological differences that emerged within the membership on questions of feminist analysis and strategy.

After years of reflection, Nancy Adamson arrived at her current understanding of the barriers to lesbian feminist organizing. She says, 'I just kept running into lesbians who were so different from me and had such different ideas about the world, about how to be sexually, about roles, about politics. "Lesbian" wasn't really a common thing between us. I kept being confronted by my notion that lesbianism would unite us. I thought that being lesbians would pull us together through bad times and our differences, but I began to see that it didn't ... I became very cynical about the possibility of organizing on the basis of being a lesbian. I wasn't convinced that being lesbians *was* a basis for organizing, and I'm still not.'

Radical versus socialist feminist perspectives split lesbian activists and weakened prospects of forging lesbian-specific projects and more generally, a lesbian-feminist movement. Indeed, the fissures that resulted from challenges posed by gay-liberationist and socialist lesbians to LOOT's radical lesbian-feminist thrust contributed to the organization's demise. However, in contradictory fashion, the emergence of a range of lesbian subject positions and discourses also attests to LOOT's profound success. Initially, LOOT played a powerful, transformative role in instituting a marvellous process through which a small group of largely white, middle-class, university-educated lesbians learned *to be* lesbian and feminist in all aspects of their lives. Unprecedented in depth and scope, the process eventually made it possible for these women to act *as lesbian feminists* in different political struggles – an increasingly necessary shift in times of scarce political resources, fortifying New Right forces, and a looming economic recession.

THE MOBILIZING NEW RIGHT

Across Canada, the late 1970s and early 1980s brought massive industrial and public-sector lay-offs, tightening wage and price controls, soaring inflation, cutbacks in social services (welfare, unemployment insurance, women's shelters, day care, employment training), and anti-union policies – the ravages of a deepening economic crisis. At the same time, monopolies and multinationals entrenched their domination of world economies, post–Cold War rhetoric was accompanied by armaments build-up, and the conservative climate of opinion served to legitimize state inactivity in such areas as unemployment and equal-pay legislation. The revolution, as members of LOOT had once heralded, was not around the corner.

A New Right backlash that began in the early 1970s in response to the growing visibility and politicization of lesbian, gay, and feminist communities continued to train its attention on the field of gender and sexual politics. By 1980, Campaign for Life, a coalition of groups such as Positive Parents and Renaissance International, and the groups of the neo-fascist right, among others, the Nationalist Party (formerly the Western Guard), the Ku Klux Klan, and the League Against Homosexuals, had intensified their pro-family, antichoice, antigay/lesbian, antifeminist, and racist lobby. Anxious to see homosexuality and feminism abolished through prayer or government legislation or, more crudely, obliterated as a solution to major social changes and crises, these groups postered the city with antilesbian and antigay hate literature during the provincial and municipal elections of 1980. That same year, right-wing Toronto School Board trustees rallied to block the introduction of lesbian/gay-positive curriculum. February 1981 marked a resurgence of the mid-1970s 'clean up Yonge Street' campaign: Metro police raided four gay bathhouses and laid charges against over three hundred men.[45] Several months later, Lesbians Against the Right reported, 'We are now becoming the target of right-wing attacks because there's something to take aim at,' and they accented the rise in police intimidation of lesbians.[46]

None of the above developments emerged in isolation from the growth of anti-abortion mobilization, the stepped-up state regulation of sex-trade workers, the escalating violence against women and children in the home and on the streets, and the increased police harassment of racial and ethnic communities most graphically evinced by the killing of Albert Johnson in Toronto in August 1979. In the United States, following the defeat of the Equal Rights Amendment, Allen Hunter argued that 'the New Right's patriarchal and heterosexist politics are also its racist and anti-working class politics ... in new right discourse, "Christian" becomes a code word for "white". The image of 'the family' operates to exclude natives, blacks, people of colour, the poor, lesbians and gay men, from the established moral framework.'[47]

Lesbian feminists who had attempted to define a lesbian public presence in Toronto realized that their heightened visibility by the decade's end was double-edged. In 1981, a member of the newly formed group Lesbians Against the Right (LAR), Amy Gottlieb, mused that 'the forces trying to push us back into the closet of the nuclear family, taking away our children, denying us jobs, harassing us on the streets are getting stronger ... and [this] backlash makes it a lot harder to survive. It also makes things a lot clearer as to who we are and who our enemies are.'[48]

As the 1980s unfolded and battle lines became more and more deeply etched, lesbian activists decided that grass-roots agitation would require creative, well-planned strategies and concerted reliance on coalition building. In May 1981, at the lesbian political forum from which Lesbians Against the Right (LAR) would later spring, Kathy Arnup announced, 'We've become scapegoats [of the right-wing], just like jews, blacks and immigrants.'[49] Borrowing the union axiom 'An injury to one is an injury to all,' members of LAR sought to forge links between lesbians and the gay movement, the women's movement, the antiracist movement, the labour movement, the reproductive-rights movement, the antinuclear movement, and antipoverty organizations. In ways that were unworkable a decade earlier, they endeavoured to define their own priorities and then work together in cooperation with other progressive people. Though LAR only survived for two years, it would not have been possible without the bedrock laid down by LOOT members.

10

Back to the future: Concluding notes

During the 1970s in Toronto and other Canadian cities, following the American lead, autonomous lesbian-feminist organizing signalled the first of many fractures within the largely heterosexual-dominated women's movement. Eager to differentiate themselves from straight women, sexist gay men, and non-political gay women, 'new lesbians' invented lesbian-feminist discourse, subject positions, and identities through avenues of life/style, sexuality, culture, and politics. In the 1980s, women of colour and immigrant women, Jewish women, disabled women, and working-class women charged feminism, and lesbian feminism, with its white, Christian, able-bodied, middle-class character.[1] Splinter groups increasingly committed to a particular brand of identity politics proliferated. The 1980s also yielded the subdivision of activist lesbians into specialized groupings: lesbians of colour, Jewish lesbians, working-class lesbians, leather dykes, lesbians against s/m, older lesbians, lesbian youth, disabled lesbians, and so on (see below).

In 1995, lesbian culture and politics have undergone an extraordinary redefinition through shifts in emphasis and group membership since the heyday of LOOT and similar lesbian-feminist projects. Today, among increasingly savvy lesbian and bisexual activists, the commitment to learning how differences of age, race, ethnicity, and class complexly intermix with sexual identity is serving to unsettle the normative 'whiteness,' unexamined class assumptions, ageism, and ableism that hobbled lesbian feminism in the 1970s. Though the drive to congregate and organize has far from disappeared, idyllic notions of 'Lesbian Nation' have all but been abandoned.

Concentrated in large urban centres, support groups include Lesbians of Colour (Toronto); Vancouver Island Support Group (Victoria);

Gays and Lesbians Aging (GALA, Toronto); Lesbian Youth Peer Support (LYPS, Toronto); Lesbian Youth Group (Vancouver); Black Socialist Dykes (Toronto); Gays and Lesbians at the University of Manitoba (Winnipeg); Fredericton Lesbians and Gays; Nice Jewish Girls (Toronto); Truro Lesbian Support Group; Asian Lesbians of Toronto (ALOT); Atish, for 'lesbigays' of South Asian Heritage (Vancouver); Two-Spirited Peoples of the First Nations (Toronto); the lesbian caucus of the Disabled Women's Network (DAWN); and Outrageous, Wiser Lesbians (OWLS, Toronto).[2] There is a range of social services: counselling services, coming-out groups, funding foundations, and community halls and centres, such as the Vancouver Gay and Lesbian Centre and the Lesbian and Gay Community Centre in Montréal. Legal issues are the focus of organizations: Equality for Gays and Lesbians Everywhere (EGALE), in Ottawa; the Coalition for Lesbian and Gay Rights in Ontario (CLGRO); Action Network for Gay and Lesbian Rights (Montréal), Canadian Committee against Customs Censorship (CCaCC); Censorstop; and lesbian and gay caucuses in unions like the Canadian Union of Educational Workers (CUEW), Bell Canada, and the Canadian Union of Public Employees (CUPE). Socially, needs are met by lesbian/gay bars and assorted 'Dyke Nites' at straight clubs; Lesbian and Gay Pride Day committees; church groups; choirs; recreation clubs; potluck dinner clubs; and lesbian softball, soccer, golf, swimming, bowling, water polo, and curling leagues. Bisexual women have also begun to build their own networks and enunciate their own political program.[3]

In the domain of representation, identified by editors of *Radical America* as the central site of queer political contests in the nineties, there are *Quota, a lesbian magazine* (Toronto), *Khush: a Newsletter of South Asian Lesbians and Gays* (Toronto), *X-tra!* (Vancouver, Toronto, Ottawa), *Sami Yoni, for Lesbians of South Asian Descent* (Toronto), *Angles* (Vancouver), *Labrys* (Ottawa), *CLUE!* magazine (Calgary), *Perceptions* (Regina), *Gayzette* (Halifax), and *Lezzie Smut* (Vancouver). Canadian lesbian anthologies have been published by the Women's Press, Sister Vision Press, Ragweed/Gynergy, and Queer Press, and there are lesbian/gay radio shows on community and campus stations. Lesbian/gay/queer issues have been published by *Border/Lines, Fireweed*, and *Fuse* magazines. Culturally, lesbians are making significant contributions to the fields of theatre, music, visual and performance art, film/video, and photography.

From my vantage point as a white, middle-class academic/activist, I devour cartoons by Noreen Stevens; prose by Dionne Brand, Jane

Rule, Makeda Silvera, and Beth Follett; computer porn by Shonagh Adelman; poetry by Brenda Brooks, Leleti Tamu, Daphne Marlatt, Betsy Warland, Carolyn Gammon, Tamai Kobayashi, and Mona Oikawa; and music by Faith Nolan, Seven Cent Posse, Sugar and Spice, k.d. lang, Ingrid Stitt, and Women With Horns. The films/videos of Midi Onodera, Candy Paulker, Michelle Mohabeer, Shanni Mootoo, Marusia Bociurkiw, Rose Gutierrez, and Gita Saxena (Gitanjali) and the art of Stephanie Martin, Grace Channer, Karen Augustine, Anna Camilleri, River Sui, and Racy Sexy examine intersections of racial identity, racism, and sexuality, and offer a stinging antidote to the sanitized and commodified white-lesbian 'flavour of the month' peddled by *Newsweek*, *Vanity Fair*, and *New York* magazines.

Academic ventures, though much less robust in Canada than in the United States, include the Toronto Centre for Lesbian and Gay Studies and their newsletter, *Centre/Fold*; a smattering of credit and non-credit courses in colleges and universities; and assorted campus-based lesbian and gay groups, conferences, and seminars.[4] Lesbians have been involved in many forms of AIDS activism, including direct-action groups like AIDS Action Now! and support groups for persons living with AIDS.[5] Moreover, lesbians continue to make up the leadership of sex workers' rights organizations such as the Canadian Organization for the Rights of Prostitutes (CORP), Maggie's – the Prostitutes' Safe Sex Project, and Sex Workers Alliance of Toronto (SWAT). Indeed, in a departure from the 1970s, there are greater numbers of lesbians who have chosen to work alongside pro-feminist gay men across a wide spectrum of community-based activities.

In contrast to LOOT, today there are no groups that attempt to be all things to all lesbians. Instead, the diffuse, partitioned character of lesbian-feminist organizing predominates. Almost all former members of LOOT are currently involved in politically oriented undertakings as lesbians and feminists, yet not in organizations that identify explicitly as lesbian feminist: for instance, alternative publishing, literacy advocacy, fiction writing, feminist teaching, counselling and healing, 'third world' solidarity work, pay-equity lobbying, cooperative housing, performance art and cultural production, local antiracist action, antipoverty organizing, the environmental movement, feminist service groups such as rape crisis and battered women's centres, self-defence, bookselling, and safe-sex education and outreach.

It is unclear to me whether communities of bar lesbians, closeted, suburban gay women, and lesbian feminists are closer together today than they were twenty years ago. The majority of lesbians (and gay men) continue to live double lives, hiding their sexuality in fear of damaging consequences. It's possible that greater numbers will come out in the 1990s, buoyed up by a splendid twenty-five-year legacy of activism and the tenacity of lesbian and lesbian/gay/queer institutions intent on realizing greater visibility, dignity, and equality in the future. Whether closeted or partially closeted lesbians then place their lesbian identity in a public, political context as a site of personal/political agitation for change remains an open question.

Since the 1970s, the presumption of an instant unity among lesbians qua lesbians has been proven both false and intolerant to differences. Given the limitations of LOOT and early lesbian-feminist praxis more generally, the increasing recognition of diversity and the naming of difference/s as a site of organizing would seem to mark a positive step. But as Cherrie Moraga warns, 'Failure to move out from there will only isolate us in our own oppression – will only insulate rather than radicalize us.'[6] And bell hooks adds that 'the ability to see and describe one's own reality is a significant step in the long process of self-recovery; but it is only a beginning.'[7] As Lilith Finkler noted in her interview with me, 'I used to identify as a separatist but one of the things I recognize now is that I am a lesbian, I'm a Jew, I'm poor with a working-class background, I'm an incest survivor, I'm a survivor of psychiatric abuse ... what's so hard is that if I decided to be a separatist and only hang out with Jewish lesbian ex-inmates who were survivors of incest, it would be a very small group.'

Within the past several years, in Toronto, Montréal, Vancouver and several smaller cities, networks of mixed-gender, multi-sexual, and multiracial coalitions have emerged in the wake of successive political crises: the police shootings of black youths in the late 1980s; the Chantal Daigle and Barbara Dodd abortion cases (1989); the Montréal Massacre (1989); police violence directed against lesbians and gay men in Montréal (1990); the invasion of First Nation territories at Kanasatake (1990); the Gulf War (1991); the police raid on the gay men's leather bar, Katacombes, in Montréal (1993); the trumped-up targeting of Somali Canadians as welfare defrauders (1993–94); the rise of anti-Semitism and anti-immigration sentiment and practices; and the recent escalation of gay/lesbian bashing in most urban centres. Throughout, lesbian, gay, and bisexual activists have struggled to forge tenuous, fragile bonds with other progressive constituencies. Reminiscent of joint organizing in the 1970s, participation in alliance building is still fraught with miscommunication, suspicion, and the fear of co-optation. Though concerted efforts have been made to promote and realize inclusivity, problems of sexism, racism, homophobia, and unexamined class privilege persist.[8]

Considering the international scene, it is striking that lesbian and gay organizing largely remains specific to white, Western, industrialized countries and, in particular, to large cities.[9] There are, however, signs of change. For example, the first-ever lesbian and gay conference was held in Moscow in the summer of 1991. Since the mid-1980s, organizing initiatives have been launched in Japan, South Africa, Cuba, Mexico, and parts of Latin America and Eastern Europe by gays and lesbians with limited resources and in opposition to sometimes life-threatening, brutal regimes. The fourth Encuentro Lesbian Feminista de Latinoamerica y del Caribe was held in Brazil in 1994.[10]

On the one hand, small victories have been secured. On the other, most Western capitalist cultures are beseiged by the ascendancy of moral and economic conservatism and the erosion of political gains, the rootedness of heterosexism deepened by the AIDS/HIV crisis, and the sluggishness of social-change movements. In Canada, two lesbians recently lost custody of their children in part because they were lesbians and deemed 'unfit' care-givers and role models by a judge in Renfrew County.[11] On sex- and gender-related issues, the state has re-tooled obscenity legislation: the Supreme Court *Butler* decision (1992) has been used by Ontario judges to confiscate lesbian and gay sexually explicit images/texts from Canadian bookstores, and Memorandum D-9-1-1 continues to dictate the U.S./Canada border seizures of lesbian/gay print and visual materials en route to lesbian/gay, women's, and left bookstores.[12] Passed hurriedly in the summer of 1993, the 'youth pornography' bill, Bill C-128 (Section 163.1 of the Criminal Code), has increased controls on sex-trade workers and criminalized young gay-male hustlers. A last-minute electoral ploy intended to advance the federal Tory government's tough anticrime agenda, the law provides for up to five years in prison for simple possession and up to ten years for production, distribution, importation, or sale of sexually explicit images of anyone under eighteen (or anyone who *appears to be* under eighteen).[13]

The federal House of Commons has yet to include sexual-orientation protection in the Charter of Rights and Freedoms, though courts ruled in the *Haig and Birch* decision (1992) that sexual orientation is an 'analogous ground' and must be 'read into' both the Charter and the Canadian Human Rights Act. The Human Rights Commission alone is currently faced with over eighty cases concerning discrimination, harassment, and employment benefits launched by lesbians and gay men in Canada. When the Canadian Union of Public Employees (CUPE) passed a resolution to amend its pension plan so its gay and lesbian workers could name their partner as beneficiary, the Ministry of Revenue denied the union eligibility for tax benefits that other employers receive for contributions to employee pension plans under the Income Tax Act.

On a positive note, over the past twenty-five years, a significant handful of victories have been secured. In 1991, the 'Douglas' decision made at the Supreme Court level determined that homosexuality is no longer grounds for discrimination in the Canadian Armed Forces.[14] A number of corporate employers have decided to extend spousal benefits to their lesbian and gay employees, including Bell Northern Research and Northern Telecom, Southam, Sears, and Dow Chemical. At the provincial government level, the Ontario legislature passed antidiscrimination legislation in 1986 to join Québec (1977), Manitoba (1987), the Yukon (1988), Nova Scotia (1991), New Brunswick (1992), British Columbia (1992), and Saskatchewan (1993). The only remaining provinces and territories that do not provide antidiscrimination legislation are Prince Edward Island, Alberta, Newfoundland, and the Northwest Territories. In June 1994, the Québec Human Rights Commission recommended that provincial legislation be amended to extend to lesbian and gay couples the same rights and benefits enjoyed by heterosexual couples, except the right to adopt children.[15]

In December 1990, the Ontario New Democratic Party (NDP) extended job benefits – including health, dental, and leave time – to same-sex couples in the civil service. In 1992, Michael Leshner won a four-year legal battle requiring the Ontario government to extend survivor pension benefits to its lesbian and gay employees. Though the body of judicial and quasi-judicial rulings recognizing the rights of lesbians and gays is growing, the process is expensive and time-consuming and deals ineffectively with discrimination on a case-by-case basis.

In 1993, the ruling Ontario NDP government introduced the omnibus Bill 167 – the Equality Rights Statute Law Amendment Act – intended to rewrite over fifty laws to provide equal rights for same-sex couples. Among the laws to be revised are the Family Law Act, Landlord and Tenant Act, Insurance Act, Cemeteries Act, and Land

Transfer Tax Act.[16] The sweeping bill championed by Attorney General Marion Boyd was designed to legalize lesbian/gay adoption, spousal pension benefits upon death of the partner, and tax benefits for lesbian and gay couples.[17] In May 1994, it passed first reading by a narrow margin of 57–52 votes; the debate in and outside the legislature whipped up considerable moral anxiety about the stability of 'the family.'[18] Indeed, an Ontario provincial by-election in the Victoria-Haliburton riding was won in April 1994 by Chris Hodgson, a Progressive Conservative candidate who campaigned exclusively against the provincial NDP's promise to extend legal rights to same-sex couples. Hodgson's campaign literature argued that 'new spending schemes' (that is, same-sex spousal benefits) will 'increase the cost of doing business in Ontario and drive jobs away.'[19]

In May 1994, the Roman Catholic Archbishop of Toronto, Aloysius Ambrozic, addressed more than one million Catholic parishioners. In a letter mailed to two hundred parishes in the greater Toronto area, he proclaimed: 'Any attempt to promote a homosexual lifestyle as the equivalent of legal marriage must be vigorously opposed. It is a matter of considerable urgency, and to that end we are asking you to write to your local member of provincial parliament to protest the proposed legislation.'[20] Dignity, a group for gay and lesbian Catholics with country-wide chapters, vociferously condemned the archbishop's decree, as did a number of progressive Catholic, Jewish, United Church, and Anglican leaders. Meanwhile, in Alberta in 1994, backed by the support of several influential church groups, provincial Tory Premier Ralph Klein appealed a court decision that would extend human-rights protection to lesbians and gay men.[21] At the same time, gays, lesbians, and supporters have mobilized bodies and resources to combat the damage of active, repressive forces.

On 9 June 1994, the second reading of Bill 167 in the Ontario Legislature was defeated by a margin of 68–59 after a charged, emotional debate. Twelve members of the majority NDP government voted against the bill. While thousands of lesbians, gays, bisexuals, and supporters protested the defeat at a downtown demonstration later that evening, fundamentalist leaders such as Ken Campbell hailed the quashing of the bill as a victory for the 'majority of the province.'[22] Over the course of several months of heated skirmishes, these fiercely competing positions approached the character of an informal national referendum on homosexuality, sexual liberation, and the family with all the properties of a full-scale moral panic reminiscent of Anita Bryant's 'Save Our Children' crusade and the police incursion on *The Body Politic* magazine in 1977.

Notwithstanding the fiery backlash, it is clear that law reform in and of itself is a limited avenue for change – a reality that lesbian feminists had predicted in the late 1970s. Sociologist Didi Khayatt has documented how lesbian teachers in Ontario continue to peform elaborate 'passing' strategies to hide their lesbian identities in spite of legal protection for sexual orientation via antidiscrimination legislation.[23] Legal scholar Didi Herman warns against the liberal thrust underlying the civil-rights reforms sought by organizations of lesbians and gay men in the Canadian context.[24] Writer Carol Allen is concerned about who will be excluded by legislation change. She cautions: 'We must stop making legal arguments which, if successful, will only help other professional, white, middle-class, able-bodied lesbians and gays whose family form looks very much like the traditional heterosexual ideal.'[25] Moreover, the law provides an inadequate measure of protection for vulnerable constituencies such as lesbian and gay teachers, child-care workers, nurses, and social workers. As such, legal reform in isolation from massive educational offensives will not necessarily dismantle homophobic and heterosexist attitudes and practices.

To chart continuities and changes over the past twenty years, I asked former members of LOOT whether they felt that it was harder or easier to come out as a lesbian in the 1990s. Their responses were wide-ranging and reflect their hopes and fears for women who have yet to begin the journey of coming to terms with their sexual identity. What follows is a sampling of their observations.

Fiona Rattray: There's so many options now, you open the phone book under the letter 'G' or 'L' and you can plug into all these different things. It seems less risky for women to come out, but there's less of that heady sense that we're doing something, we're changing things, moving things; it's more like this stuff is here and I'm coming out into it. I still sometimes feel like the giant heterosexual society is out there waiting to step on us, but it can't squash us back to where we were before. There's always going to be somebody hammering away at you so you can't really ever relax and say, 'Well, we've fought the fight.' One step forward, another back, but if you look globally, around the world, lesbian groups are happening, it's spreading out. The concept of a visible, organized, global force is exciting.

Pat Hugh: When I came out (in 1965) I had to look for women through *Tab*, this trashy newspaper; I think it's still around. I left Guyana when I was a young dyke because I knew I couldn't be a dyke there and I wrote a woman whose name I discovered in a classified ad in *Tab*. And the dykes today don't have to do that. Never again, and it's great.

Rachel: There are more books; they are more widely distributed, we have wider informal networks, and when the people down the block with the 13-year-old realize that they have lesbian neighbours, they may take that in. But I'm depressed about the situation. Lesbian teachers and guidance counsellors meet young women who are clearly struggling with lesbianism, and these older role models and mentors are scared shitless of being out and giving any kind of help because of the consequences.

Virginia Adamson: I don't think it's any easier to come out in the 90s. I know a lot of people who still haven't come out, who have supportive people around them. People are afraid of AIDS because it has brought up people's hatred toward homosexuals.

Natalie LaRoche: There seems to be a new generation of young militants, young dykes, young trade unionists, young antiracist people; I like the energy and I feel hopeful. I love what Black women and Black dykes are doing and the fact that they're getting strong. Their knowing themselves is going to change the face of feminism. Black and brown and women of colour are getting together and changing it whether white women like it or not. I have faith in a maturity that's going to happen, that's going to get beyond all the bullshit.

In the 1990s, perhaps more than ever, contests over what 'lesbian' means rage on. Exhibiting 'authentic' behavioural, ideological and style codes (however much authenticity itself is debated) is still esteemed among many politicized lesbian feminists as one method of revealing one's inner self, securing high moral rank, and locking up political credibility. Today the drive to determine identity-based codes – the ongoing preoccupation with *being a 'real' lesbian* – seems to betray an even greater urgency and intensity. And yet there seems to be re-markably less consensus among the players: a potentially liberating dilemma given the challenges posed to the silences constructed by white, middle-class lesbian-feminist discourse, icons, and narratives, yet one that may also immobilize. *Village Voice* columnist Alisa Solomon warns that 'a lesbian can wag her finger as righteously as any patriarchal puritan, defining what's acceptable according to what must not be ingested, worn and especially desired.'[26] And reporting on the National Lesbian Conference in Atlanta in 1991, Donna Minkowitz reported: 'The main business emerged: an inquisition into the sins of conference goers, from working for Uncle Sam to preferring thin women as sex partners ... Attendees were so obsessed with setting up a *cordon sanitaire* that no one organized to do anything concrete to change the real world.'[27] In 1995, most urban lesbian activists in Canada and the United States have demonstrated little enthusiasm for the prospect of bridging balkanized constituencies.

At the same time, attempts within lesbian-feminist communities to supplant old prescriptions with liberal-individualist codes for fashionable, politically sophisticated 'queerdom' in the 1990s threaten to mandate new notions of who's in and who's out. Such a focus harkens back to the inward-looking nature of preceding Lesbian Nations rather than forward to the promise of mobilizing against actual state and social discrimination. Exclusionary parameters police populations and operate to compartmentalize constituencies as acceptable or unacceptable. I argue that no movement for gender and sexual liberation can afford the evacuation of a male-to-female lesbian transsexual, a leather dyke into s/m fantasy, a lesbian (or any woman) who is HIV+, a softball-playing and factory-working gay woman, a rural lesbian who has never heard of Susie Sexpert, or a lesbian of colour who refuses to splice her self into identity-pieces with lesbian on top.[28]

Certainly, there is no obvious or guaranteed correlation between 'otherness' and community-based militancy. However, in the lesbian-feminist 1970s, formal and informal strictures worked to deny the benefits of belongingness to those least acquiescent to conformity. Positioned on the outside (though insiders did not always feel inside) were those lesbians, whether or not they identified as feminists, who came to terms with their lesbian selves primarily in lesbian/gay bars, hostels, prisons, baseball and hockey leagues, recreation clubs, house parties, and workplaces. I am not suggesting that these sites were void of codes and rules; I suspect that they were governed by a sophisticated infrastructure of norms and meanings intrinsic to every subculture. What remains worth interrogating, however slippery and contradictory, is the power wielded within social formations to make manifest certain possibilities and to preclude the attainment of others.

The knowledge and meanings of polymorphously diverse lesbian experience have been silenced, distorted, denied, and/or omitted from the historical record. During the period of 1977–80, members of the Lesbian Organization of Toronto identified lesbian visibility, lesbian-feminist pride, and the dismantling of heterosexual hegemony as fundamental to the collective fight for sexual and social freedom for all women. LOOT-goers set out to operationalize what it meant to *be* a full-time lesbian feminist in all facets of their lives – the 'unified epistemological and volitional agent,' to quote Shane Phelan.[29] Coming out – perceived as the first necessary and prideful step towards liberation – was not just a linguistic act; it was a physical and psychic dramatization of one's essential lesbianness. Members of LOOT insisted on the radical specificity of lesbian feminism through what Judith Bulter might call the self-disclosing, repetitive acts of gender and sexual insubordination.[30] Reinvesting the feminist dictum 'the personal is political' with bold, fresh lesbian faith served as an intense flash point for a newly forming feminist constituency.

Several former LOOT members claim that the genesis of all social/recreational, support, political, and legal action by and for lesbians in Toronto in the 1990s can be traced directly back to the concretization of lesbian-feminist vision/s internal to the Lesbian Organization of Toronto. Without question, young activists today owe a debt to LOOT's fecund seedbed of ideas, energy, and hutzpah. The richness of contemporary lesbian/gay/queer organizing attests to the profound impact of LOOT's existence in spite of the difficulties of transfering grass-roots political and cultural acumen from generation to generation. At the same time, LOOT's legacy is not an unproblematic one. The varied successes and limitations of the LOOT experiment at once inspire and haunt contemporary efforts to contest debilitating discourses and practices of heterosexism, as well as sexism, racism, and class inequality. Figuring out how to accomplish liberatory politics and gains without reproducing past mistakes will preoccupy grass-roots activists for decades to come.

Amid the current profusion of multi/queer/culture and identities, tensions persist between organizing autonomously and building coalitions across diverse constituencies. The often painful, exasperating, and yet indispensable work of grass-roots activism is most cogently articulated by African American Bernice Johnson Reagon in 'Coalition Politics,' a speech delivered at the West Coast Women's Music Festival in 1981.[31] Almost fifteen years later, to me it appears easier at times to abandon the commitment to devoted, militant struggle than to persevere in spite of disillusionment. Yet, in urban and rural milieux, lesbian/gay/queer and queer-positive resources are multiplying, not shrinking – a testament to the fortitude and imagination of those faced with adversity, hostility, and feelings of non-existence. Indeed, the proliferating tentacles of anti-heterosexist resistance emerge by necessity to challenge the diffuse, micro-techniques of power that socially organize heterosexuality as the only allegedly 'normal,' 'natural,' and 'universal' human sexual expression. While post-structuralist theorists illuminate the instability and performativity of identity categories to the point of deconstituting queerness altogether, many lesbians/gays/queers stubbornly promulgate their perverse identifications. And they are joined by increasing numbers of organized cross-dressers, transvestites, transsexuals, and transgenderists: a phenomenon that suggests the multiplication rather than the dissolution of identities.[32] And yet, as Judith Butler heeds, though 'outness' demands affirmation, the term may present an impossible conflict between racial, ethnic, or religious affiliation and sexual politics. In other words, we need to ask, For whom is outness an available and affordable option?[33] We need to recall that the vast majority of lesbians (and gay men) are not out, lead double lives, and struggle to be whole human beings.

Many lesbian stories need to be told, retold, and remembered. *The House That Jill Built* offers one book of stories that aims to stem the corrosive tide of amnesia. In the end, I am still uncertain as to what the determinate content of a lesbian-feminist politics might be. While some lesbian commentators argue for the assimilationist right to 'family' monopolized by heterosexuals, others hope that future queers will embrace their role as 'recruiters' of those foundering in the alien worlds of families. Some endorse the power of pink consumerism to change mainstream attitudes; others agitate for the efflorescence of a radical movement, or movements, not a market. Some are concerned to highlight the vulnerability of women (and lesbians) to sexual victimization, while others insist on the urgent need to assert sexual optimism and jouissance.

In June 1994, over one million lesbians/gays/queers and friends gathered to celebrate the twenty-fifth anniversary of the Stonewall riots in New York City. (A counter-parade of ten thousand was organized to raise the profile of issues pertaining to AIDS/HIV, to celebrate sex radicalism, and to support the North American Man/Boy Love Association.) Around the same time, cities across Canada staged their own lesbian and gay pride parades and festivals. Demands made by participants ran the gamut: lesbian/gay visibility; political, legal, and social rights; access to services; funding for HIV/AIDS-related activities and cultural projects; an end to right-wing and fundamentalist homophobia, police harassment, and state censorship.[34] Still, consensus on a definitive political program remains as elusive as it did in the 1970s. And dominant structures and attitudes seem more intractable than ever imagined by first generation post-Stonewall lesbian activists. Yet I maintain that a compassionate and critical evaluation of the past enables us to understand better the texture of lesbian political life, as well as the reactionary fear and hatred of difference, be it, sexual, gender-based, racial, or cultural.

In the end, the complexities of making a truly feminist, socialist, sexually plural, and anti-racist tomorrow were glimpsed by lesbian feminists of the 1970s. Intrepid amazons, they saw their own and other women's oppression as angering, unacceptable, and in dire need of redress. With utter irreverence, their voices and their actions, albeit imperfect, prepared the ground for subsequent community-based developments, and their influence continues to be felt. I argue that lesbian feminism 1970s-style cannot simply be dismissed as one example of 'stunted,' 'self-righteous,' and ultimately backwards or regressive identity politics.[35] I've discovered that the theoretical, personal, and political enterprise of white, middle-class Lesbian Nationalism twenty years ago commands both respectful reclamation and rigorous reflection. The iterated desire to open up a community or a movement, all the while restricting its membership, is a paradox that hampers many radical projects even today. Lesbian feminists in the 1970s were not unaware of the tension; some recall moments of their own ambivalence towards lesbian-nationalist rhetoric. Indeed, efforts to describe and analyse contradictions that arise in the process of identity production suggest new possibilities for historicizing and explicating how identity itself becomes a site of multiple and conflicting claims.

Appendix

Below, the reader will find a list of women I interviewed, and the date of the interview. With the exception of Holly Devor, whom I interviewed in Victoria, BC, the interviews took place in Toronto between the fall of 1988 and the spring of 1991.

Former LOOT members

Adamson, Nancy, 11 December 1988
Adamson, Virginia, 15 March 1989
Bearchell, Chris, and Konnie Reich, 5 November 1998, 21 May 1990
Bell, Gay, and Rosemary Barnes, 21 November 1988, 11 December 1988
Brooks, Naomi, 2 February 1989
Cole, Susan, 27 April 1989
Cordingley, Nia, 28 November 1990
Dworin, Ruth, 2 May 1990
Fernie, Lynne, 24 April 1990
Finkler, Lilith (Evelyn), 14 April 1989
Genge, Sue, and Kathy Arnup, 12 December 1989
Godfrey, Pam, 18 December 1990
Gottlieb, Amy, 23 November 1988
Hugh, Pat, 16 February 1989
Kado, Ann, 7 December 1989
LaRoche, Natalie, 22 November 1988
Leslie, Pat, 27 October 1988
Marchand, Donna, 20 March 1990
Masters, Philinda (Phil), 19 December 1989

Moores, Margaret, 23 March 1990
Murphy, Pat, 18 April 1989
Rachel [pseudonym], 29 December 1988
Rattray, Fiona, 15 November 1988
Smith, Cate (Catherine), 15 February 1989
Stinson, Deb, 15 February 1990
Valverde, Mariana, 8 January 1989
Weir, Lorna, 18 December 1989
Zaremba, Eve, 29 December 1988

LOOT Anniversary party: 25 April 1990, Women's Common, Toronto

Group Interview: Naomi Brooks, Eve Zaremba, Pat Leslie, Margaret Moores, 31 May 1990, Trinity/St Paul's, Toronto

Lesbians who were out between 1965 and 1980 and were not regular members of LOOT

Axten, Mary, 27 March 1989
Bryson, Laurie, 14 November 1990
Devor, Holly, 31 May 1990
Dina [pseudonym], 6 November 1990
Frese, Lynne, 7 January 1991
Giselle, 5 November 1990
Gwendolyn, 12 March 1991
Jain, Linda, 21 January 1991
Lowes, Tin (Virginia), 16 January 1991
MacIntosh, Carol, and Betty, 6 January 1991
Potts (Rosen), Adrienne, 3 March 1991
Schaillee, Caroline, and Susan Wells, 26 February 1991
Schembri, Maryse, 4 February 1991
Van Dyke, Jude (Judith Zutz), 13 December 1990
Walsh, Maxine, 27 November 1990

Women who were straight or bisexual feminists during LOOT's lifetime

Burstyn, Varda, 31 January 1991 and 5 March 1991
Egan, Carolyn, 31 October 1990
Sky, Laura, 26 March 1991

Archives

Canadian Lesbian and Gay Archives, 56 Temperance St., Toronto

Canadian Women's Movement Archives / Archives canadiennes du mouvement des femmes, University of Ottawa, Ottawa

Notes

INTRODUCTION

1 See Lois Stuart, interviewed by Lesbians Making History, 'People Think This Didn't Happen in Canada – But It Did,' *Fireweed, Lesbiantics II* (Spring 1989): 86.

2 Eloise Salholz, 'The Power and the Pride,' *Newsweek*, 21 June 1993: 54–60; Jeanie Russell Kasindorf, 'Lesbian Chic: The Brave, Bold World of Gay Women,' *New York*, May 1993: 30–7; Leslie Bennetts, 'k.d. lang's Edge: Crossing Over, Catching Fire,' *Vanity Fair*, August 1993: 94–8, 142–6. For criticism of 'lesbian chic' see Rachel Giese, 'I Feel Pretty, Witty and Gay,' *Border/Lines* 32 (Spring 1994): 26–9.

3 Amy Cunningham, 'Not Just Another Prom Night,' *Glamour*, June 1992: 222–5, 259–60.

4 Arlene Stein, 'All Dressed Up But No Where to Go? Style Wars and the New Lesbianism,' *Out/Look*, Winter 1989: 34–42.

5 Cherrie Moraga, 'Writing Is the Measure of My Life' (interview), *Out/Look*, Winter 1989: 56.

6 Alisa Solomon, 'In Whose Face?' *Village Voice* 2 July 1991: 41.

7 On new trends in women's music, see Arlene Stein, 'Androgyny Goes Pop: But Is It Lesbian Music?' in A. Stein, ed., *Sisters, Sexperts and Queers: Beyond the Lesbian Nation* (New York: Penguin Books 1993), 96–109.

8 Chris Bearchell was the first to use the phrase 'wet test' as a measure of the arousal potential of a sexually explicit text or image.

9 Recent contributions to lesbian and gay historical scholarship include Bob Cant and Susan Hemmings, eds, *Radical Records: Thirty Years of Lesbian and Gay History, 1957–1978* (London: Routledge and Kegan Paul 1988); Lillian Faderman, *Odd Girls and Twilight Lovers: A History of Lesbian Life in Twentieth Cen-*

tury America (New York: Columbia University Press 1991); Allan Bérubé, *Coming Out under Fire: Gay Men and Women in the Second World War* (New York: Penguin Books 1990); Martin Bauml Duberman, Martha Vicinus, and George Chauncey, Jr, eds, *Hidden from History: Reclaiming the Gay and Lesbian Past* (New York: New American Library 1989); John D'Emilio and Estelle Freedman, *Intimate Matters: A History of Sexuality in America* (New York: Harper and Row 1988); Judith Brown, *Immodest Acts* (Toronto: Oxford University Press 1986); Gary Kinsman, *The Regulation of Desire: Sexuality in Canada* (Montréal: Black Rose Books 1987); Becki Ross, ed., *Forbidden Love: The Unashamed Lives of Post-War Canadian Lesbians* (forthcoming, 1995). For a review of recent scholarship on lesbians/gays in the history of sexuality, see Jennifer Terry, 'Locating Ourselves in the History of Sexuality,' *Out/Look*, Summer 1988: 86–91.

10 On the topic of lesbian and gay studies, conferences have included 'Among Women, Among Men,' Amsterdam, 1983; 'Sex and the State,' Toronto, 1985; 'Homosexuality, Which Homosexuality?' Amsterdam, 1987; and the annual Lesbian and Gay Studies Conference in the United States, which began in 1987. Among the print resources are *GLQ: A Journal of Lesbian and Gay Studies, Journal of Homosexuality* (San Francisco), *Sociologists' Lesbian and Gay Caucus* (Claremont, Calif.), *Homologies* (University of Amsterdam), *Lesbian and Gay Studies Newsletter* (University of Toronto), *Legacy: Newsletter of the Lesbian and Gay Studies Centre at Yale* (New Haven, Conn.), and communinty-based newsletters: *San Francisco Bay Area Gay and Lesbian Historical Society Newsletter, Gay Archivist* (Toronto), *Canadian Lesbian and Gay History Network Newsletter* (Montréal and Toronto), *Lesbian Herstory Archives News* (New York), *Centre/fold, Newsletter of Toronto Centre for Lesbian and Gay Studies* (Toronto). Every three years the Berkshire Women's History Conference in the north-eastern United States programs cutting-edge sessions on lesbianism / female homoeroticism. Special issues of journals that have featured lesbianism and lesbian politics include *The Lesbian Issue, Signs, I and II* (Chicago: University of Chicago Press 1985, 1993), *The Lesbian Issue, Resources for Feminist Research* (March 1983), *Fireweed, Lesbiantics I and II* (Summer 1982; Spring 1989), *Perverse Politics: Lesbian Issues, Feminist Review* (Spring 1990), and *The Lesbian Issue, Feminist Studies* (Fall 1991).

11 I use quotation marks here to alert the reader to the ongoing definitional struggles over the use of the term 'lesbian,' particularly when women in the past did not use this category to describe themselves. Suffice it to say that the question of definition continues to be a vexing one in lesbian and feminist historiography.

12 Robert Padgug, 'Sexual Matters: On Conceptualizing Sexuality in History,' *Radical History Review*, Spring/Summer 1979: 3–23.

13 Kathy Peiss and Christina Simmons, 'Passion and Power: An Introduction,' in K. Peiss and C. Simmons, eds, *Passion and Power: Sexuality in History* (Philadelphia: Temple University Press 1989), 3–13.

14 Carole Vance, 'Pleasure and Danger: Towards a Politics of Sexuality,' in C. Vance, ed., *Pleasure and Danger: Female Sexuality Today* (Boston and London: Routledge and Kegan Paul 1984), 1–28, and 'Social Construction Theory: Problems in the History of Sexuality,' in Dennis Altman et al., eds, *Homosexuality, Which Homosexuality?* (London: GMP Publishers 1989), 13–34; Jeffrey Weeks, *Sexuality and Its Discontents* (London, Melbourne, and Henley: Routledge and Kegan Paul 1985), and *Sexuality* (London: Tavistock 1986); Frank Mort, *Dangerous Sexualities: Medico-Moral Politics in England since 1830* (London and New York: Routledge and Kegan Paul 1987). And for a brilliant essay on the social construction of heterosexuality, see Jonathon Ned Katz, 'The Invention of Heterosexuality,' *Socialist Review* 20, 1 (January/March 1990): 7–33.

15 Gayle Rubin, 'Thinking Sex: Notes for a Radical Theory of the Politics of Sexuality,' in Carole Vance, ed., *Pleasure and Danger*, 267–319.

16 Jeffrey Weeks, *Sex, Politics and Society: The Regulation of Sexuality since 1800* (London and New York: Longman 1981), 98.

17 Laurie Bell, *On Our Own Terms: A Practical Guide to Lesbian and Gay Relationships in Canada*, (Toronto: Coalition for Lesbian and Gay Rights in Ontario 1991).

18 On lesbian experience, see Adrienne Rich, 'Compulsory Heterosexuality and Lesbian Existence,' in Ann Snitow, Christine Stansell, and Sharon Thompson, eds, *Powers of Desire: The Politics of Sexuality* (New York: Monthly Review Press 1983), 177–205.

19 The collapsing of lesbian and gay experience together under the umbrella 'homosexual,' is most glaring in the early work of Dennis Altman, *Homosexual: Oppression and Liberation* (New York: Avon 1971) and *Coming Out in the Seventies* (Boston: Alyson Publications 1979), as well as in many of the essays in Kenneth Plummer's *The Making of the Modern Homosexual* (London: Hutchinson 1981).

20 Martha Bianchi Dickinson, *The Life and Letters of Emily Dickinson* (Boston: Houghton Mifflin 1924), and *Emily Dickinson Face to Face: Unpublished Letters with Notes and Reminiscences* (Boston: Houghton Mifflin 1932). For a greater discussion of the relationship between Dickinson and Sue Gilbert, see Lillian Faderman, 'Emily Dickinson's Letters to Sue Gilbert,' *Massachusetts*

Review 18, 2 (September 1977): 197–225, and 'Emily Dickinson's Homoerotic Poetry,' *Higginson Journal* 18 (June 1978): 19–27. Also see Nancy Johnston, 'The Attar from the Rose: Feminist Approaches to Textual Criticism,' in Debra Martens, ed., *Weaving Alliances* (Ottawa: Canadian Women's Studies Association 1993), 331–43.

21 Judy Grahn, *Another Mother Tongue* (Boston: Beacon Press 1986), 170.

22 Gloria T. Hull, 'Researching Alice Dunbar-Nelson: A Personal and Literary Perspective,' in G.T. Hull, Barbara Smith, and Patricia Scott, eds, *All The Women Are White, All the Blacks Are Men, But Some of Us Are Brave* (New York: Feminist Press 1982), 191.

23 Judith Schwarz, 'Questionnaire on Issues in Lesbian History,' *Frontiers* 4, 3 (1979): 2.

24 Paula Gunn Allen, *The Sacred Hoop* (Boston: Beacon Press 1986); Judy Grahn, 'Strange Country This: Lesbianism and North American Indian Tribes,' in Monika Kehoe, ed., *Historical, Literary and Erotic Aspects of Lesbianism* (New York and London: Harrington Park Press 1986), 43–57; Evelyn Blackwood, 'Sexuality and Gender in Certain Native American Tribes: The Case of Cross-Gender Females,' in Estelle Freedman et al., eds, *The Lesbian Issue, Signs* (Chicago: University of Chicago Press, 1985), 27–42. On cross-dressing, see Jonathon Katz, *Gay American History* (New York: Thomas Y. Crowell 1976), and *Gay/Lesbian Almanac* (New York: Harper and Row 1983); Julie Wheelwright, *Amazons and Military Maids* (London: Pandora 1989); Rudolf M. Dekker and Lotte Van De Pol, *The Tradition of Female Transvestism in Early Modern Europe* (London: Macmillan 1989); San Francisco Lesbian and Gay History Project, 'She Even Chewed Tobacco: A Pictorial History of Passing Women in America,' in Martin B. Duberman, Martha Vicinus, and George Chauncey Jr, eds, *Hidden from History: Reclaiming the Gay and Lesbian Past* (New York: New American Library 1989), 183–94; and Lisa Duggan, 'Dandies and Dykes: The Erotic Meanings of Female Crossdressing,' paper presented at the Berkshire Women's History Conference, June 1990. On African American/Canadian lesbian/ gay subculture, see Makeda Silvera, 'Man Royals and Sodomites: Some Thoughts on Afro-Caribbean Lesbians,' in M. Silvera, ed., *Piece of My Heart: A Lesbians of Colour Anthology* (Toronto: Sister Vision Press 1991), 14–26; Eric Garber, 'Gladys Bentley: Bulldagger Who Sang the Blues,' *Out/Look*, Fall 1988: 52–61, and 'A Spectacle in Color: The Lesbian and Gay Subculture of Jazz Age Harlem,' in M. Duberman et al., eds, *Hidden from History*, 318–31; 'Mabel Hampton's Coming Out Story,' *Lesbian Herstory Archives News* 7 (December 1981): 31–3; Anita Cornwell, *Black Lesbian in White America* (Tallahassee, Fla.: Naiad Press 1983); Hazel V. Carby, 'It

Jus Be's Dat Way Sometime: The Sexual Politics of Women's Blues,'
Radical America, June/July 1986: 9–24; Gloria Hull, '"Under the days": The
Buried Life and Poetry of Angelina Weld Grimké,' *Conditions* 12, 2 (1979):
17–25. On lesbian/gay subcultures in Germany, see Lillian Faderman and
Bridgette Eriksson, *Lesbian Feminism in Turn of the Century Germany* (Tallahas-
see, Fla.: Naiad Press 1980). And on pre-Stonewall lesbian bar culture,
see Joan Nestle, 'Butch/Fem Relationships: Sexual Courage in the 1950s,'
in J. Nestle, *A Restricted County* (Ithaca, NY: Firebrand Books 1987), 100–9;
John D'Emilio, *Sexual Politics, Sexual Communities: The Making of a Homosexual
Minority in the U.S., 1940-1970* (Chicago: University of Chicago Press
1983); Madeline Davis and Liz Kennedy, *Boots of Leather, Slippers of Gold: The
History of a Lesbian Community* (New York: Routledge 1993); Elly Bulkin,
'An Old Dyke's Tale: An Interview with Doris Lunden,' *Conditions* 6
(1980): 26–44; Donna Penn, 'Public Space and Lesbian Lives in Twentieth
Century America,' unpublished paper presented at Berkshire Women's
History Conference, Rutgers University, June 1990; Lesbians Making
History, 'People Think This Didn't Happen in Canada,' *Fireweed, Lesbiantics
II* 28 (Spring 1989): 81–94; Line Chamberland, 'Flirt et Flirt et Potins: Les
lesbiennes dans les journaux jaunes,' *Canadian Lesbian and Gay History Net-
work Newsletter* 4 (November 1990): 3–7; and Becki Ross, ed., *Forbidden Love:
The Unashamed Lives of Post-War Canadian Lesbians* (forthcoming, 1995).

25 Several very important studies have investigated themes of lesbian identity in the past twenty years; however, this work addresses questions of
external boundaries, defining and explicating lesbianism in relation to
the non-lesbian world – survival strategies, such as secrecy and 'passing,'
rather than the construction of identity in the context of lesbian-feminist
political communities. See Barbara Ponse, *Identities in the Lesbian World: The
Social Construction of Self* (Westport, Conn.: Greenwood Press 1978), and M.
Didi Khayatt, *Lesbian Teachers: An Invisible Presence* (Albany: State University
of New York Press 1992).

26 For an incomplete list, see Jo Freeman, *The Politics of Women's Liberation*
(New York and London: Longman 1975); Sheila Rowbotham, *The Past Is
before Us: Feminism in Action since the 1960s* (Winchester, Mass.: Unwin and
Hyman 1989); Lynne Segal, *Is the Future Female?* (London: Virago 1987);
Elizabeth Wilson (with Angela Weir), *Hidden Agendas* (London: Tavistock
1986); special issue on 'Presenting the Past: Twenty Years of the Women's
Movement,' *Feminist Review* 30 (Spring 1989); Nancy Adamson, Linda Bris-
kin, and Marg McPhail, *Feminist Organizing for Change: The Contemporary
Women's Movement in Canada* (Toronto: Oxford University Press 1988). In
addition, see John Cleveland, 'The Mainstreaming of Feminist Issues:

The Toronto Women's Movement, 1966–1984', M.A. thesis, Department
of Sociology, York University, 1984, and Maureen Fitzgerald, Connie
Guberman, and Margie Wolfe, eds, *Still Ain't Satisfied: Canadian Feminism
Today* (Toronto: Women's Press 1982). Important essays on the subject of
the women's movement include Ann Snitow, 'Gender Diary,' *Dissent*,
Spring 1989: 205–24; Karen Hansen, 'Women's Unions and the Search
for a Political Identity,' in K. Hansen and Ilene Philipson, eds, *Women,
Class and the Feminist Imagination* (Philadelphia: Temple University Press
1990), 213–38; Annie Popkin, 'The Social Experience of Bread and Roses,
Building a Community and Creating a Culture,' in Hansen and Philipson,
eds, *Women, Class and the Feminist Imagination*, 182–212; Carolyn Egan, Linda
Lee Gardner, and Judy Vashti Persad, 'The Politics of Transformation:
Struggles with Race, Class and Sexuality in the March 8th Coalition,' in
Frank Cunningham, Sue Findlay, Marlene Kadar, Alan Lennon, and Ed
Silva, eds, *Social Movements / Social Change: The Politics and Practice of Organizing*
(Toronto: Between the Lines 1988), 20–47; Sue O'Sullivan, 'Passionate
Beginnings, 1969–1972,' *Feminist Review* 11 (1984); Hazel V. Carby, 'White
Women Listen! Black Feminism and the Boundaries of Sisterhood,' in
Contemporary Centre for Cultural Studies, ed., *The Empire Strikes Back*
(London: Hutchinson 1982). An exception is Alice Echols, *Daring to Be
Bad: Radical Feminism in America, 1967–1975* (Minneapolis: University of
Minnesota Press 1989).
27 Susan Krieger, 'Lesbian Identity and Community: Recent Social Science
Literature,' *Signs, The Lesbian Issue* (Chicago: University of Chicago Press
1985): 224.
28 Ibid., 237.
29 Deborah Wolf, *The Lesbian Community* (Berkeley: University of California
Press 1979); Susan Krieger, *Mirror Dance: Identity in a Women's Community*
(Philadelphia: Temple University Press 1983); Michel Brody, ed., *Are We
There Yet? A Continuing History of Lavender Woman, a Chicago Lesbian Newspaper,
1971–76* (Iowa City: Aunt Lute 1985); Shane Phelan, *Identity Politics: Lesbian
Feminism and the Limits of Commmunity* (Philadelphia: Temple University Press
1989); Lillian Faderman, *Odd Girls and Twilight Lovers*; Sherry McCoy and
Maureen Hicks, 'A Psychological Retrospective on Power in the Contemporary Lesbian-Feminist Community,' *Frontiers* 4, 3 (1979): 65–9; Kathleen
Weston and Lisa Rofel, 'Sexuality, Class and Conflict in a Lesbian Workplace,' in *Signs, The Lesbian Issue* (Chicago: University of Chicago Press,
1985), 199–222; Katie King, 'The Situation of Lesbianism as Feminism's
Magical Sign: Contests for Meaning and the U.S. Women's Movement,
1968–1972,' *Communication* 9 (1986): 65–91; Michele D. Dominy, 'Lesbian-

Feminist Gender Conceptions: Separatism in Christchurch, New Zealand,' *Signs* (Winter 1986): 274–87; Susan Ardill and Sue O'Sullivan, 'Upsetting an Applecart: Difference, Desire and Lesbian Sado-Masochism,' in Christian McEwan and Sue O'Sullivan, eds, *Out the Other Side: Contemporary Lesbian Writing* (London: Virago 1988), 122–43; Wendy Clark, 'The Dyke, the Feminist and the Devil,' in *Sexuality, a Reader* (London: Virago 1987), 201–16; Arlene Stein, 'Sisters and Queers: the Decentring of Lesbian Feminism,' *Socialist Review* 1 & 2 (1992): 33–55.

30 In the first anthologies of Canadian women's movement writings, there was virtually no inclusion of lesbians or discussion of institutionalized heterosexuality. Among these texts, see *Women Unite!* (Toronto: Women's Educational Press 1972); Margaret Anderson, ed., *Mother Was Not a Person* (Montréal: Black Rose Books 1972); Myrna Kostash, *Long Way from Home* (Toronto: McClelland and Stewart 1980); Naomi Wall, 'The Last Ten Years: A Personal/Political View,' in Fitzgerald, Guberman, and Wolfe, eds, *Still Ain't Satisfied: Canadian Feminism Today* (Toronto: Women's Press 1982), 15–29. (There are two important articles that treat lesbian issues in *Still Ain't Satisfied*, one by Amy Gottlieb on organizing and one by Eve Zaremba on sexuality.) In the recent collection *Changing Patterns: Women in Canada*, edited by Lorraine Code and Sandra Burt (Toronto: McClelland and Stewart 1988), there is only cursory mention of lesbian realities. Nancy Adamson, Linda Briskin, and Margaret McPhail are much more concerned to include analysis of lesbian politics in their text, *Feminist Organizing for Change* (Toronto: Oxford University Press 1988); however, the ideas and references remain underdeveloped. A new collection, *And Still We Rise: Feminist Political Mobilizing in Contemporary Canada*, edited by Linda Carty (Toronto: Women's Press 1993), contains an edited transcript of a conversation among a multi-racial group of lesbians in Toronto. For the most part, however, the participation of lesbians of colour in lesbian-feminist politics in the 1970s has received little scholarly attention. While it is true that there were no organizations founded by lesbians of colour during this period, it is also the case that archivists have not enlarged their networks to include the solicitation of materials that document the lives of women of colour who self-identified as lesbians and feminists in the post-Stonewall era.

31 On cultural funding for lesbian groups, see Becki Ross, 'Heterosexuals Only Need Apply: The Secretary of State's Regulation of Lesbian Existence,' *Resources for Feminist Research* 17, 3 (September 1988): 35–9.

32 Lorna Weir, 'Socialist Feminist Politics,' unpublished manuscript on the politics of lesbian feminism, Toronto, 1987: 17.

33 I want to thank Megan Davies, a former member of the collective the Canadian Women's Movement Archives (CWMA)/les archives canadiennes du mouvement des femmes, for first introducing me to the LOOT collection.

34 Written accounts of social movements in Canada in the 1970s include Tania Das Gupta, *Learning from Our History: Community Development by Immigrant Women in Ontario, 1958–1986* (Toronto: Cross Cultural Communication Centre 1986); Denis W. Johnston, *Up the Mainstream: The Rise of Toronto's Alternative Theatres, 1968–1975* (Toronto: University of Toronto Press 1991); and Vern Harper, *Following the Red Path: The Native People's Caravan, 1974* (Toronto: NC Press 1979).

35 CBC Radio's Morningside, '1970s Revival,' host Peter Gzowski, 1 May 1991.

36 Geoff Pevere, 'An Exhilarating Romp through the Decade that Time Forgot,' *Globe and Mail*, 11 May 1991. On the CBC network show 'Prime Time,' Pevere also hosted a four-part series on the revival of the 1970s: 11–14 June 1991.

37 See Havelock Ellis, *Sexual Inversion: Studies in the Psychology of Sex*, vol. 2 (New York: Random House 1936; original 1910), and *The Psychology of Sex* (London: Pan Books 1959; original 1933); and Richard von Krafft-Ebing, *Psychopathia Sexualis* (Brooklyn: Physicans and Surgeons Book Co. 1931).

38 Frank Caprio, *Female Homosexuality: A Psychodynamic Study of Lesbianism* (New York: Citadel Press 1954), 171, 294.

39 Daniel Cappon, *Towards an Understanding of Homosexuality* (Toronto: Prentice Hall 1965), 5.

40 Del Martin and Phyllis Lyon, *Lesbian/Woman* (New York: Fawcett Books 1972), 1–15.

41 For one lesbian's account of her life-threatening encounter with the psychiatric profession, see Sheila Gilhooly and Persimmon Blackbridge, *Still Sane* (Vancouver: Press Gang 1985).

42 On the heterosexist regulatory practices of Street Haven staff in the mid-to-late 1960s, see Becki Ross, 'Destaining the Delinquent Body: Moral Regulatory Practices at Street Haven, 1965–1969,' in B. Ross, ed., *Forbidden Love: The Unashamed Lives of Post-War Canadian Lesbians* (forthcoming, 1995). And on lesbianism and prostitution, see Donna Penn, 'The Lesbian, the Prostitute and the Containment of Female Sexuality in Postwar America,' in Joanne Meyerowitz, ed., *Not June Cleaver: Women and Gender in Post-War America, 1945–1960* (Philadelphia: Temple University Press 1994), 358–81.

43 See Gary Kinsman, 'The Ottawa Purge Campaigns,' *Centre/Fold* 4 (Spring

1993): 12–13, and 'Character Weaknesses and 'Fruit Machines': Towards an Analysis of the Social Organization of the Anti-Homosexual Purge Campaign in the Canadian Federal Civil Service, 1959–1964,' unpublished manuscript, 1993.

44 On teenage sexuality in the 1950s and 1960s, see Mary Louise Adams, 'The Trouble with Normal: Post-War Teenagers and the Construction of Heterosexuality,' unpublished Ph.D. thesis, Department of Educational Theory, OISE, 1994.

45 Mary Louise Adams, 'Precendent-Setting Pulp: *Women's Barracks* Was Deemed "Exceedingly Frank,"' *X-tra!* 231 (3 September 1993): 21.

46 Emily Sisley and Bertha Harris, *The Joy of Lesbian Sex* (New York: Simon and Schuster 1977), 40.

47 For feminist analysis of the mass-marketed pulp novels, see Maida Tilchin and Fran Koski, 'Some Pulp Fiction,' *The Body Politic*, August 1976: 2–4; Susanna Benns, 'Sappho in Soft Cover: Some Notes on Lesbian Pulp,' *Fireweed* 11 (1981): 36–43; Roberta Yusba, 'Odd Girls and Strange Sisters: Lesbian Pulp Novels of the 50s,' *Out/Look*, Spring 1991: 34–37. And for a ground-breaking analysis of Ann Bannon's lesbian novels, see Diane Hamer, '"I am a Woman": Ann Bannon and the Writing of Lesbian Identity in the 1950s,' in Mark Lilly, ed., *Lesbian and Gay Writing* (London: Macmillan 1990), 47–75. For interviews with Ann Bannon re the reprinting of her 1950s lesbian novels by Naiad Press, see Maida Tilchin, 'Ann Bannon: The Mystery Solved!' *Gay Community News*, 8 January 1983: 8–12; Jeff Weinstein, 'In Praise of Pulp: Bannon's Lusty Lesbians,' *Village Voice Literary Supplement* 20 (October 1983): 8–9; Charlotte Rubens, '50s Lesbian Pulp Author: An Interiew with Ann Bannon,' *Coming Up!*, November 1983: 16; Tricia Lootens, 'Ann Bannon: A Lesbian Audience Discovers Its Lost Literature,' *off our backs* 8, 11 (December 1983): 12–20. The National Film Board production *Forbidden Love: The Unashamed Stories of Lesbian Lives* (1992) explores the meanings attributed to lesbian pulp fiction by Canadian lesbians in the 1950s and 1960s.

48 See Ross Higgins and Line Chamberland, 'Mixed Messages: Lesbians, Gay Men and the Yellow Press in Quebec and Ontario during the 1950s and 1960s,' in Ian McKay, ed., *The Challenge of Modernity* (Toronto: McGraw-Hill Ryerson 1992), 421–38.

49 On celebratory yet critical analysis of the Canadian lesbian bar scene in the 1950s and 1960s, see the NFB film *Forbidden Love* (1992) and Becki Ross, 'Dance to "Tie a Yellow Ribbon," Get "Churched," and Buy the "Little Lady" a Drink: Lesbian Bar Culture in Toronto, 1965–1975,' in Debra Martens, ed., *Weaving Alliances* (Ottawa: Canadian Women's Stud-

ies Association 1993), 267–88. On tensions between lesbian feminists and bar-going gay women between 1965 and 1980, see Trisha Franzen, 'Differences and Identities: Feminism and the Albuquerque Lesbian Community,' *Signs* 18, 4 (Summer 1993): 891–906.

50 Shari Zeck, 'Seeing Ourselves on Screen: New Books on Lesbians, Gay Men and Film,' *Out/Look* 13 (Summer 1991): 80.

51 On black pride and power as 'metonymic leverage for the affirmation of gay pride and the assertion that sisterhood is strength,' see Kobena Mercer, 'Welcome to the Jungle: Identity and Diversity in Postmodern Politics,' in Jonathon Rutherford, ed., *Identity: Community, Culture, Difference* (London: Lawrence and Wishart 1990), 43–71.

52 Alberto Melucci, *Nomads of the Present: Social Movements and Individual Needs in Contemporary Society* (Philadelphia: Temple University Press 1989); Barbara Epstein, 'Rethinking Social Movement Theory,' *Socialist Review* 20, 1 (January/March 1990): 35–65, David Plotke, 'What's So New about New Social Movements?' *Socialist Review* 20, 1 (January/March 1990): 81–102.

53 Cunningham et al., *Social Movements / Social Change*, and William Carroll, ed., *Organizing Dissent: Contemporary Social Movements in Theory and Practice* (Toronto: Garamond Press 1992).

54 Antonio Gramsci, *Selections from the Prison Notebooks of Antonio Gramsci*, ed. and trans. Quintin Hoare and Geoffrey Nowell Smith (New York: International Publishers 1971).

55 A.I. signifies artificial insemination – a reproductive technique that a number of lesbians have used since the late 1970s. Many of my informants joked about the 'mini lesbian baby boom' that, in part, they feel differentiates 'the lesbian community' of the 1990s from that of the 1970s.

56 For example, see Arlene Stein, *Sisters, Sexperts and Queers: Beyond the Lesbian Nation* (New York: Penguin Books 1993).

57 Faderman, *Odd Girls and Twilight Lovers*, 220, 244.

58 Sidney Abbott, 'Lesbians and the Women's Movement,' in Ginny Vida, ed., *Our Right to Love: A Lesbian Resource Book* (Englewood Cliffs, NJ: Prentice-Hall 1978), 140.

59 Vance, 'Social Construction Theory,' 29.

CHAPTER 1 Shaking the ground

1 Radicalesbians, 'Woman Identified Woman' was an essay first distributed as a leaflet at a New York City conference, and first published in *The Ladder* 11/12 (August/September 1970).

2 Across Canada, the new left emerged through the Student Union for

Peace Action (SUPA), Company of Young Canadians (CYC), and, several years later, the New Democratic Party's Waffle, Maoist, Trotskyist, and Marxist Leninist cadres like Red Morning, the International Socialists, and Rising Up Angry. Vern Harper chronicles First Nations organizing in *Following the Red Path: The Native People's Caravan, 1974* (Toronto: NC Press 1979). And, in June 1969, at the Stonewall Inn in New York, Black, Puerto Rican, and white working-class drag queens, bar dykes, and street people fought back against a routine police bar raid. Their outrage touched off rioting for three days and marked the symbolic birth of contemporary gay liberation.

3 Nancy Adamson, Linda Briskin, and Marg McPhail, *Feminist Organizing for Change* (Toronto: Oxford University Press 1988), 42.

4 See John Cleveland, 'The Mainstreaming of Feminist Issues: The Toronto Women's Movement, 1966–1984,' unpublished manuscript, housed at the CWMA, Toronto, 1984. Cleveland argues that the women's caucus within the activist Toronto Student Movement at the University of Toronto became the mainly off-campus Toronto Women's Liberation Movement (TWLM) in 1968. He suggests that its structure and activities were to foreshadow the orientation of new-left socialist feminists for the next 15 years. Feminist members of TWLM focused on reproductive choice, from birth control and abortion to day care, VD clinics, childbirth, working women and strike support, education, and media work (p. 5).

5 Mary Bolton, 'Sisterhood at the Conference,' *Toronto Women's Liberation Movement Newsletter*, May 1971: 22–3. The Leila Khaled Collective, a splinter group from TWLM with a focus on Third World solidarity, originally agreed to host the Indo-Chinese conference in Toronto, but at the last minute, pulled out. Toronto Women's Liberation took over organizing it, but confusion reigned from the start about the purpose of the conference and the role of Canadian women in it. The 'lesbian question' was only one of many wrenching debates that erupted during the three-day conference.

6 Mary Bolton, 'Lesbian Educational,' *Toronto Women's Liberation Movement Newsletter*, April 1971: 11–13. Here Bolton observed that 'the debates seemed to center less around sexual preference and more around the politics of whether or not it was necessary to totally isolate yourself from men' (12). The panel consisted of Pat Murphy, Linda Jain of the homophile society, and Judy Masters, Susan McEwan, and Aline Gregory, 'who see themselves as a combination of radical feminism-lesbianism but do not represent the views of any particular group' (p. 11). Nym Hughes, Yvonne Johnson, and Yvette Perrault in *Stepping out of Line: A Resource Book*

on Lesbian Feminism (Vancouver: Press Gang 1984) mention that lesbians also attempted to raise lesbian issues at the Vancouver Indo-Chinese conference in 1971 and were similarly silenced.

7 Sherrill Cheda, Joanna Stuckey, and Maryon Kantaroff, 'New Feminists Now,' *Canadian Woman's Studies Journal* 2, 2 (1980): 27–9; Linda Diebel, 'Man Is the Enemy of the New Feminists,' *Toronto Telegram*, 8 December 1970.

8 Cheri Dinovo, 'Growing Up Gay,' *Velvet Fist* 1, 6 (August 1971): 6; Editorial, 'Invitation to the Women's Movement,' *Velvet Fist* 2, 3 (1972): 2; Pat Murphy and Linda Jain, 'Gay Sisters,' *Velvet Fist* 2, 4 (1972): 7; 'On Lesbianism: A Selection from Feminist Anthologies,' *Velvet Fist* 2, 5 (1972): 7.

9 Judy Grahn, 'The Psychoanalysis of Edward the Dyke,' reprinted in *Bellyfull* 1, 2 (June 1972): 6.

10 Informal discussion with Dorothy E. Smith.

11 Pat Murphy and Linda Jain, 'Gay Sisters,' 7.

12 Anonymous, *The Other Woman*, 1, 1 (May–June 1972): 17.

13 Alice Echols, 'The First Sex War: Gay/Straight Splits in Early Women's Movement Organizing,' paper presented at OISE, Toronto, January 1991.

14 On dyke baiting inside the women's movement, see Barbara Abbott and Sidney Love, *Sappho Was a Right-On Woman* (New York: Stein and Day 1972). Amber Hollibaugh, in her article 'Writers as Activists,' *Out/Look*, Fall 1990, says: 'In 1966, I was a lesbian in a political movement that didn't want me – either in the Left or in the early women's movement. When I was with my lover at women's conferences and we were told that we couldn't sleep in the same room because it might look bad for the women's movement, that was hard to hear' (71).

15 Rita Mae Brown, *The Ladder*, April/May 1972, and *Plain Brown Wrapper* (Baltimore: Daughters, Inc. 1976), 11.

16 Brown, *Plain Brown Wrapper*, 15.

17 Ibid., 29.

18 Katie King, 'The Situation of Lesbianism as Feminism's Magical Sign: Contests for meaning and the U.S. Women's Movement, 1968–1972,' *Communication* 9 (1986): 65.

19 In her book *Daring to be Bad: Radical Feminism in America, 1968–1975* (Minneapolis: University of Minnesota Press 1990), Alice Echols notes that the essay 'Woman Identified Woman' was not the earliest expression of lesbian feminism – Rita Mae Brown and Martha Shelley had denounced movement homophobia in the pages of *Rat* and *Come Out* earlier (p. 216).

20 Ann Koedt, 'Lesbianism and Feminism,' in A. Koedt, Ellen Levine, and Anita Rapone, eds, *Radical Feminism* (New York: Quadrangle 1973), 250, 248.

21 Karol, 'Dyke Power,' *The Other Woman* 1, 4 (March 1973): 7.

22 Lorna, 'Dykes Unite,' *The Other Woman* 2, 2 (March 1974).

23 Adrienne Potts, 'Adrienne Potts' Speech for Gay Pride Day,' *The Other Woman*, 2, 1 (September/October 1973): 20.

24 Pat Leslie, 'Editorial,' *The Other Woman* 2, 2 (March 1974): 1.

25 Judi Morton, 'When I Grow Up I Want to Be a Lesbian,' *The Pedestal*, June/July 1975: 10–11.

26 'Montreal Lesbian Conference,' *Long Time Coming*, February 1974: 2–5.

27 As reported in *Long Time Coming* (April/May 1976), the second annual convention of the BCFW was held in November 1975. The resolutions on lesbian rights passed included: lesbianism itself should not be considered grounds for loss of custody of children; self-supporting attitudes and life/style alternatives should be discussed with women, and lesbianism is one of those alternatives; there should be no discrimination in the hiring or promotion of lesbians in jobs relating to children (day care, teaching); divorce, immigration, and age-of-consent laws should be amended so they cease to discriminate against lesbians and gays. Beginning in the fall of 1975, members of the BCFW lesbian caucus, together with the University of British Columbia Women's Office, organized a series of six seminars, entitled 'Perspective on Lesbianism.'

28 See Julia Creet, 'A Test of Unity: Lesbian Visibility in the British Columbia Federation of Women,' in Sharon Stone, ed., *Lesbians in Canada* (Toronto: Between the Lines 1990), 183–97.

29 Ibid., 25.

30 'Lesbian Caucus,' *BCFW Newsletter* 1, 1 (November 1974): 9, and 1, 4 (March 1975): 9.

31 There was an attempt to build an Ontario Coalition of feminist groups based on the BCFW model. A couple of meetings were scheduled, but it never took off. It would require considerable investigatory research to determine the reasons why the idea for such a coalition was abandoned.

32 On 25 October 1975 a Women's March on Parliament Hill was staged to protest government inaction during International Women's Year. This was the one of the first times a national women's movement march had included lesbian demands as an official part of the program. Speaking as a represenative of Gays of Ottawa, Marie Robertson outlined the two lesbian demands: (1) equal custody for lesbian mothers and (2) inclusion of sexual orientation in the Ontario Human Rights Code and the Canadian Human Rights Act.

33 Amy Gottlieb, 'Lesbian Bill of Rights,' *After Stonewall: Critical Journal of Lesbian and Gay Liberation in Prairie Canada*, 9 (Fall 1979): 10–11, 18, 20.

34 This quote, the official motto of *The Body Politic*, is attributed to Kurt Hiller, 1921.

35 John D'Emilio, *Sexual Politics, Sexual Communities: The Making of a Homosexual Minority in the United States, 1940–1970* (Chicago: University of Chicago Press 1983), 235.

36 Dell Whan, 'Elitism,' in Karla Jay and Allen Young, eds, *Out of the Closets: Voices of Gay Liberation* (New York: Douglas Books 1972), 323.

37 Martha Shelley, 'Gay Is Good,' in Jay and Young, eds, *Out of the Closets*, 32.

38 Subsequent conferences were held in Winnipeg (1974), Ottawa (1975), Toronto (1976), Saskatoon (1977), Halifax (1978), Ottawa (1979), and Calgary (1980).

39 For dates and brief descriptions of these developments, see 'Victories and Defeats: A Gay and Lesbian Chronology, 1964–1982,' in Ed Jackson and Stan Persky, eds, *Flaunting It! A Decade of Gay Journalism from The Body Politic* (Vancouver: New Star Books, Toronto: Pink Triangle Publishing 1982), 224–43. Also, see Gary Kinsman, *The Regulation of Desire*, 179–218.

40 On the liberalization of the Canadian criminal code with respect to homosexual reforms and, in particular, the influence of Britain's Wolfenden Report (1957), see Kinsman, *The Regulation of Desire*, 139–77.

41 In Canada, there was little homophile activism in the tradition of DOB or Mattachine Society. Exceptionally, between 1949 and 1964, James Egan – Canada's first openly gay activist – wrote hundreds of letters to the tabloid press (e.g., *Hush, Flash, Tab, Justice Weekly*) protesting the routinely trivializing, contemptuous portrayal of homosexuality. He met other gay people for informal discussion groups at the Music Room on Yonge Street. See Robert Champagne, *Jim Egan: Canada's Pioneer Gay Activist* (Toronto: Canadian Lesbian and Gay History Network, Publication no. 1, 1989).

42 Norma Mitchell was the ASK president from 1967 until its closure in 1968. She was interviewed by Bob Cummings in a three-part series on 'The Lesbians' for *Georgia Straight*, Vancouver's left, counter-cultural magazine, (13–19 September 1968: 9–12; 4–10 October 1968: 9–12; and 1–7 November 1968: 9–12).

43 Del Martin and Phyllis Lyon, *Lesbian/Woman* (New York: Bantam Books 1972), 248.

44 *York University Homophile Association Newsletter*, March 1971: 3.

45 *Backchat*, April 1971: 3.

46 *Backchat*, June 1972: 4.

47 This aggressive disruption by the Western Guard was reported on by *Bellyfull* in their June 1972 issue (p. 3). A few years following the attack on the CHAT centre, the Western Guard (which was related to the Ed-

mund Burke Society) vandalized Toronto's first Black bookstore, Third
World Books – windows were smashed and the building was spray-
painted. The tactics used by members of the Edmund Burke Society were
not unfamiliar to some gay activists. Gary Kinsman recalls that in 1971,
at Convocation Hall on the campus of the University of Toronto, the Society stormed an event that was staged in support of the political prison-
ers jailed in accordance with the *War Measures Act* in Québec during the
October Crisis in 1970.

48 See interview with Chris Fox in Marion Foster and Kent Murray, *A Not
So Gay World* (Toronto: McClelland and Stewart 1972), 142. The absence
of lesbians or gay women was even more acute for women living in
smaller cities. Writing in the *Ontarion* (22 November 1973), Heather Ramsay, a gay activist in Guelph, made an impassioned pitch to other gay
women: 'I seem to be the only gay woman attending the University of
Guelph ... Where are you? I want to meet you, talk to you, and most importantly, grow with you ... Lesbian oppression is feeling you are all
alone' (p. 9).

49 *BackChat*, May 1972: 7.

50 Press release, CUNTS, on file at the CWMA.

51 Pat Smith, 'Why I Didn't Go to the Gay Pride Rally,' *The Pedestal*, January
1974: 3.

52 Gillean Chase, 'Gay Pride Week?' *The Other Woman*, August 1974: 16.

53 Marie Roberston, 'Notes from the Full-Hipped Polish Dyke: The Long
and Winding Road to Lesbian Separatism,' *The Body Politic* 24 (May/June
1976): 17. In *Long Time Coming*, April/May 1976, an unsigned commentary
took up similar themes: 'We are tired of lesbians being presented by *The
Body Politic* and other male publications and organizations as not being involved in organizations. In both Canada and the US the majority of radical grass-roots feminist organizations were organized and run by lesbians. A lesbian travelling across Canada and visiting women's centres and
feminist publications and other media groups will find that a large percentage (sometimes 100%) of women working are lesbians. It is time that
gay men realized that lesbians are political and are active in organizations; if these organizations are feminist or lesbian rather than gay male
then it's an indication of both where lesbians' heads are at and also
where gay males' heads are at' (38).

54 Robertson, 'Notes from the Full-Hipped Polish Dyke,' 17.

55 For mainstream accounts of this market, see Philip Marchand, 'Cruising,'
Toronto Life, March 1975: 33–6; Ken Waxman, 'The Rise of Gay Capitalism,' *Toronto Life*, September 1976: 34–6, 48–51, 149–53. For critical ac-

counts of the emergence of a gay market in the seventies, see Gary Kinsman, *The Regulation of Desire*, 179–97; and Michael Lynch's critique of Ken
Waxman's article 'Rise of Gay Capitalism' in *The Body Politic*, November
1976.

56 Kinsman, *The Regulation of Desire*, 223.

57 Clearly, this period in the history of the revolutionary left in Toronto
(and elsewhere in the country) requires much more investigation: e.g.,
the roles played by women and lesbians in formulating positions and policy, and the relationship of left groups to other protest movements –
women's and gay movements, the Waffle faction of the NDP, peace and
environmental movements, and Third World solidarity work. See back
issues of *Old Mole*, *Socialist Voice*, and *Guerilla*.

58 Informal discussion with Dorothy E. Smith.

59 Pat Leslie, 'Guerilla Theatre,' *Velvet Fist* 2, 3 (1972): 4.

60 Ibid.

61 Interview with Susan Cole, 1989. Robin Morgan, in her famous essay
'Goodbye to All That,' first published in the *Rat* (January 1970) and
widely anthologized, claimed that the male-dominated left was counter-
feit and that women constituted the real left. Her public pillorying of the
new left was one of many feminist critiques at the time that named the
intransigent sexism of left men.

62 On Wages for Housework, the Toronto chapter, modelled after the international vision of Selma St James (England) and Maria Della Costa
(Italy), see Judy Ramirez, 'Wages for Housework, May Day speeches,' *The
Other Woman*, May/June 1975: 20. Wages for Housework's history of activism included a successful campaign to win reinstatement of baby-
bonus indexing in 1978, agitation for welfare rights in Regent Park (Toronto), May Day rallies (because all women are workers), participation in
Women Against Violence Against Women marches and anti-Anita Bryant
demonstrations in 1977, the organization of domestic workers and immigrant women's centres, the formation of the Lesbian Mothers Defense
Fund in 1978, and solidarity work with prostitutes in the prostitutes'
rights group BEAVER. According to historian John Cleveland, in 'The
Mainstreaming of the Women's Movement,' Wages for Housework was
boycotted by almost every other group in the women's movement. As
Chris Bearchell stated in her 'Dykes' column (*The Body Politic*, September
1977), 'There is no attempt to convince women that the chains of
drudgery should be broken, not paid for' (25). Wages for Housework fell
apart in Toronto owing to internal wrangling in the International in
1979–80.

63 For an illuminating discussion of the ways in which the left 'dragged its feet' in the 1970s on subjects of sexuality and sexual politics, see Varda Burstyn, 'The Left and the Porn Wars: A Case Study in Sexual Politics,' in H. Buchbinder, V. Burstyn, D. Forbes, and M. Stedman, *Who's on Top? The Politics of Heterosexuality* (Toronto: Garamond Press 1987), 13–46.

64 'Letter,' *The Other Woman*, May/June 1972: 16–17.

65 In a letter to *The Body Politic*, December/January 1976–7, Walter Davis, a founder of the Revolutionary Marxist Group, says that the RMG fully supports gay liberation and has an overall analysis of sexual oppression, which sees gay oppression as part of the sickness of capitalism. He argues that the RMG has openly gay supporters, incorporates it into the program and has militants taking part in the gay struggle and other struggles as open gays (p. 2). In its September/October 1974 issue, *The Body Politic* published the RMG's 'Proposition from the Left' (pp. 14–15), which was a preliminary statement on gay liberation prepared and distributed by the RMG at gay events in Toronto during the summer of 1974.

CHAPTER 2 Independent lesbian-feminist organizing

1 Adrienne Rich, 'The Meaning of Our Love for Women Is What We Have Constantly to Expand,' first published by Out and Out Books 1977, reprinted in Rich's collection, *On Lies, Secrets and Silence, Selected Prose, 1968–1977* (New York: W.W. Norton 1980), 225.

2 Judy Grahn, 'A History of Lesbianism,' in *Edward the Dyke and Other Poems* (Oakland: Women's Press Collective 1971).

3 Co-founders of Daughters of Bilitis Del Martin and Phyllis Lyon outline their perspective in *Lesbian/Woman* (1972): 'From the beginning, DOB was a self help organization ... DOB set about to redirect the self pity, self consciousness and self abasement that had always been the Lesbian's lot through the paths of self awareness, self knowledge and self observation towards another self – that of self acceptance, self confidence and self esteem' (220).

4 For a useful distinction between community or ghetto and political liberation movement, see Gary Kinsman, *The Regulation of Desire: Sexuality in Canada* (Montréal: Black Rose Books 1987), 223–4.

5 Chris Bearchell, 'Images of Lesbians in the Media, Part II,' *The Body Politic*, December/January 1977/78: 35.

6 The CLIT Statement, first published in January 1974 in *off our backs*, is reprinted in its entirety (35 pp.) in *Long Time Coming* (January 1975).

7 Sidney Abbott and Barbara Love, 'Is Women's Liberation a Lesbian Plot?'

in Vivian Gornick and Barbara Moran, eds, *Woman in Sexist Society* (New York: Basic Books 1971), 601–21; Anne Koedt, 'Lesbianism and Feminism,' in A. Koedt, Ellen Levine, and Anita Rapone, eds, *Radical Feminism* (New York: Quadrangle 1973), 246–58; Charlotte Bunch and Nancy Myron, eds, *Lesbianism and the Women's Movement* (Baltimore: Diana Press 1975); *Notes from the First Year: Women's Liberation* (New York: New York Radical Women 1968); *Notes from the Second Year: Women's Liberation* (New York: New York Radical Women 1970); *Notes from the Third Year: Women's Liberation* (New York: New York Radical Women 1971); *Sisterhood Is Powerful* (New York: Random House 1970); *Voices from Women's Liberation* (New York: Signet Books 1970); *Feminist Revolution* (New Paltz, NY: Redstockings 1975); *The Rebirth of Feminism* (New York: Quadrangle 1971).

8 Charlotte Bunch, 'Lesbians in Revolt,' in *The Furies*, January 1972, reprinted in Bunch and Myron, eds, *Lesbianism and the Women's Movement*, 24–30.

9 Jill Johnston, *Lesbian Nation* (New York: Touchstone Press 1973), 85.

10 There is a serious need for much more empirical research on the origins, substance, and directions of lesbian-feminist organizing in all parts of both English and French Canada. Virtually all the early lesbian drop-ins and rap groups either were connected to the local women's centre or had access to institutional space at a college or university. Small numbers of lesbian Québécoises were active in the following groups: Front de libération homosexuelle (1971); Centre homophile d'aide et de libération (CHAL); GAY, later Gay McGill, where Denise Goyette was a leader of this self-help and counselling support group (1972, 1973); GMAH – Gay Montreal Association / Association homophile de Montréal (1974); CHUM – Centre homophile urbain de Montréal (1974); GHAP – Groupe homosexuel d'action politique (1975); and, CHAR/GCAR – Comité homosexuel anti-repression / Gay Coalition Against Repression (1976), which later became ADGQ, Association pour les droits des gai(e)s du Québec (1976).

11 For a sampling of small, community-based newsletters of value to gay men and, to a lesser extent, lesbians in the 1970s, see: *Windsor Gay Community Newsletter* (1975), *Homophile Association of London* (1974–83), *Go Info, Ottawa* (1975 to present), *Dialogue Hamilton* (1976–7), *Gemini II, Waterloo University Gay Liberation Movement* (1973–4), *London Lesbian Collective Newsletter* (1977–8), *Gay Saskatchewan Newsletter* (1978–9), *Gay Alliance for Equality Newsletter, Halifax* (1978), and *Waves: A Lesbian Feminist Newsletter, Victoria* (1978–9). Back issues are on file at the Canadian Women's Archives (Ottawa) and the Canadian Lesbian and Gay Archives (Toronto).

12 Informal discussion with Dorothy E. Smith.

13 Susan, 'A Conversation,' *The Other Woman* 2, 1 (September/October 1973): 3, 17.

14 A Woman's Place existed as a basement room in the YMCA for several months before moving to Dupont Street in the summer of 1972. It housed the office of *The Other Woman*, abortion and legal referrals, wen-do referrals, the women's bookstore – Lettuce Out Books, the lesbian drop-in. More than one woman I interviewed mentioned to me that she discovered A Woman's Place (and other lesbians) through a listing of Canadian women's centres in the back pages of *Lesbian/Woman* (1972) by Del Martin and Phyllis Lyon. In Downsview, a northern suburb of Toronto, at Vanier Residence, York University, there was also a lesbian drop-in.

15 'Announcement,' *The Other Woman* 2, 4 (April 1974): 22.

16 Toronto Women's bookstore, which had homes on Dupont Street and Kensington Avenue before moving to Harbord Street in 1975, stocked American lesbian poetry and fiction published by Diana Inc., Daughters, and Naiad; the albums of lesbian musicians recorded in the studios of Olivia, Redwood, and Wise Womon; and lesbian and feminist periodicals.

17 Margret Anderson, ed., *Mother Was Not a Person* (Montréal: Black Rose Books 1972); Marylee Stephenson, ed., *Women in Canada* (Don Mills, Ont.: General Publishing 1977); and *Women Unite!* (Toronto: Women's Educational Press 1972).

18 'Women's Lib: A Second Look,' *Time*, 8 December 1970: 50.

19 'Alcoholism and Homosexuality Degraded Lee Bryant's Life for 10 years Until Her Conversion to Christianity,' *Toronto Star*, September 1970; 'Three Women Claim Police Abused Them in Garage,' ibid., 28 May 1974: A4; 'Lesbians Win Custody Case Provided They Live Apart,' ibid., 23 February 1973; 'Female Soldiers Wed and Shock U.S. Army,' ibid., 28 January 1973; 'Lesbianism "Rampant" [in Kingston's Prison for Women],' *London Free Press*, 9 March 1973; 'My Lesbian Lover Threatened to Kill Me,' *Toronto Star*, 15 September 1977.

20 'Editorial,' *Toronto Sun*, 29 March 1973: 8.

21 See Becki Ross, 'Tracking Lesbian Speech: The Social Organization of Lesbian Periodical Publishing in English Canada, 1973–1988,' in Claudine Potvin and Janice Williamson, eds, *Women's Writing and the Literary Institution* (Edmonton: University of Alberta Press 1992), 173–87.

22 Guthrie, 'A Letter,' *The Other Woman* 2, 1 (September/October 1973): 1.

23 'A Reply,' *The Other Woman* 2, 1 (September/October 1973): 1.

24 Ibid.

25 The lyrics to 'I Enjoy Being a Dyke' are as follows:

> When I see a man who's sexist
> and who does something I don't like
> I just tell him that he can fuck off
> I enjoy being a dyke.
> I've always been an uppity woman
> I refuse to run I stand and strike
> cuz I'm gay and I'm proud and I'm angry
> and I enjoy being a dyke.

26 For coverage of the event in the gay, lesbian, and feminist press, see 'The Brunswick Tavern Dykes,' *Long Time Coming*, May/June 1974: 6; 'Women Harassed and Arrested,' *The Other Woman*, April 1974: 17; 'Brunswick Four Minus One – The Trial,' ibid., June 1974: 2; 'Uppity Women,' *The Body Politic*, March/April 1974: 1; 'Partial Win for the Brunswick Four,' ibid., July/August 1974: 6; Michael Riordan, 'Gay Woman Recounts Police Violence,' ibid., May/June 1975: 8.

27 See mainstream news coverage, see 'Three Women Claim That Police Abused Them in Garage,' *Toronto Star*, 28 May 1975; 'Woman Guilty, Two Cleared in Disturbance,' *Globe and Mail*, 1 June 1974; 'Sentence Suspended for Tavern Incident,' *Toronto Star*, 3 June 1974.

28 In 1975, a Royal Commission into Metropolitan Toronto Police Practices was established 'to determine whether or not the alleged mistreatment or use of excessive force is a tendency or practice in the said Police Force' (p. i). Chaired by Mr Justice Donald R. Morand, the report was released on 30 June 1976. In chapter 10, entitled 'Patricia Murphy,' the commissioner concluded: 'I am satisfied on the evidence before me that no excessive force was used by the police officers ... I should point out at this time that the actions of the women in abusing the police for doing their duty were reprehensible ... The police were required to use force to arrest the women. Again, I find that this force was reasonable under the circum-stances ... I am further satisfied that the attitude of the 4 women, partic-ularly Patricia Murphy, was very antagonistic to the police who were only carrying out their duties ... On the evidence before me the [Brunswick Tavern] management was entirely justified in calling for the assistance of the police and the police were justified not only in requesting the women to leave the premises but also in forceably removing them when they re-fused to leave' (p. 70). See Mr Justice Donald R. Morand, Royal Commis-sion into Metropolitan Toronto Police Practices, 30 June 1976.

29 For a critical, feminist assessment of the limitations of Opportunity for Youth grants, see Pat Shafer, 'OFY Exposé: Autonomy or Co-option?' *The Other Woman*, July 1974: 7.

30 The Labyris Collective announced its formation in the Fall 1974 issue of *The Other Woman*: 'It's a place to come together, meet sisters, relax and read, eat and drink, play pool, participate in political forums, read and hear poetry, theatre, music' (22).

31 See 'Women's Café,' *The Other Woman*, February 1975, for a description of the Clementyne's space at 342 Jarvis St.

32 On the street sweeps of street prostitutes and massage parlour workers on Yonge Street in the 1970s, see Deborah Brock, 'Regulating Prostitution/Regulating Prostitutes', Ph.D. dissertation, Department of Educational Theory, University of Toronto, 1989.

33 Phil Masters, 'Clementyne's Café,' *Women's Information Centre Newsletter*, May, 1975: 2.

34 The zoning hassle is reported in *Long Time Coming*, September 1975: 6.

35 One of my narrators explained that the offices of the WIC and the Rape Crisis Centre (at Queen St. and Spadina Ave.) were broken into by police and firemen in the fall of 1974. She described the break-in during the summer of 1975 this way: 'Wages for Housework and Wages Due were happening and the Queen was coming that summer. The RCMP phoned them and told them they better watch their step ... And the house was broken into that summer. They targeted the Women's Centre and Wages for Housework. They broke a radio, they stomped on a tube of Gestetner ink – big cop boot-prints stamped everywhere. They threw things around, they stole copies of the newsletter, put tea in the coffeepot, they were definitely making their mark. There was a cubby-hole that held our list of 300 names and they must have come back and stolen the list of subversives ... So the RCMP could have been intercepting our mail.'

36 Pat Leslie, 'Interview with Paulette and Artemis,' *The Other Woman*, November/December 1976: 12–13.

37 Gay Bell interview of Dougall Haggart and Marie Zemask, 29 July 1986; audio-tape available on file at CWMA (Toronto).

38 'Toronto Women's Coffeehouse,' *Long Time Coming*, April/May 1976: 39.

39 Gay Bell interview of Haggart and Zemask.

40 Informal discussion with Dorothy E. Smith.

41 'Gay Women Unlimited,' *Backchat*, April 1976: 3.

42 'Gay Women Unlimited,' *The Other Woman*, December/January 1976: 7.

43 Ibid., 4.

44 For more information on Wages Due Lesbians, see Wages Due, 'Lesbian Autonomy and the Gay Movement,' *The Body Politic*, August 1976: 8; Boo Watson, 'Lesbian Conference Urges Autonomy,' ibid., August 1976: 17; Heather Stirling, 'Conference Explores Lesbian Autonomy,' ibid., September 1976: 8; Wages Due, 'Lesbians Struggle at Nellie's Women's Hostel,' ibid., October 1976: 17; Wages Due, 'Women Speak Out,' ibid., December/January 1976–7: 1; Dorothy Kidd, 'Letter,' ibid., June 1977: 2; Chris Bearchell, 'The Wages of Disunity,' ibid., September 1977: 19; Judy Ramirez and Ellen Woodsworth, 'Wages for Housework, May Day Speeches,' ibid., May/June 1975: 20–1; 'Wages Due Lesbians,' *Long Time Coming*, April 1975: 10–11; Ellen Agger, 'Address to the March 11 Cut-Backs Rally,' *The Body Politic* 24 (June 1976): 6.

45 Agger, 'Address,' 6.

46 Ibid.

47 Ramirez and Woodsworth, 'May Day Speeches,' 21.

48 See back issues of the Toronto Lesbian Mothers Defense Fund newsletter, *Grapevine*, housed at the CWMA. For a partial list of Canadian writings on lesbian mothering in the 1970s, see Ellen Agger, 'Lesbians Fight to Keep Kids,' *The Body Politic*, December/January 1976–7: 3; Gerald Hannon, 'Marie Robertson: Upfront Dyke and Loving Women,' ibid., December/January 1976–7: 9; Chris Bearchell, 'Custody Rights for Lesbian Mothers,' ibid., May 1977: 10; Francie Wyland, *Motherhood, Lesbianism and Child Custody* (Toronto: Falling Wall Press 1977); Debbie Bodinger, 'Lesbian Mothers,' *LOOT Newsletter*, April 1979: 6; Kate Middleton, 'Custody Battles – Not Child's Play,' *Broadside*, April 1980: 8; Francie Wyland, 'Lesbian Mothers Defense Fund,' ibid., February 1981: 8; Sharon Stone, 'Lesbian Mothers Organizing,' in S. Stone, ed., *Lesbians in Canada* (Toronto: Between the Lines 1990), 198–208. See Kathryn Ferris, 'Child Custody and the Lesbian Mother: An Annotated Bibliography,' in *The Lesbian Issue, Resources for Feminist Research* (March 1983): 106–9.

49 For reports on the Montréal conferences in January 1974, and January 1975, see *Long Time Coming*, February 1974 and April/May 1975, *The Body Politic*, March/April 1974 and January/February 1975.

50 Cited in the *University of Toronto Homophile Newsletter* 3 (Spring 1971): 3.

CHAPTER 3 'Family of Womon We've Begun'

1 'Family of Womon We've Begun' is a line from Linda Shear's song of the same name on the album *Lesbian Portrait* (Northhampton: Old Lady Blue Jeans 1975).

2 Alix Dobkin, 'Talking Lesbian,' from the album *Lavender Jane Loves Women* (Durham, NC: Ladyslipper Music 1975).

3 *Lesbian Canada Lesbienne* was published by six women from Halifax who consituted themselves as APPLE, Atlantic Provinces Political Lesbians for Equality. On the first page, editor Anne Fulton describes the aim of the magazine: 'To keep the hot feminist blood flowing, to keep the lesbian pride burning and to keep our political minds and our hearts in touch with our sisters across the country.'

4 M. Anne Fulton, 'My Personal Love Affair with the National Lesbian Movement,' *The Body Politic*, March 1977: 10.

5 There had been some discussion about forming a Toronto lesbian centre at the Kingston conference, 'The Not So Invisible Woman: Lesbian Perspectives in the Gay Movement,' held from 22–24 May 1976, but nothing concrete emerged.

6 See the full text of the letter on file at the CWMA in Toronto.

7 Joyce Rock, 'Dykes, Dancing and Politics,' *The Body Politic*, June 1976: 17.

8 As reported in the article 'Lesbians Call for Autonomy' in *The Body Politic*, October 1976, 'the Lesbian Caucus got together again Monday morning, with forty women left. Topics discussed were: child custody, child care, rape and defense of women victimized by police or male violence, fundraising, job discrimination, lesbian community centres, education on legal rights, National Lesbian Conference. During the discussion, reps from Wages Due arrived and urged women to go to Nellie's [Hostel] and then they left. When the subject of a strategy for lesbian liberation was tackled, it became apparent that a very broad spectrum of political views was represented in the group. Suggestions ranged from starting businesses which would make money for and hire only women, to public actions around lesbian rights, to the formation of an anti-capitalist lesbian movement. Women from Ottawa agreed to have a workshop in October 1976 on lesbian liberation strategies. Fifteen women signed a phone list and GATE agreed to stage another meeting' (p. 1).

9 See Sharon Stone's analysis of mainstream media coverage of the second wave women's liberation movement (unpublished Ph.D. manuscript, Department of Sociology, York University, 1992).

10 Nancy Adamson, Linda Briskin, and Marg McPhail, *Feminist Organizing for Change* (Toronto: Oxford University Press 1988), esp. chap. 1.

11 There was some interest in setting up an Ontario Coalition based on the BC model of the federation, but after several meetings the idea fizzled and died.

12 'Lesbian Autonomy or Cooptation' (editorial), *The Other Woman*, September/October 1976: 1.

13 Del Martin and Phyllis Lyon, *Lesbian/Woman* (New York: Bantam Books 1972), 214.

14 'Seize the time' was a popular civil-rights, new-left, and antiwar slogan shot through with the idealized promise of social change.

15 From a taped interview with the LOOT Task Force, February 1978; housed at CWMA.

16 The oft-quoted phrase coined by the New York Radicalesbians in their manifesto 'Woman-Identified Woman' was reprinted countless times. It can be found in *For Lesbians Only: A Separatist Anthology*, ed. Sarah Lucia Hoagland and Julia Penelope (London: Onlywoman Press 1988), 17–22.

17 See the November/December 1976 issue of *The Other Woman*. This statement was also released as (part of) LOOT's first newsletter in March 1977.

18 Cited in Sharlene Sheard-Robertson, 'Rosemary Barnes,' *The Body Politic*, July/August 1977: 26.

19 There is some debate over whether 342 Jarvis Street was understood by everyone involved in the planning stages to be a 'lesbian' centre or a 'women's' centre. The confusion stemmed from a dispute over the advantages and disadvantages of an upfront, unambiguously lesbian identification.

20 Gayle Rubin, 'The Leather Menace: Comments on Politics and S/M,' in Samois, ed., *Coming to Power* (Boston: Alyson Publications 1987), 219.

21 Ann Bannon, *I Am a Woman* (Greenwich, Conn.: Fawcett Publications 1959; repr. Tallahassee, Fla.: Naiad Press 1977); and David George Kin, *Women without Men: True Stories of Lesbian Love in Greenwich Village* (New York: Brookwood Publishing 1958), dust jacket.

22 Verena Stefan, *Shedding* (Plainfield, Vt.: Daughters, Inc. 1978 [1975]); Rita Mae Brown, *Rubyfruit Jungle* (Plainfield, Vt.: Daughters, Inc. 1973; repr. New York: Bantam Books 1977); Elizabeth Lang, *Anna's Country* (Tallahassee, Fla.: Naiad Press 1981); and Carol Anne Douglas, *To the Cleveland Station* (Tallahassee: Naiad Press 1982).

23 Lorna Weir, 'Exorcising Ghosts of Friendships Past,' *The Body Politic*, August 1980: 43.

24 An exception (among the LOOT founders) is Chris Bearchell. Beginning in 1974 when she arrived in Toronto from Edmonton, Alberta, Chris ran an informal phone line from her home, invited young lesbians who were just coming out to her home, and acted as a one-woman resource guide, counsellor, and political contact.

25 Pat Leslie, former member of *The Other Woman* editorial collective, officially founded the Women's Movement Archives (which later became the

Canadian Women's Movement Archives) in the summer of 1977 to combat amnesia. See Pat's article, 'Women's Movement Archives,' *Lesbian/Lesbienne*, August–December 1979: 11.

26 Among the activists who left for the west coast before LOOT's opening were Holly Devor, Ellen Woodsworth, and Adrienne Potts.

27 Throughout the 1960s, 'The Man' symbolized all that was corrupt and ugly about powerful institutions like governments and the 'military-industrial complex.' The usage of the term was thus widespread among anti-establishment activists like civil-rights workers, student antiwar activists, and other radicals. By the mid-1970s in Toronto, among lesbian feminists, 'The Man' came to assume a much narrower meaning with a shift from its left, anticapitalist connotation to a focus on 'The Man' as signifier of patriarchy and women's (especially lesbians') oppression at the hands of men in general.

28 Sue Genge, a member of CUPE (Canadian Union of Public Employees) from the late 1970s to the mid-1980s, was a primary lobbyist for the successful inclusion of sexual-orientation protection in the CUPE collective agreement in 1979. In September 1976, in Toronto, gay activist Brian Mossop was expelled from the Communist party for being openly gay and advocating homosexuality.

29 Heterosexual bias, or privilege, or even the institution of heterosexuality (following from Charlotte Bunch's early writings) were terms used in the mid-to-late 1970s to describe what would later be named heterosexism, compulsory heterosexuality, or heterosexual hegemony. The first reference to 'homophobia' I've found in the Canadian feminist/lesbian press is the Gays of Ottawa booklet, *Understanding Homophobia* (1975), which was mentioned in the October/November 1975 issue of *The Pedestal* (Vancouver).

30 For examples of the utopian visions of feminist activists at different historical junctures, see Barbara Taylor, *Eve and the New Jerusalem: Socialism and Feminism in the Nineteenth Century* (London: Virago 1983); Shari Bentstock, *Women of the Left Bank: Paris, 1900–1940* (Austin: University of Texas Press 1986); and Joan Sangster, *Dreams of Equality: Women on the Canadian Left, 1920–1950* (Toronto: McClelland and Stewart 1989).

31 Sue Cartledge, 'Bringing It All Back Home: Lesbian Feminist Morality,' in Gay Left Collective, ed., *Homosexuality: Power and Politics* (London: Allison and Busby 1980), 102; and John Marshall, 'The Politics of Tea and Sympathy,' in ibid., 77–84.

32 Annie Popkin, 'The Social Experience of Bread and Roses: Building a Community and Creating a Culture,' in Karen V. Hansen and Ilene Phi-

lipson, eds, *Women, Class and the Feminist Imagination: A Socialist Feminist Reader* (Philadelphia: Temple University Press 1990), 182–212.

33 Barbara Taylor, *Eve and the New Jerusalem*, ix.

34 Carl Wittman, 'Refugees from Amerika,' in Joseph McCaffery, ed., *The Homosexual Dialectic* (Englewood Cliffs, NJ: Prentice-Hall 1972).

35 Monique Wittig and Sandra Zweig, *Lesbian Peoples: Materials for a Dictionary* (New York: Avon Books 1976); Bertha Harris, *Lover* (Plainfield, Vt.: Daughters, Inc. 1976); Joanna Russ, *The Female Man* (New York: Bantam Books 1975); Sally Gearhart, *The Wanderground* (Watertown, Mass.: Persephone Press 1978; repr. Boston: Alyson Publications 1984). The *Wanderground* was reviewed favourably in *Broadside*, December 1979. For an excellent discussion of the lesbian utopian novel, see Bonnie Zimmerman, *The Safe Sea of Women: Lesbian Fiction, 1969–1989* (Boston: Beacon Press 1990), 143–63.

36 Philip Marchand, 'Getting on with the 70s,' *Maclean's*, January 1975: 21, 23.

37 Shane Phelan, *Identity Politics: Lesbian Feminism and the Limits of Community* (Philadelphia: Temple University Press 1989), 18.

38 See Dorothy E. Smith, *The Everyday World as Problematic: A Feminist Sociology* (Toronto: University of Toronto Press 1987) for further discussion of 'the line of fault' and the 'bifurcation of consciousness,' 49–104.

39 *LOOT Newsletter*, March 1977: 1.

40 *Ibid.*

41 DOB members played an active role in providing support for lesbian bars that were the focus of state and police harassment in California and New Jersey. So, contrary to the claims made by several lesbian researchers, the DOB's disdain towards bar lesbians, though certainly expressed and reflective of the organization of class differences between lesbians, was neither uniform nor absolute. On DOB, see 'Dual Identity and Lesbian Autonomy: The beginning of Separate Organizing among Women,' in John D'Emilio, *Sexual Politics, Sexual Communities: The Making of a Homosexual Minority in the United States, 1940–1960* (Chicago: University of Chicago Press 1983), 92–107.

42 *LOOT pamphlet*, on file at CWMA.

43 Conference report in *Long Time Coming*, February 1974: 92–107.

44 See the article 'In Amerika They Call Us Dykes,' by Boston Women's Health Collective in *Our Bodies, Our Selves* (New York: Simon and Shuster 1973), 65.

45 Adrienne Potts and Lydia Gross, 'We Do a Lot of the Talking,' *The Other Woman*, October 1973: 7–8.

46 M. Julia Creet, 'A Test of Unity: Lesbian Visibility in the British Columbia Federation of Women,' in Sharon Stone, ed., *Lesbians in Canada* (Toronto: Between the Lines 1990), 191.

47 Charlene D., 'Come Out – All the Way,' *The Other Woman*, October/November 1975: 13.

48 Mariana Valverde, 'Beyond Guilt: Lesbian Feminism and Coming Out,' *Resources for Feminist Research* 12, 1 (March 1983): 65.

49 Barbara Ponse, *Identities in the Lesbian World: The Social Construction of Self* (Westport, Conn.: Greenwood Press 1978): 74.

50 Wendy Clark, 'The Dyke, the Feminist and the Devil,' *Sexuality, a Reader* (London: Virago 1987), 208.

51 Bertha Harris, 'What We Mean to Say: Notes towards Defining the Nature of Lesbian Literature,' *Heresies* 3 (1977): 5–8.

52 'Introduction,' in Julia Penelope Stanley and Susan Wolfe, eds, *The Coming Out Stories* (Watertown, Mass.: Persephone Press 1980), 5.

53 Bonnie Zimmerman, 'The Politics of Transliteration: Lesbian Personal Narratives,' in *Signs, The Lesbian Issue* (Chicago University of Chicago Press 1985), 261.

54 Rita Mae Brown, *Rubyfruit Jungle*; June Arnold, *Sister Gin* (Plainfield, Vt.: Daughters, Inc. 1975; repr. New York: Feminist Press 1989); Elana Nachmann, *Riverfinger Women* (Plainfield, Vt.: Daughters, Inc. 1974).

55 Sara Diamond and Helen Mintz, Interview with Lisa Steele: 'Fighting the Right,' *Fuse*, August/September 1981: 211–15.

56 Judith Quinlan, 'Lesbian Relationships,' *Resources for Feminist Research* 12, 2 (March 1983): 50.

57 Judi Morton, 'When I Grow Up I Want to Be a Lesbian,' *The Pedestal*, June–July 1975: 11.

58 For discussion of the difficulty of translating personal consciousness into political action, see John Marshall, 'The Politics of Tea and Sympathy,' and Keith Burch, 'The Politics of Autonomy,' in Gay Left Collective, ed., *Homosexuality: Power and Politics* (London: Alison and Busby 1980), 82, 86.

59 Alice Echols, *Daring to Be Bad: Radical Feminism in America, 1967–1975* (Minneapolis: University of Minnesota Press 1989), 233.

60 Mariana Valverde, 'Beyond Guilt,' 65.

61 Ibid.

62 Nym Hughes, Yvonne Johnson, and Yvette Perrault, *Stepping out of Line: A Workbook on Lesbianism and Feminism* (Vancouver: Press Gang 1984), 173.

63 As Jeffrey Weeks says of England in the mid-seventies: 'Media coverge focused almost exclusively in the 70s on gay men and their "astonishing revolution" and ignored lesbianism, compounding the image of homosex-

uality as a male phenomenon' (*Coming Out: Homosexual Politics in Britain, from the Nineteenth Century to the Present* [London: Quartet Books 1977], 28). Also, see Susan Hemmings, 'Horrific Practices: How Lesbians Were Presented in the Newspapers of 1978,' in Gay Left Collective, ed., *Homosexuality: Power and Politics* (London: Alison and Busby 1980), 157–71.

64 Chris Bearchell, 'Media Madness and Lesbian Images,' *The Body Politic*, November 1977: 10, and 'Knowing Who Your Friends Are or Lesbian Images Part II,' ibid., December/January 1977–8: 35.

65 Kathy Arnup, '"Mothers Just Like Others": Lesbians, Divorce and Child Custody in Canada,' *Canadian Journal of Women and the Law* 3 (1987): 8–32. For a discussion of Canadian and U.S. decisions, see Wendy L. Gross, 'Judging the Best Interests of the Child: Child Custody and the Homosexual Parent,' *Canadian Journal of Women and the Law* 1 (1986): 505–31.

66 See *The Body Politic* June 1977, July/August 1977, and September 1977 for reports of the dismissals of Thornborrow and Cameron.

67 See *Life Together*, Ontario Human Rights Code Review Committee report to the Ontario Legislature, June 1977. Though a 1977 Gallup poll about the inclusion of sexual orientation in the Canadian Human Rights Act indicated that 52 per cent of Canadians supported such a move (with 30 per cent opposed), it would be another ten years before such antidiscrimination legislation was officially passed by Ontario members of parliament. The anti-homosexual reference in Canada's Immigration Act was deleted in 1976, and sexual orientation was included in Québec's human-rights charter in 1977.

CHAPTER 4   The politics of lesbian-feminist life/style

1 This was not the first set of challenges made by women to restrictive conventions. Feminist and socialist members of Owenite and other communitarian settlements agitated tirelessly for dress reform in the 1800s and early 1900s, and upper-class women pressured to adapt clothing to their increasingly more active lives. See Elizabeth Wilson, *Adorned in Dreams* (Berkeley: University of California Press 1985), and Helen Lenskyj, *Out of Bounds: Women, Sport and Sexuality* (Toronto: Women's Press 1986).

2 In November 1975, ten women, all of whom were lesbians, stormed the stage of the Miss Canada Pageant in Toronto to protest the degrading and sexist nature of the contest. They handed out leaflets announcing 'Happy International Women's Year and Smash Sexism' and disrupted the evening proceedings before being ushered off stage by police officers. See coverage in *The Other Woman*, December/January 1976: 2–3.

3 In contrast to 1970s lesbian style, Dennis Altman argues that in the mid-to-late 1970s, visible white, gay-male culture was signified by 'theatrically macho clothing (denim, leather and the ubiquitous key rings) rather than by feminine style drag; the new masculine homosexual is likely to be non-apologetic about his sexuality, self-assertive, highly consumerist and not at all revolutionary, though prepared to demonstrate for gay rights' (52). See Altman, *The Homosexualization of America* (Boston: Beacon Press 1982). For fictional accounts of white gay-male style in the 1970s, see John Rechy, *The Sexual Outlaw* (New York: Grove 1977), and Larry Kramer, *Faggots* (New York: Bantam Books 1978). Also, see Gregg Blatchford, 'Male Dominance and the Gay World,' in Kenneth Plummer, ed., *The Making of the Modern Homosexual* (London: Hutchinson 1981), 184–210; and Hal Fischer, *Gay Semiotics: A Photographic Study of Visual Codes among Homosexual Men* (San Francisco: NFS Press 1979).

4 On the construction of style in new social movements, see John Clarke, Stuart Hall, Tony Jefferson, and Brian Roberts, 'Subcultures, cultures and class,' *Cultural Studies* 7/8 (Summer 1975): 5–74; Dick Hebdige, *Subculture: The Meaning of Style* (New York: Metheun 1979); Michael de Certeau, *The Practice of Everyday Life* (Berkeley: University of California Press 1984); Myrna Kostash, *Long Way from Home* (Toronto: McClelland and Stewart 1980); Sara Evans, *Personal Politics: The Roots of the Women's Liberation Movement in the Civil Rights Movement and the New Left* (New York: Vintage Books 1979); Jo Freeman, *Politics of Women's Liberation* (New York and London: Longman 1975); Elizabeth Wilson, *Adorned in Dreams*, and 'Deviant Dress,' *Feminist Review*, Summer 1990: 65–74; Michael Bronski, *Culture Clash: The Making of a Gay Sensibility* (Boston: South End Press 1984); Inge Blackman and Kathryn Perry, 'Skirting the Issue: Lesbian Fashion for the 1990s,' *Feminist Review*, Spring 1990: 67–78; Wendy Chapkis, *Beauty Secrets: Women and the Politics of Appearance* (Boston: South End Press 1986); Manning Marable, *Race, Reform and Rebellion: The Second Reconstruction in Black America, 1945–1982* (New York: Macmillan 1984); and Michael Omi and Howard Winant, *Racial Formation in the United States from the 1960s to the 1980s* (New York: Routledge and Kegan Paul 1986).

5 See Del Martin and Phyllis Lyon, *Lesbian/Woman* (New York: Bantam Books 1972), 84.

6 For an early, brilliant psychoanalytic account of lesbian community-making, see Rosemary Barnes, 'Dykes in Search of Affection and Independence,' in *Resources for Feminist Research*, March 1983: 46.

7 These were the major publishing houses for lesbian literature in the 1970s. Only Naiad Press (Tallahassee, Fla.) continues to thrive in the 1990s. There were no independent lesbian presses in Canada or Québec

in the 1970s, and women's publishing houses like Press Gang (Vancouver, 1975) and The Women's Educational Press (Toronto, 1972) did not publish lesbian-specific material until the 1980s.

8 With the closure of *Lesbian Canada Lesbienne* and *Long Time Coming* in 1976 and of lesbian-feminist editions of *The Pedestal* in 1975, the only regularly produced English Canadian lesbian periodical available at LOOT was the organization's own newsletter. This lack of material produced outside of Toronto not only mandated a heavier reliance on American texts; it also disorganized LOOT's connection to other lesbian initiatives across the country and contributed to the insular, inward-looking character of the organization. At peak distribution, 400 copies were made of the *LOOT Newsletter*.

9 *The Body Politic* reports that 1977 was the 'Year of the Queer in Television': both Gays of Ottawa and the Gay Offensive Collective in Toronto launched television shows. In Toronto, 'Gay News and Views' was later followed up by 'This Show May Be Offensive to Heterosexuals.' See David Mole, 'Rights of Access,' *The Body Politic*, November 1977: 1,4; and Michael Riordon, 'Proselytizing vs. Protecting Your Ass on the Boob Tube,' ibid., December/January 1977–8: 16–17. 'Gay News and Views' was carried on three cable stations: Metro, Rogers, and Maclean Hunter. 'This Show May Be Offensive to Heterosexuals' was produced by the Gay Offensive Collective and members of the Dyke Brigade (all of whom were members of LOOT).

10 Philip Marchand, 'Getting on with the Seventies,' *Maclean's*, January 1975: 25.

11 There is some evidence that several post-Stonewall lesbians in Toronto, Montréal, and Vancouver subscribed to *The Ladder*, or read it occasionally, when they could find it. Pat Murphy remembers leafing through a copy of *The Ladder* in the Parkside Tavern on Yonge Street in 1971.

12 See Gay Bell, 'Lesbians in the Mirror,' *The Body Politic*, June 1979: 33.

13 On 'textual mediation' and 'documentary reality,' see Dorothy E. Smith, *The Everyday World Is Problematic: A Feminist Sociology* (Toronto: University of Toronto Press 1987).

14 In a similar way, and decades before the rise of lesbian-feminist music, according to Ian Chambers, 'black music provided one of the strongest means of survival – a secret language of solidarity, a way of articulating oppression, a means of cultural resistance, a cry of hope.' See Chambers, 'A Strategy for Living,' *Cultural Studies*, Summer 1975: 161. On the subject of folk music, many Canadian and American lesbian-feminist performers (like Rita McNeil, Beverly Glenn Copeland, Ferron, Heather Bishop, Meg

Christian, and Alix Dobkin) had roots in the folk music tradition of the late 1960s. In the 1970s, some played at the Philadelphia Folk Festival, the Mariposa Folk Festival (Toronto), the Vancouver Folk Festival, the Winnipeg Folk Festival, and local folk-music clubs like Toronto's Riverboat in Yorkville Village, the Penny Farthing, Eggerton's, the Nervous Breakdown, and the Trojan Horse.

15 Especially engaging and disruptive are Hammer's films 'X' (1974), *Dyketactics* (1975), and *Women I Love* (1978).

16 Dorothy Sangster, 'Gay Women: A Minority Report,' *Chatelaine*, July 1977: 24, 79–84.

17 Marchand, 'Getting on with the Seventies,' 24, 21.

18 The LOOT logo – two women's signs joined and partly enclosed in a rectangle – was designed by Lynnie Johnston. She says, 'The idea was to graphically communicate togetherness and strength, openness and freedom.'

19 Cited in *The Other Woman*, Winter 1975: 4.

20 Val Edwards, 'The Invisible Community,' *Broadside*, September 1980: 4.

21 John Gagnon and William Simon, 'The Lesbians: A Preliminary Overview,' in *Sexual Deviance* (New York: Harper and Row 1972), 261.

22 Rosemary Barnes remembers that 'hot items' like calling up Bell Canada to list the organization in the phone book and opening up the LOOT bank account created a public lesbian presence.

23 In *The Other Woman* (October/November 1976), Pat Leslie reported that five lesbian members of Berkeley Music Collective were detained at the Canada/U.S. border, harassed for several hours, and given a ministerial permit to enter the country on the condition that they would not perform musically and would be willing to post a $150 bond to ensure their return (p. 7). Harassment of lesbians surfaces again with Donna Marchand's account of her aborted trip to the Michigan Womyn's Music Festival in August 1979 (see *LOOT Newsletter*, September 1979). In the December 1979 issue of *Broadside*, Chris Bearchell charged the editors with downplaying the lesbian harassment at the U.S. border and trying to distance themselves from lesbian issues. Bearchell argued that the harassment is not 'random' – it is directed at *visibly* gay and lesbian people. Moreover, it was an issue that stretched beyond Toronto's community, she stated: because of a discriminatory immigration policy, gays from Mexico and Germany had been subject to detainment and questions, as had gay men from Vancouver, an Israeli, and two Italian women carrying a copy of the Gay Yellow Pages.

24 Val Edwards, 'The Invisible Community,' 5.

25 For a more detailed discussion of the lesbian film and video production of Marg Moores and Almerinda Travassos, see Becki Ross, 'Having the Last Laugh,' in *Fuse* 13, 5 (June/July 1990): 26–30.

26 For several entertaining and sensitive fictional accounts of lesbian feminist living in the 1970s written by gay men, see Armistead Maupin's *Significant Others* (New York: Harper and Row 1987), and David Leavitt's *Equal Affections* (New York: Harper and Row 1989).

27 Women's self-defence courses sprang up in response to feminist recognition of women's vulnerability to male violence.

28 See unsigned column in *The Other Woman*, October 1973: 24.

29 In the summer of 1976, Chris Bearchell and Konnie Reich were assaulted by a man wielding a belt in Toronto's Annex area. See *The Body Politic*, July 1976: 7. He called the women 'diseased' and wanted to know why they couldn't get a man. Nia Cordingley was beaten up several times by straight men outside lesbian bars. She was hospitalized once and had her nose broken.

30 Kathleen Barry, 'West Coast Conference: Not Purely Academic,' *off our backs* 3, 10 (September 1973): 25; Robin Morgan, 'The Proper Study of Womankind,' in R. Morgan, ed., *Going Too Far* (New York: Random House 1978). (Morgan originally gave the talk at the West Coast Women's Studies Conference in 1973).

31 Rita Mae Brown, 'The Shape of Things to Come,' in Charlotte Bunch and Nancy Myron, eds, *Lesbianism and the Women's Movement* (Baltimore: Diana Press 1975), 75.

32 See Gillean Chase, 'Class: Thrashing It out in Ontario,' *The Other Woman*, January/February 1977: 14.

33 See Pat Leslie, 'More on Bolton: Feminist Wants Class Analysis,' *The Other Woman*, January/February 1977: 15.

34 The interpretation of class as class background within lesbian feminism is evident in Charlotte Bunch and Nancy Myron, eds, *Class and Feminism* (Baltimore: Diana Press 1975), and Joan Gibbs and Sara Bennett, eds, *Top Ranking: A Collection of Articles on Racism and Classism in the Lesbian Community* (New York: Come! Unity Press 1980). American researchers Kathleen M. Weston and Lisa B. Rofel make the point that the liberalism underlying this conception of class is not unique to lesbian feminism, but has intellectual antecedents that extend far back in the Western tradition. For a study of the ways in which the 'politics of trust, grounded in interpersonal relationships' supported interpretations that reduced class-based conflict among lesbians to a matter of individuals acts, intentions, and capabilities, see their article 'Sexuality, Class and Conflict in a Lesbian

Workplace,' *Signs: The Lesbian Issue* (Chicago: University of Chicago Press 1985), 199–222.

35 Interview with Rosemary Barnes.

36 Pat Leslie, 'Feminist Businesses,' *The Other Woman*, March/April 1976: 4.

37 As advertised in the *LOOT Newsletter*, December/January 1978/9, a 'redistribution event' or rummage sale of clothing, furniture, appliances, and home baking was scheduled as a LOOT fund-raiser. In the same newsletter, a 'swap meet' – the exchange of goods you don't need for stuff you do – was also advertised for the same month. For a discussion of 'downward mobility' from the perspective of women of colour, see Gloria Anzaldua and Cherrie Moraga, *This Bridge Called My Back: Writings by Radical Women of Colour* (New York: Kitchen Table Press 1981).

38 On communal living according to utopian socialist philosophy, see Barbara Taylor, *Eve and the New Jerusalem: Socialism and Feminism in the Nineteenth Century* (London: Virago 1983), 238–60.

39 See Colin Webster, 'Communes,' *Cultural Studies* 7, 8 (Summer 1975): 128.

40 Referring to Toronto in the late sixties, Myrna Kostash, in her book *Long Way From Home*, claims: 'On the edge of Yorkville was the educational commune Rochdale College: big, free, unstructured, nurturing Rochdale. You could live your whole life here with your friends: cooking for each other, putting dances and parties together; showing movies, turning each other on, sharing books and manuscripts' (126). Also, see David Sharpe, *Rochdale: The Runaway College* (Toronto: Anansi 1987), and Henry Mietkiewicz and Bob Mackowycz, *Dream Tower: The Life and Legacy of Rochdale College* (Toronto and Montreal: McGraw-Hill Ryerson 1988). Other movement-inspired households sprang up in major cities like Edmonton, Vancouver, Halifax, Saskatoon, Winnipeg, and Ottawa. In *Heroine* (Toronto: Coach House 1988), Gail Scott provides a fictional account of grass-roots leftist organizing in Montréal, including descriptions of communal living and crash pads.

41 On lesbian communal living in the U.S., see Alice Echols, *Daring to Be Bad: Radical Feminism in America, 1967–1975* (Minneapolis: University of Minnesota Press 1989), 228. Also see Deborah Wolf, *The Lesbian Community* (Berkeley: University of California Press 1979), 100.

42 In Toronto in 1976, Pat Hugh and Charlene Sheard (later both LOOT members) were denied accommodation in a one-bedroom apartment at York University. The women were informed that same-gender couples were only permitted to rent two-bedroom suites, even though one-bedrooms were commonly assigned to heterosexual couples. See Coalition for Gay Rights in Ontario, 'Discrimination against Lesbians and Gay

Men: The Ontario Human Rights Omission,' (1986), and 'Lesbians Expose Landlord [in Waterloo, Ontario],' *The Body Politic*, May/June 1975: 9.

43 See, Sue, Nelly, Dian, Carol, Billie, *Country Lesbians* (Grants Pass, Ore.: Womanshare Books 1976).

44 Alix Dobkin's 'Living with Lesbians' was released by Wax Woman Records in 1976. The album is reviewed by Ruth Dworin in *The Other Woman*, May/June 1976.

45 CLIT Statements, originally published in *off our backs*, reprinted in *Long Time Coming*, January 1975: 1–35.

46 Lorna Weir, 'Exorcising Ghosts of Friendships Past,' *The Body Politic*, August 1980: 43.

47 Gillean Chase, 'Review of Jill Johnston's *Lesbian Nation*,' *The Other Woman*, August 1974: 13.

48 Naomi Brooks, group interview, 1990.

49 See Jan Clausen's controversial essay, 'My Interesting Condition,' *Out/Look*, Winter 1990: 11.

50 In the summer of 1974, the 'Bare Breast Brigade' (BBB) was formed by several Toronto lesbian feminists. Incensed that women could be fined for 'gross indecency' for bareing their chests 'while Yonge St. dives thrive and pig males pin Playboy photos in their walls,' members of the BBB announced their strategy: 'Let's set the precedent now! Let's get an 'even' tan for the first year in our lives. Women take off your shirts and join the BBB.' The July 1974 issue of *The Other Woman* carries several photos of topless white women proudly holding up their BBB banner.

51 Adrienne Rich, *Blood, Bread and Poetry* (New York: W.W. Norton 1986), 199.

52 Todd Gitlin, *The Sixties*, 430.

53 Ti-Grace Atkinson, *Amazon Odyssey* (New York: Links 1974), 132.

54 Interviews with Gay Bell and Linda Jain. Evidence of some diversity in lesbian-feminist dress disrupts oversimplified, shorthand descriptions of 1970s lesbian fashion rigidity or the 'drab, nun-like devotion to dreary' found in some current scholarship. See Lisa Duggan, 'The Anguished Cry of an 80s Fem: "I want to be a drag queen," in *Out/Look*, Spring 1988: 62–5; Wendy Clark, 'The Dyke, the Feminist and the Devil,' *Feminist Review* 11 (Summer 1982): 30–9; and Shane Phelan, *Identity Politics: Lesbian Feminism and the Limits of Community* (Philadelphia: Temple University Press 1989).

55 On the struggles of First Nations peoples across Canada for self-determination in the 1970s, see Vern Harper, *Following the Red Path: The Native People's Caravan, 1974* (Toronto: NC Press 1979), and Joy McBride, 'One Step Forward? The Canadian Native Movement, 1968–1974,' unpublished paper, Queen's University, 1989.

56 See the *LOOT Newsletter*, December/January, 1978: 9. Evelyn Torton Beck's path-clearing anthology, *Nice Jewish Girls: A Lesbian Anthology* (Watertown, Mass.: Persephone Press), was published in 1982.

57 See Lilith, 'A Dykey Kike, or a Kikey Dyke, Which Will It Be? 'Oy Vey,' *Lesbian Perspective*, February 1980: 2.

58 In the June/July 1975 issue of the *Pedestal, a Lesbian Feminist Newspaper* from Vancouver, there was a call for submissions to 'The Dream Page' on 'psychic experiences, astral travel, déjà vu, mediumistic experiences or philosophies on where dreams can lead.' And on the theme of spirituality, in the December/January 1978/9 issue of *The Body Politic*, Judith Crewe reviewed *The Fourteenth Witch* (Watertown, Mass.: Persephone Press 1977) – a book of photography and poetry by five lesbians.

59 Rosemary Barnes, 'Dykes in Search of Affection and Independence,' 46.

60 On time, see Jane Mansbridge, 'Time, Emotion and Inequality: Three Problems of Participatory Groups,' in *Journal of Applied Behavioural Science*, May 1973: 351–68.

61 The Furies in Washington, DC, assumed a hard line on male children: women should not waste energies on boys, but should relinquish custody to fathers. As part of her commitment to a lesbian separatist politic, Furies member Coletta Reid gave up her two-year-old son. And, by the late 1970s, age and spatial restrictions were placed on the attendance of boy children at Michigan Womyn's Music Festival.

62 Dina, a working-class lesbian mother, told me about the informal childcare collective she helped to establish in 1975 at the Cameo Club on Howard Park Drive for gay women who had kids (from heterosexual marriages) and wanted a night out. They didn't think about it as a collective then, says Dina, but the practical ways they accomplished the care prefigured arrangements that would later be instituted by lesbians at the Toronto Rape Crisis Centre and other organizations where lesbian mothers worked.

63 Correspondence with Midi Onodera.

64 See Sharon D. Stone, 'Must Disability Always Be Visible? The Meaning of Disability for Women,' *Canadian Woman's Studies Journal* 13, 4 (Winter 1993): 11–13.

65 Barbara Ponse, *Identities in the Lesbian World: The Social Construction of Self* (Westport, Conn.: Greenwood Press 1978), 60. On passing as a survival strategy for Northern Ontario lesbian teachers in the classroom and outside of it, see M. Didi Khayatt, *Lesbian Teachers: An Invisible Presence* (Albany, NY: SUNY Press 1992). And see the *Sinister Wisdom* special issue on passing (Summer/Fall 1988).

66 Todd Gitlin, *The Sixties*, 5.
67 See Joreen (Jo Freeman), 'The Tyranny of Structurelessness,' in Anne Koedt, Ellen Levine, and Anita Rapone, eds, *Radical Feminism* (New York: Quadrangle 1973).
68 Jan Clausen, 'My Interesting Condition,' 15.
69 Sherry McCoy and Maureen Hicks, 'A Psychological Retrospective on Power,' *Frontiers* 4, 3 (1979): 66.
70 Kenneth Plummer, 'Building a Sociology of Homosexuality,' in Kenneth Plummer, ed., *The Making of the Modern Homosexual* (London: Hutchinson 1981), 29.
71 Wendy Clark, 'The Dyke, the Feminist and the Devil,' in *Sexuality, a Reader* (London: Virago 1987), 201.
72 On performance of gender and sexual identity, see Judith Butler's essay 'Imitation and Gender Insubordination,' in Diana Fuss, ed., *Inside Out: Lesbian Theories, Gay Theories* (New York and London: Routledge 1991), 13–31.
73 Diana Fuss develops the concept of 'gravitational point' in 'Lesbian and Gay Theory: The Question of Identity Politics,' in D. Fuss, *Essentially Speaking: Feminism, Nature and Difference* (New York and London: Routledge 1989), 101.
74 Katie King, 'The Situation of Lesbianism as Feminism's Magical Sign: Contests for Meaning in the U.S. Women's Movement, 1968–1972,' *Communication* 9 (1986): 65–91.

CHAPTER 5 Mining lesbian-feminist sexual discourse and practice

1 Cris Williamson, 'Dream Child,' on *The Changer and The Changed* (San Francisco: Olivia Records 1975).
2 See Judy Gill, Diana Chastain, Linda Carmen, Mary Bolton, and Jenny Robinson, 'Sexual Myths,' in *Women Unite! An Anthology of the Canadian Women's Movement* (Toronto: Women's Educational Press 1972), 162–9.
3 *Toronto Women's Liberation Newsletter* (1969): 7.
4 Judy Bernstein, Peggy Morton, Linda Seese, and Myrna Wood, 'Sisters, Brothers, Lovers, Listen ... ,' in *Women Unite!*, 35.
5 See Naomi Wall, 'The Last Ten Years: A Personal/Political View,' in Maureen Fitzgerald, Connie Guberman, and Margie Wolfe, eds, *Still Ain't Satisfied* (Toronto: Women's Press 1983), 15–29. The liberalization of the Criminal Code in 1969 also made the distribution of birth-control information and the sale of birth-control devices legal for the first time in Canada.
6 Dana Densmore, 'On Celibacy,' *No More Fun and Games* (1969); on masturbation, see Betty Dodson, *Liberating Masturbation* (New York: Bodysex

Designs 1974), and Carolyn Smith, Toni Ayres, and Maggie Rubenstein, *Getting in Touch: Self-Sexuality for Women* (San Francisco: Multimedia Resource Centre 1974); and on clitoral orgasm, see Anne Koedt, 'Myth of the Vaginal Orgasm,' in A. Koedt, Ellen Levine, and Anita Rapone, eds, *Radical Feminism* (New York: Quadrangle 1973), 198–207; and see Rita Mae Brown, 'Coitus Interruptus,' *Rat* 2, 27 (February 1970): 6–23. For popular texts, see Lonnie Barbach, *For Yourself: The Fulfillment of Female Sexuality* (Garden City, NY: Doubleday 1975), and Barbara Seaman, *Free and Female* (Greenwich, Conn.: Fawcett 1973).

7 Kate Millett, *Sexual Politics* (New York: Avon Books 1970), 112.

8 See Dorothy Sangster, 'Gay Women: A Minority Report,' *Chatelaine*, July 1977: 24.

9 Myrna Kostash, 'Courting Sappho: If I Only Could, I Surely Would,' in *Maclean's*, November 1974: 19.

10 In their first action following the protest of 5 November 1977, Toronto WAVAW women and members of the spin-off group 'Snuff Out Snuff' postered downtown Toronto streets. They maintained that 'mutilating, patriarchal sexual speech' shot through *Snuff* culminated in the sexual climax of a woman's death, though this was later proven to be an elaborate hoax.

11 Increasingly sophisticated theories of women's sexual victimization and men's predisposition to violate were devised and published by radical-feminist writers. See Kate Millett, *Sexual Politics*; Susan Brownmiller, *Against Our Will: Men, Women and Rape* (New York: Simon and Schuster 1975); Mary Daly, *Gyn/Ecology: The Metaethics of Radical Feminism* (Boston: Beacon Press 1978); and Robin Morgan, 'Theory and Practice, Pornography and Rape,' in *Going Too Far* (New York: Random House 1978), 163–9.

12 In the March 1980 issue of *Lesbian Perspective*, the LOOT newsletter, Mary Syrett calls for the formation of a lesbian incest survivors support group.

13 Sharon Stone, column in *LOOT Newsletter*, August 1979: 4.

14 Gay Bell, 'Lesbians in the Mirror,' *The Body Politic*, June 1979: 33.

15 Audre Lorde, in her essay 'Uses of the Erotic' (pamphlet, Out & Out Books: New York 1978; repr. in *Sister Outsider* [Freedom, Calif: Crossing Press 1984]), describes the erotic as 'a resource within each of us that lies in a deeply female and spiritual plane' (53).

16 B. Ruby Rich, 'Feminism and Sexuality in the 1980s,' *Feminist Review* 12, 3 (Fall 1986): 508.

17 Jane Rule, 'Homophobia and Romantic Love,' in *Outlander: Short Stories and Essays* (Tallahassee, Fla.: Naiad Press 1981), 181.

18 *LOOT Newsletter*, July 1977: 1.

19 Anne Koedt, 'Lesbianism and Feminism,' in Koedt, Levine, and Rapone, eds, *Radical Feminism* 254.

20 'In Amerika They Call us Dykes,' in Boston Women's Health Collective, eds, *Our Bodies, Our Selves* (New York: Simon and Schuster 1973), 56.

21 Alix Dobkin, 'Talking Lesbian,' on *Lavender Jane Loves Women* (Durham, NC: Ladyslipper Music, Inc. 1975).

22 Rita Mae Brown, 'The Shape of Things to Come,' in Charlotte Bunch and Nancy Myron, eds, *Lesbianism and the Women's Movement* (Baltimore: Naiad Press), 70.

23 Brown, *Plain Brown Wrapper* (Baltimore: Daughters, Inc. 1976), 14.

24 Lorna Weir, 'Feminist Sexual Politics,' unpublished manuscript, 1987: 18. Later published in revised form, 'Socialist Feminism and the Politics of Sexuality,' in Meg Luxton and Heather Jon Maroney, eds, *Feminism and Political Economy* (London: Methuen 1987), 69–83.

25 'Lesbian Feminist Statement: On a Queer Day,' *The Other Woman*, October 1973: 25.

26 Hari Matta, 'Stolen Pages,' *The Other Woman*, September/October 1976: 20.

27 See Dinah Forbes, 'Difficult Loves,' in Howard Buchbinder, Varda Burstyn, D. Forbes, and Mercedes Steedman, *Who's on Top? The Politics of Heterosexuality* (Toronto: Garamond Press 1987), 47. For an early autobigraphical account of her struggles as a straight feminist, see Joanne Kates, 'Once More with Feeling: Heterosexuality and Feminist Consciousness,' in Fitzgerald, Guberman, and Wolfe, eds, *Still Ain't Satisfied*, 76–84.

28 For more on the perils of bisexuality, see Jan Clausen, 'My Interesting Condition,' *Outlook*, Winter 1989–90: 11–21. And see Linda Silber, 'Negotiating Sexual Identity: Non-Lesbians in a Lesbian Feminist Community,' *Journal of Sex Research* 27, 1 (February 1990): 131–9.

29 'Bisexual Woman,' unsigned, *Long Time Coming*, July 1975: 9–14.

30 Lilith Finkler, 'Lesbians Who Sleep with Men,' *Broadside*, November 1983: 4.

31 Rowena Hunnisett, 'Gay Pride Week,' *The Other Woman*, October 1973: 18.

32 'Adrienne Potts' Speech for Gay Pride March,' *The Other Woman*, October 1973: 20.

33 Gillean Chase, 'Gay Pride? Week,' *The Other Woman*, August 1974: 16.

34 See Adrienne Rich on gay men's sex in her essay 'The Meaning of Our Love for Women Is What We Have Constantly to Expand,' pamphlet (Brooklyn, NY: Out and Out Books, 1977). And see John Grube, 'Queens and Flaming Virgins: Towards a Sense of Gay Community,' *Rites* 2, 9 (April 1986): 14–17.

35 Rita Mae Brown, 'A Stranger in Paradise: Rita Mae Brown Goes to the Baths,' *The Body Politic*, April 1976: 15.

36 On the tensions and overlaps between lesbian and gay sex and sexual representation in the 1990s, see Julia Creet, 'Lesbian Sex / Gay Sex: What's the Difference?' *Out/Look*, Winter 1991: 29–34.

37 'Classifieds,' *The Body Politic*, November 1977: 31.

38 For further references to racism in gay-male pornography, see Kobena Mercer and Isaac Julien, 'White Gay Racism,' in *Male Order: Unwrapping Masculinity* (London: Lawrence and Wishart 1988), 104–10; Gary Kinsman, Interview with Pei Lim: 'Racism and Gay Male Porn,' *Rites*, February 1987: 14–15; Kobena Mercer, 'Skin Head Sex Thing: Racial Difference and the Homoerotic Imaginary,' in Bad Object-Choices, eds, *How Do I Look? Queer Film and Video* (Seattle: Bay Press 1991), 169–210; and Richard Fung, 'Looking for My Penis: The Eroticized Asian in Gay Video Porn,' in *How Do I Look?*, 145–60.

39 Adrienne Rich, *Dream of a Common Language* (New York: W.W. Norton 1978), 31.

40 See Martha Vicinus, 'Sexuality and Power: A Review of Current Work in the History of Sexuality,' *Feminist Studies* 8, 1 (Spring 1982), 133–56; and Mary Louise Adams, 'Disputed Desire: The "Feminine" Women in Lesbian History,' unpublished paper delivered at Berkshire Women's History Conference, Rutgers University, June 1990.

41 'Some Workshop Reports,' National Lesbian Conference, Ottawa 1976: 1; on file at CWMA.

42 Judith Quinlan, 'Letter,' *Broadside*, October/November 1980: 8.

43 The emphasis on lesbian sexual prudery and prescriptivism, with little attention to the often untidy, contradictory, and ambiguous character of lesbian sex, is found in Alice Echols, 'Taming of the Id: Feminist Sexual Politics, 1968–1983,' in Carole Vance, ed., *Pleasure and Danger* (New York: Routledge and Kegan Paul 1984), 50–72; Susan Ardill and Sue O'Sullivan, 'Sex in the Summer of '88,' *Feminist Review* 31 (1989): 126–34; Wendy Clark, 'The Dyke, the Feminist and the Devil,' in *Sexuality, a Reader* (London: Virago 1987), 201–16; Esther Newton and Shirley Walton, 'The Misunderstanding: Toward a More Precise Sexual Vocabulary,' in Vance, ed., *Pleasure and Danger*, 242–50; Lisa Duggan, 'The Anguished Cry of an 80s Fem: I Want to Be a Drag Queen,' *Out/Look*, Spring 1988: 62–5; and Jan Zita Grover, 'Words to Lust By,' *Women's Review of Books*, November 1990: 21–3.

44 In *Sinister Wisdom*, Summer/Fall 1988, Marilyn Frye observed that lesbian sex is utterly 'inarticulate.'

45 Teresa Trull, *The Ways a Woman Can Be* (Oakland: Olivia Records 1976).

46 In order, these quotes are taken from Bannon's novels *Beebo Brinker* (Tallahassee, Fla.: Naiad Press 1986; original pub. 1962), 207; *Odd Girl Out* (Tallahassee: Naiad Press 1986; orig. pub. 1957), 60; and *Journey to a Woman* (Tallahassee: Naiad Press 1986; orig. pub. 1960), 64.

47 Ellen, 'A Conversation,' *The Other Woman*, October 1973: 1.

48 Holly Devor, 'Lesbian Feminism,' *The Other Woman*, October 1973: 11.

49 'Smash Phallic Imperialism,' unsigned, *The Other Woman*, Summer 1973: 6.

50 Karen Henderson, 'Review of Barbara Hammer's Dyke Films,' *LOOT Newsletter*, March 1979: 7.

51 Michele Landsberg, 'Lesbians Shouldn't Be Isolated,' *Toronto Star*, 28 May 1979: D1, 1.

52 Rosemary Barnes, cited in Coalition for Gay Rights in Ontario brief 'The Human Rights Omission,' submitted to Ontario Legislature, 1981: 7.

53 Grover, 'Words to Lust By,' 22.

54 'Classifieds,' *The Body Politic*, June 1977: 31. Ruth Roach Pierson suggested to me that personal ads placed by women in publications like the *New York Review of Books*, while not explicitly sexual, are implicitly so.

55 See *The Other Woman*, January/February 1976: 5.

56 Emily Sisley and Bertha Harris, *The Joy of Lesbian Sex* (New York: Simon and Schuster 1977), 4.

57 Non-monogamy vs. monogamy was not a new debate. See the Montréal Lesbian Conference report, *Long Time Coming*, February 1974: 7–8. And see Gloria Geller, 'The Issue of Nonmonogamy among Lesbians,' *Resources for Feminist Research* 12, 1 (March 1983): 44–45.

58 See the Ottawa Lesbian Conference Report, 1978, on file at CWMA.

59 Kate Middleton, 'The Coldwater Dyke,' *The Body Politic*, September 1976: 20.

60 On the difficulties of living up to the 'wonderdyke' image, see Laura S. Brown, 'Confronting Internalized Oppression,' in Monika Kehoe, ed., *Historical, Literary and Erotic Aspects of Lesbianism* (New York: Harrington Park Press 1986), 99; and Paula Webster, 'The Forbidden: Eroticism and Taboo,' in C. Vance, ed., *Pleasure and Danger*, 385–98.

61 Though Heather Bishop re-recorded Bessie Smith's 'Prove It on Me Blues,' there was little to no knowledge among lesbian feminists of the rich tradition of black women's blues in the 1920s and 1930s, particularly during the Harlem Renaissance. See Hazel V. Carby, 'It Jus Be's Dat Way Sometime: The Sexual Politics of Women's Blues,' *Radical America*, June/July 1986: 9–22.

62 Nomadic Sisters, *Loving Women* (San Francisco: Amazon Art Works 1975); Godiva, *What Lesbians Do* (San Fransciso: Amazon Art Works 1976); Dodson, *Liberating Masturbation*.

63 Tee Corrinne, *Cunt Coloring Book* (Weather Lake, Mo.: Naiad Press 1977); Sisley and Harris, *The Joy of Lesbian Sex*; Samois, *What Color Is Your Handkerchief? A Lesbian S/M Reader* (Boston: Alyson Publications 1979).

64 Webster, 'The Forbidden: Eroticism and Taboo,' 386.

65 Gay Bell, 'Margaret Dwight Spore at the Ottawa Lesbian Conference,' *The Other Woman*, November/December 1976: 5. Margaret Dwight Spore was the founder of BEAVER (Better End to All Vicious Erotic Repression) in Toronto in 1978, a small organization of sex-trade workers, some of whom identified as lesbians.

66 Meg Christian, 'Ode to a Gym Teacher,' on *I Know You Know* (Los Angeles: Olivia Records 1974).

67 Joan Bridi Miller, 'S/M, Another Point of View,' *Gay Community News*, October 1976, was one of the first on this subject. Pat Califia's sex-help book *Sapphistry: The Book of Lesbian Sexuality* (Tallahassee, Fla.: Naiad Press) was published in 1980. Sold under the counters of some feminist bookstores, it quickly became the focus of much-heated debate.

68 In the 'Introduction' to *Home Girls: A Black Feminist Anthology* (New York: Kitchen Table Press 1983), Black lesbian feminist Barbara Smith says, 'Until now, Black women have been peripheral to these [sex] debates and I am not sure that it will be helpful to us to step into the middle of white-rooted interpretations of these issues. The history of sexual exploitation of black women, both at the level of myth and of daily life, by a white culture has understandably made many women wary of participating in this particular controversy' (xlv). Notably, there were no lesbians of colour who contributed to Samois's initial *What Color Is Your Handkerchief?* reader, nor their expanded collection *Coming to Power* (Boston: Alyson Publications 1981).

69 In the early 1980s, the voice of sex radical Sue Golding was one to be reckoned with. See Golding's 'Sex at Issue: Time for Questioning in Bed,' *The Body Politic*, October 1981: 35; 'Exposed for Debate,' ibid., November 1981: 35; and 'Thoughts about Lesbian Sex, Politics and Community Standards,' *Fireweed: Lesbiantics I* 13 (1982): 80–100. Also see Chris Bearchell, 'Art, Trash and Titillation: A Consumer's Guide to Lezzy Smut,' *The Body Politic*, May 1983: 29–33.

70 See Chris Bearchell's article 'Why I Am a Gay Liberationist: Thoughts on Sex, Freedom, the Family and the State,' *Resources for Feminist Research* 12, 1

(March 1983): 57–60. A disclaimer was printed at the top of Bearchell's article by editorial collective members of this lesbian issue: 'The views expressed here are the author's and we welcome the continuation of this debate in the pages of other journals and magazines across the country.'

71 Ellen Willis, 'Feminism, Moralism and Pornography,' in Ann Snitow, Chistine Stansell, and Sharon Thompson, eds, *Powers of Desire* (New York: Monthly Review Press 1983), 464.

72 'Amy Vanderdyke,' *Long Time Coming*, April/May 1976: 23.

73 Jan Brown, 'Sex, Lies and Penetration: A Butch Finally 'Fesses Up,' *Out/Look* 7 (Winter 1990): 30.

74 Customs Canada seizures of lesbian/gay materials have escalated in the 1980s and 1990s. See Becki Ross, 'Launching Lesbian Cultural Offensives,' *Resources for Feminist Research* 17, 2 (June 1988): 12–16; Marusia Bociurkiw, 'Territories of the Forbidden: Lesbian Culture, Sex and Censorship,' *Fuse*, April 1988: 27–32; and Becki Ross, 'Wunna His Fantasies: The State/d Indefensibility of Lesbian Smut,' *Fireweed* 38 (Spring 1993): 38–47.

75 Chris Fox, 'Review of *Loving Women* by the Nomadic Sisters,' *The Other Woman*, March/April 1976: 17–18.

76 Ann Cognita, 'Slut Perspective,' *Lavender Sheets*, Summerish [sic] 1989: 7.

77 'Dear Lezzy,' *Lavender Sheets*, Summerish [sic] 1980: 14.

78 Mariana Valverde, 'Confessions of a Lesbian Ex-Masochist,' *The Body Politic*, September 1979: 18.

79 Robin Tyler, *Always a Bridesmaid, Never a Groom* (Los Angeles: Olivia Records 1979).

80 Val Edwards, 'Robin Tyler: Comic in Contradiction. A Profile,' *The Body Politic*, September 1979: 23.

81 Margaret Hunt, 'A Fem's Own Story: An Interview with Joan Nestle,' in Christian McEwen and Sue O'Sullivan, eds, *Out the Other Side: Contemporary Lesbian Writing* (London: Virago 1988), 235.

82 Maida Tilchin and Fran Koski, 'Some Pulp Sappho,' *The Body Politic*, August 1976: 2.

83 For lesbian-feminist repudiations of the butch/femme stance see Sidney Abbott and Barbara Love, *Sappho Was a Right-On Woman* (New York: Stein and Day 1972), 19–44; and Eleanor Cooper, 'Social Outlets,' in Ginny Vida, ed., *Our Right to Love: Lesbian Resource Book* (Englewood Cliffs, NJ: Prentice-Hall 1978), 48–50. In *The Joy of Lesbian Sex*, Sisley and Harris comment: 'Pathetically, [butch/femme] behaviour was a parody of the worst heterosexual coupling; the butch stomping and hen-pecked, the femme kittenish and nagging' (40). For contemporary condemnation of butch/femme relations, see Sheila Jeffreys, 'Butch and Femme: Now and Then,'

in Lesbian History Group, ed., *Not a Passing Phase: Reclaiming Lesbian History, 1840–1985* (London: Women's Press 1989), 158–87.

84 Lorna Weir, 'So Much for the Woman-Identified Woman,' *The Body Politic,* June 1979: 31.

85 Interview with Natalie LaRoche. Natalie continues: 'I have my theory about the roots of butch/femme identities: I think femmes were little girls who needed boys, and butches were little girls who wanted to be boys and that's the karma that we all work out. Even today, you always hear, "butch is better." I do my stint with long red nails and dresses because I'm sick of it.'

86 Chase, 'Gay Pride? Week,' 16.

87 In her article 'Speaking Up for Our Sisters: Decriminalization of Prostitution,' *Fireweed* 1, 1 (1978), Margaret Dwight Spore describes BEAVER as 'Canada's first organizational voice for prostitutes and other workers of the flesh; i.e., strippers, porno actresses, etc. It advocates: the removal of soliciting and bawdy house charges from the Criminal Code of Canada; the recognition of prostitutes as legitimate workers with an independent status; equal police protection for prostitutes and other workers of the flesh; an end to use of non-related legislation (i.e., loitering) to control prostitution' (26).

88 See Laurie Bell, ed., *Good Girls / Bad Girls: Sex Trade Workers and Feminists Face to Face* (Toronto: Women's Press 1987); Frederique Delacoste and Priscilla Alexander, eds, *Sex Work: Writings by Women in the Sex Industry* (Pittsburgh: Cleis Press 1987).

89 Gay Bell, 'Snuff, Violence and Waking Up Mad,' *The Body Politic,* December/January 1977–8: 28.

90 See Janice Raymond, *The Transsexual Empire* (Boston: Beacon Press 1979); and Mary Daly, *Gyn/Ecology: The Metaethics of Radical Feminism* (Boston: Beacon Press 1978).

91 Sound Recording of the Transsexual Debate, LOOT, October 1978; on file at CWMA.

92 Interview with Pat Murphy. It would have been interesting had a female-to-male (FTM) transsexual asked permission to join the LOOT membership. Given the emphasis on biological femaleness, an FTM should have been welcomed at LOOT, though I suspect that had such an individual appeared, 'he' would have been denied entrance.

93 'Transsexual Debate,' *LOOT Newsletter,* November 1978: 4.

94 There were several transsexual and transvestite organizations formed in Toronto in the early 1970s. ACT, the Association of Canadian Transsexuals, was founded in 1972 and held regular meetings at the CHAT com-

munity centre. From available documents, it is unclear whether there were any self-identified lesbian members.

95 Large sheets of newsprint covered with wonderful graffiti are housed at the CWMA.

96 The disclosure that Sandy Stone, a member of the publicly lesbian separatist music-distribution label Olivia, was a male-to-female lesbian transsexual scandalized many lesbians across the U.S., Canada, and Québec in the late 1970s.

97 I like Judith Butler's discussion of instability in 'Imitation and Gender Insubordination: The Instability of Gay/Lesbian Identity,' at York University, 23 January 1991. For other provocative accounts that draw from psychoanalysis see Jessica Benjamin, 'Master and Slave: The Fantasy of Erotic Domination,' in Snitow, Stansell, and Thompson, eds, *Powers of Desire*, 280–99; and Diane Hamer, 'Significant Others: Lesbianism and Psychoanalytic Theory,' *Feminist Review* 34 (Spring 1990): 134–51.

CHAPTER 6 LOOT's structure and program

1 See Nancy Adamson, Linda Briskin, and Margaret McPhail, *Feminist Organizing for Change: The Contemporary Women's Movement in Canada* (Toronto: Oxford University Press 1988), 229–55.

2 Darlene Lawson, taped debate on lesbian-feminist strategy at LOOT, February 1978; housed at CWMA.

3 I place 'non-political' in quotations to signal my ambivalence with its usage. The term implies a dichotomy – good lesbians are self-consciously feminists, bad lesbians are falsely conscious non-feminists (or antifeminists) – which obscures the particularities of women's experience and the material conditions under which they navigated their everyday/everynight lives. A fully investigated and elaborated explication of different relationships to feminism awaits future research. Several women I interviewed suggested that a pool table at 342 Jarvis Street might have made possible linkages between these communities of lesbians, hence a more diverse LOOT membership.

4 Barbara Gittings and Kay Tobin, 'Lesbians and the Gay Movement,' in Ginny Vida, ed., *Our Right to Love: A Lesbian Resource Book* (Englewood Cliffs, NJ: Prentice-Hall 1978), 151.

5 Nym Hughes, Yvonne Johnson, and Yvette Perrault, *Stepping out of Line: A Workbook on Lesbianism and Feminism* (Vancouver: Press Gang 1984), 173.

6 Ilona Laney, 'Lesbian Organization Opens Its Doors,' *The Body Politic*, May 1977: 4.

7 Over the group's three-year history, members of Mama Quilla II, fashioned after Sara Ellen Dunlop's short-lived band, Mama Quilla, included Linda Robitaille (saxophone), Maxine Walsh (congas), Linda Jain (drums), Lorraine Segato (vocals), Susan Cole (vocals and piano), Donna Marchand (guitar), and Susan Sturman (guitar).

8 See 'Annoucing the Birth of Atthis Theatre,' *LOOT Newsletter*, June 1979: 1. For more information on the beginnings of lesbian theatre in Toronto, see Gay Bell, 'From a Resistance to Lesbian Theatre to a Lesbian Theatre of Resistance,' *Resources for Feminist Research* 12, 1 (March 1983): 30–3; and Amanda Hale, 'A Dialectical Drama of Facts and Fiction on the Feminist Fringe,' in Rhea Tregebov, ed., *Work in Progress: Building Feminist Culture* (Toronto: Women's Press 1987), 77–100.

9 Gay Bell, 'Michigan Womyn's Music Festival,' *LOOT Newsletter*, September 1977: 4.

10 Susan Cole, taped debate on lesbian-feminist strategy at LOOT, February 1978; housed at CWMA.

11 Chris Bearchell, debate on lesbian-feminist strategy at LOOT, February 1978.

12 Lorna Weir and Eve Zaremba, 'Boys and Girls Together: Feminism and Gay Liberation,' *Broadside* 4, 1 (1982): 10–11.

13 Pat Leslie, 'An Independent Women's Movement,' *The Other Woman*, May/June 1975: 10, 24. Though the shift from radical to cultural feminism was more sharply delineated in the U.S. than in Canada, Pat Leslie's use of the term in 1975 in the context of grass-roots Toronto feminism is instructive.

14 Ibid.

15 *The Other Woman*, January 1977: 2.

16 Letter to LOOT membership by Gay Bell, July 1977; on file at the CWMA.

17 'Wasn't LOOT itself a political action committee?' asked Judith Bennett. Debate on lesbian-feminist strategy at LOOT, February 1978.

18 *LOOT Newsletter*, December/January 1977–8: 3.

19 Brenda Lang, debate on lesbian-feminist strategy at LOOT, February 1978.

20 *LOOT Newsletter*, June 1978: 1.

21 Pat Leslie, Task Force minutes, June 1978, on file at CWMA.

22 *LOOT Newsletter*, May 1978: 4.

23 See a report on 1977 National Gay Rights Conference in Saskatoon by Gary Kinsman and Andrea Goth, members of the Revolutionary Marxist Group, 'Lesbians and Gays Move to Support Women's Struggles,' *The*

Militant, 18 July 1977. At this conference, lesbian feminists were encouraged by the passage of a motion securing 50 per cent of the decision-making power for lesbians despite the fact that lesbians did not make up 50 per cent of the delegates. Unfortunately, the optimism generated by the motion was short-lived. At the 1978 NGRC conference in Halifax, the 50 per cent resolution struck in Saskatoon – where almost all the women present, and a handful of gay men, supported it – was overturned. Recalls Naomi Brooks, 'The guys who voted it down called us fascists and Nazi operators because we weren't doing what they wanted.' For an analysis of this defeat, see Bill Fields, 'The Rise and the Fall of the Fifty Per Cent Solution: Lesbians in the Canadian Gay Rights Movement,' Faculty of Social Work, University of Regina, 1983; on file at Canadian Lesbian and Gay Archives.

24 Karen Henderson, *LOOT Newsletter*, November 1977): 4.
25 Judith Bennett, LOOT Task Force meeting, February 1978; sound recording housed at CWMA.
26 See Joreen (Jo Freeman), 'The Tyranny of Structurelessness,' in Anne Koedt, Ellen Levine, and Anita Rapone, eds., *Radical Feminism* (New York: Quadrangle 1973), 285–300; Adamson et al., *Feminist Organizing for Change*, 229–55; and Saskatoon Women's Liberation Papers, Steering Committee, Constitution Proposal, January 1978: 3; on file at CWMA.
27 Meredith Tax, 'The Sound of One Hand Clapping: Women's Liberation and the Left,' *Dissent*, Fall 1988: 461. And for more discussion of the internal processes of feminist organizing, see the case study by Red Apple Collective, 'Socialist Feminist Women's Unions: Past and Present,' *Socialist Review* 8, 2 (March/April 1978): 37–57; Annie Popkin, 'The Social Experience of Bread and Roses: Building a Community and Creating a Culture,' in Karen V. Hansen and Ilene J. Philipson, eds, *Women, Class and the Feminist Imagination* (Philadelphia: Temple University Press 1990), 182–212; Karen Hansen, 'Women's Unions and the Search for a Political Identity,' in Hansen and Philipson, eds., *Women, Class and the Feminist Imagination*, 213–38; Judith Sealander and Dorothy Smith, 'The Rise and Fall of Feminist Organizations in the 1970s: Dayton as a Case Study,' in ibid., 239–57; and Janice Ristock, 'Feminist Collectives: The Struggles and Contradictions in Our Quest for a 'Uniquely Feminist Structure,' in Janice Ristock and Jeri D. Wine, eds, *Women and Social Change: Feminist Activism in Canada* (Toronto: James Lorimer 1991), 41–55.
28 See Pat Leslie, 'Do You Want To See Our Queer Pass?' *The Other Woman*, November/December 1976. Leslie writes about the Berkeley Women's Music Collective: '[They] practice collectivity in their music by exchang-

ing instruments for each song. As Susan humourously put it, "We're so collective, we're afraid to get good at one thing". Neither do they have the traditional lead singer as so many bands do; but each person sings her own original song ... Sisterhood is more than a feeling' (21).

29 Rosemary Barnes, 'Dykes in Search of Affection and Independence,' *Resources for Feminist Research* 12, 1 (March 1983): 46.

30 Dorothy E. Smith, 'Where There Is Oppression, There Is Resistance,' *Branching Out* 6, 1 (1979): 11.

31 On trashing, see Smith, ibid., 14.

CHAPTER 7 Lesbian feminists meet gay liberationists

1 This song was composed by Michael Riordan and Heather Ramsay for the anti-Bryant mass rally held at the St Lawrence Market in January 1978. It was sung, en masse, to the tune of 'The Battle Hymn of the Republic.' On file at the Canadian Lesbian and Gay Archives.

2 On Anita Bryant, see Gayle Rubin, 'Thinking Sex: Notes for a Radical Theory of the Politics of Sexuality,' in Carole Vance, ed., *Pleasure and Danger* (Boston: Routlege and Kegan Paul 1984), 271, and Pat Califia, 'A Personal View of the History of the Lesbian S/M Community and Movement in San Francisco,' in *Coming to Power* (Boston: Alyson 1987), 245–83. Califia states: 'Bryant's hate campaign painted the ugliest, most sensationalistic picture of the gay community, she focused on the fringe and minority elements of the community. This created a mean-spirited and frightened attitude in the mainstream gay movement. Pedophiles, transsexuals, transvestites, tearoom cruisers, hustlers, young gays and s/mers were disavowed and urged to keep quiet and become invisible' (274).

3 There were similar Stop Anita Bryant coalitions that sprang up in Winnipeg, Saskatoon, Edmonton, and Vancouver.

4 At the end of 1977, *Good Housekeeping* magazine named Anita Bryant 'the most admired woman of the year.'

5 The 'Lunacy' editorial (*Toronto Sun* 28 September 1977) links the rights of gays to adopt children to the 'death-wish that infects Western civilization.' For other pro-Bryant coverage see 'Anita's Day,' editorial, *Toronto Sun*, 15 January 1978, and a column by Mackenzie Porter, ibid., 16 January 1978. One exception to the media attacks led by the likes of Claire Hoy of the *Toronto Sun* is a short article by Betty Lee, 'Bitter Oranges,' *Toronto Star, Canada Magazine*, 23 July 1977.

6 Claire Hoy, 'Stop the Bleeding Hearts,' *Toronto Sun*, 8 September 1977; 'Gay Rights ... continuing saga,' ibid., 13 November 1977; 'Morality vs.

Perversity,' ibid., 21 December 1977; 'Kids, Not Rights, Their Craving,' ibid., 24 December 1977; 'Bryant Speaks Our Mind,' ibid., 15 January 1978.

7 There was some reluctance on the part of *The Body Politic* collective to take up the Anita Bryant crusade seriously because of the editors' anti-American stance. So, GATE took the organizing lead and called the first meeting at the CHAT office on Church Street. At the first demonstration, a large paper maché effigy of Anita Bryant was burned.

8 The term 'hysterical hate campaign' is coined in the article, 'Anita Must Go!' by Andrea Goth in *The Militant*, 18 July 1977.

9 The *Life Together* report proposed over one hundred changes to the Human Rights Code, and in particular identified native people, the physically disabled, youth, and homosexuals as disadvantaged by the current legislation. Released in the summer of 1977, the report strongly recommended the extension of civil rights to homosexuals in the areas of services, employment, and housing.

10 On 26 June 1977, more than a quarter of a million people poured into the streets of San Francisco against the Briggs Initiative – a policy that intended to prohibit lesbian/gay curriculum in schools and the hiring of lesbian/gay teachers – screaming 'no more Miamis' and 'gay rights now.' For analysis of the defeat of the Briggs Initiative, see Amber Hollibaugh, 'Sexuality and the State: The Defeat of the Briggs Initiative and Beyond,' *Socialist Review*, May/June 1979: 55–71.

11 'Crisis: In the Midst of Danger, A Chance to Unite,' editorial, *The Body Politic*, February 1978: 1

12 None of the meetings was held at 342 Jarvis Street because no men were allowed on the premises. It's possible that had mixed-gender meetings been held at LOOT, members might have been able to exert more influence over the structure and content of the community forums.

13 Demands made at the Anita Bryant rally, 14 January 1978, were: stop Anita's crusade; defend *The Body Politic* and freedom of the press; include sexual orientation in the human-rights code along with custody for lesbian mothers; defend Bob and Dave – two gay men who were busted for a week for postering; drop charges against people busted at the WAVAW demo; drop charges against Montreal gays – 140 busted at Truxx bar; and ensure full sexual rights for youth, no discrimination against teachers and social-service workers, sexual self-determination for children, and economic independence for women.

14 In January, a bus-load of Toronto gay and lesbian activists travelled to Pe-

terborough to protest Anita Bryant's visit to that community. The rally and demonstration were co-organized by the Ad Hoc Coalition, the Trent Student Union, and the Trent Homophile Association. According to Pat Murphy, 'We weren't sure whether we were going to get out of there alive. Going to Peterborough was a statement that "You will not bury us."'

15 Adrienne Rich 'The Meaning of Our Love for Women Is What We Have Constantly to Expand,' in *On Lies, Secrets and Silence* (New York: W.W. Norton 1980), 223. The essay was first printed as a pamphlet by Brooklyn, New York's Out and Out Books as the first in a series on lesbian feminism.

16 Olivia Records released the album *Lesbian Concentrate: A Lesbianthology of Songs and Poems, 100% Undiluted* (1977) as a protest against Anita Bryant forces in the U.S., with a percentage of profits going to the National Lesbian Mothers Defense Fund. On the album, African American Linda Tillery informs Bryant, 'You're one of our sisters, and you're going to find that out.'

17 See Susan Cole, 'Sunkist Marriage Goes Sour,' *Broadside*, July/August 1980: 9. In her interview, Susan Cole told me: 'After the crusade died down, Bryant ended up suing for divorce on the basis of mental and physical cruelty and she took back everything she said. She said that her husband forced her to do it, which is something a lot of us had been saying or thinking. *The Body Politic* buried a notice about this in the back of the paper.'

18 See Val Edwards, 'The Invisible Community,' *Broadside*, September 1980, who argues, 'When I took over the LOOT newsletter in 1978, I found that it was virtually impossible to persuade lesbians to contribute meaty political articles' (5). Jeffrey Weeks reports that, not unlike LOOT, *Sappho* in London was founded in 1972 as a grass-roots publication, 'designed more to keep its subscribers in touch with each other's preoccupations than to advance political perspectives.' See Weeks, *Coming Out: Homosexual Politics in Britain, from the Nineteenth Century to the Present* (London: Quartet Books 1977), 214.

19 Anita Bryant debate, taped at LOOT, January 1978; housed at CWMA.

20 Ed Jackson and Stan Persky, the editors of *Flaunting It!* (Toronto and Vancouver: New Star Books and Pink Triangle Press 1982) state: 'A full debate about lesbian political priorities never found its way into the pages of *The Body Politic* ... the volatile nature of the issue and the fragility of existing alliances apparently inhibited free-wheeling discussion, at least

in print. A survey of *TBP* issues spanning the Seventies reveals only fragmentary attempts at dealing with the perceived causes of the problems or at proposing solutions to them' (175).

21 'Lesbians and the Ontario Human Rights Code' was a printed statement made by members of the Lesbian Organization of Toronto outlining their demand for inclusion of sexual orientation in the Ontario Human Rights Code. On file at the Canadian Lesbian and Gay Archives, Toronto.

22 According to Gary Kinsman, members of the revolutionary left, in particular the League for Socialist Action and the Revolutionary Marxist Group, were also critical of the 'human rights' approach for dealing with formal levels of equality rather than substantive social change. But, to quote Gary, 'even though I think our analysis was accurate, we were saying that the alternative was socialist revolution, which was too abstract, not very concrete and not very credible' (personal correspondence with Gary Kinsman). There was a Gay Marxist Study Group at Toronto's Marxist Institute in the mid-1970s, with Tim McCaskell, Richard Fung, Walter Davis, Gary Kinsman, Ken Popert, Brian Mossop, Herb Spiers, Ed Jackson, and Peter Lancastle. This was an early attempt to theorize the connectedness of sexism, homophobia, and class oppression.

23 In her article 'Lesbian Feminism and the Gay Rights Movement: Another View of Male Supremacy, Another Separatism,' in Frye, *The Politics of Reality: Essays in Feminist Theory* (New York: The Crossing Press 1983), Marilyn Frye argues, 'Being gay [male] is not at all inconsistent with being loyal to masculinity and committed to contempt for women' (137).

24 For mainstream news accounts, see 'Gay Community Is Appalled,' *Toronto Star*, 3 August 1977; 'Nobody Else Wants Yonge Street Blight,' ibid., 11 August 1977; 'Editorial,' *Globe and Mail*, 12 August 1977; and 'Sin Strip Victim,' *Toronto Sun*, 3 August 1977. It was argued in the *Toronto Sun* (5 August 1977) that 'the strip does contribute to a climate of sexual permissiveness that is unwholesome and unhealthy. It is an environment for perversions and degradations that are unimagined by "straight" people.' To counteract the vilifying mainstream accounts, GATE leafletted the bars with their position paper on what the murder of Jacques meant to the gay community. Five men who did not self-identify as gay or as members of Toronto's gay-male community were eventually arrested, charged, and jailed for Jaques's brutal slaying. An important exception to the moralistic and often hateful critiques made by mainstream journalists was Joanne Kates's 'Impolitic Moves,' *Toronto Star, Fanfare Magazine*, 4 January 1978: 13.

25 Ulli Diemer, 'Death on Yonge Street,' *Ward Seven News*, 13 August 1977. As

Deanne Bogdan suggested to me, the Portuguese reaction of outrage at the horror of a child's murder must be taken into account, and must not be understood solely as homophobic fury.

26 Yvonne Chi-Ying Ng, 'Ideology, Media and Moral Panics: An Analysis of the Jaques Murder,' M.A. thesis, Centre for Criminology, University of Toronto, 1981. See also Gary Kinsman, 'The Jaques Murder: An Anatomy of a Moral Panic,' in *The Regulation of Desire* (Montréal: Black Rose Books 1986), 204-5.

27 Gerald Hannon, 'Men Loving Boys Loving Men,' *The Body Politic*, November 1977: 30-3. The standpoint of sexually active young gays and lesbians was explored by Hannon in 'Seven Years to Go: the Plight of Gay Youth,' in *The Body Politic*, September 1976: 1, 14-15.

28 Claire Hoy, 'Stop the Bleeding Hearts,' *Toronto Sun*, 30 October 1977; 'The Limp Wrist Lobby,' ibid., 2 November 1977; 'Gay Rights, Continuing Saga,' ibid., 13 November 1977; 'Morality vs. Perversity,' ibid., 21 December 1977; *Toronto Sun*, 22 December 1977; 'Kids, Not Rights, Their Craving,' ibid., 25 December 1977.

29 Armed with a warrant, officers from the Metropolitan Toronto Police force and the Ontario Provincial Police carted away twelve shipping cartons filled with documents and records: subscription lists dating back years, distribution and advertising records, corporate and financial records (even the cheque book), classified ad records and addresses, manuscripts for publication, and letters to the editors. Personal and business mail was opened and the Canadian Gay Archives was ransacked.

30 L. Phillips, 'Letter: The Straight Goods,' and Marlowe Amber, 'Letter: Boys Noise,' *The Body Politic*, March/April 1979: 4.

31 Darlene Lawson, 3-hour taped debate, 'Men Loving Boys Loving Men,' at LOOT, January 1978; housed at CWMA.

32 Francie Wyland, quoted in the *Toronto Star*, 10 January 1978. At the National Gay Rights Coalition conference in Halifax in 1978, Neil Glickman, a Wages Due speaker told delegates that lesbian mothers could justifiably support Anita Bryant. 'After all,' he chimed, 'if they don't put the welfare of their kids first, what kind of mothers are they?' See Ken Popert, 'Bryantism and Wages Due: Recruiting within Our Own Movement,' *The Body Politic*, September 1978: 5.

33 Robin Tyler, quoted in *The Body Politic*, December/January 1978/9: 9.

34 Darlene Lawson, debate, 'Men Loving Boys Loving Men,' at LOOT, January 1978.

35 'Editorial,' *The Body Politic*, December/January 1977: 1. In a gesture of reconciliation (seen by many lesbian feminists as too little too late), *The Body*

Politic reprinted the original 'Men Loving Boys Loving Men' article in April 1979. It was accompanied by a long, self-critical essay, 'Another Look,' that sought to embrace a feminist analysis of social, physical, and economic inequities in adult/child sexual relations.

36 Lorna Weir is quoted in the essay 'Another Look' that accompanied the reprint of 'Men Loving Boys Loving Men' in *The Body Politic*, April/May 1979: 25.

37 Pat Leslie, 'Doing Our Own Work,' *The Body Politic*, September 1978: 2.

38 See Eve Zaremba, 'Porn Again,' *The Body Politic*, October 1978: 4.

39 Ibid.

40 Darlene Lawson, debate, 'Men Loving Boys Loving Men,' at LOOT, January 1978.

41 Claire Hoy, 'The Limp Wrist Lobby,' *Toronto Sun*, 2 November 1977. And see Christina Blizzard, 'Gay Pap Appealing Tax Waste,' ibid., 25 January 1992: 14; 'Gay Flier Furor: Pamphlet Says Homosexuality "Natural,"' ibid., 25 September 1992: 4; 'Gay Case for Fliers Is Bizarre,' ibid., 25 September 1992: 14; 'Personal Problem? Yes It Is,' ibid., 15 October 1992: 16; and 'Buddies in Bad Times,' ibid., 15 June 1993: A18.

42 In *The Body Politic*, February 1976, Chris Bearchell reports that at the third annual NGRC conference in the summer of 1975, members voted to include a demand for the abolition of all age-of-consent laws. The alternative was a demand for a uniform age of consent for all, gay and straight. The age of consent varied interprovincially, from 14 to 18 (p. 1).

43 It is hypothesized in the article 'Incest and Other Sexual Taboos: A Dialogue between Men and Women' (*Out/Look*, Fall 1989) that 'the feminist/lesbian movements may be anti-sexual because many of the women involved may have been sexually abused. Whether they remember it or not' (53). I would submit that the connections between women's histories of sexual abuse, feminist politics, and actual sexual practice require much more rigorous investigation.

44 In an article entitled 'Divided We Stand' in *The Body Politic* (February 1977) Andrew Hodges observed: 'Comment on the enormous spectrum of male sexual possibilities has been restricted within the movement, sometimes explicitly for fear of offending lesbian sensibilities' (21).

45 Jane Rule's original article, 'Teaching Sexuality,' appeared in issue no. 53 (June 1979) of *The Body Politic* and has been reprinted in her collection *Outlander: Short Stories and Essays* (Tallahassee, Fla.: Naiad Press 1982), 157–62. Here Rule adds: '[I would want] to make adults easier to seduce, less burdened with fear or guilt, less defended by hypocrisy. If we accepted sexual behaviour between children and adults, we would be far more able

to protect our children from abuse and exploitation than we are now'
(160–1).

46 Chris Bearchell, 'Why I'm a Gay Liberationist,' *Resources for Feminist Research*
12, 1 (March 1983): 60.

47 At the Bi-National Lesbian Conference in Toronto, May 1979, a workshop of six young lesbians recommended that the conference pass a resolution condemning age-of-consent laws that did not reach the floor of
the plenary. See Chris Bearchell's article on lesbian cross-generational relations, 'I Was 15, She Was 43,' *The Body Politic*, December/January 1977–8:
14.

48 See Kate Millett, 'Beyond Politics? Children and Sexuality,' in Vance, ed.,
Pleasure and Danger, 217–24. In 1975, *Show Me! a Picture Book of Sex for Children
and Parents* by H. Fleischauer-Hardt, was banned by Customs Canada officials at the border. Though fully heterosexual in content, the book, especially the photographs, attempted to offer a positive portrayal of children
as active and curious sexual agents.

49 Gayle Rubin, 'Thinking Sex: Notes for a Radical Theory on the Politics
of Sexuality,' in Vance, ed., *Pleasure and Danger*, 268.

50 Reported by Ken Popert in 'Lesbian Group Supports Age of Consent
Laws,' *The Body Politic*, April 1976: 1.

51 Robin Hardy reports that the National Gay Youth Coalition, formed in
Toronto in May 1978, did not resolve the age-of-consent laws issue. He
writes: 'Delegates were divided over whether the demand should be for
abolition of age of consent laws or for an equalization which would bring
the age for gay youth in line with that for straight youth.' See 'Gay Youth
Plan Assault on School System,' *The Body Politic*, June/July 1978: 4.

52 Chris Bearchell, NGRC report, *The Other Woman*, October/November
1975: 4.

53 Lisa, debate, 'Men Loving Boys Loving Men,' at LOOT, January 1978.

54 Gayle Rubin, 'Letter,' *The Body Politic*, February 1978: 2.

55 Judy Springer, in her letter to *The Body Politic* (April 1978), points out 'the
lack of feminist viewpoint' in *The Body Politic* on the subject of pedophiles
(p. 3). Unfortunately, she herself does not offer a feminist analysis.

CHAPTER 8 Lesbian feminists meet women's liberationists

1 Adrienne Rich, 'Twenty-One Love Poems,' in *Dream of a Common Language*
(New York: W.W. Norton 1978), 34.

2 Interview with Varda Burstyn. Burstyn explains that, for several years,
socialist feminists had used May Day celebrations to highlight a slate of

women's demands, including universal child care, abortion on demand, and equal pay for work of equal value.

3 Deborah Wolf, in *The Lesbian Community* (Berkeley: University of California Press 1979), states that on 8 March 1857 women textile workers in New York first protested their working conditions. In August 1910 at the Second International Conference of Socialist Working Women, the celebration of International Working Women's Day was established. Only later was the date of March 8th chosen.

4 See Carolyn Egan, Linda Lee Gardiner, and Judy Vashti Persad, 'The Politics of Transformation: Struggles with Race, Class and Sexuality in the March 8th Coalition,' in F. Cunningham, S. Findlay, M. Kadar, A. Lennon, and E. Silva, eds, *Social Movements / Social Change: The Politics and Practice of Organizing*, (Toronto: Between the Lines 1988), 20–47.

5 Ibid., 21.

6 Interestingly, in 1989 at the Women's Common, a private women's club in Toronto, Rosemary Barnes told me that at a general meeting, the hottest item on the agenda was whether to have an open house once a year where men could come. The motion was voted down after a very heated discussion.

7 Quoted from Maureen Fitzgerald, 'Toronto International Women's Day Committee,' *Canadian Woman's Studies* 2, 2 (1980): 33.

8 The following statement was printed in *The Other Woman* (June 1975): 'Let this be a lesson to us that the Women's Movement will not do anything until we can resolve this one, most important question once and for all – that of Man as Enemy. Unity builds strategy builds Revolution' (7).

9 Darlene Lawson, taped debate, 'Lesbian Feminist Strategy,' at LOOT, 18 March 1979; housed at CWMA.

10 This phrase is found in the WAVAW leaflet distributed at the IWD rally and demonstration in March 1978; on file at CWMA.

11 Pat Murphy, taped debate, 'Child Sexuality,' February 1978, at LOOT; housed at CWMA.

12 WAVAW leaflet distributed at the IWD rally and demonstration in March 1978; on file at CWMA.

13 Ibid.

14 Unidentified speaker, debate, 'Child Sexuality,' February 1978 at LOOT.

15 Eve Zaremba, debate on lesbian-feminist strategy, 18 March 1979, at LOOT.

16 Eve Zaremba, 'Now You See It, Now You Don't,' *Broadside*, May 1979: 19. The accompanying photo, by Bev Allinson, focused on the presence of

male leftists at the rear of the march, all the while framing this presence as primary. The placards in the image read: 'Fight for Our Rights, Fight for Socialism,' 'The Right to a Job,' 'Revolutionary Feminism, International Socialism,' 'Working Women to Fight the Crisis,' 'Only Solution to Women's Oppression Is Socialism.'

17 In her article 'Toronto International Women's Day Committee,' Maureen Fitzgerald's use of the two terms 'socialist feminist' and 'anti-capitalist feminist' indicates that in early 1978, when IWDC was formed, the term 'socialist feminist' was not in full currency (p. 34). IWDC did not officially name itself a socialist-feminist organization until 1979, though many of its members identified as socialists before its naming.

18 This now famous poster, 'Feminists Are Everywhere,' is part of the Graphic Feminism travelling show of Canadian Women's Movement Archives print and visual artefacts.

19 IWDC was formed in 1978 by making the follow-up committee of the first March 8th Coalition into a permanent committee. See Carolyn Egan, 'Socialist Feminism: Activism and Alliances,' in Heather Jon Maroney and Meg Luxton, eds, *Socialist Feminism and Political Economy* (Toronto: Methuen 1987), 109–19.

20 Gay Days was not the first celebration of gay pride in Toronto – in 1971, small-scale festivities were organized at Queen's Park. In 1973, a number of gay activists approached Mayor David Crombie with a request for official recognition of Gay Pride Day, but the request was flatly denied. Throughout his twelve years as Toronto's mayor, Art Eggleton also refused to grant Lesbian and Gay Pride Day status as one of the city's official days of celebration. However, in the fall of 1990, Toronto city council voted in favour of the motion and overrode the mayor's homophobic resistance.

21 Egan et al., 'The Politics of Transformation,' 32. For another account of early March 8th Coalition organizing, see Naomi Wall, 'The Last Ten Years,' in Maureen Fitzgerald, Connie Guberman, and Margie Wolf, eds, *Still Ain't Satisfied* (Toronto: Women's Press 1982), 15–29.

22 Gay Bell, debate on lesbian-feminist strategy, 18 March 1979, at LOOT.

23 As reported in Egan et al., 'The Politics of Transformation,' in 1985 the section of the leaflet written to highlight sexuality and women's right to live freely and openly as lesbians was inadvertently omitted from the text sent to the typesetter. Thousands of the leaflets were printed and distributed before the mistake was realized. They concluded that 'the Coalition was much criticized,' but if 'an anti-heterosexist perspective had been in-

tegrated throughout the leaflet, the omission would not have had the same effect' (34). At the IWD rally in Toronto in 1986, there was not one public mention of lesbianism.

24 Sue Genge, 'Lesbians and Gays in the Union Movement,' in Linda Briskin and Lynda Yanz, eds, *Union Sisters: Women in the Labour Movement* (Toronto: Women's Press 1983), 167.

25 Arja Lane, 'Wives Supporting the Strike,' in Briskin and Yanz, eds, *Union Sisters*, 327.

26 Chris Bearchell, 'The Cloak of Feminism,' *The Body Politic*, June 1979: 20.

27 Pat Leslie, 'Lesbians and Feminists: A Fine Kettle of Fish,' *LOOT Newsletter*, April 1979: 2.

28 Pat Leslie tape-recorded the opening performance by 'Personal Friends,' the three speeches, and the short discussion period before the small group discussions, which were not taped. The tape is housed at CWMA. Unless otherwise indicated, subsequent quotes that reference the skit were drawn from this taped recording.

29 Lilith Finkler, 'When Lesbians Sleep with Men,' *Broadside*, November 1983: 4.

30 Bearchell, 'The Cloak of Feminism,' 20.

31 Leslie, 'Lesbians and Feminists,' 2.

32 Over its two-year history, WAVAW organized rallies, protests, petitions, violence-against-women educationals, pickets, meetings with city councillors, and letters to newspaper editors and advertisers. Those who had been involved in antiviolence organizing (like the Rape Crisis Centre and Nellie's Hostel), and those who were new to feminism, became caught up in WAVAW's feverish pace. Male sexual violence (in particular, its 'celebration' in mass media and straight male pornography) came to represent a 'life and death' reality to many feminists, both lesbian and straight.

33 The short-lived PLOT was the forerunner of Lesbians Against the Right in 1981. Having dubbed the group PLOT, Natalie LaRoche told me that she took delight in knowing that the French meaning of plot was cunt.

34 Owing to internal strife, the Coalition itself collapsed in 1979. Part of the collapse was directly related to the deteriorating relationship between lesbians and gay men.

35 'Lesbian Conference High on Culture, Low on Politics,' *The Body Politic*, June/July 1978: 6.

36 *Dyke Daily* 1, 1 (December 1978): 2. There was the suggestion that lesbian feminists connected to bi-national lesbian organizing approach *The Body Politic* to ask for a monthly column rather than expend womanpower trying to keep a flagging lesbian newsletter alive.

37 Following the Fine Kettle forum, several lesbian feminists published short essays expressing their concern with what they perceived as the rise in lesbian separatist sentiment and their own critique of 'living in a lavender ghetto.' See Kitchener-Waterloo Gay Media Collective, 'Lesbians in the Feminist Movement,' *Lesbian/Lesbienne*, August/December 1979: 5–6; Ruth Dworin, 'Separatism: Strategy or Solution?' *LOOT Newsletter*, May 1979: 7–8; and the angry retort to Dworin by the pseudonymous Cellan Jay, Marion Lay, and Susan Quipp, 'Separatists Respond,' *LOOT Newsletter*, July 1979: 5.

38 In *Broadside*, October 1979, IWDC responded to Eve's 'Movement Comment' by denouncing the misrepresentation of the article and accompanying photograph, which suggested that men outnumbered women in the IWD march (p. 19). Women outnumbered men, IWDC argued, and they were absolutely clear about the feminist content of their demands. A broad spectrum of women's groups led the march; there was an all-women's party in the evening and the proceeds went to the organizing committee for the Bi-national Lesbian Conference. It is also important to note that IWDC was not mentioned in the description of various Toronto feminist groups in the pilot issue of *Broadside* in May 1979, and an apology for this oversight was not issued by the editors.

39 Bi-National Lesbian Conference program, Toronto, 1979: 3; on file at CWMA.

40 To Gay Bell, the Hart House location had special significance: 'The euphoria for me was that I was a lesbian for four or five years while I was a University of Toronto student in the 60s and had searched in vain for another lesbian. I fell in love with a female professor who was sympathetic but didn't go along with it. So it was real interesting to be on campus and give a big holler and say, "Look at all these god-damned lesbians here now!"'

41 For conference coverage, see Gay Bell and Natalie LaRoche, '400 Attend First Ever Bi-national Lesbian Conference,' *Socialist Voice* 3, 10 (18 June 1979): 4.

42 'LOOT Changes,' *LOOT Newsletter*, June 1979: 1, 5.

43 Amy Gottlieb, 'Lesbian Bill of Rights,' *After Stonewall: Critical Journal of Lesbian and Gay Liberation in Prairie Canada* (Fall 1979): 10, 18, 20.

44 Pat Leslie, 'Opinion,' *Lesbian Perspective*, November 1979: 2.

45 In June 1979, the Feminist Party of Canada was formed to work towards founding a permanent political party with a feminist perspective. For more on the philosophy of the party, see the October 1979 and the February 1980 issues of *Broadside*. The first unofficial issue of *Broadside*, ap-

peared in May 1979. It was followed by volume 1, number 1, in October 1979. Many of the women I interviewed felt 'cheated' and 'ripped off' by the editorial collective, who chose not to mention the word lesbian in the introductory issue. In particular, the absence of a stated commitment to anti-heterosexist thought and practice was especially irritating. Naomi Brooks commented: 'I was furious and ready to wipe these women into the dustbin of history. They had a fucking newspaper, they were all dykes, and they wouldn't talk about us.' In response to this criticism, former member of the *Broadside* collective Susan Cole told me: 'We had more letters to *Broadside* complaining about too much lesbian content than we ever got from anybody complaining about too little. The feminism that pushed the paper out every month had a strong lesbian presence and god knows the Secretary of State Women's Program [our funders] started to get heavy with us around that issue in 1988.' The Fly By Night, a women-only lounge, was opened on 27 April 1979 by Pat Murphy and a collective of women, most of whom had been involved to varying degrees in LOOT. Known in the community as a family-run lesbian bar 'where you could go and be entertained and not be responsible for it,' 'the Fly' was a popular spot until its close in 1981. It was located at the back of the Stage 212 hotel, behind a strip bar, and most lesbians I interviewed agreed that it attracted a more diverse clientele than LOOT ever did.

CHAPTER 9 LOOT's closure: An evaluation

1 Interview with Natalie LaRoche, 1988.
2 Maureen, 'We Have an Empty House,' *Lesbian Perspective* (September 1979): 1.
3 'Butchford and Bulldyke,' *LOOT Newsletter*, July 1979: 4, and November 1979: 3.
4 'Open Letter to the Lesbian Community, I' and 'Open Letter to the Lesbian Community, II,' October 1979; housed at CWMA.
5 *LOOT Newsletter*, 'Editorial,' October 1979: 3.
6 Sharon Stone, 'Help,' *Lesbian Perspective*, September 1979: 6.
7 'Do You Want a Newsletter?' *Lesbian Perspective*, March 1980: 1.
8 'With Mixed Emotions,' *Lavender Sheets*, May 1980: 4.
9 Maureen, 'We Have an Empty House,' 1.
10 This observation is recorded in the September 1979 issue of *Lesbian Perspective*, 4.
11 'General Meeting,' *Lesbian Perspective* (November 1979): 1.
12 Val Edwards, 'The Invisible Community,' *Broadside*, September 1980: 4.

13 Ibid.

14 Judith Quinlan, 'Letter: Response to Val Edwards,' *Broadside*, October/November 1980: 3, 8.

15 Gay Bell and Cate Smith presented a brief to the Canadian Radio and Television Commission (CRTC) task force on sex-role stereotyping in the media in March 1980. As Gay remembers it: 'Cate and I asked each other, since when do you see a bunch of lesbians at the bar toasting each other with a bottle of Labbatt's Blue? Or two lesbians in a hair-cutting ad, arms around each other and one says, "That's a real snazzy butch hairdo"? Never. So we presented this three-page paper to this panel. There were ten or twelve guys who were reps from the radio and television stations and these guys were mindboggled, their balls were falling out of their pants into their shoes, they could not believe what they were hearing.' And Cate adds: 'We held hands for moral support and for each other, so they could see. They had never even thought about it. It was totally outside their realm of experience.' For an excerpt of their text, see 'PLUM's Brief,' *Lavender Sheets*, May 1980: 4–5.

16 On Lesbians Against the Right (LAR), see Sharon Stone, 'Lesbians Against the Right,' in Jeri Wine and Janice Ristock, eds, *Feminist Activism in Canada* (Toronto: James Lorimer 1991), 236–53. Lorna Weir prepared a short section on LAR that was, unfortunately, edited out of her article 'Socialist Feminism and the Politics of Sexuality,' in Heather Jon Maroney and Meg Luxton, eds, *Feminism and Political Economy* (Toronto: Methuen 1987). Here, Weir delves into the accomplishments of LAR and some of the reasons why the organization folded when it did – many of which are similar to those that account for LOOT's demise. For a wonderful collection of speeches delivered at the 9 May 1981 forum out of which Lesbians Against the Right was formally constituted, see *Lesbians Are Everywhere: Fighting the Right* (Toronto: LAR 1981). LAR had an overt and intentional political focus: it was an explicitly lesbian, feminist, anti-right, anti-Klan, antiracist, coalition-building group and yet, according to Weir, it collapsed because of political differences, the absence of leadership, and confusion about priorities and direction beyond being a 'hit squad' vis-à-vis other movements.

17 Edwards, 'The Invisible Community,' 4.

18 Sherry McCoy and Maureen Hicks, 'A Psychological Retrospective on Power in the Contemporary Lesbian-Feminist Community,' *Frontiers* 4, 3 (1979): 67.

19 Sharon Stone, 'Lesbians Against the Right'; John Cleveland, 'The Mainstreaming of Feminist Issues: The Toronto Women's Movement,

1966–1984,' unpublished M.A. thesis, Department of Sociology, York University, 1984: 11.

20 This line is repeated from an earlier quote by Judith Quinlan.

21 Edwards, 'The Invisible Community,' 4.

22 Name withheld, 'Letter,' *Broadside*, October/November 1980: 3.

23 Ibid.

24 Rosemary Barnes, 'Dykes in Search of Affection and Independence,' *Resources for Feminist Research*, March 1983: 46.

25 Cleveland, 'The Mainstreaming of Feminist Issues,' 6.

26 Name withheld, 'Letter,' 3.

27 Adrienne Potts (Rosen), 'We Do a Lot of Talking,' *The Other Woman*, September/October 1973: 7.

28 Nym Hughes, Yvonne Johnson, and Yvette Perrault, *Stepping Out of Line* (Vancouver: Press Gang 1984), 167.

29 Chela Sandoval, 'Comment on Susan Krieger's 'Lesbian Identity and Community: Recent Social Science Literature,' in *Signs: The Lesbian Issue* (Chicago: University of Chicago Press, 1985), 243.

30 Ruth Dworin, 'Separatism: Strategy or Solution?' *LOOT Newsletter*, May 1979: 4.

31 Chris Bearchell, 'Review of Ti-Grace Atkinson's *Amazon Odyssey*,' *The Body Politic*, June 1976: 19.

32 Edwards, 'The Invisible Community,' 4.

33 Sue Cartledge, 'Bringing It All Back Home: Lesbian Feminist Morality,' in Gay Left Collective, ed., *Homosexuality: Power and Politics* (London and New York: Allison and Busby 1980), 95.

34 Lillian Faderman, *Odd Girls and Twilight Lovers* (New York: Columbia University Press 1991), 188–245. And see Alice Echols, 'The Taming of the Id: Feminist Sexual Politics, 1968–83,' in Carole Vance, ed., *Pleasure and Danger* (New York and London: Routledge and Kegan Paul 1984), 50–72; Shane Phelan, *Identity Politics* (Philadelphia: Temple University Press 1989), 37–80. In Toronto, though lesbian political ideology was heavily informed by separatism, it was mediated by other political influences, in part owing to the small size of the activist lesbian community, which would not have supported a fully developed lesbian separatist faction.

35 In her May 1979 article 'Separatism: Strategy or Solution?' for the *LOOT Newsletter*, Ruth Dworin attacked the 'fascism' of a 'new wave of separatism' that proclaimed, 'Males are genetically inferior, all male babies should be destroyed at birth' and 'Death to all mutants (i.e. men)' (p. 4). Angered by Dworin's dismissal, three pseudonymous 'radical separatists' declared: '[Developing our own strength] means freedom from the con-

ception of women as perpetually nice, polite, passive, guilty, unable to withstand criticism or disagreement, i.e., DEAD and it means life to LES-BIAN SEPARATISM' (emphasis in original). See Cellan Jay, Marion Lay, and Susan Quipp, 'Separatists Respond,' *LOOT Newsletter*, July 1979: 4.

36 Jan Clausen, 'My Interesting Condition,' *Out/Look*, Winter 1990: 20.

37 John Cleveland, quoting Susan Cole in 'The Mainstreaming of Feminist Issues,' 27.

38 Lorna Weir, 'Feminist Sexual Politics,' 22 (unpublished manuscript).

39 Pat Leslie, 'Lesbian Organization of Toronto Herstory,' in the Bi-National Lesbian Conference program, Toronto, 1979: 20.

40 Michele Landsberg, 'Lesbians Shouldn't Be Isolated,' *Globe and Mail*, 28 May 1979.

41 I would also argue that the failure of the left to make gender/sexual politics a priority contributed to their crises in membership and direction in the late 1970s and the virtual disappearance of Marxist/Leninist organizations by the early 1980s.

42 Lorna Weir, 'Socialist Feminism and the Politics of Sexuality,' in Heather Jon Maroney and Meg Luxton, eds, *Feminism and Political Economy* (Toronto: Methuen 1987), 69-83.

43 Personal correspondence with Dorothy E. Smith.

44 Pat Leslie, 'Lesbian Organization of Toronto: A Herstory,' a two-page document on file at CWMA: 1 (originally prepared for the Fine Kettle of Fish forum).

45 For a critical, ethnographic account of the bath raids, see George Smith, 'The Political Activist as Ethnographer,' *Social Problems* 37, 4 (November 1990): 629-48, and 'Policing the Gay Community: Inquiry into Textually-Mediated Social Relations,' *International Journal of the Sociology of Law* 16 (1988): 163-83.

46 Lorna Weir, 'Lesbians Against the Right: An Introduction,' in *Lesbians Are Everywhere: Fighting the Right* (Toronto: Lesbians Against the Right 1981), 2.

47 Allan Hunter, 'In the Wings: New Right Ideology and Organization,' *Radical America* 5, 1-2 (Spring 1981): 24; and see Lisa Steele's interview, 'Fighting the Right' in *Fuse*, August/September 1982.

48 Amy Gottlieb, 'The Gay Movement,' in Lesbians Against the Right, ed., *Lesbians Are Everywhere*, 7.

49 Kathy Arnup, 'Sexual Orientation and the Trade Union Movement,' in Lesbians Against the Right, ed., *Lesbians Are Everywhere*, 14. For a useful summary of the antigay and antilesbian lobby in the early 1980s, see Gary Kinsman, *The Regulation of Desire* (Montreal: Black Rose Books 1987), 206-11.

298 Notes to p. 219

CHAPTER 10 Concluding notes

1 Much has been written on diversity from a lesbian standpoint since the
late 1970s. For a sampling, see Joan Gibbs and Sara Bennett, eds, *Top
Ranking: A Collection of Articles on Racism and Classicism in the Lesbian Community*
(Brooklyn, NY: February Third Press 1980); Gloria Anzaldua and Cherrie
Moraga, eds, *This Bridge Called My Back: Writings by Radical Women of Colour*
(New York: Kitchen Table Press 1981); Evelyn Torton Beck, *Nice Jewish
Girls: A Lesbian Anthology* (Watertown, Mass.: Persephone Press 1982);
Hortense Spillers, 'Interstices: A Small Drama of Words,' in Carole Vance,
ed., *Pleasure and Danger: Female Sexuality Today* (Boston and London: Rou-
tledge and Kegan Paul 1984), 73–100; Audre Lorde, *Sister Outsider: Essays
and Speeches* (New York: The Crossing Press 1984), and *A Burst of Light*
(Ithaca, NY: Firebrand Books 1988); Juanita Ramos, ed., *Companeras: Latina
Lesbians* (New York: Latina Lesbian History Project 1987); Jackie Goldsby,
'What It Means to Be Colored Me,' *Out/Look*, Summer 1990: 8–17, and
'Queen for 307 Days: Looking B(l)ack at Vanessa Williams and the Sex
Wars,' in Arlene Stein, ed., *Sisters, Sexperts and Queers: Beyond the Lesbian
Nation* (New York: Penguin Books 1993), 110–28; Ekua Omosupe, 'Black/
Lesbian/Bulldagger,' *differences: A Journal of Feminist Cultural Studies* 3, 2
(1991): 101–11; Kate Rushin, 'Clearing a Space for Us: A Tribute to Audre
Lorde,' *Radical America* 24, 4 (1993): 85–8; Margaret Randall, 'To Change
Our Own Reality and the World: A Conversation with Lesbians in Nica-
ragua,' *Signs*, Summer 1993: 907–24; Karin Aguilar-San Juan, 'Landmarks
in Literature by Asian American Lesbians,' ibid., 936–43; Jewelle Gomez,
'Speculative Fiction and Black Lesbians,' ibid., 950–5; Barbara Smith and
Jewelle Gomez, 'Taking the Home out of Homophobia: Black Lesbians
Look in Their Own Backyard,' *Out/Look* 8 (Spring 1990): 32–7; and Alicia
Gaspar de Alba, 'Tortillerismo: Work by Chicana Lesbians,' *Signs*, Sum-
mer 1993: 956–63. For an introduction to new, Canadian-based voices,
see the work of Black, Native, and Asian lesbians living in Canada: Leleti
Tamu, 'Casselberry Harvest,' *Fireweed*, Spring 1989: 47; Donna Barker, 'S
& M Is an Adventure,' *Fireweed* 28 (Spring 1989): 115–21; Li Yuen, 'Inter-
national Lesbian Sex Week Poster,' *Angles*, September 1987: 15–16; Tamai
Kobayashi, 'Untitled,' *Fireweed* 30 (Spring 1990): 52–3; Milagros Parades,
'Christmas Eve Imaginings,' *Fireweed*, Spring 1989: 79; Makeda Silvera,
ed., *Piece of My Heart: A Lesbian of Colour Anthology* (Toronto: Sister Vision
Press 1992); Karen Augustine, 'Bizaare Women, Exotic Bodies and Outrageous Sex,' *Border/Lines*, Winter 1994. On lesbians and disability, see the
recent NFB film *Towards Intimacy*, and the 1993 pamphlet 'Women with

Disabilities Talk About Sexuality,' produced by the Disabled Women's Network (DAWN) of Toronto; Joanne Doucette, 'Redefining Difference: Disabled Lesbians Resist,' in Sharon Stone, ed., *Lesbians in Canada* (Toronto: Between the Lines 1990), 61-72. On aging see Jeanette Auger, 'Lesbians and Aging: Triple Trouble or Tremendous Thrill,' in Stone, ed., *Lesbians in Canada*, 25-34. On class in the 1950s, see Line Chamberland, 'Projet de communication: Sur la culture lesbienne, les années 1950s à Montréal' (trans. as 'Social Class and Integration in the Lesbian Sub-Culture'), in Sandra Kirby, Dayna Daniels, Kate McKenna, and Michelle Pujol, eds, *Women Changing Academe* (Winnipeg: Sororal Publishing 1991), 75-88. And from her research on sexualities in Egypt, Didi Khayatt has written 'A Subject in Limbo: Redefining the Categories,' paper presented at Queer Sites conference, Toronto, May 1993.

2 On issues specific to small-town lesbian/gay life, see Eleanor Brown, 'Lives Are Changing in Small Towns: Lesbians and Gay Men across Ontario Are Risking Much to Come out in Support of Family Rights,' *X-tra!* 252 (24 June 1994): 18.

3 Bisexuality is taken up by CKLN radio, 'Bi and Out: Discussing the Les/Bi Divide on Queer Radio,' *Fireweed*, Summer 1992: 62-7; Carol Queen, 'Strangers at Home: Bisexuals in the Queer Movement,' *Out/Look*, Spring 1992: 23-33; and Lorraine Hutchins and Lani Kaahumanu, *Bi Any Other Name: Bisexual People Speak Out* (Boston: Alyson Publications 1990).

4 The Toronto Centre for Lesbian and Gay Studies sponsors an annual 'Lesbian and Gay Academic Forum,' the University of British Columbia planned a lesbian/gay speakers' series for the fall of 1993, and lesbian/gay/queer conferences have been held at Concordia/Université du Québec à Montréal (1992), New College, University of Toronto (1993), and York University (1994).

5 On the topic of lesbians, AIDS, and HIV, see Mary Louise Adams, 'All That Rubber, All That Talk,' in Inez Rieder and Patricia Ruppelt, eds, *AIDS: The Women* (San Francisco: Cleis Press 1988), 130-3; Mona Oikawa, 'Safer Sex in Santa Cruz,' *Fireweed: Asian Canadian Women* 30 (Spring 1990): 31-4; Diane Richardson, *Women and the AIDS Crisis* (London: Pandora 1987); Pat Califia, *Macho Sluts* (Boston: Alyson Publications 1989); The ACT UP/NY Women and AIDS Book Group, eds, *Women, AIDS and Activism* (Toronto: Between the Lines 1990); Sue O'Sullivan's interview with Cindy Patton, 'Mapping: Lesbians, AIDS and Sexuality,' *Feminist Review*, Spring 1990: 120-33; Jackie Winnow, 'Lesbians Working on AIDS: Assessing the Impact of Health Care for Women,' *Out/Look*, Summer 1989: 10-18; and Ruth L. Schwartz, 'New Alliances, Strange Bedfellows: Lesbi-

ans, Gay Men and AIDS,' in Stein, ed., *Sisters, Sexperts and Queers*, 230–44. For a cogent analysis of African American women and AIDS, see Evelynn Hammonds, 'Missing Persons: African American Women, AIDS and the History of Disease,' *Radical America* 24, 2 (1992): 7–23.

6 Cherrie Moraga, 'La Güera,' in Moraga and Anzaldua, eds, *This Bridge Called My Back*, 29.

7 bell hooks, *From the Margin to the Centre* (Boston: South End Books 1984), 24.

8 On the problem of theorizing and implmenting a class-conscious lesbian and gay politics, see Dorothy Allison, 'A Question of Class,' in Stein, ed., *Sisters, Sexperts and Queers*, 133–55; and Steven Maynard, 'When Queer Is Not Enough,' *Fuse*, Fall 1991: 14–18. And see Alexander Chee, 'Queer Nationalism,' Steve Cosson, 'Queer Voices,' and Maria Maggenti, 'Women as Queer Nationals' *Out/Look*, Winter 1991: 12–23. On homophobia in racial communities, see bell hooks, 'Reflections on Homophobia and Black Communities,' *Out/Look*, Summer 1988: 22–5; and Smith and Gomez, 'Taking the Home out of Homophobia,' 32–7.

9 For an excellent summary of lesbian and gay organizing in Sweden over the past fifteen years, see Catharina Landstrom, 'Lesbian Rights, Lesbian Organizing and Social Policy,' paper presented at York University, August 1994.

10 See the *New Internationalist* special issue 'Pride and Prejudice: Homosexuality' (November 1989) and the *International Lesbian and Gay Association Pink Book: A Global View of Lesbian and Gay Oppression and Liberation* (Amsterdam: COC-magazijn 1985, 1988). On lesbian/gay experience internationally, see Stephan Likosky, ed., *Coming Out: An Anthology of International Gay and Lesbian Writings* (New York: Pantheon Books 1992). The now-defunct *Out/Look* magazine in San Francisco was a leading voice in introducing international perpsectives. For a sampling of its articles, see John Parsons, 'East Germany Faces Its Past: A New Start for Socialist Sexual Politics,' *Out/Look*, Summer 1989: 43–52; Barry Adam, 'Homosexuality without a Gay World: Pasivos y Activos en Nicaragua,' Winter 1989: 74–82; Masha Gessen, 'We Have No Sex: Soviet Gays and AIDS in the Era of Glasnost,' Summer 1990: 42–53, and 'Comrade in Arms: The First Out Lesbian in the USSR Visits the USA,' Spring 1991: 66–71; Leonore Norrgard, 'Opening the Hong Kong Closet,' Winter 1990: 56–61; and Miras Soliwoda, 'Did You Ever Have Sex in Poland?' Summer 1991: 77–9. See also Elena Lonero, 'Women Meet in El Salvador Despite Hate Campaigns: Caribbean and Latin American Lesbians Make a splash,' *X-tra!* 237 (26 November 1993): 11.

11 Gay Doherty, 'The Trauma of Our Justice System,' *Quota*, September 1993: 1, 4.

12 The categories of public and private have been, and continue to be, integral to the state regulation and administration of sex. Most recently announced sex legislation includes Bill C-49, which criminalizes 'communication for the purposes of prostitution,' and Bill C-61, which criminalizes 'corrupting morals' (Section 159), 'keeping a common bawdy house' (Section 193) ,and 'procuring and living on the avails of prostitution' (Section 195). Bill C-128 provides for up to ten years' imprisonment for the production, distribution, and importation or sale of 'child pornography': the sexually explicit representation of anyone under 18, or anyone who appears to be under 18. For criticism of the federal 'Kiddie Porn' bill, see Brenda Cossman, 'How the State Created a Bunch of Paedophiles,' *X-tra!* 236 (12 November 1993): 17.

13 For analysis of the debate that swirled around the passage of the new youth-pornography law, see Heather Cameron, 'Who's Really Being Targeted? Kiddie Porn Will Allow Police a "Foot in the Door,"' *X-tra!* 226 (25 June 1993): 15. Also see Brenda Cossman, 'How the State Created a Bunch of Paedophiles,' 17. Cossman argues that the North American Man-Boy Love Association (NAMBLA) was used and demnonized to justify the new youth-pornography law. 'The message conveyed was that all gay men are paedophiles ... [which] is a central element in the hate campaign being waged by the religious right and its efforts to depict gay men and lesbians as the new evil enemy. The debates around Bill 128 gave reasoned legitimacy to this homophobic rhetoric.' And see Eleanor Brown, 'Hustler Speaks Out on Obscenity Charge,' *X-Tra!*, 13 May 1994: 11.

14 Eleanor Brown, 'Canadian Forces Surrender: Court Decision Opens Gates for Lesbian and Gay Soldiers,' *X-Tra!* 209 (30 October 1992): 15.

15 Richard Mackie, 'Quebec Urged to Follow Ontario on Gay Benefits,' *Globe and Mail*, 2 June 1994: A5.

16 In 'Who Gets to Be Family,' Carol Allen makes the valuable point that poor lesbians on social assistance might suffer economically when the definition of spouse changes in the Family Benefits Act. It is possible, Allen argues, that one woman might then be considered financially dependent on her (female) spouse, which would make the couple vulnerable to cut-backs in family benefits (in Linda Carty, ed., *And Still We Rise: Feminist Political Mobilizing in Contemporary Canada* [Toronto: Women's Press 1993], (105). For a compelling argument in favour of same-sex spousal benefits from the standpoint of a lesbian mother, see Katherine Arnup, '"We Are Family": Lesbian Mothers in Canada,' *Resources for Feminist Re-*

search 20, 3 & 4 (Fall 1991): 101–7. Also see Coalition of Lesbian and Gay Rights of Ontario, *Happy Families: The Recognition of Same-Sex Spousal Relationships*, 1993.

17 Two days before the second reading of Bill 167, Attorney General Marion Boyd elected to remove a provision that would have given same-sex couples the right to apply for child adoption. She also agreed not to change the current legal definition of spouse or of marital status. Lesbian and gay activists expressed outrage and disappointment that the amendments weakened the initial bill and capitulated to the right wing. See Craig McInnes, 'Boyd Backs Off on Gay Spouses,' *Globe and Mail*, 9 June 1994: A1, A10.

18 Craig McInnes, 'To Homosexual Parents, A Family Is a Family,' *Globe and Mail*, 2 June 1994: A1, A4. In 1993, an Unemployment Insurance Commission appeals board ruled that two women are spouses. The ruling argued that one of the women had 'just cause' to quit her job (to relocate to be with her lover) and should receive unemployment benefits. The UI Commission is appealing the decision to a federal-court judge. See Eleanor Brown, 'These Two Women Are Spouses,' *X-tra!*, 7 January 1994: 1.

19 Chris Hodgson Campaign, 'Same-Sex Benefits,' *Lindsay Post*, 11 March 1994.

20 Julie Smith, 'Archbishop Assails Same-Sex Benefits,' *Globe and Mail*, 30 May 1994: A5.

21 Scott Feschuk, 'Alberta Tories in a Bind over Gay-Rights Decision,' *Globe and Mail*, 14 April 1994.

22 Craig McInnes, Martin Mittelstaedt, and James Rusk, 'Ontario Bill on Gay Rights Defeated,' *Globe and Mail*, 10 June 1994: A1, A10.

23 Didi Khayatt, 'Legalized Invisibility: The Effect of Bill 7 on Lesbian Teachers,' *Women's Studies International Forum* 13, 3 (1990): 185–93.

24 For an informative, well-argued consideration of the limitations of civil-rights strategies pursued by lesbian and gay activists, see Didi Herman, *Rights of Passage: Struggles for Lesbian and Gay Legal Equality* (Toronto, University of Toronto Press 1994).

25 Allen, 'Who Gets to Be Family,' in Carty, ed., *And Still We Rise*, 103.

26 Alisa Solomon, 'Dykotomies: Scents and Sensibility,' in Stein, ed., *Sisters, Sexperts and Queers*, 215. In the same collection, see Lisa Kahaleole Chang Hall, 'Bitches in Solitude: Identity Politics and Lesbian Community,' 218–29.

27 Donna Minkowitz, 'The Well of Correctness,' *Village Voice*, 21 May 1991: 39.

28 Susie Bright (a.k.a. Susie Sexpert), *Susie Sexpert's Lesbian Sex World* (San

Francisco: Cleis Press 1990), and *Susie Bright's Sexual Reality: A Virtual Sex World Reader* (San Francisco: Cleis Press 1992).

29 Shane Phelan, *Identity Politics: Lesbian Feminism and the Limits of Community* (Philadelphia: Temple University Press 1983), 138.

30 Judith Butler, 'Imitation and Gender Insubordination,' in Diana Fuss, ed., *Inside Out: Lesbian Theories, Gay Theories* (London and New York: Routledge 1991), 13-31.

31 Bernice Johnson Reagon, 'Coalition Politics: Turning the Century,' in Barbara Smith, ed., *Home Girls: A Black Feminist Anthology* (New York: Kitchen Table Press 1983), 356-69.

32 On transsexuality, see Chris Martin, 'World's Greatest Cocksucker: Transsexual Interviews,' *Fiction International* 22 (San Diego: San Diego University Press 1992), 101-22.

33 Judith Butler poses this question in her essay 'Critically Queer,' *GLQ: A Journal of Lesbian and Gay Studies* 1, 1 (1993): 18.

34 See the vast range of comments made by contributors to 'Living Pride: Twenty-five Years of Pride,' *X-tra!* 252 (24 June 1994): insert.

35 For selected essays on identity politics, see Mary Louise Adams, 'There's No Place Like Home: On the Place of Identity in Feminist Politics,' *Feminist Review*, Spring 1989: 22-33; Jenny Bourne, 'Homelands of the Mind: Jewish Feminism and Identity Politics,' *Race and Class* 29 (1987): 1-24; Steven Epstein, 'Gay Politics, Ethnic Identity: The Limits of Social Constructionism,' *Socialist Review*, May/August 1987: 9-54; Diana Fuss, 'Lesbian and Gay Theory: The Question of Identity Politics,' in D. Fuss, *Essentially Speaking: Feminism, Nature and Difference* (New York and London: Routledge 1989), 97-112; Melanie Kay Kantrowitz, 'To Be a Radical Jew in the Late Twentieth Century,' in Christia McEwen and Sue O'Sullivan, eds, *Out the Other Side: Contemporary Lesbian Writing* (London: Virago 1988), 243-68; L.A. Kauffman, 'The Anti-Politics of Identity,' *Socialist Review* 20, 1 (January/March 1990), 67-79; Kobena Mercer, 'Welcome to the Jungle: Identity and Diversity in Postmodern Politics,' in Jonathon Rutherford, ed., *Identity: Community, Culture and Difference* (London: Lawrence and Wishart 1990), 43-71; Pratibha Parmar, 'Other Kinds of Dreams: An Interview with June Jordan,' *Spare Rib* 184 (1981): 12-15; Shane Phelan, *Identity Politics: Lesbian Feminism and the Limits of Community* (Philadelphia: Temple University Press 1989); Chela Sandoval, 'Comment on Susan Krieger's 'Lesbian Identity and Community: Recent Social Science Literature,' in Estelle B. Freedman, Barbara Gelpi, Susan Johnson, and Kathleen Weston, eds, *The Lesbian Issue: Essays from Signs* (Chicago: University of Chicago Press 1985), 241-4; Joan Scott, 'Experience,' in Judith Butler and Joan

Scott, eds, *Feminists Theorize the Political* (New York: Routledge 1992),
22–40; Bonnie Zimmerman, 'The Politics of Transliteration: Lesbian Personal Narratives,' in Freedman, Gelpi, Johnson, and Weston, eds, *The Lesbian Issue*, 251–70; Lisa M. Walker, 'How to Recognize a Lesbian: The
Cutural Politics of Looking Like What You Are,' *Signs*, Summer 1993:
866–90; Margaret Cerullo, 'Hope and Terror: The Paradox of Gay and
Lesbian Politics in the 1990s,' *Radical America* 24, 3 (1993): 10–16; Shane
Phelan, '(Be)coming Out: Lesbian Identity and Politics,' *Signs*, Summer
1993: 765–89; ki Namaste, 'The Politics of Inside/Out: Queer Theory,
Poststructuralism, and a Sociological Approach to Sexuality,' *Sociological
Theory* 12, 2 (July 1994): 220–31; and Janice M. Irvine, 'A Place in the
Rainbow: Theorizing Lesbian and Gay Culture,' ibid.: 232–48.

Bibliography

Unpublished Manuscripts

Adams, Mary Louise. 'The Trouble with Normal: Post-War Teenagers and the Construction of Heterosexuality.' Ph.D. thesis, Department of Educational Theory, OISE (Toronto), 1994.
- 'Disputed Desire: The "Feminine" Woman in Lesbian History.' Paper presented at the Berkshire Women's History Conference, Rutgers University, June 1990.
Brock, Deborah. 'Regulating Prostitution / Regulating Prostitutes: Some Canadian Examples, 1970–1989.' Ph.D. dissertation, Department of Educational Theory, University of Toronto, 1989.
Cleveland, John. 'The Mainstreaming of Feminist Issues: The Toronto Women's Movement, 1966–1984.' M.A. thesis, Department of Sociology, York University, 1984.
Duggan, Lisa. 'Dandies and Dykes: The Erotic Meanings of Female Cross-dressing.' Paper presented at the Berkshire Women's History Conference, Rutgers University, June 1990.
Echols, Alice. 'The First Sex War: Gay/Straight Splits in Early Women's Movement Organizing.' Paper presented at OISE, Toronto, January 1991.
Fields, Bill. 'The Rise and the Fall of the Fifty Per Cent Solution: Lesbians in the Canadian Gay Rights Movement.' Paper, Faculty of Social Work, University of Regina, 1983. On file at the Canadian Lesbian and Gay Archives.
Khayatt, Didi. 'A Subject in Limbo: Redefining the Categories.' Paper presented at the Queer Sites conference, Toronto, May 1993.
Kinsman, Gary. 'Character Weaknesses and "Fruit Machines": Towards an Analysis of the Social Organization of the Anti-Homosexual Purge Campaign in the Canadian Federal Civil Service, 1959–1964.' Manuscript, 1993.

– 'Official Discourse as Sexual Regulation.' Ph.D. dissertation, Department of Educational Theory, University of Toronto, 1988.

McBride, Joy. 'One Step Forward? The Canadian Native Movement, 1968–1974.' Paper, Queen's University, Kingston, 1989.

Ng, Yvonne Chi-Ying. 'Ideology, Media and Moral Panics: An Analysis of the Jaques Murder.' M.A. thesis, Centre for Criminology, University of Toronto, 1981. On file at Canadian Lesbian and Gay Archives.

Penn, Donna. 'Public Space and Lesbian Lives in Twentieth Century America.' Paper presented at the Berkshire Women's History Conference, Rutgers University, June 1990.

Saskatoon Women's Liberation Papers, Steering Committee, Constitution Proposal, January 1978. On file at the Canadian Women's Movement Archives (CWMA).

Stone, Sharon. 'Mainstream Media Coverage of the Women's Movement.' Ph.D. dissertation, Sociology Department, York University, 1992.

Weir, Lorna. 'Socialist Feminist Politics.' Manuscript on the politics of lesbian feminism, Toronto, 1987.

Albums

Dobkin, Alix. 'Talking Lesbian.' On *Lavender Jane Loves Women*. Durham, NC: Ladyslipper Music, Inc. 1975.

– *Living with Lesbians*. Wax Woman Records 1976.

Christian, Meg. *Meg Christian: Face the Music*. Los Angeles: Olivia Records 1977.

Lesbian Concentrate: a lesbianthology of songs and poems, 100% undiluted. Los Angeles: Olivia Records 1977.

Shear, Linda. 'Family of Womon We've Begun.' On *Lesbian Portrait*. Northampton, Mass.: Old Lady Blue Jeans 1975.

Trull, Teresa. *The Ways a Woman Can Be*. Los Angeles: Olivia Records 1976.

Tyler, Robin. *Always a Bridesmaid, Never a Groom*. Los Angeles: Olivia Records 1979.

Williamson, Cris. 'Dream Child.' On *The Changer and The Changed*. Los Angeles: Olivia Records 1975.

Commission Reports

Coalition for Gay Rights in Ontario. 'The Human Rights Omission.' 1981. On file at the Canadian Lesbian and Gay Archives, Toronto.

– 'Discrimination against Lesbians and Gay Men: The Ontario Human Rights

Omission.' 1986. On file at the Canadian Lesbian and Gay Archives, Toronto.

Coalition for Lesbian and Gay Rights of Ontario. 'Happy Families: The Recognition of Same-Sex Spousal Relationships.' Toronto, 1993.

Lesbian Organization of Toronto. 'Lesbians and the Ontario Human Rights Code.' 1978. On file at the Canadian Lesbian and Gay Archives, Toronto.

Morand, Mr Justice Donald R. The Royal Commission into Metropolitan Toronto Police Practices. Toronto, June 1976.

Ontario Human Rights Code Review Committee. Report to the Ontario Legislature: *Life Together.* June 1977. On file at the Canadian Lesbian and Gay Archives, Toronto.

Community Reports

Bi-National Lesbian Conference Program. Toronto, 1979. On file at the Canadian Women's Movement Archives.

Leslie, Pat. 'Lesbian Organization of Toronto: A Herstory.' A two-page document on file at the CWMA. Originally prepared for the Fine Kettle of Fish forum.

'Open Letter to the Lesbian Community, I' and 'Open Letter to the Lesbian Community, II.' October 1979. Housed at the CWMA.

Ottawa Lesbian Conference Report. 1978. On file at the CWMA.

Articles in Community Newspapers

Adam, Barry. 'Homosexuality Without a Gay World: Pasivos y Activos en Nicaragua.' *Out/Look* 8 (Winter 1989): 74–82.

Adams, Mary Louise. 'Precendent-Setting Pulp: *Women's Barracks* Was Deemed "Exceedingly Frank."' *X-tra!* 231 (3 September 1993): 21.

Agger, Ellen. 'Address to the March 11 Cut-Backs Rally.' *The Body Politic* 24 (June 1976): 6.

– 'Lesbians Fight to Keep Kids.' *The Body Politic*, December/January 1976–7: 3.

Anonymous. *York University Homophile Association Newsletter*, March 1971: 3.

– *University of Toronto Homophile Newsletter* 3 (Spring 1971): 3.

– *Backchat*, April 1971: 3.

– *Backchat*, May 1972: 7.

– *Backchat*, June 1972: 4.

– 'Letter.' *The Other Woman*, May/June 1972: 16, 17.

– Editorial: 'Invitation to the Women's Movement.' *Velvet Fist* 2, 3 (1972): 2.

- 'On Lesbianism: A Selection from Feminist Anthologies.' *Velvet Fist* 2, 5 (1972): 7.
- 'Smash Phallic Imperialism.' *The Other Woman* 1, 5 (Summer 1973): 6.
- 'A Reply.' *The Other Woman* 2, 1 (September/October 1973): 1.
- 'Lesbian Feminist Statement: On a Queer Day.' *The Other Woman*, October 1973: 25.
- 'Montréal Lesbian Conference.' *Long Time Coming*, February 1974: 2–5.
- 'Announcement.' *The Other Woman* 2, 4 (April 1974): 22.
- 'Bisexual Woman.' *Long Time Coming*, July 1975: 9–14.
- 'Beauty Pageant.' *The Other Woman* December 1975/January 1976: 2–3.
- *Long Time Coming*, April/May 1976: 38.
- 'Toronto Women's Coffeehouse.' *Long Time Coming*, April/May 1976: 39.
- 'Gay Women Unlimited.' *Backchat*, May 1976: 4.
- Editorial: 'Lesbian Autonomy or Cooptation.' *The Other Woman*, September/October 1976: 1.
- *LOOT Newsletter*, March 1977: 1.
- 'Transsexual Debate.' *LOOT Newsletter*, November 1978: 4.
- 'LOOT Changes.' *LOOT Newsletter*, June 1979: 1, 5.
- 'Letter.' *Broadside*, October/November 1980: 3.
Arnup, Kathy. 'Sexual Orientation and the Trade Union Movement.' In Lesbians Against the Right, ed., *Lesbians Are Everywhere: Fighting the Right* [community chapbook], 11–14. Toronto, 1981.
Barry, Kathleen. 'West Coast Conference: Not Purely Academic.' *off our backs* 3, 10 (September 1973): 25.
Bearchell, Chris. 'NGRC Report.' *The Other Woman*, October/November 1975:4.
- Review of Ti-Grace Atkinson's *Amazon Odyssey. The Body Politic*, June 1976: 19.
- 'Custody Rights for Lesbian Mothers.' *The Body Politic*, May 1977: 10.
- 'Wages Dues.' *The Body Politic*, September 1977: 25.
- 'The Wages of Disunity.' *The Body Politic*, September 1977: 19.
- 'Media Madness and Lesbian Images, Part I.' *The Body Politic*, November 1977: 10.
- 'Knowing Who Your Friends Are or Lesbian Images, Part II.' *The Body Politic*, December/January 1977/78: 35.
- 'I Was 15, She Was 43.' *The Body Politic*, December/January 1977/78: 14.
- 'Lesbian Conference High on Culture, Low on Politics.' *The Body Politic*, June/July 1978: 6.
- 'The Cloak of Feminism.' *The Body Politic*, June 1979: 20.
Bell, Gay. 'Margaret Dwight Spore at the Ottawa Lesbian Conference.' *The Other Woman*, November/December 1976: 5.

- 'Michigan Womyn's Music Festival.' *LOOT Newsletter*, September 1977: 4.
- 'Snuff, Violence and Waking Up Mad.' *The Body Politic*, December/January 1977/78: 28.
- 'Lesbians in the Mirror.' *The Body Politic*, June 1979: 33.
Bell, Gay, and Natalie LaRoche. '400 Attend First Ever Bi-National Lesbian Conference.' *Socialist Voice* 3, 10 (18 June 1979): 4.
Bell, Gay, and Cate Smith. 'PLUM's Brief.' *Lavender Sheets*, May 1980: 4–5.
Bociurkiw, Marusia. 'Territories of the Forbidden: Lesbian Culture, Sex and Censorship.' *Fuse*, April 1988: 27–32.
Bodinger, Debbie. 'Lesbian Mothers.' *LOOT Newsletter*, April 1979: 6.
The Body Politic Collective. 'Uppity Women.' *The Body Politic*, March/April 1974: 1.
- 'Partial Win for the Brunswick Four.' *The Body Politic*, July/August 1974: 6.
- 'Proposition from the Left.' *The Body Politic*, September/October 1974: 14–15.
- 'Lesbians Expose Landlord [in Waterloo, Ontario].' *The Body Politic*, May/June 1975: 9.
- 'Lesbians Call for Autonomy.' *The Body Politic*, October 1976: 1.
- 'Classifieds.' *The Body Politic*, June 1977: 31.
- 'Classifieds.' *The Body Politic*, November 1977: 31.
- Editorial: 'Crisis: In the Midst of Danger, A Chance to Unite.' *The Body Politic*, February 1978: 1
- 'Men Loving Boys, Loving Men: Another Look.' *The Body Politic*, April/May 1979: 24–7.
Bolton, Mary. 'Lesbian Educational.' *Toronto Women's Liberation Movement Newsletter*, April 1971: 11–13.
- 'Sisterhood at the Conference.' *Toronto Women's Liberation Movement Newsletter*, May 1971: 22–3.
Brown, Jan. 'Sex, Lies and Penetration: A Butch Finally "Fesses Up."' *Out/Look* 10 (Winter 1990): 30–5.
Brown, Rita Mae. 'Coitus Interruptus.' *Rat* 2, 27 (February 1970): 6–23.
- 'A Stranger in Paradise: Rita Mae Brown Goes to the Baths.' *The Body Politic*, April 1976: 15.
Butchford and Bulldyke. 'Column.' *LOOT Newsletter*, July 1979: 4; November 1979: 3.
Chamberland, Line. 'Flirt et Flirt et Potins: Les lesbiennes dans les journaux jaunes.' *Canadian Lesbian and Gay History Network Newsletter* 4 (November 1990): 3–7.
Champagne, Rob. 'An Interview with Jim Egan: Canada's First Gay Activist.' *Rites*, December 1986 / January 1987: 8–9.

– *Jim Egan: Canada's Pioneer Gay Activist* [chapbook]. Toronto: Canadian Lesbian and Gay History Network, Publication no. 1, 1989.

Chase, Gillean. 'Gay Pride? Week.' *The Other Woman*, August 1974: 16.

– 'Review of Jill Johnston's *Lesbian Nation*.' *The Other Woman*, August 1974: 13.

– 'Class: Thrashing It Out in Ontario.' *The Other Woman*, January/February 1977: 14.

Chee, Alexander. 'Queer Nationalism.' *Out/Look* 11 (Winter 1991): 12–23.

Clausen, Jan. 'My Interesting Condition.' *Out/Look* 7 (Winter 1990): 11–21.

CLIT Statements. *Long Time Coming*, January 1975: 1–35.

Cognita, Ann. 'Slut Perspective.' *Lavender Sheets*, Summerish [sic] 1979: 7.

Cole, Susan. 'Sunkist Marriage Goes Sour.' *Broadside*, July/August 1980: 9.

Cossman, Brenda. 'How the State Created a Bunch of Paedophiles.' *X-tra!* 236 (12 November 1993): 17.

Cosson, Steve. 'Queer Voices.' *Out/Look* 11 (Winter 1991): 12–23.

Creet, Julia. 'Lesbian Sex / Gay Sex: What's the Difference?' *Out/Look* 11 (Winter 1991): 29–34.

Crewe, Judith. 'Review of *The Fourteenth Witch*.' *The Body Politic*, December/January 1978–9: 21.

Cummings, Bob. 'The Lesbians.' *Georgia Straight*, 13–19 September 1968: 9–12; 4–10 October 1968: 9–12; 1–7 November 1968: 9–12.

D., Charlene. 'Come Out – All the Way.' *The Other Woman*, October/November 1975: 13.

Davis, Walter. 'Letter.' *The Body Politic*, December/January 1976/77: 2.

Densmore, Dana. 'On Celibacy.' *No More Fun and Games*, 1969.

Devor, Holly. 'Lesbian Feminism.' *The Other Woman* 2, 1 (September/October 1973): 10–11.

Diamond, Sara, and Helen Mintz. Interview with Lisa Steele: 'Fighting the Right.' *Fuse*, August/September 1981: 211–15.

Diemer, Ulli. 'Death on Yonge Street.' *Ward Seven News*, 13 August 1977: 8.

Dinovo, Cheri. 'Growing Up Gay.' *Velvet Fist* 1, 6 (August 1971): 6.

Doherty, Gay. 'The Trauma of Our Justice System.' *Quota*, September 1993: 1, 4.

Duggan, Lisa. 'The Anguished Cry of an 80s Fem: "I Want to Be a Drag Queen."' *Out/Look* 1 (Spring 1988): 62–5.

Dworin, Ruth. 'Separatism: Strategy or Solution?' *LOOT Newsletter*, May 1979: 7–8.

Edwards, Val. 'Robin Tyler: Comic in Contradiction. A Profile.' *The Body Politic*, September 1979: 21–3.

– 'The Invisible Community.' *Broadside*, September 1980: 4–5.

Ellen. 'A Conversation.' *The Other Woman*, October 1973: 1.

Finkler, Lilith. 'Lesbians Who Sleep With Men.' *Broadside*, November 1983: 4.

Fox, Chris. 'Review of *Loving Women* by the Nomadic Sisters.' *The Other Woman*, March/April 1976: 17–18.

Fulton, M. Anne. 'My Personal Love Affair with the National Lesbian Movement.' *The Body Politic*, March 1977: 10.

Gessen, Masha. 'We Have No Sex: Soviet Gays and AIDS in the Era of Glasnost.' *Out/Look* 9 (Summer 1990): 42–53.

– 'Comrade in Arms: The First Out Lesbian in the USSR Visits the USA.' *Out/Look* 13 (Spring 1991): 66–71.

Goth, Andrea. 'Anita Must Go!' *The Militant*, 18 July 1977: 5.

Gottlieb, Amy. 'The Gay Movement.' In Lesbians Against the Right, ed., *Lesbians Are Everywhere: Fighting the Right*, 7–10. Toronto, 1981.

Grahn, Judy. 'The Psychoanalysis of Edward the Dyke.' Reprinted in *Bellyfull* 1, 2 (June 1972): 6.

Grover, Jan Zita. 'Words to Lust By.' *Women's Review of Books*, November 1990: 21–3.

Grube, John. 'Queens and Flaming Virgins: Towards a Sense of Gay Community.' *Rites*, April 1986: 14–17.

Guthrie. 'A Letter.' *The Other Woman* 2, 1 (September/October 1973): 1.

Hannon, Gerald. 'Seven Years to Go: The Plight of Gay Youth.' *The Body Politic*, September 1976: 1, 14–15.

– 'Marie Robertson: Upfront Dyke and Loving Women.' *The Body Politic*, December/January 1976/77: 9.

– 'Men Loving Boys Loving Men.' *The Body Politic*, November 1977: 30–3.

Hardy, Robin. 'Gay Youth Plan Assault on School System.' *The Body Politic*, June/July 1978: 4.

Henderson, Karen. 'Review of Barbara Hammer's Dyke Films.' *LOOT Newsletter*, March 1979: 7.

Hodges, Andrew. 'Divided We Stand.' *The Body Politic*, February 1977: 20–2.

Hollibaugh, Amber. 'Writers as Activists.' *Out/Look*, Fall 1990: 69–71.

hooks, bell. 'Reflections on Homophobia and Black Communities.' *Out/Look*, Summer 1988: 22–5.

Hunnisett, Rowena. 'Gay Pride Week.' *The Other Woman* 2, 1 (September/October 1973): 18.

Jay, Cellan, Marion Lay, and Susan Quipp [pseudonyms]. 'Separatists Respond.' *LOOT Newsletter*, July 1979: 5.

Karol. 'Dyke Power.' *The Other Woman* 1, 4 (March 1973): 7.

Kidd, Dorothy. 'Letter.' *The Body Politic*, June 1977: 2.

Kinsman, Gary. Interview with Pei Lim: 'Racism and Gay Male Porn.' *Rites*, February 1987: 14–15.

– 'The Ottawa Purge Campaigns.' *Centre/Fold* 4 (Spring 1993): 12–13.

Kinsman, Gary, and Andrea Goth. 'Lesbians and Gays Move to Support Women's Struggles.' *The Militant*, 18 July 1977: 4.

Kitchener-Waterloo Gay Media Collective. 'Lesbians in the Feminist Movement.' *Lesbian/Lesbienne* 1, 1 (August/December 1979): 5–6.

Laney, Ilona. 'Lesbian Organization Opens Its Doors.' *The Body Politic*, May 1977: 4.

Lavender Sheets Collective. 'With Mixed Emotions.' *Lavender Sheets*, May 1980: 4.

– 'Dear Lezzy.' *Lavender Sheets*, Summerish [sic] 1980: 14.

Lesbian Caucus. 'Lesbian Caucus Report.' *BCFW Newsletter* 1, 1 (November 1974): 9; 1, 4 (March 1975): 9.

Lesbian Perspective Collective. 'General Meeting.' *Lesbian Perspective*, November 1979: 1.

– 'Do You Want a Newsletter?' *Lesbian Perspective*, March 1980: 1.

Leslie, Pat. 'Guerilla Theatre.' *Velvet Fist* 2, 3 (1972): 4.

– 'An Independent Women's Movement.' *The Other Woman*, May/June 1975: 10, 24.

– 'Feminist Businesses.' *The Other Woman*, March/April 1976: 4.

– 'Do You Want to See Our Queer Pass?' *The Other Woman*, November/December 1976: 21.

– 'Interview with Paulette and Artemis.' *The Other Woman*, November/December 1976: 12–13.

– 'More on Bolton: Feminist Wants Class Analysis.' *The Other Woman*, January/February 1977: 15.

– 'Women's Movement Archives.' *The Other Woman*, January/February 1977: 4.

– 'Doing Our Own Work.' *The Body Politic*, September 1978: 2.

– 'Lesbians and Feminists: A Fine Kettle of Fish.' *LOOT Newsletter*, April 1979: 2.

– 'Lesbian Organization of Toronto Herstory.' In the Bi-National Lesbian Conference program, 20. Toronto, 1979.

– 'Women's Movement Archives.' *Lesbian/Lesbienne*, August–December 1979: 11.

– 'Opinion.' *Lesbian Perspective*, November 1979: 2.

Lilith. 'A Dykey Kike, or a Kikey Dyke, Which Will It Be? Oy Vey.' *Lesbian Perspective*, February 1980: 2.

Lonero, Elena. 'Women Meet in El Salvador Despite Hate Campaigns: Caribbean and Latin American Lesbians Make a Splash.' *X-tra!* 237 (26 November 1993): 11.

Long Time Coming Collective. 'The Brunswick Tavern Dykes.' *Long Time Coming,* May/June 1974: 6.
- 'Wages Due Lesbians.' *Long Time Coming,* April 1975: 10–11.
- 'Toronto Women's Coffeehouse.' *Long Time Coming,* April/May 1976: 39.
LOOT Newsletter Collective. 'LOOT Changes.' *LOOT Newsletter,* June 1979: 1, 5.
- 'Editorial.' *LOOT Newsletter,* October 1979: 3.
Lootens, Tricia. 'Ann Bannon: A Lesbian Audience Discovers Its Lost Literature.' *off our backs* 8, 11 (December 1983): 12–20.
Lorna. 'Dykes Unite.' *The Other Woman* 2, 2 (March 1974): 5.
Lynch, Michael. 'Critique of Ken Waxman's article, "Rise of Gay Capitalism."' *The Body Politic,* November 1976: 20.
'Mabel Hampton's Coming Out Story.' *Lesbian Herstory Archives News* 7 (December 1981): 31–3.
Maggenti, Maria. 'Women as Queer Nationals.' *Out/Look,* Winter 1991: 12–23.
Masters, Phil. 'Clementyne's Café.' *Women's Information Centre Newsletter,* May 1975: 2.
Matta, Hari. 'Stolen Pages.' *The Other Woman,* September/October 1976: 20.
Maureen. 'We Have an Empty House.' *Lesbian Perspective,* September 1979: 1.
Maynard, Steven. 'The Hunk on the Train: Some Reflections on Class and Desire.' *Rites,* June 1989: 9.
- 'The Ruling Class Doesn't Ride the Train.' *Rites,* May 1990: 9.
Middleton, Kate. 'The Coldwater Dyke.' *The Body Politic,* September 1976: 20.
- 'Custody Battles – Not Child's Play.' *Broadside,* April 1980: 8.
Miller, Joan Bridi. 'S/M, Another Point of View.' *Gay Community News,* October 1976: 17.
Mole, David. 'Rights of Access.' *The Body Politic,* November 1977: 1, 4.
Morton, Judi. 'When I Grow Up I Want to Be a Lesbian.' *The Pedestal,* June/July 1975: 10–11.
Murphy, Pat, and Linda Jain. 'Gay Sisters.' *Velvet Fist* 2, 4 (1972): 7.
National Lesbian Conference. 'Some Workshop Reports,' 1. Ottawa, 1976. On file at the CWMA.
Norrgard, Leonnore. 'Opening the Hong Kong Closet.' *Out/Look* 7 (Winter 1990): 56–61.
Oikawa, Mona. 'Safer Sex in Santa Cruz.' *Fireweed* 30 (Spring 1990): 31–4.
The Other Woman Collective. 'Women Harassed and Arrested.' *The Other Woman,* April 1974: 17.
- 'Brunswick Four Minus One – The Trial.' *The Other Woman,* June 1974: 2.
- 'Women's Café.' *The Other Woman,* February 1975.

Out/Look Collective. 'Incest and Other Sexual Taboos: A Dialogue between Men and Women.' *Out/Look* 6 (Fall 1989): 50–7.

Parsons, John. 'East Germany Faces Its Past: A New Start for Socialist Sexual Politics.' *Out/Look* 6 (Summer 1989): 43–52.

Phillips, L. Letter: 'The Straight Goods.' *The Body Politic*, March/April 1979: 4.

– 'Lesbian Group Supports Age of Consent Laws.' *The Body Politic*, April 1976: 1.

Popert, Ken. 'Bryantism and Wages Due: Recruiting within Our Own Movement.' *The Body Politic*, September 1978: 5.

Potts (Rosen), Adrienne. 'Adrienne Potts' Speech for Gay Pride Day.' *The Other Woman* 2, 1 (September/October 1973): 20.

Potts (Rosen), Adrienne, and Lydia Gross. 'We Do a Lot of the Talking.' *The Other Woman* 2, 1 (September/October 1973): 7–8.

Quinlan, Judith. 'Letter.' *Broadside*, October/November 1980: 3, 8.

Radicalesbians. 'Woman Identified Woman.' *The Ladder* 11/12 (August/September 1970).

Ramirez, Judy, and Ellen Woodsworth. 'Wages for Housework, May Day Speeches.' *The Other Woman*, May/June 1975: 20–1.

Ramsay, Heather. 'Where Are You?' *Ontarion*, 22 November 1973: 9.

Riordan, Michael. 'Gay Woman Recounts Police Violence.' *The Body Politic*, May/June 1975: 8.

– 'Flaunting It!' *The Body Politic*, September 1977: 15.

– 'Proselytizing vs. Protecting Your Ass on the Boob Tube.' *The Body Politic*, December/January 1977/78: 16–17.

Robertson, Marie. 'Notes from the Full-Hipped Polish Dyke: The Long and Winding Road to Lesbian Separatism.' *The Body Politic* 24 (May/June 1976): 17.

Rock, Joyce. 'Dykes, Dancing and Politics.' *The Body Politic*, June 1976: 17.

Rubens, Charlotte. '50s Lesbian Pulp Author: An Interview with Ann Bannon.' *Coming Up!*, November 1983: 16

Rubin, Gayle. 'Letter.' *The Body Politic*, February 1978: 2.

Shafer, Pat. 'OFY Exposé: Autonomy or Co-option?' *The Other Woman*, July 1974: 7.

Sheard-Robertson, Sharlene. 'Rosemary Barnes.' *The Body Politic*, July/August 1977: 26–7.

Smith, Barbara, and Jewelle Gomez. 'Taking the Home out of Homophobia: Black Lesbians Look in Their Own Backyard.' *Out/Look* 8 (Spring 1990): 32–7.

Smith, Dorothy. 'Where There Is Oppression, There Is Resistance.' *Branching Out* 6, 1 (1979): 10–15.

Smith, Pat. 'Why I Didn't Go to the Gay Pride Rally.' *The Pedestal*, January 1974: 3.

Soliwoda, Miras. 'Did You Ever Have Sex in Poland?' *Out/Look* 13 (Summer 1991): 77–9.

Springer, Judy. 'Letter.' *The Body Politic*, April 1978: 3.

Stirling, Heather. 'Conference Explores Lesbian Autonomy.' *The Body Politic*, September 1976: 8.

Stone, Sharon. Column in *LOOT Newsletter*, August 1979: 4.

– 'Help.' *Lesbian Perspective*, September 1979: 6.

Susan. 'A Conversation.' *The Other Woman* 2, 1 (September/October 1973): 3, 17.

Terry, Jennifer. 'Locating Ourselves in the History of Sexuality.' *Out/Look*, Summer 1988: 86–91.

Tilchin, Maida. 'Ann Bannon: The Mystery Solved!' *Gay Community News*, 8 January 1983: 8–12.

Tilchin, Maida, and Fran Koski. 'Some Pulp Fiction.' *The Body Politic*, August 1976: 2–4.

Valverde, Mariana. 'Freedom, Violence and Pornography.' *The Body Politic*, March/April 1979: 19.

– 'Confessions of a Lesbian Ex-Masochist.' *The Body Politic*, September 1979: 18.

Vanderdyke, Amy. Column in *Long Time Coming*, April/May 1976: 23.

Wages Due. 'Lesbian Autonomy and the Gay Movement.' *The Body Politic*, August 1976: 8.

– 'Lesbians Struggle at Nellie's Women's Hostel.' *The Body Politic*, October 1976: 17.

– 'Women Speak Out.' *The Body Politic*, December/January 1976/77: 1.

Watson, Boo. 'Lesbian Conference Urges Autonomy.' *The Body Politic*, August 1976: 17.

Weir, Lorna. 'So Much for the Woman-Identified Woman.' *The Body Politic*, June 1979: 31.

– 'Exorcising Ghosts of Friendships Past.' *The Body Politic*, August 1980: 43.

– 'Lesbians Against the Right: An Introduction.' In Lesbians Against the Right, ed., *Lesbians Are Everywhere: Fighting the Right*, 2–4. Toronto, 1981.

Winnow, Jackie. 'Lesbians Working on AIDS: Assessing the Impact of Health Care for Women.' *Out/Look*, Summer 1989: 10–18.

Wyland, Francie. 'Lesbian Mothers Defense Fund.' *Broadside*, February 1981: 8.

Yuen, Li. 'International Lesbian Sex Week Poster.' *Angles*, September 1987: 15–16.

Yusba, Roberta. 'Odd Girls and Strange Sisters: Lesbian Pulp Novels of the 50s.' *Out/Look* 12 (Spring 1991): 34–7.

Zaremba, Eve. 'Porn Again.' *The Body Politic*, October 1978: 4.

– 'Now You See It, Now You Don't.' *Broadside*, May 1979: 19.

– 'Speaking the Unspeakable.' *Broadside*, July 1981: 19.

Zeck, Shari. 'Seeing Ourselves on Screen: New Books on Lesbians, Gay Men and Film.' *Out/Look* 13 (Summer 1991): 80–2.

Articles in Mainstream Press

Bennetts, Leslie. 'k.d lang's Edge: Crossing Over, Catching Fire.' *Vanity Fair*, August 1993: 94–8, 142–6.

Blizzard, Christina. 'Gay Pap Appealing Tax Waste.' *Toronto Sun*, 25 January 1992: 14

– 'Gay Flier Furor: Pamphlet Says Homosexuality "Natural."' *Toronto Sun*, 25 September 1992: 4

– 'Gay Case for Fliers Is Bizarre.' *Toronto Sun*, 25 September 1992: 14.

– 'Personal Problem? Yes It Is.' *Toronto Sun*, 15 October 1992: 16.

– 'Buddies in Bad Times.' *Toronto Sun*, 15 June 1993: A18.

Cunningham, Amy. 'Not Just Another Prom Night.' *Glamour*, June 1992: 222–5, 259–60.

Diebel, Linda. 'Man Is the Enemy of the New Feminists.' *Toronto Telegram*, 8 December 1970.

Globe and Mail Staff. 'Woman Guilty, Two Cleared in Disturbance.' *Globe and Mail*, 1 June 1974.

– 'Editorial.' *Globe and Mail*, 12 August 1977.

Hoy, Claire. 'Stop the Bleeding Hearts.' *Toronto Sun*, 8 September 1977.

– 'The Limp Wrist Lobby.' *Toronto Sun*, 2 November 1977.

– 'Gay Rights ... Continuing Saga.' *Toronto Sun*, 13 November 1977.

– 'Morality vs. Perversity.' *Toronto Sun*, 21 December 1977.

– 'Kids, Not Rights, Their Craving.' *Toronto Sun*, 24 December 1977.

– 'Bryant Speaks Our Mind.' *Toronto Sun*, 15 January 1978.

Kates, Joanne. 'Impolitic Moves.' *Fanfare*, 4 January 1978: 13.

Kostash, Myrna. 'Courting Sappho: If I Only Could, I Surely Would.' *Maclean's*, November 1974: 19.

Landsberg, Michele. 'Lesbians Shouldn't Be Isolated.' *Toronto Star*, 28 May 1979: D1, 1.

Lee, Betty. 'Bitter Oranges.' *Toronto Star, Canada Magazine*, 23 July 1977: 25.

London Free Press Staff. 'Lesbianism "Rampant" [in Kingston's Prison for Women].' *London Free Press*, 9 March 1973.

Marchand, Philip. 'Getting on with the 70s.' *Maclean's*, January 1975: 23, 25.

– 'Cruising.' *Toronto Life*, March 1975: 33–6.

Pevere, Geoff. 'An Exhilarating Romp through the Decade That Time Forgot.' *Globe and Mail*, 11 May 1991: 1.

Porter, Mackenzie. 'Anita Bryant.' *Toronto Sun*, 16 January 1978.

Salholz, Eloise. 'The Power and the Pride.' *Newsweek*, 21 June 1993: 54–60.

Sangster, Dorothy. 'Gay Women: A Minority Report.' *Chatelaine*, July 1977: 24, 79–84.

Time Magazine Staff. 'Women's Lib: A Second Look.' *Time*, 8 December 1970: 50.

Toronto Star Staff. 'Female Soldiers Wed and Shock U.S. Army.' *Toronto Star*, 28 January 1973.

– 'Lesbians Win Custody Case Provided They Live Apart.' *Toronto Star*, 23 February 1973.

– 'Three Women Claim Police Abused Them in Garage.' *Toronto Star*, 28 May 1974: A4.

– 'Sentence Suspended for Tavern Incident.' *Toronto Star*, 3 June 1974.

– Editorial: 'Gay Community Is Appalled.' *Toronto Star*, 3 August 1977.

– Editorial: 'Nobody Else Wants Yonge Street Blight.' *Toronto Star*, 11 August 1977.

– 'My Lesbian Lover Threatened to Kill Me.' *Toronto Star*, 15 September 1977.

– 'Alcoholism and Homosexuality Degraded Lee Bryant's Life for 10 Years Until Her Conversion to Christianity.' *Toronto Star*, September 1978.

Toronto Sun Staff. 'Editorial.' *Toronto Sun*, 29 March 1973: 8.

– Editorial: 'Sin Strip Victim.' *Toronto Sun*, 3 August 1977.

– 'Editorial.' *Toronto Sun*, 5 August 1977.

– Editorial: 'Lunacy.' *Toronto Sun*, 28 September 1977.

– Editorial: 'Anita's Day.' *Toronto Sun*, 15 January 1978.

Weinstein, Jeff. 'In Praise of Pulp: Bannon's Lusty Lesbians.' *Village Voice Literary Supplement* 20 (October 1983): 8–9.

Articles in Journals

Adams, Mary Louise. 'There's No Place Like Home: On the Place of Identity in Feminist Politics.' *Feminist Review* 31 (Spring 1989): 22–33.

Aguilar–San Juan, Karin. 'Landmarks in Literature by Asian American Lesbians.' *Signs*, Summer 1993: 936–43.

Ardill, Susan, and Sue O'Sullivan. 'Sex in the Summer of '88.' *Feminist Review* 31 (Spring 1989): 126–34.

Arnup, Katherine. '"Mothers Just Like Others": Lesbians, Divorce and Child Custody in Canada.' *Canadian Journal of Women and the Law* 3 (1987): 8–32.

Augustine, Karen. 'Bizarre Women, Exotic Bodies and Outrageous Sex.' *Border/Lines*, Winter 1994: 22–4.

Barker, Donna. 'S & M Is an Adventure.' *Fireweed* 28 (Spring 1989): 115–21.

Barnes, Rosemary. 'Dykes in Search of Affection and Independence.' *Resources for Feminist Research* 12, 1 (March 1983): 46–7.

Bearchell, Chris. 'Why I'm a Gay Liberationist: Thoughts on Sex, Freedom, the Family and the State.' *Resources for Feminist Research* 12, 1 (March 1983): 57–60.

Bell, Gay. 'From a Resistance to Lesbian Theatre to a Lesbian Theatre of Resistance.' *Resources for Feminist Research* 12, 1 (March 1983): 30–3.

Benns, Susanna. 'Sappho in Soft Cover: Some Notes on Lesbian Pulp.' *Fireweed* 11 (1981): 36–43.

Blackman, Inge, and Kathryn Perry. 'Skirting the Issue: Lesbian Fashion for the 1990s.' *Feminist Review* 34 (Spring 1990): 67–78.

Blackwood, Evelyn. 'Sexuality and Gender in Certain Native American Tribes: The Case of Cross-Gender Females.' In Estelle Freedman et al., eds, *Signs, The Lesbian Issue*, 27–42. Chicago: University of Chicago Press 1985.

Bourne, Jenny. 'Homelands of the Mind: Jewish Feminism and Identity Politics.' *Race and Class* 29 (1987): 1–24.

Bronski, Michael. 'Eros and Politicization: Sexuality, Politics and the Idea of Community.' *Radical America*, January/February 1988: 45–52.

Bulkin, Elly. 'An Old Dyke's Tale: An Interview with Doris Lunden.' *Conditions* 6 (1980): 26–44.

Butler, Judith. 'Critically Queer.' *GLQ: A Journal of Lesbian and Gay Studies* 1, 1 (1993): 17–32.

Carby, Hazel V. 'It Jus Be's Dat Way Sometime: The Sexual Politics of Women's Blues.' *Radical America*, June/July 1986: 9–24.

Cerullo, Margaret. 'Hope and Terror: The Paradox of Gay and Lesbian Politics in the 1990s.' *Radical America* 24, 3 (1993): 10–16.

Chambers, Ian. 'A Strategy for Living.' *Cultural Studies*, Summer 1975: 157–66.

Cheda, Sherrill, Joanna Stuckey, and Maryon Kantaroff. 'New Feminists Now.' *Canadian Woman's Studies Journal* 2, 2 (1980): 27–9.

CKLN Caucus. 'Bi and Out: Discussing the Les/Bi Divide on Queer Radio.' *Fireweed*, Summer 1992: 62–7.

Clarke, John, Stuart Hall, Tony Jefferson, and Brian Roberts. 'Subcultures, Cultures and Class.' *Cultural Studies* 7/8 (Summer 1975): 5–74.

Dominy, Michele D. 'Lesbian-Feminist Gender Conceptions: Separatism in Christchurch, New Zealand.' *Signs: A Journal of Women in Culture and Society*, Winter 1986: 274–87.

Epstein, Barbara. 'Rethinking Social Movement Theory.' *Socialist Review* 20, 1 (January/March 1990): 35–65.

Epstein, Steven. 'Gay Politics, Ethnic Identity: The Limits of Social Constructionism.' *Socialist Review* 17 (May/August 1987): 9–54.

Faderman, Lillian. 'Emily Dickinson's Letters to Sue Gilbert.' *Massachusetts Review* 18, 2 (September 1977): 197–225.

– 'Emily Dickinson's Homoerotic Poetry.' *Higginson Journal* 18 (June 1978): 19–27.

Ferris, Kathryn. 'Child Custody and the Lesbian Mother: An Annotated Bibliography.' *Resources for Feminist Research*, March 1983: 106–9.

Fitzgerald, Maureen. 'Toronto International Women's Day Committee.' *Canadian Woman's Studies* 2, 2 (1980): 33–4.

Franzen, Trisha. 'Differences and Identities: Feminism and the Albuquerque Lesbian Community.' *Signs* 18, 4 (Summer 1993): 891–906.

Frye, Marilyn. 'Review of *The Coming Out Stories*.' *Sinister Wisdom* 14 (1980): 97–8.

Garber, Eric. 'Gladys Bentley: Bulldagger Who Sang the Blues.' *Out/Look* 3 (Fall 1988): 52–61.

Gaspar de Alba, Alicia. 'Tortillerismo: Work by Chicana Lesbians.' *Signs* 18, 4 (Summer 1993): 956–63.

Geller, Gloria. 'The Issue of Nonmonogamy among Lesbians.' *Resources for Feminist Research* 12, 1 (March 1983): 44–5.

Giese, Rachel. 'I Feel Pretty, Witty and Gay.' *Border/Lines* 32 (Spring 1994): 26–9.

Goldsby, Jackie. 'What It Means to Be Colored Me.' *Out/Look*, Summer 1990: 8–17.

Golding, Sue. 'Sexual Issue: Time for Questioning in Bed.' *The Body Politic*, November, 1981: 35.

– 'Thoughts about Lesbian Sex, Politics and Community Standards.' *Fireweed: Lesbiantics I* 13 (1982): 80–100.

Gomez, Jewelle. 'Speculative Fiction and Black Lesbians.' *Signs* 8, 4 (Summer 1993): 950–5.

Gottlieb, Amy. 'Lesbian Bill of Rights.' *After Stonewall: Critical Journal of Lesbian and Gay Liberation in Prairie Canada* 9 (Fall 1979): 10–11, 18, 20; reprinted in *Lesbian/Lesbienne* 1, 1 (Fall 1979).

Gross, Wendy L. 'Judging the Best Interests of the Child: Child Custody and the Homosexual Parent.' *Canadian Journal of Women and the Law* 1 (1986): 505–31.

Hamer, Diane. 'Significant Others: Lesbianism and Psychoanalytic Theory.' *Feminist Review* 34 (Spring 1990): 134–51.

Hammonds, Evelynn. 'Missing Persons: African American Women, AIDS and the History of Disease.' *Radical America* 24, 2 (1992): 7–23.

Harris, Bertha. 'What We Mean to Say: Notes towards Defining the Nature of Lesbian Literature.' *Heresies* 3 (1977): 5–8.

Hollibaugh, Amber. 'Sexuality and the State: The Defeat of the Briggs Initiative and Beyond.' *Socialist Review*, May/June 1979: 55–71.

Hull, Gloria. '"Under the days": The Buried Life and Poetry of Angelina Weld Grimké.' *Conditions* 12, 2 (1979): 17–25.

Hunter, Allen. 'In the Wings, New Right Ideology and Organization.' *Radical America* 5, 1–2 (Spring 1981): 23–35.

Irvine, Janice M. 'A Place in the Rainbow: Theorizing Lesbian and Gay Culture.' *Sociological Theory* 12, 2 (July 1994): 232–48.

Katz, Jonathon Ned. 'The Invention of Heterosexuality.' *Socialist Review* 20, 1 (January/March 1990): 7–33.

Kauffman, L.A. 'The Anti-Politics of Identity.' *Socialist Review* 20, 1 (January/March 1990): 67–79.

King, Katie. 'The Situation of Lesbianism as Feminism's Magical Sign: Contests for Meaning and the U.S. Women's Movement, 1968–1972.' *Communication* 9 (1986): 65–91.

Kobayashi, Tamai. 'Untitled.' *Fireweed* 30 (Spring 1990): 52–3.

Krieger, Susan. 'Lesbian Identity and Community: Recent Social Science Literature.' *Signs, The Lesbian Issue*, 223–40. Chicago: University of Chicago Press 1985.

Lesbians Making History. 'People Think This Didn't Happen in Canada.' *Fireweed, Lesbiantics II* 28 (Spring 1989): 81–94.

McCoy, Sherry, and Maureen Hicks. 'A Psychological Retrospective on Power in the Contemporary Lesbian-Feminist Community.' *Frontiers* 4, 3 (1979): 65–9.

Mansbridge, Jane. 'Time, Emotion and Inequality: Three Problems of Participatory Groups.' *Journal of Applied Behavioural Science*, May 1973: 351–68.

Martin, Chris. 'World's Greatest Cocksucker: Transsexual Interviews.' *Fiction International* 22 (1992): 101–22.

Maynard, Steven. 'Rough Work and Rugged Men: The Social Construction of Masculinity in Working Class History.' *Labour/Le travail* (Spring 1989): 159–69.

– 'When Queer Is Not Enough.' *Fuse*, Fall 1991: 14–18.

Minkowitz, Donna. 'The Well of Correctness.' *Village Voice*, 21 May 1991: 39.

Moraga, Cherrie. Interview: 'Writing Is the Measure of My Life.' *Out/Look* 4 (Winter 1989): 53–7.

Namaste, Ki. 'The Politics of Inside/Out: Queer Theory, Poststructuralism and a Sociological Approach to Sexuality.' *Sociological Theory* 12, 2 (July 1994): 220-31.

New Internationalist. 'Pride and Prejudice: Homosexuality.' Special issue, November 1989.

Omosupe, Ekua. 'Black/Lesbian/Bulldagger.' *differences: A Journal of Feminist Cultural Studies* 3, 2 (1991): 101-11.

O'Sullivan, Sue. 'Passionate Beginnings, 1969-1972.' *Feminist Review* 11 (1984).

- 'Interview with Cindy Patton: 'Mapping: Lesbians, AIDS and Sexuality.' *Feminist Review*, Spring 1990: 120-33.

Padgug, Robert. 'Sexual Matters: On Conceptualizing Sexuality in History.' *Radical History Review*, Spring/Summer 1979: 3-23.

Parades, Milagros. 'Christmas Eve Imaginings.' *Fireweed*, Spring 1989: 79.

Parmar, Pratibha. 'Other Kinds of Dreams: An Interview with June Jordan.' *Spare Rib* 184 (1981): 12-15.

Phelan, Shane. '(Be)coming Out: Lesbian Identity and Politics.' *Signs* 18, 4 (Summer 1993): 765-89.

Plotke, David. 'What's So New About New Social Movements?' *Socialist Review* 20, 1 (January/March 1990): 81-102.

Popkin, Annie. 'An Early Moment in Women's Liberation: The Social Experience within Bread and Roses.' *Radical America*, January/February 1988: 19-34.

Quinlan, Judith. 'Lesbian Relationships.' *Resources for Feminist Research* 12, 2 (March 1983): 50-1.

Randall, Margaret. 'To Change Our Own Reality and the World: A Conversation with Lesbians in Nicaragua.' *Signs* (Summer 1993): 907-24.

Red Apple Collective. 'Socialist Feminist Women's Unions: Past and Present.' *Socialist Review* 8, 2 (March/April 1978): 37-57.

Rich, B. Ruby. 'Feminism and Sexuality in the 80s.' *Feminist Studies* 12, 3 (Fall 1986): 525-61.

Ross, Becki. 'Launching Lesbian Offensives.' *Resources for Feminist Research* 17, 2 (June 1988): 12-16.

- 'Heterosexuals Only Need Apply: The Secretary of State's Regulation of Lesbian Existence.' *Resources for Feminist Research* 17, 3 (September 1988): 35-9.

- 'The House That Jill Built.' *Rites*, February 1989: 8.

- 'L'organisme lesbienne de Toronto, 1976-1980.' *Treize*, mars 1989: 11-14.

- 'The House That Jill Built: Lesbian Feminist Organizing in Toronto, 1976-1980.' *Feminist Review* 35 (Summer 1990): 75-91.

- 'Having the Last Laugh.' *Fuse Magazine*, June/July 1990: 26-30.

- 'Lesbian History Quiz.' *Rites*, June 1990: 10; September 1990: 11.

- 'Like Apples and Oranges: Lesbian Feminists Respond to the Politics of *The Body Politic.*' *Fuse,* Spring 1993: 19–28.
- 'Wunna His Fantasies: The State/d Indefensibility of Lesbian Smut.' *Fireweed* 38 (Spring 1993): 38–47.

Rushin, Kate. 'Clearing a Space for Us: A Tribute to Audre Lorde.' *Radical America* 24, 4 (1993): 85–8.

Schwarz, Judith. 'Questionnaire on Issues in Lesbian History.' *Frontiers* 4, 3 (1979): 2–10.

Silber, Linda. 'Negotiating Sexual Identity: Non-Lesbians in a Lesbian Feminist Community.' *Journal of Sex Research* 27, 1 (February 1990): 131–9.

Smith, George. 'Policing the Gay Community: An Inquiry into Textually-mediated Social Relations.' *International Journal of the Sociology of the Law* 16 (1988): 163–83.

- 'The Political Activist as Ethnographer.' *Social Problems* 37, 4 (November 1990): 629–48.

Snitow, Ann. 'Gender Diary.' *Dissent,* Spring 1989: 205–24.

Solomon, Alisa. 'In Whose Face?' *Village Voice,* 2 July 1991: 41.

Spore, Margaret Dwight. 'Speaking Up for Our Sisters: Decriminalization of Prostutition.' *Fireweed* 1 (1978): 23–6.

Stein, Arlene. 'All Dressed Up But No Where to Go? Style Wars and the New Lesbianism.' *Out/Look,* Winter 1989: 34–42.

- 'Androgyny Goes Pop: But Is It Lesbian Music?' *Out/Look* 13, Spring 1991: 26–33.
- 'Sisters and Queers: The Decentring of Lesbian Feminism.' *Socialist Review* 1 & 2 (1992): 33–55.

Stone, Sharon D. 'Must Disability Always Be Visible? The Meaning of Disability for Women.' *Canadian Woman's Studies Journal* 13, 4 (Winter 1993): 11–13.

Tamu, Leleti. 'Casselberry Harvest.' *Fireweed,* Spring 1989: 47.

Tax, Meredith. 'The Sound of One Hand Clapping: Women's Liberation and the Left.' *Dissent* (Fall 1988): 457–62.

Valverde, Mariana. 'Beyond Guilt: Lesbian Feminism and Coming Out.' *Resources for Feminist Research* 12, 1 (March 1983): 65–7.

Vicinus, Martha. 'Sexuality and Power: A Review of Current Work in the History of Sexuality.' *Feminist Studies* 8, 1 (1982): 133–56.

Walker, Lisa M. 'How to Recognize a Lesbian: The Cutural Politics of Looking Like What You Are.' *Signs* (Summer 1993): 866–90.

Webster, Colin. 'Communes.' *Cultural Studies* 7, 8 (Summer 1975): 127–34.

Weir, Lorna, and Eve Zaremba. 'Boys and Girls Together: Feminism and Gay Liberation.' *Broadside* 4, 1 (1982): 10–11.

Weston, Kathleen, and Lisa Rofel. 'Sexuality, Class and Conflict in a Lesbian Workplace.' *Signs, The Lesbian Issue* (Chicago: University of Chicago Press 1985), 199–222.

Wilson, Elizabeth. 'Deviant Dress.' *Feminist Review* 35 (Summer 1990): 65–74.

Zimmerman, Bonnie. 'The Politics of Transliteration: Lesbian Personal Narratives.' *Signs, The Lesbian Issue* (1985), 251–70.

Books/Chapters in Books

Abbott, Sidney. 'Lesbians and the Women's Movement.' In Ginny Vida, ed., *Our Right To Love: A Lesbian Resource Book*, 139–44. Englewood Cliffs, NJ: Prentice-Hall 1978.

Abbott, Sidney, and Barbara Love. 'Is Women's Liberation a Lesbian Plot?' In Vivian Gornick and Barbara Moran, eds, *Woman in Sexist Society*, 601–21. New York: Basic Books 1971.

– *Sappho Was a Right-On Woman*. New York: Stein and Day 1972.

ACT UP/NY Women and AIDS Book Group, eds, *Women, AIDS and Activism*. Toronto: Between the Lines 1990.

Adam, Barry. *The Rise of a Gay and Lesbian Movement*. Boston: Twayne Publishers 1987.

Adams, Mary Louise. 'All That Rubber, All That Talk.' In Inez Rieder and Patricia Ruppelt, eds, *AIDS: The Women*, 130–3. San Francisco: Cleis Press 1988.

Adamson, Nancy, Linda Briskin, and Marg McPhail. *Feminist Organizing for Change: The Contemporary Women's Movement in Canada*. Toronto: Oxford University Press 1988.

Allen, Carol. 'Who Gets to Be Family?' In Linda Carty, ed., *And Still We Rise*.

Allison, Dorothy. 'A Question of Class.' In Arlene Stein, ed., *Sisters, Sexperts and Queers: Beyond the Lesbian Nation*, 133–55. New York: Penguin Books 1993.

Altman, Dennis. *Homosexual: Oppression and Liberation*. New York: Avon 1971.

– *Coming Out in the Seventies*. Boston: Alyson Publications 1979.

Anderson, Margaret, ed. *Mother Was Not a Person*. Montréal: Black Rose Books 1972.

Ardill, Susan, and Sue O'Sullivan. 'Upsetting An Applecart: Difference, Desire and Lesbian Sado-Masochism.' In Christian McEwann and Sue O'Sullivan, eds, *Out the Other Side: Contemporary Lesbian Writing*, 122–43. London: Virago 1988.

Arnold, June. *Sister Gin*. Plainfield, Vt.: Daughters, Inc. 1975; repr. New York: Feminist Press 1989.

Atkinson, Ti-Grace. *Amazon Odyssey*. New York: Links 1974.

Auger, Jeanette. 'Lesbians and Aging: Triple Trouble or Tremendous Thrill.' In Sharon Stone, ed., *Lesbians in Canada*, 25–34. Toronto: Between the Lines 1990.

Bannon, Ann. *I Am a Woman*. Greenwich, Conn.: Fawcett Publications 1959; repr. Tallahassee, Fla.: Naiad Press 1977.

– *Beebo Brinker*. Tallahassee, Fla.: Naiad Press 1986.

– *Women in the Shadows*. Tallahassee, Fla.: Naiad Press 1986.

– *Odd Girl Out*. Tallahassee, Fla.: Naiad Press 1986.

– *Journey to a Woman*. Tallahassee, Fla.: Naiad Press 1986.

Barbach, Lonnie. *For Yourself: The Fulfillment of Female Sexuality*. Garden City, NY: Doubleday 1975.

Beck, Evelyn Torton, ed. *Nice Jewish Girls: A Lesbian Anthology*. Watertown, Mass.: Persephone Press 1982.

Bell, Laurie. *Good Girls / Bad Girls: Sex Trade Workers and Feminists Face to Face*. Toronto: Women's Press 1987.

– *On Our Own Terms: A Practical Guide to Lesbian and Gay Relationships in Canada*. Toronto: Coalition for Lesbian and Gay Rights in Ontario 1991.

Benjamin, Jessica. 'Master and Slave: The Fantasy of Erotic Domination.' In Ann Snitow, Christine Stansell, and Sharon Thompson, eds, *Powers of Desire*, 280–99. New York: Monthly Review Press 1983.

Bentstock, Shari. *Women of the Left Bank: Paris, 1900–1940*. Austin: University of Texas Press 1986.

Bernstein, Judy, Peggy Morton, Linda Seese, and Myrna Wood. 'Sisters, Brothers, Lovers, Listen ... ' In *Women Unite! An Anthology of the Canadian Women's Movement*, 31–9. Toronto: Women's Educational Press 1972.

Bérubé, Allan. *Coming Out under Fire: Gay Men and Women in the Second World War*. New York: Penguin Books 1990.

Blatchford, Gregg. 'Male Dominance and the Gay World.' In Kenneth Plummer, ed., *The Making of the Modern Homosexual*, 184–210. London: Hutchinson 1981.

Boston Women's Health Collective. 'In Amerika They Call Us Dykes.' In *Our Bodies, Our Selves*, 56–73. New York: Simon and Shuster 1973.

Bright, Susie. *Susie Sexpert's Lesbian Sex World*. San Francisco: Cleis Press 1990.

– *Susie Bright's Sexual Reality: A Virtual Sex World Reader*. San Francisco: Cleis Press 1992.

Brody, Michel, ed. *Are We There Yet? A Continuing History of Lavender Woman, a Chicago Lesbian Newspaper, 1971–76*. Iowa City: Aunt Lute 1985.

Bronski, Michael. *Culture Clash: The Making of a Gay Sensibility*. Boston: South End Press 1984.

Brown, Judith. *Immodest Acts*. Toronto: Oxford University Press 1986.

Brown, Laura S. 'Confronting Internalized Oppression.' In Monika Kehoe, ed., *Historical, Literary and Erotic Aspects of Lesbianism*, 99–108. New York: Harrington Park Press 1986.

Brown, Rita Mae. *Rubyfruit Jungle*. Plainfield, Vt.: Daughters, Inc. 1973; repr. New York: Bantam Books 1977.

- 'The Shape of Things to Come.' In Charlotte Bunch and Nancy Myron, eds, *Lesbianism and the Women's Movement*, 75–80. Baltimore: Diana Press 1975.

- *Plain Brown Wrapper*. Baltimore: Daughters, Inc. 1976.

Brownmiller, Susan. *Against Our Will: Men, Women and Rape*. New York: Simon and Schuster 1975.

Bunch, Charlotte. 'Lesbians in Revolt.' In C. Bunch and Nancy Myron, eds, *Lesbianism and the Women's Movement*, 24–30. Baltimore: Diana Press 1975.

- 'Lesbian Feminist Theory.' In Ginny Vida, ed., *Our Right to Love: A Lesbian Resource Book*, 180–2. Englewood Cliffs, NJ: Prentice-Hall 1978.

- *Passionate Politics: Feminist Theory in Action, 1968–1986*. New York: St Martin's Press 1987.

Bunch, Charlotte, and Nancy Myron, eds. *Lesbianism and the Women's Movement*. Baltimore: Diana Press 1975.

- *Class and Feminism*. Baltimore: Diana Press 1975.

Burstyn, Varda. 'The Left and the Porn Wars: A Case Study in Sexual Politics.' In Howard Buchbinder, V. Burstyn, Dinah Forbes, and Mercedes Steedman, *Who's on Top? The Politics of Heterosexuality*, 13–46. Toronto: Garamond Press 1987.

Butler, Judith. 'Imitation and Gender Insubordination.' In Diana Fuss, ed., *Inside Out: Lesbian Theories, Gay Theories*, 13–31. New York and London: Routledge 1991.

Califia, Pat. *Sapphistries: The Book of Lesbian Sexuality*. Tallahassee, Fla.: Naiad Press 1980.

- 'A Personal View of the History of the Lesbian S/M Community and Movement in San Francisco.' In Samois, ed., *Coming to Power*, 245–83. Boston: Alyson Publications 1987.

- *Macho Sluts*. Boston: Alyson Publications 1988.

Cant, Bob, and Susan Hemmings, eds. *Radical Records: Thirty Years of Lesbian and Gay History, 1957–1978*. London: Routledge and Kegan Paul 1988.

Cappon, Daniel. *Towards an Understanding of Homosexuality*. Toronto: Prentice-Hall 1965.

Caprio, Frank. *Female Homosexuality: A Psychoanalytic Study of Lesbianism*. London: Icon Books 1955; repr. 1965.

Carby, Hazel V. 'White Women Listen! Black Feminism and the Boundaries of Sisterhood.' In Contemporary Centre for Cultural Studies, ed., *The Empire Strikes Back*. London: Hutchinson 1982.

Carroll, William, ed. *Organizing Dissent: Contemporary Social Movements in Theory and Practice*. Toronto: Garamond Press 1992.

Cartledge, Sue. 'Bringing It All Back Home: Lesbian Feminist Morality.' In Gay Left Collective, ed., *Homosexuality: Power and Politics*, 93–103. London: Allison and Busby Ltd 1980.

de Certeau, Michael. *The Practice of Everyday Life*. Berkeley: University of California Press 1984.

Chamberland, Line. 'Projet de communication: Sur la culture lesbienne, les années 1950s à Montréal.' Translated as 'Social Class and Integration in the Lesbian Sub-Culture.' In Sandra Kirby, Dayna Daniels, Kate McKenna, and Michelle Pujol, eds, *Women Changing Academe*, 75–88. Winnipeg: Sororal Publishing 1991.

Chapkis, Wendy. *Beauty Secrets: Women and the Politics of Appearance*. Boston: South End Press 1986.

Clark, Wendy. 'The Dyke, the Feminist and the Devil.' In *Sexuality, a Reader*, 201–16. London: Virago 1987.

Code, Lorraine, and Sandra Burt, eds. *Changing Patterns: Women in Canada*. Toronto: McClelland and Stewart 1988.

Cooper, Eleanor. 'Social Outlets.' In Ginny Vida, ed., *Our Right to Love: Lesbian Resource Book*, 48–50. Englewood Cliffs, NJ: Prentice-Hall 1978.

Corinne, Tee. *Cunt Coloring Book*. Weather Lake, Mo.: Naiad Press 1977.

Cornwell, Anita. *Black Lesbian in White America*. Tallahassee, Fla.: Naiad Press 1983.

Creet, Julia. 'A Test of Unity: Lesbian Visibility in the British Columbia Federation of Women, 1974–5.' In Sharon Stone, ed., *Lesbians in Canada*, 183–97. Toronto: Between the Lines 1990.

Cunningham, Frank, Sue Findlay, Marlene Kadar, Alan Lennon, and Ed Silva, eds. *Social Movements / Social Change: The Politics and Practice of Organizing*. Toronto: Between the Lines 1988.

Daly, Mary. *Gyn/Ecology: The Metaethics of Radical Feminism*. Boston: Beacon Press 1978.

Das Gupta, Tania. *Learning from Our History: Community Development by Immigrant Women in Ontario, 1958–1986*. Toronto: Cross Cultural Communication Centre 1986.

Davis, Madeline, and Elizabeth Kennedy. *Boots of Leather, Slippers of Gold: The History of a Lesbian Community*. New York: Routledge 1993.

Dekker, Rudoloph M., and Lotte Van De Pol. *The Tradition of Female Transvestism in Early Modern Europe*. London: Macmillan 1989.

Delacoste, Frederique, and Priscilla Alexander, eds. *Sex Work: Writings by Women in the Sex Industry*. Pittsburgh: Cleis Press 1987.

D'Emilio, John. *Sexual Politics, Sexual Communities: The Making of a Homosexual Minority in the U.S., 1940–1970*. Chicago: University of Chicago Press 1983.

D'Emilio, John, and Estelle Freedman. *Intimate Matters: A History of Sexuality in America*. New York: Harper and Row 1988.

Dickinson, Martha Bianchi. *The Life and Letters of Emily Dickinson*. Boston: Houghton Mifflin 1924.

– *Emily Dickinson Face to Face: Unpublished Letters with Notes and Reminiscences*. Boston: Houghton Mifflin 1932.

Dodson, Betty. *Liberating Masturbation*. New York: Bodysex Designs 1974.

Doucette, Joanne. 'Redefining Difference: Disabled Lesbians Resist.' In Sharon Stone, ed., *Lesbians in Canada*, 61–72. Toronto: Between the Lines 1990.

Douglas, Carole Anne. *To the Cleveland Station*. Tallahassee, Fla.: Naiad Press 1982.

Duberman, Martin Bauml, Martha Vicinus, and George Chauncey, Jr, eds. *Hidden from History: Reclaiming the Gay and Lesbian Past*. New York: New American Library 1989.

Echols, Alice. 'The Taming of the Id: Feminist Sexual Politics, 1968–1983.' In Carole Vance, ed., *Pleasure and Danger*, 50–72. Boston and London: Routledge and Kegan Paul 1984.

– *Daring to Be Bad: Radical Feminism in America, 1967–1975*. Minneapolis: University of Minnesota Press 1989.

Egan, Carolyn. 'Socialist Feminism: Activism and Alliances.' In Heather Jon Maroney and Meg Luxton, eds, *Feminism and Political Economy*, 109–19. Toronto: Methuen 1987.

Egan, Carolyn, Linda Lee Gardner, and Judy Vashti Persad. 'The Politics of Transformation: Struggles with Race, Class and Sexuality in the March 8th Coalition.' In Frank Cunningham, Sue Findlay, Marlene Kadar, Alan Lennon, and Ed Silva, eds, *Social Movements / Social Change: The Politics and Practice of Organizing*, 20–47. Toronto: Between the Lines 1988.

Ellis, Havelock. *Sexual Inversion: Studies in the Psychology of Sex*, volume 2. New York: Random House 1936; original, 1910.

– *The Psychology of Sex*. London: Pan Books 1959; original, 1933.

Evans, Sara. *Personal Politics: The Roots of the Women's Liberation Movement in the Civil Rights Movement and the New Left*. New York: Vintage Books 1979.

Faderman, Lillian. *Odd Girls and Twilight Lovers: A History of Lesbian Life in Twentieth Century America*. New York: Columbia University Press 1991.

Faderman, Lillian, and Bridgette Eriksson. *Lesbian Feminism in Turn of the Century Germany*. Tallahassee, Fla.: Naiad Press 1980.

Feminist Revolution. New Paltz, NY: Redstockings 1975.

Fischer, Hal. *Gay Semiotics: A Photographic Study of Visual Codes among Homosexual Men.* San Francisco: NFS Press 1979.

Forbes, Dinah. 'Difficult Loves.' In Howard Buchbinder, Varda Burstyn, D. Forbes, and Mercedes Steedman, *Who's on Top? The Politics of Heterosexuality,* 47–62. Toronto: Garamond Press 1987.

Foster, Marion, and Kent Murray. 'Interview with Chris Fox.' In M. Foster and K. Murray, *A Not So Gay World: Homosexuality in Canada,* 139–54. Toronto: McClelland and Stewart 1972.

Freeman, Jo. 'The Tyranny of Structurelessness.' In Anne Koedt, Ellen Levine, and Anita Rapone, eds, *Radical Feminism.* New York: Quadrangle 1973.

– *The Politics of Women's Liberation.* New York and London: Longman 1975.

Frye, Marilyn. 'Lesbian Feminism and the Gay Rights Movement: Another View of Male Supremacy, Another Separatism.' In M. Frye, *The Politics of Reality: Essays in Feminist Theory,* 128–51. New York: The Crossing Press 1983.

Fung, Richard. 'Looking for My Penis: The Eroticized Asian in Gay Video Porn.' In *How Do I Look: Queer Film and Video,* 145–60. Seattle: Bay Press 1991.

Fuss, Diana. 'Lesbian and Gay Theory: The Question of Identity Politics.' In D. Fuss, *Essentially Speaking: Feminism, Nature and Difference,* 97–112. New York and London: Routledge 1989.

Gagnon, J.H., and William Simon. 'The Lesbians: A Preliminary Overview.' In *Sexual Deviance,* 260–9. New York: Harper and Row 1972.

– *Sexual Conduct.* Chicago: Aldine 1973.

Garber, Eric. 'A Spectacle in Color: The Lesbian and Gay Subculture of Jazz Age Harlem.' In Martin B. Duberman, Martha Vicinus, and George Chauncey Jr, eds, *Hidden from History: Reclaiming the Gay and Lesbian Past,* 318–31. New York: New American Library 1989.

Gearhart, Sally. *The Wanderground.* Watertown, Mass.: Persephone Press 1978; repr. Boston: Alyson Publications 1984.

Genge, Sue. 'Lesbians and Gays in the Union Movement.' In Linda Briskin and Lynda Yanz, eds, *Union Sisters: Women in the Labour Movement,* 161–70. Toronto: Women's Press 1983.

Gibbs, Joan, and Sara Bennett, eds. *Top Ranking: A Collection of Articles on Racism and Classism in the Lesbian Community.* New York: Come! Unity Press 1980.

Gilhooly, Sheila, and Persimmon Blackbridge. *Still Sane.* Vancouver: Press Gang 1985.

Gill, Judy, Diana Chastain, Linda Carmen, Mary Bolton, and Jenny Robinson. 'Sexual Myths.' In *Women Unite! An Anthology of the Canadian Women's Movement,* 162–9. Toronto: Women's Educational Press 1972.

Gitlin, Todd. *The Sixties: Years of Hope, Days of Rage.* New York: Bantam 1987.

Gittings, Barbara, and Kay Tobin. 'Lesbians and the Gay Movement.' In Ginny
  Vida, ed., *Our Right to Love: A Lesbian Resource Book*, 149–54. Englewood Cliffs,
  NJ: Prentice-Hall 1978.
Godiva. *What Lesbians Do*. San Fransciso: Amazon Art Works 1976.
Goldsby, Jackie. 'Queen for 307 Days: Looking B(l)ack at Vanessa Williams
  and the Sex Wars.' In Arlene Stein, ed., *Sisters, Sexperts and Queers: Beyond the
  Lesbian Nation*, 110–28. New York: Penguin Books 1993.
Gottlieb, Amy. 'Mothers, Sisters, Lovers, Listen ... ' In Maureen Fitzgerald,
  Connie Guberman, and Margie Wolfe, eds, *Still Ain't Satisfied: Canadian Femi-
  nism Today*, 234–42. Toronto: Women's Press 1982.
Grahn, Judy. 'A History of Lesbianism.' In J. Grahn, *Edward the Dyke and Other
  Poems*. Oakland: Women's Press Collective 1971.
– *Another Mother Tongue*. Boston: Beacon Press 1986.
– 'Strange Country This: Lesbianism and North American Indian Tribes.' In
  Monika Kehoe, ed., *Historical, Literary and Erotic Aspects of Lesbianism*, 43–57.
  New York and London: Harrington Park Press 1986.
Gunn Allen, Paula. *The Sacred Hoop*. Boston: Beacon Press 1986.
Hale, Amanda. 'A Dialectical Drama of Facts and Fiction on the Feminist
  Fringe.' In Rhea Tregebov, ed., *Work in Progress: Building Feminist Culture*,
  77–100. Toronto: Women's Press 1982.
Hall, Lisa Kahaleole Chang. 'Bitches in Solitude: Identity Politics and Lesbian
  Community.' In Arlene Stein, ed., *Sisters, Sexperts and Queers: Beyond the Lesbian
  Nation*, 218–29. New York: Penguin Books 1993.
Hansen, Karen. 'Women's Unions and the Search for a Political Identity.' In
  K. Hansen and Ilene Philipson, eds, *Women, Class and the Feminist Imagination*,
  213–38. Philadelphia: Temple University Press 1990.
Hamer, Diane. '"I am a Woman": Ann Bannon and the Writing of Lesbian
  Identity in the 1950s.' In Mark Lilly, ed., *Lesbian and Gay Writing*, 47–75. Lon-
  don: Macmillan 1990.
Harper, Vern. *Following the Red Path: The Native People's Caravan, 1974*. Toronto:
  NC Press 1979.
Harris, Bertha. *Lover*. Plainfield, Vt.: Daughters, Inc. 1976.
Hebdige, Dick. *Subculture: The Meaning of Style*. New York: Methuen 1979.
Hemmings, Susan. 'Horrific Practices: How Lesbians Were Presented in the
  Newspapers of 1978.' In Gay Left Collective, ed., *Homosexuality: Power and Pol-
  itics*, 157–71. London: Alison and Busby 1980.
Higgins, Ross, and Line Chamberland. 'Mixed Messages: Lesbians, Gay Men
  and the Yellow Press in Quebec and Ontario during the 1950s and 1960s.'
  In Ian McKay, ed., *The Challenge of Modernity*, 421–38. Toronto: McGraw-Hill
  Ryerson 1992.

Hoagland, Sarah, and Julia Penelope, eds. *For Lesbians Only: A Separatist Anthology*. London: Onlywomen Press 1988.

Hollibaugh, Amber, and Cherrie Moraga. 'What We're Rollin Around in Bed With.' In Ann Snitow, Christine Stansell, and Sharon Thompson, eds, *Powers of Desire*, 394–405. New York: Monthly Review Press 1983.

hooks, bell. *From the Margin to the Centre*. Boston: South End Books 1984.

Hughes, Nym, Yvonne Johnson, and Yvette Perrault. *Stepping out of Line: A Resource Book on Lesbian Feminism*. Vancouver: Press Gang 1984.

Hull, Gloria T. 'Researching Alice Dunbar-Nelson: A Personal and Literary Perspective.' In G.T. Hull, Barbara Smith, and Patricia Scott, eds, *All The Women Are White, All the Blacks Are Men, But Some of Us Are Brave*. New York: Feminist Press 1982.

Hunt, Margaret. 'A Fem's Own Story: An Interview with Joan Nestle.' In Christian McEwen and Sue O'Sullivan, eds, *Out the Other Side: Contemporary Lesbian Writing*, 232–42. London: Virago 1988.

Hutchins, Lorraine, and Lani Kaahumanu. *Bi Any Other Name: Bisexual People Speak Out*. Boston: Alyson Publications 1990.

International Lesbian and Gay Association. *International Lesbian and Gay Association Pink Book: A Global View of Lesbian and Gay Oppression and Liberation*. Amsterdam: COC-magazijn 1985, 1988.

Jackson, Ed, and Stan Persky, eds. *Flaunting It! A Decade of Gay Journalism from The Body Politic*. Vancouver: New Star Books; Toronto: Pink Triangle Press 1982.

Jeffreys, Sheila. 'Butch and Femme, Now and Then.' In Lesbian History Group, ed., *Not a Passing Phase: Reclaiming Lesbians in History, 1840–1985*, 158–87. London: Women's Press 1989.

Johnston, Jill. *Lesbian Nation*. New York: Touchstone 1973.

Johnston, Nancy. 'The Attar from the Rose: Feminist Approaches to Textual Criticism.' In Debra Martens, ed., *Weaving Alliances*, 331–43. Ottawa: Canadian Women's Studies Association 1993.

Kantrowitz, Melanie Kay. 'To Be a Radical Jew in the Late Twentieth Century.' In Christian McEwen and Sue O'Sullivan, eds, *Out the Other Side: Contemporary Lesbian Writing*, 243–68. London: Virago 1988.

Kates, Joanne. 'Once More with Feeling: Heterosexuality and Feminist Cor sciousness.' In Maureen Fitzgerald, Connie Guberman, and Margie Wolfe, eds, *Still Ain't Satisfied: Canadian Feminism Today*, 76–84. Toronto: Women's Press 1982.

Katz, Jonathon Ned. *Gay American History*. New York: Thomas Y. Crowell 1976.

– *Gay/Lesbian Almanac*. New York: Harper and Row 1983.

Khayatt, M. Didi. *Lesbian Teachers: An Invisible Presence.* Albany: State University of New York 1992.

Kin, David George. *Women without Men: True Life Stories of Lesbian Love in Greenwich Village.* New York: Brookwood Publishing Corp. 1958.

Kinsman, Gary. *The Regulation of Desire: Sexuality in Canada.* Montréal: Black Rose Books 1987.

Koedt, Anne. 'Lesbianism and Feminism.' In A. Koedt, Ellen Levine, and Anita Rapone, eds, *Radical Feminism,* 246–58. New York: Quadrangle 1973.

– 'Myth of the Vaginal Orgasm.' In Koedt, Levine, and Rapone, eds, *Radical Feminism,* 198–207.

Kostash, Myrna. *Long Way from Home.* Toronto: McClelland and Stewart 1980.

Krafft-Ebing, Richard von. *Psychopathia Sexualis.* New York: C.P. Putnam's Sons 1965.

Kramer, Larry. *Faggots.* New York: Bantam Books 1978.

Krieger, Susan. *The Mirror Dance: Identity in a Women's Community.* Philadelphia: Temple University Press 1983.

Lane, Arja. 'Wives Supporting the Strike.' In Linda Briskin and Lynda Yanz, eds, *Union Sisters: Women in the Labour Movement,* 321–32. Toronto: Women's Press 1983.

Lang, Elizabeth. *Anna's Country.* Tallahassee, Fla.: Naiad Press 1981.

Leavitt, David. *Equal Affections.* New York: Harper and Row 1989.

Lenskyj, Helen. *Out of Bounds: Women, Sport and Sexuality.* Toronto: Women's Press 1986.

Likosky, Stephan, ed. *Coming Out: An Anthology of International Gay and Lesbian Writings.* New York: Pantheon Books 1992.

Lorde, Audre. *Zami: A New Spelling of My Name.* New York: Crossing Press 1982.

– 'Uses of the Erotic.' In *Sister Outsider: Essays and Speeches,* 53–9. New York: Crossing Press 1984.

– *A Burst of Light.* Ithaca, NY: Firebrand Books 1988.

Marable, Manning. *Race, Reform and Rebellion: The Second Reconstruction in Black America, 1945–1982.* New York: Macmillan 1984.

Marshall, John. 'The Politics of Tea and Sympathy.' In Gay Left Collective, ed., *Homosexuality: Power and Politics,* 77–84. London: Allison and Busby 1980.

Martin, Del, and Phyllis Lyon. *Lesbian/Woman.* New York: Fawcett Books 1972.

Maupin, Armistead. *Significant Others.* New York: Harper and Row 1987.

Melucci, Alberto. *Nomads of the Present: Social Movements and Individual Needs in Contemporary Society.* Philadelphia: Temple University Press 1989.

Mercer, Kobena. 'Welcome to the Jungle: Identity and Diversity in Postmodern Politics.' In Jonathon Rutherford, ed., *Identity: Community, Culture, Difference,* 43–71. London: Lawrence and Wishart 1990.

- 'Skin Head Sex Thing: Racial Difference and the Homoerotic Imaginary.' Bad Object-Choices, eds, *How Do I Look? Queer Film and Video*, 169–210. Seattle: Bay Press 1991.

Mercer, Kobena, and Isaac Julien. 'White Gay Racism.' In *Male Order: Unwrapping Masculinity*, 104–10. London: Lawrence and Wishart 1988.

Mietkiewicz, Henry, and Bob Mackowycz. *Dream Tower: The Life and Legacy of Rochdale College*. Toronto and Montreal: McGraw-Hill Ryerson 1988.

Millett, Kate. *Sexual Politics*. New York: Avon Books 1970.

- 'Beyond Politics? Children and Sexuality.' In Carole Vance, ed., *Pleasure and Danger*, 217–24. Boston and London: Routledge and Kegan Paul 1984.

Moraga, Cherrie. 'La Guera.' In C. Moraga and Gloria Anzaldua, eds, *This Bridge Called My Back: Writings by Radical Women of Color*, 27–34. New York: Kitchen Table, Women of Color Press 1981.

Moraga, Cherrie, and Gloria Anzaldua, eds, *This Bridge Called My Back: Writings by Radical Women of Color*. New York: Kitchen Table, Women of Color Press 1981.

Morgan, Robin, ed. *Sisterhood Is Powerful*. New York: Random House 1970.

- 'The Proper Study of Womankind: On Women's Studies.' In R. Morgan, ed., *Going Too Far*, 189–201. New York: Random House 1978.

- 'Theory and Practice, Pornography and Rape.' In Morgan, ed., *Going Too Far*, 163–9.

Mort, Frank. *Dangerous Sexualities: Medico-Moral Politics in England since 1830*. London and New York: Routledge and Kegan Paul 1987.

Nachmann, Elana. *Riverfinger Women*. Plainfield, Vt.: Daughters, Inc. 1974.

Nestle, Joan. 'Butch/Fem Relationships: Sexual Courage in the 1950s.' In J. Nestle, *A Restricted County*, 100–9. Ithaca, NY: Firebrand Books 1987.

Newton, Esther, and Shirley Walton. 'The Misunderstanding: Toward a More Precise Sexual Vocabulary.' In Carole Vance, ed., *Pleasure and Danger*, 242–50. Boston and London: Routledge and Kegan Paul 1984.

Nomadic Sisters. *Loving Women*. San Francisco: Amazon Art Works 1975.

Notes from the First Year: Women's Liberation. New York: New York Radical Women 1968.

Notes from the Second Year: Women's Liberation. New York: New York Radical Women 1970.

Notes from the Third Year: Women's Liberation. New York: New York Radical Women 1971.

Omi, Michael, and Howard Winant. *Racial Formation in the United States from the 1960s to the 1980s*. New York: Routledge and Kegan Paul 1986.

Peiss, Kathy, and Christina Simmons. 'Passion and Power: An Introduction.'

In K. Peiss and C. Simmons, eds, *Passion and Power: Sexuality in History*, 3–13. Philadelphia: Temple University Press 1989.

Penn, Donna. 'The Lesbian, the Prostitute and the Containment of Female Sexuality in Post-War America.' In Joanne Meyerowitz, ed., *Not June Cleaver: Women and Gender in Post-War America*, 358–81. Philadelphia: Temple University Press 1994.

Phelan, Shane. *Identity Politics: Lesbian Feminism and the Limits of Community.* Philadelphia: Temple University Press 1989.

Plummer, Kenneth. 'Building a Sociology of Homosexuality.' In K. Plummer, ed., *The Making of the Modern Homosexual.* London: Hutchinson 1981.

Ponse, Barbara. *Identities in the Lesbian World: The Social Construction of Self.* Westport, Conn.: Greenwood Press 1978.

Popkin, Annie. 'The Social Experience of Bread and Roses, Building a Community and Creating a Culture.' In Karen V. Hansen and Ilene J. Philipson, eds, *Women, Class and the Feminist Imagination*, 182–212. Philadelphia: Temple University Press 1990.

Ramos, Juanita, ed., *Companeras: Latina Lesbians.* New York: Latina Lesbian History Project 1987.

Raymond, Janice. *The Transsexual Empire.* Boston: Beacon Press 1979.

Reagon, Bernice Johnson. 'Coalition Politics: Turning the Century.' In Barbara Smith, ed., *Home Girls: A Black Feminist Anthology*, 356–69. New York: Kitchen Table Press 1983.

The Rebirth of Feminism. New York: Quadrangle 1971.

Rechy, John. *The Sexual Outlaw.* New York: Grove 1977.

Rich, Adrienne. *Dream of a Common Language: Poems 1974–1977.* New York: W.W. Norton 1978.

– 'It Is the Lesbian in Us.' In A. Rich, *On Lies, Secrets and Silence*, 199–202. New York: W.W. Norton 1980.

– 'The Meaning of Our Love for Women Is What We Have Constantly to Expand.' In A. Rich, *On Lies, Secrets and Silence*, 223–30.

– 'Compulsory Heterosexuality and Lesbian Existence.' In Ann Snitow, Christine Stansell, and Sharon Thompson, eds, *Powers of Desire: The Politics of Sexuality*, 177–205. New York: Monthly Review Press 1983.

– *Blood, Bread and Poetry.* New York: W.W. Norton 1986.

Richardson, Diane. *Women and the AIDS Crisis.* London: Pandora 1987.

Ristock, Janice. 'Feminist Collectives: The Struggles and Contradictions in Our Quest for a Uniquely Feminist Structure.,' In J. Ristock and Jeri D. Wine, eds, *Women and Social Change: Feminist Activism in Canada*, 41–55. Toronto: James Lorimer 1991.

Ross, Becki. 'Sex, Lives and Archives: Pleasure/Danger Debates in 1970s Lesbian Feminism.' In Dayna Daniels, Sandi Kirby, Kate McKenna, and Michele Pujol, eds, *Women Changing Academe*, 89–112. Winnipeg: Sororal Publishing 1991.

– 'Tracking Lesbian Speech: The Social Organization of Lesbian Periodical Publishing in English Canada, 1973–1988.' In Claudine Potvin and Janice Williamson, eds, *Women's Writing and the Literary Institution*, 173–87. Edmonton: University of Alberta Press 1992.

– 'Destaining the Delinquent Body: Moral Regulatory Practices at Street Haven, 1965–1969.' In Ross, ed., *Forbidden Love: The Unashamed Lives of Post-War Canadian Lesbians*. Forthcoming, 1995.

Rowbotham, Sheila. *The Past Is before Us: Feminism in Action since the 1960s*. Winchester, Mass.: Unwin and Hyman 1989.

Rubin, Gayle. 'Thinking Sex: Notes for a Radical Theory of the Politics of Sexuality.' In Carole Vance ed., *Pleasure and Danger: The Politics of Female Sexuality*, 267–319. New York and London: Routledge and Kegan Paul 1984.

– 'The Leather Menace: Comments on Politics and S/M.' In Samois, ed., *Coming to Power*, 194–229. Boston: Alyson Publications 1987.

Rule, Jane. 'Homophobia and Romantic Love.' In J. Rule, *Outlander: Short Stories and Essays*, 181–5. Tallahassee, Fla.: Naiad Press 1981.

– 'Teaching Sexuality.' In Rule, *Outlander*, 157–62.

Russ, Joanna. *The Female Man*. New York: Bantam Books 1975.

Samois. *What Colour Is Your Handkerchief? A Lesbian S/M Reader*. Boston: Alyson Publications 1979.

– *Coming to Power: Writings and Graphics on Lesbian S/M*. Boston: Alyson Publications 1981.

San Francisco Lesbian and Gay History Project. 'She Even Chewed Tobacco: A Pictorial History of Passing Women in America.' In Martin B. Duberman, Martha Vicinus, and George Chauncey Jr, eds, *Hidden from History: Reclaiming the Gay and Lesbian Past*, 183–94. New York: New American Library 1989.

Sandoval, Chela. Comment on Susan Krieger's 'Lesbian Identity and Community: Recent Social Science Literature.' In *Signs, The Lesbian Issue*, 241–4. Chicago: University of Chicago Press 1985.

Sangster, Joan. *Dreams of Equality: Women on the Canadian Left, 1920–1950*. Toronto: McClelland and Stewart 1989.

Schwartz, Ruth L. 'New Alliances, Strange Bedfellows: Lesbians, Gay Men and AIDS.' In Arlene Stein, ed., *Sisters, Sexperts and Queers: Beyond the Lesbian Nation*, 230–44. New York: Penguin Books 1993,

Scott, Gail. *Heroine*. Toronto: Coach House Press 1988.

Scott, Joan. 'Experience.' In Judith Butler and J. Scott, eds, *Feminists Theorize the Political*, 22–40. New York: Routledge, 1992.

Sealander, Judith, and Dorothy Smith. 'The Rise and Fall of Feminist Organizations in the 1970s: Dayton as a Case Study.' In Karen Hansen and Ilene Philipson, eds, *Women, Class and the Feminist Imagination*, 239–57. Philadelphia: Temple University Press 1990.

Seaman, Barbara. *Free and Female*. Greenwich, Conn.: Fawcett 1973.

Segal, Lynne. *Is the Future Female?* London: Virago 1987.

Sharpe, David. *Rochdale: The Runaway College*. Toronto: Anansi 1987.

Shelley, Martha. 'Gay Is Good.' In Karla Jay and Allen Young, eds, *Out of the Closets: Voices of Gay Liberation*, 31–4. New York: Douglas Books 1972.

Silvera, Makeda. 'Man Royals and Sodomites: Some Thoughts on Afro-Caribbean Lesbians.' In Lynne Fernie, ed., *Sight Specific: Lesbians and Representation*, 36–43. Toronto: A Space Gallery 1987.

Sisley, Emily, and Bertha Harris. *The Joy of Lesbian Sex*. New York: Simon and Schuster 1977.

Smith, Barbara. 'Introduction.' In B. Smith, ed., *Home Girls: A Black Feminist Anthology*, xix–lvi. New York: Kitchen Table Press 1983.

Smith, Carolyn, Toni Ayres, and Maggie Rubenstein. *Getting in Touch: Self-Sexuality for Women*. San Francisco: Multimedia Resource Centre 1974.

Smith, Dorothy. *The Everyday World as Problematic: A Feminist Sociology,*. Toronto: University of Toronto Press 1987.

Solomon, Alisa. 'Dykotomies: Scents and Sensibility.' In Arlene Stein, ed., *Sisters, Sexperts and Queers: Beyond the Lesbian Nation*, 210–17. New York: Penguin Books 1993.

Spillers, Hortense. 'Interstices: A Small Drama of Words.' In Carole Vance, ed., *Pleasure and Danger*, 73–100. Boston and London: Routlege and Kegan Paul 1984.

Stanley, Julia Penelope, and Susan Wolfe, eds. *The Coming Out Stories*. Watertown, Mass.: Persephone Press 1980.

Stefan, Verna. *Shedding*. Plainfield, Vt.: Daughters, Inc. 1978 [1975].

Stein, Arlene. *Sisters, Sexperts and Queers: Beyond the Lesbian Nation*. New York: Penguin Books 1993.

Stephenson, Marylee, ed. *Women in Canada*. Don Mills, Ont.: General Publishing 1977.

Stone, Sharon. 'Lesbian Mothers Organizing.' In S. Stone, ed., *Lesbians in Canada*, 198–208. Toronto: Between the Lines 1990.

– 'Lesbians Against the Right.' In Jeri Wine and Janice Ristock, eds, *Feminist Activism in Canada*, 236–53. Toronto: James Lorimer 1991.

Sue, Nelly, Dian, Carol, Billie. *Country Lesbians*. Grants Pass, Ore.: Womanshare Books 1976.

Taylor, Barbara. *Eve and the New Jerusalem: Socialism and Feminism in the Nineteenth Century*. London: Virago 1983.

Vance, Carole. 'Pleasure and Danger: Towards a Politics of Sexuality.' In C. Vance, ed., *Pleasure and Danger: Female Sexuality Today*, 1–28. Boston and London: Routledge and Kegan Paul 1984.

– 'Social Construction Theory: Problems in the History of Sexuality.' In Dennis Altman et al., eds, *Homosexuality, Which Homosexuality?*, 13–34. London: GMP Publishers 1989.

Voices from Women's Liberation. New York: Signet Books 1970.

Wall, Naomi. 'The Last Ten Years: A Personal/Political View.' In Maureen Fitzgerald, Connie Guberman, and Margie Wolfe, eds, *Still Ain't Satisfied: Canadian Feminism Today*, 15–29. Toronto: Women's Press 1982.

Webster, Paula. 'The Forbidden: Eroticism and Taboo.' In Carole Vance, ed., *Pleasure and Danger*, 385–98. Boston and London: Routledge and Kegan Paul 1984.

Weeks, Jeffrey. *Coming Out: Homosexual Politics in Britain, from the Nineteenth Century to the Present*. London: Quartet Books 1977.

– *Sex, Politics and Society: The Regulation of Sexuality since 1800*. London: Longman 1981.

– *Sexuality and Its Discontents*. London, Melbourne, and Henley: Routledge and Kegan Paul 1985.

– *Sexuality*. London: Tavistock 1986.

Weir, Lorna. 'Socialist Feminism and the Politics of Sexuality.' In Meg Luxton and Heather Jon Maroney, eds, *Socialist Feminism and Political Economy*, 69–83. London: Methuen 1987.

Whan, Dell. 'Elitism.' In Karla Jay and Allen Young, eds, *Out of the Closets: Voices of Gay Liberation*, 318–23. New York: Douglas Books 1972,

Wheelwright, Julie. *Amazons and Military Maids*. London: Pandora 1989.

Willis, Ellen. 'Feminism, Moralism and Pornography.' In Ann Snitow, Christine Stansell, and Sharon Thompson, eds, *Powers of Desire*, 460–7. New York: Monthly Review Press 1983.

Wilson, Elizabeth. *Adorned in Dreams*. Berkeley: University of California Press 1985.

Wilson, Elizabeth (with Angela Weir). *Hidden Agendas*. London: Tavistock 1986.

Wittig, Monique, and Sandra Zweig. *Lesbian Peoples: Materials for a Dictionary*. New York: Avon Books 1976.

Wittman, Carl. 'Refugees from Amerika.' In Joseph McCaffery, ed., *The Homosexual Dialectic*. Englewood Cliffs, NJ: Prentice-Hall 1972.

Wolf, Deborah. *The Lesbian Community.* Berkeley: University of California Press 1979.

Wyland, Francie. *Motherhood, Lesbianism and Child Custody.* Toronto: Falling Wall Press 1977.

Zimmerman, Bonnie. *The Safe Sea of Women: Lesbian Fiction, 1969–1989.* Boston: Beacon Press, 1990.

Illustration credits

Index

7